Amillennialism
and the
Age to Come

A Premillennial Critique of the Two-Age Model

MATT WAYMEYER

Kress Biblical Resources
www.kressbiblical.com

Amillennialism and the Age to Come

Copyright © 2016 by Matt Waymeyer

ISBN 978-1-934952-25-2

All rights reserved. No portion of this book may be reproduced in any form without the written permission of the copyright owner, except for brief excerpts quoted in critical reviews.

Unless otherwise indicated, all Scripture is taken from the NEW AMERICAN STANDARD BIBLE®, Copyright © 1960, 1962, 1963, 1968, 1971, 1972, 1975, 1977, 1995 by the Lockman Foundation. Used by permission.

Cover design by Cherith Festa
Interior design and typeset by Katherine Lloyd, theDESKonline.com

To Michael Vlach,
whose friendship and faithful example
continually spur me on to greater diligence
in my study of God's Word

Contents

Preface vii

Abbreviations ix

Chapter 1   Introduction to the Two-Age Model 1

PART 1: The Intermediate Kingdom in the Old Testament

Chapter 2   The Intermediate Kingdom in the Psalms and Prophets . . . 19

Chapter 3   The Intermediate Kingdom in Isaiah 65:17–25 31

Chapter 4   The Intermediate Kingdom in Zechariah 47

Chapter 5   The Intermediate Kingdom in Isaiah 24:21–23 69

PART 2: The Two-Age Argument in the New Testament

Chapter 6   The Succession of the Two Ages 87

Chapter 7   The Characteristics of the Two Ages 97

Chapter 8   The Resurrection and Judgment of All Mankind 107

Chapter 9   The Destruction and Renewal of the Cosmos 129

Chapter 10 The Final Victory over Sin and Death 147

PART 3: The Intermediate Kingdom in Revelation 20

Chapter 11 The Timing of Satan's Binding 175

Chapter 12 The Nature of the First Resurrection 207

Chapter 13 The Duration of the Thousand Years 243

Chapter 14 The Chronology of John's Visions 263

Chapter 15 Conclusion 301

Appendix   The Intermediate Kingdom in Intertestamental Judaism . . . 305

Scripture Index 315

Preface

One of the most encouraging developments in evangelicalism over the past several decades has been the remarkable resurgence of reformed theology. This rediscovery of the doctrines of grace has not only captured the Bible's emphasis on the sovereignty of God in salvation but also strengthened the unity of the church around the centrality of the gospel. In the area of eschatology, however, I have noticed two concerning trends among those who have joined this reformation.

The first involves what I call *eschatological agnosticism*. To be sure, eschatology is one of the most difficult theological issues to understand, especially when it comes to the finer details. But some Christians, although diligent students of Scripture in every other area, avoid the topic altogether and appear content to place themselves in the category of undecided. Some even seem proud of their agnosticism, as if ignorance about the meaning of biblical prophecy is evidence of a commitment to more significant matters. But affirming the centrality of the gospel should not mean dismissing the importance of how God will accomplish the restoration of all things to Himself. Scripture reveals too much about the subject of eschatology for Christians to be content in the dark, especially those who preach the Word and shepherd the flock.

A second trend is the way that some Christians are quick to embrace amillennialism simply because they see it as the reformed position on the end times. This appears to be most common among former Arminians. After an initial exposure to reformed theology, they spend the next several years diligently studying the Bible's teaching on predestination before finally identifying themselves as Calvinists. But their subsequent conversion to amillennialism takes place overnight—and oftentimes with very little first-hand study of the biblical text—simply because they see it as an indispensable part of the reformed system. In contrast, the commitment to *sola scriptura* at the heart of reformed theology should drive us to a careful exegesis of the relevant biblical passages, in search of what God has revealed about the end times. Only then is the student of Scripture ready to take a firm position on this difficult issue.

This book presents an invitation to those who may find themselves caught up in either one of these trends. Whether an eschatological agnostic who has never studied the millennial debate, or an amillennialist who has failed to give this issue the careful attention it deserves, the reader is challenged to consider this premillennial response to the most compelling arguments for amillennialism. The goal of this book is not only to clarify the key differences between these two competing millennial views, but also to provide an exegetical critique of the two-age model of amillennialism. In considering this response, the reader is encouraged to be diligent in his own study of Scripture, weighing carefully the arguments on both sides of the debate. Just as importantly, he is also encouraged to let that study spur him on to greater holiness as he eagerly awaits the blessed hope and appearing of our great God and Savior, the Lord Jesus Christ.

Matt Waymeyer
Jupiter, Florida
March 2016

Abbreviations

ASV	American Standard Version
BDAG	Bauer, W., F. W. Danker, W. F. Arndt, and F. W. Gingrich. *Greek-English Lexicon of the New Testament and Other Early Christian Literature.* 3d ed. Chicago, 1999
BECNT	Baker Exegetical Commentary on the New Testament
Bib	*Biblica*
BSac	*Bibliotheca Sacra*
CBQ	*Catholic Biblical Quarterly*
EBC	Expositor's Bible Commentary
EDNT	*Exegetical Dictionary of the New Testament.* Edited by H. Balz, G. Schneider. ET. Grand Rapids, 1990–1993
EGT	*The Expositor's Greek Testament.* Edited by W. Robertson Nicoll. 5 vols. Grand Rapids, 1974
ESV	English Standard Version
GTJ	*Grace Theological Journal*
HALOT	Koehler, L., Buamgartner and J. J. Stamm, *The Hebrew and Aramaic Lexicon of the Old Testament.* Translated and edited under the supervision of M. E. J. Richardson. 4 vols. Leiden. 1994–1999
HCSB	Holman Christian Standard Bible
HOTC	Holman Old Testament Commentary
ICC	International Critical Commentary
JBL	*Journal of Biblical Literature*
JETS	*Journal of the Evangelical Theological Society*
KJV	King James Version
L&N	*Greek-English Lexicon of the New Testament: Based on Semantic Domains.* Edited by J. P. Louw and E. A. Nida. 2d ed. New York, 1989
MSJ	*The Master's Seminary Journal*

NAC	New American Commentary
NASB	New American Standard Bible
NCBC	The New Century Bible Commentary Series
NCV	New Century Version
NET	New English Translation (NET Bible)
NIBC	New International Biblical Commentary
NIBCNT	New International Biblical Commentary on the New Testament
NICNT	New International Commentary on the New Testament
NICOT	New International Commentary on the Old Testament
NIDNTT	*New International Dictionary of New Testament Theology.* Edited by Colin Brown. 4 vols. Grand Rapids, 1975–85
NIDOTTE	*New International Dictionary of Old Testament Theology and Exegesis.* Edited by W. A. VanGemeren. 5 vols. Grand Rapids, 1997
NIGTC	New International Greek Testament Commentary
NIV	New International Version
NKJV	New King James Version
NLT	New Living Translation
NRSV	New Revised Standard Version
NTC	New Testament Commentary
PCS	The Preacher's Commentary Series
PNTC	The Pillar New Testament Commentary
R&R	*Reformation & Revival*
RefJ	*The Reformed Journal*
RevExp	*Review and Expositor*
RSV	Revised Standard Version
TDNT	*Theological Dictionary of the New Testament.* Edited by G. Kittel and G. Friederich. Translated by G. W. Bromiley. 10 vols. Grand Rapids, 1964–1976
Them	*Themelios*
TNTC	Tyndale New Testament Commentaries
WBC	Word Biblical Commentary
WTJ	*Westminster Theological Journal*
ZECNT	Zondervan Exegetical Commentary on the New Testament

Chapter 1

Introduction to the Two-Age Model

INTRODUCTION

In the debate between premillennialism and amillennialism, the most fundamental disagreement concerns the thousand-year reign of Christ in Revelation 20. Premillennialists believe the thousand years refers to a future reign of Jesus on earth, an intermediate kingdom between His Second Coming and the final consummation. But amillennialists believe it describes the current reign of Christ throughout the present age. For this reason, while premillennialism affirms an earthly kingdom between the present age and the eternal state, amillennialism denies this intermediate kingdom, arguing instead that the present age will be followed immediately by the new heavens and new earth.

THE TWO-AGE MODEL OF AMILLENNIALISM

One of the strongest arguments for the amillennial view involves what is known as the "two-age model," an eschatological framework first highlighted by Geerhardus Vos in the early twentieth century. According to Vos, whose contributions are considered "nothing less than epochal in their significance for the history of eschatological thought,"[1] the fundamental structure of biblical eschatology is presented in two successive ages, "this age" and "the age to come."[2] Vos believed that these two ages

---

1 Samuel E. Waldron, *The End Times Made Simple: How Could Everyone Be So Wrong About Biblical Prophecy?* (Amityville, NY: Calvary Press, 2003), 244.
2 Geerhardus Vos, "Eschatology of the New Testament," in *Redemptive History and Biblical Interpretation*, ed. Richard B. Gaffin, Jr. (Phillipsburg, NJ: Presbyterian and Reformed Publishing, 1980), 25–29.

cover biblical history and thereby constitute the basic framework of New Testament eschatology.[3]

Although several amillennialists built upon the foundation laid by Vos,[4] this model was not fully developed as a key argument in the millennial debate until the 2003 publication of *A Case for Amillennialism* by Kim Riddlebarger. In this landmark work, which was revised and expanded in 2013, Riddlebarger argued that the two-age model "enables us to make sense of eschatological language in the New Testament, specifically as it relates to the future and the millennial age."[5] Riddlebarger popularized this model as a polemic against premillennialism and placed it at the center of the case for amillennialism.[6] Since then, the two-age model has become the primary argument for the amillennial view.

THE TWO-AGE MODEL AS AN ESCHATOLOGICAL FRAMEWORK

To establish the two-age model as the eschatological framework of the New Testament, amillennialists point to the various passages in the gospels and epistles which refer to "this age" and "the age to come."[7] Some of these passages refer only to this age (Matt 13:39, 40, 49; 24:3; 28:20; Rom 12:2; 1 Cor 1:20; 2:6, 8; 3:18; 2 Cor 4:4; Gal 1:4; Eph 2:2; 1 Tim 6:17–19;

---

[3] Geerhardus Vos, *The Pauline Eschatology* (1930; repr., Phillipsburg, NJ: Presbyterian and Reformed Publishing, 1994), 12–15.

[4] E.g., William E. Cox, *Amillennialism Today* (Phillipsburg, NJ: Presbyterian and Reformed Publishing, 1966), 65; Anthony Hoekema, *The Bible and the Future* (Grand Rapids: Eerdmans Publishing, 1979), 19–22, 185–86; Bruce K. Waltke, "Kingdom Promises as Spiritual," in *Continuity and Discontinuity: Perspectives on the Relationship Between the Old and New Testaments*, ed. John S. Feinberg (Westchester, IL: Crossway Books, 1988), 275; Robert B. Strimple, "An Amillennial Response to Craig A. Blaising," in *Three Views on the Millennium and Beyond*, ed. Darrell L. Bock (Grand Rapids: Zondervan Publishing, 1999), 268–69.

[5] Kim Riddlebarger, *A Case for Amillennialism: Understanding the End Times*, expanded ed. (Grand Rapids: Baker Books, 2013), 23.

[6] In the past few years, at least two major works employ the two-age model as a primary argument against premillennialism (Jonathan Menn, *Biblical Eschatology*, [Eugene, OR: Resource Publications, 2013]; Dean Davis, *The High King of Heaven: Discovering the Master Keys to the Great End Time Debate* [Enumclaw, WA: WinePress Publishing, 2014]), and a third work argues from this framework even though it does not use the language of the two-age model (Sam Storms, *Kingdom Come: The Amillennial Alternative* [Ross-shire, Scotland: Mentor, 2013]).

[7] Riddlebarger, *A Case for Amillennialism*, 80, 103–4; Waldron, *The End Times Made Simple*, 32–34; Davis, *The High King of Heaven*, 165.

Titus 2:12); another refers only to the age to come (Heb 6:5); and still others refer to both this age *and* the age to come (Matt 12:32; Mark 10:30; Luke 18:30; 20:34–35; Eph 1:21).[8] The two-fold division of this temporal framework is seen most explicitly in this final category, the five passages which present a clear contrast between the two ages:

- Matthew 12:32: "either in this age or in the age to come"
- Mark 10:30: "now in the present age ... and in the age to come"
- Luke 18:30: "at this time and in the age to come"
- Luke 20:34–35: "this age ... that age"
- Ephesians 1:21: "not only in this age but also in the one to come"

According to Riddlebarger, the New Testament describes these ages as two successively and qualitatively distinct eschatological periods of time.[9] At the same time, even though believers live in this age and eagerly await the arrival of the age to come, because the kingdom of God is present here and now, the age to come is also seen as a current reality for those who are in Christ.[10] For this reason, Christians are said to live in the eschatological tension between the *already* and the *not yet*, as citizens of the coming age who wait for the fullness of its arrival.[11] This results in an overlap of the two ages in which the age to come is considered both present and future.[12]

---

8 In referring to the two ages, a variety of similar terminology is used. To designate the present age, the New Testament refers to "an age" (αἰῶνός) (Matt 13:39); "the age" (τοῦ αἰῶνος) (Matt 13:40, 49; 24:3; 28:20); "this age" (τῷ αἰῶνι τούτῳ) (Rom 12:2; 1 Cor 3:18; Eph 1:21); "this age" (τοῦ αἰῶνος τούτου) (1 Cor 1:20; 2:6 [2x], 8; 2 Cor 4:4; Luke 20:34); "this age" (τούτῳ τῷ αἰῶνι) (Matt 12:32); "this present evil age" (τοῦ αἰῶνος τοῦ ἐνεστῶτος πονηροῦ) (Gal 1:4); "the age of this world" (τὸν αἰῶνα τοῦ κόσμου τούτου) (Eph 2:2); "this present age" (τῷ νῦν αἰῶνι) (1 Tim 6:17; Titus 2:12); and "this time" (τῷ καιρῷ τούτῳ) (Mark 10:30; Luke 18:30). To designate the coming age, the New Testament refers to "the age to come" (μέλλοντος αἰῶνος) (Heb 6:5); "the [age] to come" (τῷ μέλλοντι) (Matt 12:32; Eph 1:21); "the age to come" (τῷ αἰῶνι τῷ ἐρχομένῳ) (Mark 10:30; Luke 18:30); "that age" (τοῦ αἰῶνος ἐκείνου) (Luke 20:35); and "the ages to come" (τοῖς αἰῶσιν τοῖς ἐπερχομένοις) (Eph 2:7).
9 Riddlebarger, *A Case for Amillennialism*, 96.
10 Ibid.
11 Ibid., 103.
12 Ibid., 80, 107, 124, 127, 130. According to Riddlebarger, even though the age to come will not be fully experienced until the Second Coming, it was realized in principle through the resurrection of Christ (107).

The Two-Age Model as an Interpretive Grid

Because it serves as the overall framework of the New Testament, Riddlebarger argues that the two-age model also functions as "the interpretive grid through which amillennialists should understand the biblical concept of future history."[13] Riddlebarger laments that "the two ages have not been properly considered as a major interpretive grid,"[14] but amillennialists have increasingly regarded this model as the hermeneutical lens through which the rest of Scripture, including Revelation 20, should be viewed.[15]

To validate this interpretive approach, amillennialists typically appeal to the hermeneutical principle known as *the analogy of faith*.[16] As Riddlebarger explains:

> This refers to the importance of interpreting an unclear biblical text in light of clear passages that speak to the same subject rather than taking the literal sense in isolation from the rest of Scripture. Texts that speak of last things must, therefore, be interpreted by other biblical passages.[17]

Because amillennialists consider Revelation 20 to be "unclear," "difficult," and "obscure," they insist it must be interpreted in light of the clear two-age passages in the gospels and epistles.[18] According to this approach, "any exposition of Revelation 20 should take place with the

---

13 Ibid., 23.
14 Ibid., 98.
15 Waldron describes the two-age model as "the Bible's own system" and the most basic and formative issue for understanding the structure of biblical eschatology (*The End Times Made Simple*, 30). Menn identifies it as "the key concept for understanding biblical eschatology" and "a clear, consistent, and comprehensive eschatological interpretive structure" (*Biblical Eschatology*, 38–39).
16 Storms, *Kingdom Come*, 138–43; Riddlebarger, *A Case for Amillennialism*, 234; Robert B. Strimple, "Amillennialism," in *Three Views on the Millennium and Beyond*, ed. Darrell L. Bock (Grand Rapids: Zondervan Publishing, 1999), 119–20; Cox, *Amillennialism Today*, 65.
17 Riddlebarger, *A Case for Amillennialism*, 51, 234. According to Cox, "All passages are equally inspired and true, but the plain must interpret the figurative" (*Amillennialism Today*, 107).
18 Riddlebarger, *A Case for Amillennialism*, 234–35; Storms, *Kingdom Come*, 138–43; Waldron, *The End Times Made Simple*, 28; Strimple, "Amillennialism," 119–20. In the words of Riddlebarger, "The amillennial interpretation of Revelation 20 attempts to build on clear texts in the Gospels and Paul's epistles" (*A Case for Amillennialism*, 235). According to Riddlebarger, the absence of an earthly millennium in the teaching of Jesus and Paul implies that Revelation 20 must not entail an intermediate kingdom either (80).

broader eschatology of the New Testament firmly in mind."[19] This means using the two-age model as the interpretive key to understanding John's vision of the millennial reign of Christ.[20]

With this model as the hermeneutical grid for the rest of Scripture, amillennialists come to Revelation 20 with the assumption that it does not—and indeed *cannot*—teach the existence of an intermediate kingdom between the present age and the eternal state.[21] As amillennialist William Cox explained a generation ago:

> Amillenarians reached their conclusions on the millennium by comparing Revelation 20 with the clear passages of Scripture.... No clear passage of Scripture anywhere speaks of an earthly, materialistic millennium like the one put forth like the millenarians. As a matter of fact, their alleged millennium militates against many clear passages of the Bible. The Scriptures outline but two ages: the present age and the age to come. The age to come is everywhere said to be eternal, and would therefore be in complete contradistinction to an interregnum of one thousand years.[22]

For that reason, amillennialists argue that "John's single apocalyptic passage in Revelation 20 *cannot be allowed* to contradict the clear teachings of the entire New Testament."[23]

This same hermeneutical approach is reflected in the argument of amillennialist Anthony Hoekema:

> Since a millennial earthly reign of Christ is taught nowhere else in Scripture, and since the characteristics of this millennial reign conflict with what Scripture teaches elsewhere about the Second

---

19 Riddlebarger, *A Case for Amillennialism*, 234.
20 In the words of amillennialist G. K. Beale, the correct hermeneutical approach is that "the rest of the Bible (e.g., Paul's epistles) should be understood as the main interpretive lens for eschatology and not any particular interpretation of Revelation 20." This statement comes from Beale's published endorsement at the front of *Kingdom Come* by Sam Storms. For some amillennialists this approach means importing meaning from other passages into Revelation 20—for example, Cox, who writes: "Since [Revelation 20] itself gives no explanation of John's meaning, its meaning must be garnered elsewhere in the Bible" (*Amillennialism Today*, 65).
21 Cox, *Amillennialism Today*, 107; Strimple, "Amillennialism," 120.
22 Cox, *Amillennialism Today*, 65.
23 Ibid., 107; emphasis added.

Coming and about the age to come which follows it, why should we affirm that Revelation 20:1–6 teaches that there will be such a reign? Instead of insisting that Revelation 20 affirms a teaching which is not found elsewhere in the Bible, is it not wiser to interpret these difficult verses in an apocalyptic book in the light of and in harmony with the clear teachings of the rest of Scripture?[24]

In a similar way, amillennialist Sam Storms argues that "the statements in other New Testament books concerning end-time chronology *necessarily and logically preclude* the notion of a post-parousia millennial age in Revelation 20."[25] For this reason, amillennialists argue that for premillennialists to affirm the existence of an intermediate kingdom in Revelation 20, they must be willing "to set aside the entire New Testament, or force it into artificial interpretations."[26] Whatever Revelation 20 means, amillennialists insist that it absolutely cannot be understood to teach premillennialism.[27]

The Two-Age Model as an Amillennial Argument

The two-age model is used not merely as an argument for the amillennial view of Revelation 20, but also as a decisive refutation of the messianic kingdom of premillennialism. More specifically, amillennialists have used the two-age model to argue against the possibility of this intermediate kingdom in three distinct ways:

1. Because "the age to come" will immediately follow this present age (Matt 12:32; Eph 1:21), there is no gap of time between the two ages to allow for the intermediate kingdom of premillennialism.

---

24 Hoekema, *The Bible and the Future*, 186.
25 Storms, *Kingdom Come*, 140; emphasis original. In the introduction to his discussion of Revelation 20, Riddlebarger argues that the two-age model makes it clear that non-glorified saints cannot exist on the renewed earth after the return of Jesus (*A Case for Amillennialism*, 234), which rules out the possibility of a future millennium before the details of John's vision are even considered.
26 Strimple, "Amillennialism," 120.
27 This assumption is held so strongly that amillennialist Sam Storms recently said, "If Revelation 20 teaches a premillennial view ... I have to abandon biblical inerrancy" (1:15:20ff. of http://www.desiringgod.org/resource-library/conference-messages/an-evening-of-eschatology).

2. Because the qualities ascribed to "the age to come" are all eternal in nature (Mark 10:30; Luke 18:30; 20:34–36), the temporal aspects of premillennialism's intermediate kingdom—such as sin, death, and procreation—render it incompatible with the coming age.

3. Because the Second Coming is the line of demarcation between the two ages—and because it will be accompanied by the resurrection and judgment of all mankind (Dan 12:2; John 5:28–29; Acts 24:15; Matt 25:31–46; 2 Thess 1:6–10), the destruction and renewal of the cosmos (2 Pet 3:10–13; Rom 8:18–23), and the final victory over sin and death (1 Cor 15:20–28, 50–57; Rom 8:17–23)—there is no gap of time to allow for the intermediate kingdom of premillennialism.

The Need for a Premillennial Response

Despite the growing popularity and influence of the two-age model, none of the major premillennial works in recent years has directly and substantially addressed this amillennial argument.[28] Because any compelling defense of premillennialism must respond to the strongest and most recent argumentation of its theological opponents, a premillennial critique of the two-age model is long overdue. The purpose of this book is to provide such a critique.

The need for this critique is strengthened further by the way the two-age model is used as a hermeneutical lens for the rest of Scripture. Because this model functions as an interpretive grid, amillennialists come to Revelation 20:1–6 with the assumption that it cannot describe an intermediate kingdom between the present age and the eternal state. Therefore, when the premillennialist appeals to Revelation 20 as evidence for his position,

---

28 For example, John MacArthur and Richard Mayhue, eds. *Christ's Prophetic Plans: A Futuristic Premillennial Primer* (Chicago: Moody Publishers, 2012); David L. Allen and Steve W. Lemke, eds., *The Return of Christ: A Premillennial Perspective* (Nashville: Broadman & Holman, 2011); Craig L. Blomberg, and Sung Wook Chung, eds. *A Case for Historic Premillennialism: An Alternative to "Left Behind" Eschatology* (Grand Rapids: Baker Books, 2009); Craig A. Blaising, "Premillennialism," in *Three Views on the Millennium and Beyond*, 157–227; Mal Couch, ed. *Dictionary of Premillennial Theology: A Practical Guide to the People, Viewpoints, and History of Prophetic Studies* (Grand Rapids: Kregel Publications, 1996); Donald K. Campbell and Jeffrey L. Townsend, eds. *A Case for Premillennialism: A New Consensus* (Chicago: Moody Press, 1992).

his argument falls on deaf ears because the two-age model has already settled the issue in the mind of the amillennialist. Likewise, when the amillennialist appeals to the two-age model as evidence that the eternal state immediately follows the Second Coming—thereby precluding an intermediate kingdom—his argument is equally unconvincing because Revelation 20 has already settled the issue in the mind of the premillennialist. In this way, the debate often consists of the two sides talking past one another, never substantially responding to the strongest arguments of the other.

In contrast, this critique takes seriously the need to engage with the case for amillennialism at its most compelling point by addressing the question of whether the two-age model precludes the possibility of an intermediate kingdom. In the process, its goal is to represent the teaching of amillennialists as fairly and accurately as possible, presenting their views and arguments in a way that they themselves would eagerly embrace. It also takes seriously the need to harmonize the entirety of Scripture's teaching about the age to come, including Revelation 20, in order to construct a truly biblical eschatology.

Revisiting the Hermeneutical Foundation

Such a critique must begin in the realm of hermeneutics. At the outset, two hermeneutical problems plague the two-age argument for amillennialism. The first problem concerns identifying Revelation 20 as an unclear passage which needs to be interpreted by clearer passages in the gospels and epistles. Even though Revelation is indeed the most symbolic book in the New Testament—and even though some passages in the Apocalypse are difficult to understand—no other biblical passage contains nearly the amount of clarity and chronological detail regarding the sequence of events that will take place after the Second Coming. This clarity is often obscured by the intricate interpretations of Revelation 20 offered by amillennialists, but a straightforward reading of the events described in Revelation 19–21 is neither confusing nor difficult to follow.[29] For this

---

29 This will be demonstrated in chapters 11–14. As premillennialist Wayne Grudem explains, the various amillennial interpretations of Revelation 20 "all have the disadvantage of having to labor under the burden of explaining away what seems to be a straightforward understanding of the text because they are convinced that the rest of Scripture does not

reason, to use passages containing far less detail (and therefore far less clarity) to interpret Revelation 20 is an unsound hermeneutical approach.

Part of the difficulty with using "clear" passages to interpret "unclear" passages is the subjectivity involved in deciding which passages belong in which category. Identifying as "clear" those passages which appear to support one's view may inadvertently become a means of silencing those passages which contradict it. Rather than using one passage to interpret another, the more objective approach is to interpret each passage in its own context and then to harmonize the contribution of each passage into a systematic understanding of the doctrine under consideration. If theological harmony is not possible, the interpreter may need to patiently and diligently revisit his exegesis of some or all of the relevant passages.

The second problem concerns the use of the two-age model as an interpretive grid. To use any passage or theological system as the lens through which the rest of Scripture is viewed tends to reinforce what the interpreter already believes while shielding him from theological correction and refinement.[30] Therefore, when the interpreter comes to a passage which challenges (or perhaps even contradicts) his beliefs, his interpretive grid often silences the contribution of those passages by forcing them to conform to his theological system. In this way, systematic theology is used to determine exegesis rather than vice versa. No interpreter is immune to this temptation, but the problem is magnified when the use of an interpretive lens is considered a valid methodology to be enthusiastically embraced rather than a dangerous pitfall to be carefully avoided. It is one thing to guard against the tendency to view Scripture through the lens of one's theological system; it is quite another to defend it as a constructive hermeneutical approach.

For example, when the amillennialist reads Old Testament prophecy through the lens of the two-age model, his interpretive grid does not allow him to acknowledge the presence of sin and death at any point in the future eschatological kingdom. Therefore, when he comes to prophecies

---

teach a future earthly millennium. But if the rest of Scripture does not deny it (and in some places hints at it), and if this text does teach it, then it would seem much more appropriate to accept it" (Wayne Grudem, *Systematic Theology: An Introduction to Biblical Doctrine* [Grand Rapids: Zondervan Publishing, 1994], 1121).

30 After all, the one who looks at the world through purple-colored lenses will tend to see only things that are purple, regardless of what color various objects may actually be.

describing the presence of sin and death in the eschatological kingdom (Ps 72:1–20; Isa 2:1–3//Mic 4:2–4; Isa 11:1–9; 65:17–25; Zech 14:16–19), he must find some other way to interpret those passages. Likewise, when the amillennialist views Revelation 20 through the lens of the two-age model, his interpretive grid does not allow him to acknowledge the existence of a messianic reign between the present age and the eternal state. Therefore, when he interprets this passage, he must do so in a way that coincides with his view of the two ages, even though that interpretation may not be faithful to the intention of the biblical author.

Reconsidering the Starting Point

This raises the more fundamental question of the appropriate starting point in formulating a biblical theology of the coming kingdom. Rather than beginning in the Old Testament and tracing the development of the kingdom through the progress of revelation, the amillennialist parachutes into the middle of the New Testament and insists that the two-age passages serve as "the starting point"[31] and "interpretive grid"[32] for the rest of Scripture. From there, whether looking backward at prophetic predictions in the Old Testament or forward to John's prophetic visions in Revelation 20, the amillennialist views every other passage through an interpretive lens which appears to have been chosen arbitrarily.

To justify his use of that lens, the amillennialist insists that "figurative passages should be interpreted within the doctrinal boundaries set by the literal passages."[33] In this case, the prophecies in the Old Testament and in Revelation 20 are considered figurative and therefore must be interpreted within the doctrinal boundaries of the two-age model, which is constructed from "literal" passages in the New Testament. But what if these Old Testament prophecies do indeed indicate an intermediate phase of the coming kingdom? And what if Revelation 20 does indeed set forth a future millennium preceding the eternal state? If so, then the interpretive lens of the amillennialist has reinforced his erroneous understanding of the two ages and his doctrinal boundaries have prevented much-needed theological refinement from taking place.

---

31 Riddlebarger, *A Case for Amillennialism*, 96.
32 Ibid., 23, 98.
33 Waldron, *The End Times Made Simple*, 28.

The amillennial approach borders on the fallacy of appealing to selective evidence. In this fallacy, one appeals only to evidence which supports his view while either neglecting or failing to consider the full import of evidence which weighs against it. As Craig Blaising notes, one of the criteria for evaluating the plausibility of a belief system is the refusal to exclude crucial data in the formulation of the system.[34] In other words, the most likely theological view is able to accommodate all of the relevant biblical data, neither ignoring nor dismissing the significance of any key passages in the process. The amillennial approach does not ignore relevant biblical data entirely, but its use of the two-age interpretive grid often diminishes the full significance of those passages or forces them to conform to the eschatology of amillennialism.

Rather than using an interpretive grid, the best way to honor the divine authority of every passage, as well as Scripture as a whole, is to trace the doctrine of the coming kingdom throughout biblical revelation. This means starting in the Old Testament and progressively moving through the entirety of Scripture—from Genesis to Revelation—allowing each passage to make its own unique, contextual contribution as it builds upon previous revelation. In the process, it must be recognized that later revelation often supplements and thereby clarifies previous revelation by providing broader context or additional detail, but it never changes the meaning of earlier passages in the process.[35] In the end, the interpreter should seek to harmonize the exegesis of all the relevant passages—much like one seeks to harmonize parallel accounts in the synoptic gospels—refusing to allow any passage to silence or twist the contribution of another.

---

34 Craig A. Blaising, "Israel and Hermeneutics," in *The People, the Land, and the Future of Israel: Israel and the Jewish People in the Plan of God*, eds. Darrell L. Bock and Mitch Glaser (Grand Rapids: Kregel Publications, 2014), 158. According to Blaising, to the extent that a theological system does not account for relevant portions of Scripture, it is weak at best. In his discussion of these criteria, Blaising acknowledges his dependence on David L. Wolfe, *Epistemology: The Justification of Belief* (Downers Grove, IL: InterVarsity Press, 1982), 50–55.

35 For example, even though the Old Testament contains several indications of plurality within God (Gen 1:26; 3:22; 11:7; Ps 45:6–7; 110:1; Isa 6:8; 48:16; 61:1; 63:10; Hos 1:2, 7; Mal 3:1–2), the doctrine of the Trinity is not clarified and fully revealed until the New Testament.

THE CLARIFYING ROLE OF REVELATION 20

With this approach, Revelation 20 is not to function as an interpretive lens for the rest of Scripture,[36] and yet—as the fullest and most comprehensive presentation of the eschatological events surrounding the Second Coming—it should be allowed to clarify previous revelation about the coming kingdom.[37] In doing so, Revelation 20 should not be used to reinterpret and distort the meaning of earlier passages, but rather should be carefully harmonized with them so that the divine authority and progressive nature of biblical revelation are appropriately honored.[38]

The primary way that Revelation 20 brings clarity to earlier revelation is by describing a millennial reign of Christ between the present age and the eternal state. Harmonizing this intermediate kingdom with previous revelation does not require that truths taught in earlier passages be altered or denied, but it does mean acknowledging the existence of a gap of time between various eschatological events, a gap not clearly revealed

---

36 According to amillennialist Sam Storms, most premillennialists read the New Testament through the grid of Revelation 20: "Often the premillennial interpretation of Revelation 20 has become so deeply embedded in the minds of its advocates that it borders on unconscious assumption. This makes it difficult for them to read other portions of God's word through anything other than premillennial spectacles" (*Kingdom Come*, 142). This hermeneutical hazard must be avoided by making sure that one's interpretation of Revelation 20 does not distort the meaning of other passages in the process of harmonizing the various texts.

37 This leads premillennialist Daniel Wallace to describe Revelation 20 as "the pinnacle of revelation about the kingdom" (Daniel B. Wallace, "Is Intra-Canonical Theological Development Compatible with a High Bibliology?" accessed on August 7, 2014, https://bible.org/article/intra-canonical-theological-development-compatible-high-bibliology).

38 Premillennialist Millard Erickson contends that the interpreter should "weight later developments *more heavily* than earlier ones" (Millard J. Erickson, *Christian Theology* [Grand Rapids: Baker Books, 1985], 123; emphasis added), and premillennialist Daniel Wallace insists that earlier revelation "must *yield* to later revelation" in the area of eschatology (Daniel B. Wallace, "New Testament Eschatology in the Light of Progressive Revelation," accessed on August 7, 2014, https://bible.org/article/new-testament-eschatology-light-progressive-revelation; emphasis added). Although this sounds similar to the approach commended here in this critique, giving more weight to later revelation—or insisting that earlier revelation must "yield" to later revelation—seems to imply an actual conflict between biblical passages, consequently requiring that one passage be granted more authority than others, an approach that must be rejected. In a similar way, premillennialist George Eldon Ladd's insistence that all other considerations be "subservient" to the exegesis of Revelation 20 (George Eldon Ladd, *Crucial Questions About the Kingdom of God* [Grand Rapids: Eerdmans Publishing, 1952], 183) seems to imply that the meaning of one passage should be trumped by the meaning of another. This approach appears to deny the equal authority of all Scripture and therefore should likewise be rejected.

in those earlier passages. This gap of time is the "thousand years" of Revelation 20.

There is a clear biblical precedent for this very dynamic within the progress of divine revelation. As most biblical interpreters recognize,[39] sometimes a given prophecy will predict two or more future events and present them in such a way that it appears they will occur simultaneously, and yet later revelation clarifies that a significant gap of time separates them.[40] Commonly referred to as "telescoping," "prophetic perspective," or "prophetic foreshortening," this phenomenon is often compared to seeing two mountain peaks off in the distance—initially they appear to be right next to each other, but a closer look reveals that they are separated by a valley.

Most amillennialists recognize this use of prophetic perspective. As Riddlebarger himself explains: "There are specific instances in the Scriptures when a prophet foretold what appears to be a single future event, but as history unfolded it became clear that the original prophecy referred to multiple events."[41] According to Riddlebarger, the mountain peak analogy is a fitting way to illustrate this dynamic:

> As I stand in the greater Los Angeles basin and look toward the mountains to the northeast, I see a single mountainous ridge on the horizon. Yet, if I were to drive directly toward the mountains,

---

39 See Gordon D. Fee and Douglas Stuart, *How to Read the Bible for All Its Worth*, 3rd ed. (Grand Rapids: Zondervan Publishing, 2003), 200; Walter C. Kaiser and Moisés Silva, *An Introduction to Biblical Hermeneutics: The Search for Meaning* (Grand Rapids: Zondervan Publishing, 1994), 143–44; Robert L. Plummer, *40 Questions About Interpreting the Bible* (Grand Rapids: Kregel Academic & Professional, 2010), 210; William W. Klein, Craig L. Blomberg, and Robert L. Hubbard, *Introduction to Biblical Interpretation* (Nashville: W Publishing Group, 1993), 304–5; Henry A. Virkler and Karelynne Gerber Ayayo, *Hermeneutics: Principles and Processes of Biblical Interpretation*, 2nd ed. (Grand Rapids: Baker Academic, 2007), 169–70; Walter C. Kaiser, Jr., *The Use of the Old Testament in the New* (Eugene, OR: Wipf and Stock Publishers, 1985), 63–68; J. Scott Duvall and J. Daniel Hays, *Grasping God's Word: A Hands-On Approach to Reading, Interpreting, and Applying the Bible* (Grand Rapids: Zondervan Publishing, 2001), 370–71; Kenneth L. Barker, "The Scope and Center of Old and New Testament Theology," in *Dispensationalism, Israel and the Church: The Search for Definition*, eds. Craig A. Blaising and Darrell L. Bock (Grand Rapids: Zondervan Publishing, 1992), 324–25; George Eldon Ladd, *The Presence of the Future: The Eschatology of Biblical Realism* (Grand Rapids: Eerdmans Publishing, 1974), 64–65.
40 See, for example, Isa 9:6–7; 40:1–5; 61:1–2 (cf. Luke 4:16–21); Jer 29:10–14; Zech 9:9–10; and Joel 2:28–32.
41 Riddlebarger, *A Case for Amillennialism*, 71.

I would soon realize that what appeared to be a single ridge was actually a series of hills, valleys, and mountains separated by many miles. So it is with some Old Testament prophecies.[42]

For example, there is no clear evidence in the Old Testament alone that there would be two distinct comings of the Messiah separated by a significant period of time. But once later revelation in the New Testament arrived, it became clear that what the Old Testament writers seemed to depict as a single event must now be recognized as two events with a gap of time separating the two.[43] As a more specific example, the events prophesied in Isaiah 61:1–2 appear to take place at the same time, and yet later revelation in Luke 4:16–21 clarifies a gap of time between the first-century fulfillment of Isaiah 61:1–2a and the eschatological fulfillment of Isaiah 61:2b. Luke 4 does not reinterpret, diminish, or distort the original meaning of Isaiah 61:1–2, but it does bring clarity to the timing of the events that were prophesied.

In the same way, even though various New Testament passages appear to teach that the Second Coming will immediately usher in the final state of perfection, Revelation 20 clarifies that a lengthy gap of time—an intermediate earthly kingdom of a thousand years—will separate the present age and the eternal state. This gap is not apparent in most of the passages cited by amillennialists, but it is implied in various Old Testament prophecies—even being designated a lengthy period of "many days" in Isaiah 24:21–23—and it is made explicit by the apostle John in his description of the millennial reign of Christ. In this way, unlike the two-age model of amillennialism, premillennialism is able to synthesize the entirety of biblical teaching on the age to come as revealed throughout Scripture.

The Approach of This Critique

In addressing the question of whether the two-age model precludes an intermediate kingdom, this critique moves progressively through Scripture. The first section (chapters 2–5) focuses on the Old Testament, with an exegesis of several prophetic passages which predict a period of time

---

42 Ibid.
43 Hoekema, *The Bible and the Future*, 89.

that is distinct from both the present age and the eternal state (Ps 72:1–20; Isa 2:1–3//Mic 4:2–4; Isa 11:1–9; 65:17–25; Zech 8:4–5; 14:16–19; Isa 24:21–23). A careful examination of these passages will demonstrate not only that the two-age model of amillennialism has difficulty accommodating these prophetic predictions, but also that they are best understood as providing evidence for an intermediate kingdom between the present age and the eternal state.

The second section (chapters 6–10) transitions to the New Testament and responds directly to the three ways that the two-age model is used as an argument against premillennialism. This section focuses on specific eschatological events which amillennialists cite as forming the dividing line between the two ages: the resurrection and judgment of all mankind (Dan 12:2; John 5:28–29; Acts 24:15; Matt 25:31–46; 2 Thess 1:6–10), the destruction and renewal of the cosmos (2 Pet 3:10–13; Rom 8:18–23), and the final victory over sin and death (1 Cor 15:20–28, 50–57; Rom 8:17–23). This examination will demonstrate that none of those arguments or New Testament passages preclude the possibility of an intermediate kingdom, and at least one of these passages refers to a messianic reign of Christ between the present age and the eternal state (1 Cor 15:20–28).

The final section of this critique (chapters 11–14) focuses on Revelation 20:1–6, commonly considered a *crux interpretum* in the debate over the millennium. This passage is critical because Revelation 20 appears to present the most obvious and formidable challenge of the two-age model by describing an intermediate reign of Christ between the Second Coming (Rev 19) and the eternal state (Rev 21). This section will evaluate the various arguments for the amillennial interpretation of Revelation 20:1–6, giving particular attention to four key exegetical issues in this passage—the timing of Satan's binding, the nature of the first resurrection, the duration of the thousand years, and the chronology of John's visions.

If Revelation 20 clearly teaches an earthly reign of Christ between the present age and the eternal state, there must be some way to harmonize this intermediate kingdom with the two ages in the New Testament. This critique will demonstrate not only that the messianic kingdom of premillennialism is unmistakably clear in Revelation 20, but also that this kingdom is perfectly compatible with all the passages cited by amillennialists as disproving it. In the end, harmonizing the entirety of biblical revelation leads to the conclusion that the thousand years in Revelation 20 describes a millennial kingdom that will take place between the present age and the eternal state, just as premillennialism teaches.

PART 1

The Intermediate Kingdom
in the
Old Testament

Chapter 2

The Intermediate Kingdom in the Psalms and Prophets

INTRODUCTION

In the two-age model of amillennialism, there is no room for the intermediate kingdom of premillennialism. As the Old Testament looks ahead to the coming kingdom, however, several prophetic passages seem to predict a period of time that is distinct from both the present age and the eternal state.[1] Because these passages describe conditions which do not fit in either time period, they appear to "indicate some future stage in the history of redemption which is far greater than the present church age but which still does not see the removal of all sin and rebellion and death from the earth."[2]

As premillennialist Robert L. Saucy notes, the conditions presented in these Old Testament passages reveal "a tension in the prophetic picture between a millennial restoration that is not yet complete and the final perfection of the eternal state."[3] On one hand, the eschatological kingdom is characterized by peace, righteousness, eternal blessing, and immortality; but on the other hand, some prophetic passages include conditions of sin,

---

1 Michael J. Vlach, "The Kingdom of God and the Millennium," *MSJ* 23, no. 2 (Fall 2012): 227, 233–40.
2 Wayne Grudem, *Systematic Theology: An Introduction to Biblical Doctrine* (Grand Rapids: Zondervan Publishing, 1994), 1127.
3 Robert L. Saucy, *The Case for Progressive Dispensationalism: The Interface Between Dispensational and Non-Dispensational Theology* (Grand Rapids: Zondervan Publishing, 1993), 237–38.

rebellion, and human death.[4] For this reason, "it is certainly possible that these conditions might be fulfilled in a historical phase of the kingdom prior to the final fulfillment" of the eternal state.[5]

Because the prophetic picture includes a portrayal of the Messiah reigning in a yet imperfect world,[6] premillennialists point to these passages as Old Testament evidence for the necessity of an intermediate kingdom.[7] According to this argument, the best way to account for all the biblical data and to resolve the aforementioned tension in the prophetic picture is to recognize the existence of two phases of the coming kingdom—the millennium (Rev 20) and the eternal state (Rev 21–22).[8] In contrast, the two-age model of amillennialism has difficulty accommodating those Old Testament passages which indicate an intermediate kingdom.

These prophetic passages include Psalm 72:1–20, Isaiah 2:1–3 // Micah 4:2–4, Isaiah 11:1–9, Isaiah 65:17–25, Zechariah 8:4–5, Zechariah 14:16–19, and Isaiah 24:21–23. In chapters 2–5 of this book, each of these passages will be considered to determine if the Old Testament provides

---

4 Craig A. Blaising and Darrell L. Bock, *Progressive Dispensationalism* (Grand Rapids: Baker Books, 1993), 274.

5 Ibid. Elsewhere Blaising is more dogmatic about the implications of this tension: "A number of prophecies while highlighting conditions of blessedness in the future kingdom also describe conditions of sin and death that can only precede the final judgment. This can be true only if the future, eschatological kingdom is first established some time before the final judgment; the final judgment then will separate two phases of that kingdom, one temporary, the other eternal" (Craig A. Blaising, "The Kingdom that Comes with Jesus: Premillennialism and the Harmony of Scripture," in *The Return of Christ: A Premillennial Perspective*, eds. David L. Allen and Steve W. Lemke [Nashville: Broadman & Holman, 2011], 145).

6 Robert L. Saucy, "Response to *Understanding Dispensationalists*, by Vern S. Poythress," *GTJ* 10, no. 2 (Fall 1989): 144. According to Saucy, this lack of perfection is "indicated by the presence of continuing sin and the corresponding presence of the saving activity of God" (*Progressive Dispensationalism*, 238).

7 Craig A. Blaising, "Premillennialism," in *Three Views on the Millennium and Beyond*, ed. Darrell L. Bock (Grand Rapids: Zondervan Publishing), 200–4; Vlach, "The Kingdom of God and the Millennium," 233–40; Grudem, *Systematic Theology*, 1127–30; Blaising, "The Kingdom that Comes with Jesus," 143–45; Saucy, *Progressive Dispensationalism*, 237–41; Blaising and Bock, *Progressive Dispensationalism*, 274–76. According to Kenneth Kantzer, the 20th-century shift toward premillennialism in evangelical scholarship was due in part to this realization that "much of what the Old Testament prophets predicted for the 'end times' could not legitimately be applied to heaven" (Kenneth S. Kantzer, "Foreword," in *A Case for Premillennialism: A New Consensus*, eds. Donald K. Campbell and Jeffrey L. Townsend [Chicago: Moody Press, 1992], 8).

8 Saucy, "Response to *Understanding Dispensationalists*," 140; Blaising, "The Kingdom that Comes with Jesus," 145.

clear evidence of an intermediate kingdom consistent with the eschatology of premillennialism.

The Intermediate Kingdom in Psalm 72:1–20

In Psalm 72, Solomon looks beyond his own experience as king over Israel to speak of the glories of the reign of the coming Messiah.[9] This future kingdom will consist of the righteous and peaceful reign of Christ over the entirety of the world (vv. 2–4, 7, 12), extending "from sea to sea" and "to the ends of the earth" (v. 8). During this coming reign of Messiah—in which "all kings bow down before him" and "all nations serve him" (v. 11; cf. v. 15)—all the peoples of the earth will be blessed (vv. 7, 16–17), and the whole world will be filled with His glory (v. 19). The coming kingdom of Psalm 72 clearly extends not only beyond the reign of Solomon, but also beyond anything experienced in the present age.

At the same time, Solomon's description of this future reign of Messiah also includes conditions that clearly fall short of the eternal state. In the coming kingdom of Psalm 72, the Messiah will defend and vindicate the afflicted (vv. 2, 4); save the children of the needy (v. 4); crush the oppressor (v. 4); subdue His enemies (v. 9); deliver the needy and afflicted in response to their cries for help (v. 12); have compassion on the poor (v. 13); and deliver the oppressed and the victims of violence (vv. 13b–14). The existence of the afflicted, needy, oppressed, and poor—along with the enemies of God who mistreat those who are victimized—is incompatible with the final consummation of the final state.

As premillennialist Wayne Grudem writes, "All of this speaks of an age far different from the present age but short of the eternal state in which there is no more sin or suffering."[10] Because this description in Psalm 72 cannot be harmonized either with our present world or with the final state of sinless immortality, it must refer to a future reign of Messiah between the present age and the eternal state.[11] In this intermediate

---

9 Walter C. Kaiser, Jr., *The Messiah in the Old Testament* (Grand Rapids: Zondervan Publishing, 1995), 133–35.
10 Grudem, *Systematic Theology*, 1129. Saucy describes it as "a picture of universal blessing for the nations, but not yet perfection" (*Progressive Dispensationalism*, 239).
11 Grudem, *Systematic Theology*, 1129; Saucy, *Progressive Dispensationalism*, 239; Michael J. Vlach, "Is Revelation 20 the Only Supporting Text for Premillennialism?," accessed on April 4, 2014, http://theologicalstudies.org/files/resources/Rev_20_an_d_OT.pdf.

kingdom, Christ will reign in peace and righteousness—bringing an abundance of blessing to the entire earth—and yet the presence of sin will continue to prevail, leaving some in need of deliverance. Affirming the existence of an intermediate kingdom is the only way to accommodate all that Psalm 72 says about this future reign of Messiah.[12]

The Intermediate Kingdom in Isaiah 2:2–4 // Micah 4:1–3

In Isaiah 2:2–4 and Micah 4:1–3, the prophets describe the worldwide kingdom that God will establish in the last days:

> Now it will come about that in the last days the mountain of the house of the Lord will be established as the chief of the mountains, and will be raised above the hills; and all the nations will stream to it. And many peoples will come and say, "Come, let us go up to the mountain of the Lord, to the house of the God of Jacob; that He may teach us concerning His ways and that we may walk in His paths." For the law will go forth from Zion and the word of the Lord from Jerusalem. And He will judge between the nations, and will render decisions for many peoples; and they will hammer their swords into plowshares and their spears into pruning hooks. Nation will not lift up sword against nation, and never again will they learn war (Isa 2:2–4).

> And it will come about in the last days that the mountain of the house of the Lord will be established as the chief of the mountains. It will be raised above the hills, and the peoples will stream to it. Many nations will come and say, "Come and let us go up to the mountain of the Lord and to the house of the God of Jacob, that He may teach us about His ways and that we may walk in His

---

[12] The strongest amillennial response to this argument is that the messianic reign predicted in Psalm 72 will be partially fulfilled in the present age and partially fulfilled in the eternal state (e.g., Dean Davis, *The High King of Heaven: Discovering the Master Keys to the Great End Time Debate* [Enumclaw, WA: WinePress Publishing, 2014], 284–85). Although this view is difficult to disprove definitively because of the possibility of prophetic conflation, it appears to separate what is joined together as a single reign in Psalm 72. The straightforward reading of the psalm portrays the various conditions as simultaneously descriptive of the Messiah's reign and therefore indicative of an intermediate kingdom.

paths." For from Zion will go forth the law, even the word of the Lord from Jerusalem. And He will judge between many peoples and render decisions for mighty, distant nations. Then they will hammer their swords into plowshares and their spears into pruning hooks; nation will not lift up sword against nation, and never again will they train for war (Mic 4:1–3).

According to these virtually identical prophecies,[13] Mount Zion will tower in prominence above all others, and the nations of the world will stream to Jerusalem to learn to walk in the ways of Yahweh. The word of the Lord will go forth as the Messiah rules from Jerusalem, judging between the nations of the world and rendering decisions for the people. As a result of this righteous reign of the Messiah, the nations will live in peace, and never again will they prepare for war. According to premillennialists, these prophecies describe an intermediate kingdom in which Jesus will reign from Jerusalem between the present age and the eternal state.

In contrast to the premillennial view, some amillennialists believe that these prophecies are being fulfilled in the present age. According to Kim Riddlebarger, Hebrews 12:18–24 indicates that Isaiah 2:2–4 and Micah 4:1–3 have already been fulfilled in the person and work of Jesus Christ and therefore that the conditions they describe are a present reality.[14] Amillennialist Robert B. Strimple takes the same view, asserting that the prophetic description of the nations streaming to Jerusalem in Isaiah 2:3 and Micah

---

13 As John Sailhamer notes, there are only slight differences between the two prophecies: "Micah does not have the formal introduction of Isa 2:1, but rather the oracle follows immediately on the description of the destruction of the Jerusalem Temple in Mic 3:12. Also, both oracles have different conclusions. Isaiah's closes with a call of exhortation to the house of Jacob to follow the Torah like the nations in the last days, while Micah's ends with a contrast between the nations who follow their own gods and Israel who worships only the Lord. Micah also contains an additional line describing the time of peace, Micah 4:4" (John H. Sailhamer, "Evidence from Isaiah 2," in *A Case for Premillennialism: A New Consensus*, eds. Donald K. Campbell and Jeffrey L. Townsend [Chicago: Moody Press, 1992], 84–85).
14 Kim Riddlebarger, *A Case for Amillennialism: Understanding the End Times*, expanded ed. (Grand Rapids: Baker Books, 2013), 87–89. Similarly, amillennialist E. J. Young believes these prophecies began their fulfillment during the present age and will reach their final realization at the Second Coming. According to Young, this passage "is difficult to interpret," and his interpretation of it "has difficulties, but it is all that one can do if he would be faithful to the language of the Bible" (Edward J. Young, *The Book of Isaiah*, [Grand Rapids: Eerdmans Publishing, 1965], 1:108–9).

4:2 "is being fulfilled *now* as men and women of every tribe on the face of the earth call upon the name of Zion's King and become citizens of 'the Jerusalem that is above,' the mother of all who are in Christ by faith."[15]

But as Saucy observes, a straightforward reading of Isaiah 2 and Micah 4 exposes the obvious difficulties with this view:

> Are the nations at present streaming to the church to learn the ways of God and walk in his paths? Is Christ really "settling disputes" today for many peoples with the result that the nations are turning their weapons into plowshares? It is plain that these questions cannot be answered positively except by an unnatural bending of the text—a bending that would have been quite foreign to the original readers.[16]

The most glaring problem with the amillennial view, which sees a present-day fulfillment of these passages, is its prediction of international harmony among the nations of the world. According to these prophecies, because of the kingdom reign of Messiah—and more specifically, because of the judgments and decisions rendered by Him as He rules from Jerusalem (Isa 2:3; Mic 4:2)—the nations of the world will live in peace, no longer having need of military weapons, for never again will they wage war against one another (Isa 2:4; Mic 4:3).[17] It is impossible to argue that

---

15 Robert B. Strimple, "Amillennialism," in *Three Views on the Millennium and Beyond*, ed. Darrell L. Bock (Grand Rapids: Zondervan Publishing), 93; emphasis original. Davis explains the present-day fulfillment of these prophecies in a similar way: "Even now, through the faithful preaching of the Gospel, many nations of new believers are ascending this Mountain, there to worship the God of Jacob. Even now—through Christ—the High Prophet of Heaven—God is teaching his people his ways. Even now, the instruction of the Gospel is going forth from Zion; even now the Word of the LORD is going forth from the Jerusalem above, of which the Church on earth is a member in good (heavenly) standing (Gal. 4:26, Heb. 12:22)" (*The High King of Heaven*, 251). According to Davis, however, "on a second reading of this prophecy, we may just as easily view it as being fulfilled ... in the new heavens and the new earth" for "the same immutable blessings of the Eternal Covenant belong to God's people in both stages of the Kingdom."

16 Saucy, *Progressive Dispensationalism*, 239. According to Sailhamer, several features of Isa 2:2–4 suggest that this vision was meant to be taken literally and physically, that is, "that Isaiah is here looking forward to the physical restoration of Jerusalem and reign of the Messiah on earth in the 'last days'" ("Evidence from Isaiah 2," 95). Sailhamer argues that the literal/physical meaning of this passage is specifically indicated by its literary genre, its literary context, and its literary type (95–101).

17 This understanding of Isa 2:4 and Mic 4:3 does not result from a hyper-literalistic interpretation illegitimately imposed upon the text. Instead it arises from the recognition that

this kind of international harmony among the nations exists as a present reality, and therefore Isaiah 2:2–4 and Micah 4:1–3 cannot be understood as being fulfilled in the current age.[18]

Other amillennialists believe that Isaiah 2:2–4 and Micah 4:1–3 will be fulfilled in the eternal state. According to Anthony Hoekema, these prophecies portray "the joyful participation of all nations in the worship of the one true God," providing "an inspiring picture, not of the millennial reign, but of conditions on the new earth."[19] But this view fails to account for at least two important details which are incompatible with the eternal state of the new heavens and earth.

First, according to these prophecies, during this righteous and peaceful reign of Messiah, the nations of the world will stream to the

---

these verses use symbolic language—hammering swords into plowshares and spears into pruning hooks—to predict a literal harmony among the literal nations of the world. In fact, amillennialist Sam Storms takes the same approach to these verses. After explaining how Isa 2:4 and Mic 4:3 contain clear examples of figurative language in Old Testament prophecy, Storms concludes that the meaning of this symbolic lanuage is that "God will restore order to the earth in the sense that political peace among all nations and the complete absence of military conflict will come to pass" (Sam Storms, *Kingdom Come: The Amillennial Alternative* [Ross-shire, Scotland: Mentor, 2013], 32). This is undoubtedly the meaning of swords being hammered into plowshares because of how this symbolic language is immediately explained in both passages as nations no longer waging war against each other. At the same time, Storms fails to comment on how or when he believes this prediction of international harmony will be fulfilled.

18 Michael Vlach notes three additional problems with this view. First, Isa 2:1 indicates that this oracle concerns Judah and Jerusalem, and therefore "any view that divorces the Jewish geographical element from the prophecy is violating the context of the passage." Second, in response to Riddlebarger's argument from Heb 12:18–24, Christians today are positionally related to a city that is yet to come (Heb 13:4), but this positional relationship to the coming New Jerusalem does not prove that Isa 2:2–4 is fulfilled today. Third, the spiritualized interpretation of Isaiah 2 presents an imbalanced and unfair understanding of the blessing/curse motif with regard to the nation of Israel by arguing for the literal fulfillment of the curses but not the blessings (Michael J. Vlach, "Isaiah and International Harmony Among the Nations [Part 2]: Does the Church Fulfill Isaiah 2?," accessed on April 4, 2014, http://www.mikevlach.com/blog/2013/11/Isaiah-and-International-Harmony-Among-the-Nations-Part-2-Does-the-Church-Fulfill-Isaiah-2-). Even some amillennialists see the weakness of this view that Isa 2:2–4 and Mic 4:1–3 are fulfilled in the church during the present age—for example, Anthony Hoekema, who describes it as "an impoverishment of the meaning of these passages" (Anthony Hoekema, *The Bible and the Future* [Grand Rapids: Eerdmans, 1979], 205–6). As Sailhamer notes, "Taken at face value Isaiah's visions appear to speak of a literal fulfillment in Jerusalem itself and thus are not easily pressed into a reference to the establishment of the church" ("Evidence from Isaiah 2," 101).

19 Hoekema, *The Bible and the Future*, 205. According to Hoekema, "All too often, unfortunately, amillennial exegetes fail to keep biblical teaching on the new earth in mind when interpreting Old Testament prophecy" (205–6).

city of Jerusalem to be taught the ways of God so they might walk in His paths.[20] As Saucy notes, this implies "an imperfection that still requires what might be called the divine saving action of sanctification."[21] Because neither imperfection nor the consequent need for sanctification will exist in the eternal state, this prophetic picture is inconsistent with the conditions of perfection that will characterize the new heavens and new earth.

Second, according to Isaiah and Micah, as the Messiah reigns from Jerusalem He will "judge between the nations" and "render decisions for many peoples" (Isa 2:4; cf. Mic 4:3).[22] This need for the Lord to render judgments and settle disputes among the people of the nations is clear evidence that sin will still be present during this time.[23] Therefore, "while this activity obviously belongs to the time of the Messiah's reign, it cannot yet be assigned to the perfected state of eternity" and must point instead

---

20 As Sailhamer observes, "The pilgrimage of Gentiles into Jerusalem, where they receive God's law, recalls Israel's own historical experiences, including their initial pilgrimage to Mount Sinai to receive God's Torah and their yearly journeys to Jerusalem. What had been Israel's experience in the past would one day be that of all the nations" ("Evidence from Isaiah 2," 90). Sailhamer argues effectively that the "law" which goes forth from Zion in Isa 2:3 refers not to the Mosaic Law but to the New Covenant law mentioned in passages like Jer 31:33 and Ezek 36:27 (91).

21 Saucy, *Progressive Dispensationalism*, 238.

22 As Leslie Allen explains: "Jerusalem was to become the international court whose findings would be accepted without quibble. Disputes would be settled amicably, for such would be Yahweh's prestige that even great nations in far-flung corners of the world would acknowledge his equity" (Leslie C. Allen, *The Books of Joel, Obadiah, Jonah, and Micah*, NICOT [Grand Rapids: Eerdmans Publishing, 1976], 325). Isa 2:4 and Mic 4:3 indicate that these judgments and decisions from the Lord will result in harmony among the nations. As Vlach writes, "These nations, which appear to disagree at times or have conflicts of interests, will accept His announcements peacefully without taking matters into their own hands" (Michael J. Vlach, "International Harmony Under the Messiah According to Isaiah 2:1–4: Part 1," accessed on April 4, 2014, http://www.mike vlach.com/blog/ 2013/11/International -Harmony-under-the-Messiah-According-to-Isaiah-2-1-4-Part-1).

23 Saucy, *Progressive Dispensationalism*, 234, 238. Here in Isa 2:4 and Mic 4:3, the verb translated "render decisions" (יָכַח) refers to settling quarrels or judiciously arbitrating disputes among people (William L. Holladay, *A Concise Hebrew and Aramaic Lexicon of the Old Testament: Based upon the Lexical Work of Ludwig Koehler and Walter Baumgartner* [Grand Rapids: Eerdmans Publishing, 1972], 134; Ludwig Koehler and Walter Baumgartner, *HALOT*, rev. Walter Baumgartner and Johann Jakob Stamm, trans. and ed. under the supervision of M. E. J. Richardson [Leiden, The Netherlands: Brill, 1994–2000], 1:410; John E. Hartley, "יכח," in *NIDOTTE*, ed. Willem A. VanGemeren [Grand Rapids: Zondervan Publishing, 1997], 2:443), and the verb "judge" (שָׁפַט) means to settle disputes among people (Holladay, *A Concise Hebrew and Aramaic Lexicon*, 380; Koehler and Baumgartner, *HALOT*, 2:1623; Richard Schultz, "שפט" in *NIDOTTE*, 4:215).

"to what has been called a millennial reign of the Messiah before the eternal conditions have commenced."[24]

As premillennialist John H. Sailhamer concludes:

> The attempt of amillennial scholars ... to find a literal fulfillment of Isaiah's visions in an earthly eternal state does not do full justice to the content of the visions themselves. Though commendable for its focus on the physical dimensions of Isaiah's visions, the interpretation of the visions as a description of the eternal state overlooks the manifest "this-worldly" scope of the prophecies themselves.[25]

Rather than finding their fulfillment in the present age or the eternal state, then, Isaiah 2:2–4 and Micah 4:1–3 must point ahead to an intermediate kingdom that will take place between the two. During this earthly messianic reign, the nations will flock to Jerusalem to worship the Lord and learn His ways, living in harmony as the Messiah renders judgment and settles disputes that arise among them. Sin will continue in the messianic kingdom, but the justice of the Lord will prevail and the nations of the world will live together in peace.[26]

---

[24] Saucy, *Progressive Dispensationalism*, 238. Vlach notes two additional problems with this view. First, Isa 9:6–7 indicates that the kingdom of Isaiah is directly related to the Davidic reign of the Son of David, but this view separates the fulfillment of Isa 2:2–4 from the Davidic reign of Jesus. Second, the kingdom promises of Isaiah 2 involve the restoration of national Israel with a unique role to the nations of the world, but according to this view Israel's role during the fulfillment of Isaiah 2 is either "non-existent or transcended" ("Isaiah and International Harmony [Part 2]").

[25] Sailhamer, "Evidence from Isaiah 2," 101.

[26] According to amillennialist Anthony Hoekema, the description in Isa 2:4 that "never again will they learn war" does not fit with the intermediate kingdom of premillennialism because of the final war that is waged in Rev 20:7–9 (*The Bible and the Future*, 205). Hoekema sees this promise as evidence that Isaiah's prophecy will be fulfilled in the new heavens and earth. This is the strongest argument against the premillennial interpretation of Isa 2:2–4 and Mic 4:1–3. Perhaps the best response that can be offered is that Isa 2:4 and Mic 4:3 have specific reference to the absence of war between the nations of the world during the millennial kingdom of Rev 20:1–6, whereas the battle of Rev 20:7–9 consists of Satan deceiving the nations of the world to attack Jesus and His saints after the thousand years are completed.

The Intermediate Kingdom in Isaiah 11:1–9

In Isaiah 11:1–9, the prophet Isaiah sets forth the righteous and peaceful reign of the Messiah. This description of the coming kingdom "clearly speaks of a momentous renewal of nature that takes us far beyond the present age, a time in which 'the earth shall be full of the knowledge of the LORD as the waters cover the sea' (v. 9)."[27] Not only will the Messiah reign with justice (vv. 3–5), but "the wolf will dwell with the lamb, and the leopard will lie down with the young goat, and the calf and the young lion and the fatling together; and a little boy will lead them" (v. 6). The coming reign of Messiah will indeed be characterized by peace and righteousness.

But Isaiah 11 also indicates that certain aspects of this kingdom rule will be coercive, and even punitive.[28] According to verse 4, as the Messiah reigns over this coming kingdom, He will judge the poor with righteousness (v. 4a), defend the afflicted with fairness (v. 4b), strike the earth with the rod of His mouth (v. 4c), and slay the wicked with the breath of His lips (v. 4d). This need for the Messiah to defend the poor and afflicted and to bring punitive judgment upon the wicked "indicates the presence of rebellious activity not in keeping with the eternal kingdom order in which sin in absent."[29]

Because the coming kingdom of Isaiah 11 exceeds what is currently manifest in the current age—and because the presence of the poor, the afflicted, and the wicked are incompatible with the eternal state—premillennialists point to this passage as evidence of an intermediate kingdom between the two.[30] During this reign between the present age and the

---

27 Grudem, *Systematic Theology*, 1128.
28 Blaising, "The Kingdom that Comes with Jesus," 158–59.
29 Ibid., 144. Amillennialists Anthony Hoekema and Corenelis Venema insist that Isa 11:6–10 should not be spiritualized in a non-earthly sense and therefore see it being fulfilled in the future state of the new heavens and earth rather than in heaven during the present age (Hoekema, *The Bible and the Future*, 203; Cornelis P. Venema, *The Promise of the Future* [Carlisle, PA: Banner of Truth, 2000], 292). But neither Hoekema nor Venema comment on the meaning of verse 4 or its significance for the timing of the fulfillment of Isaiah 11.
30 Blaising, "The Kingdom that Comes with Jesus," 143–44, 158–59; Saucy, *Progressive Dispensationalism*, 239; Blaising, "Premillennialism," 202–3; Grudem, *Systematic Theology*, 1128; Blaising and Bock, *Progressive Dispensationalism*, 274. According to Hoekema, the words in Isa 11:9—"the earth will be full of the knowledge of the Lord"—"are not an accurate description of the millennium, for during the millennium there will be those who do not know or love the Lord" (*The Bible the Future*, 203; also see Davis, *The High King of Heaven*, 289). But the earth being full of the knowledge of the Lord need not imply that every single person in the world knows and loves the Lord.

eternal state, Jesus will rule over a righteous and peaceful kingdom, and yet some degree of rebellion will continue, resulting in "a certain amount of tension between the King and the nations, a tension which is easily suppressed."[31] Affirming the existence of an intermediate kingdom is the best way to account for the entirety of Isaiah 11.

According to amillennialist Sam Storms, the divine judgment in Isaiah 11:4 "could easily be what the reigning Lord Jesus exercises throughout the course of the present church age as well as the judgment that he will inflict at the time of his second coming."[32] Unfortunately, the only evidence Storms provides for this view is that Isaiah 11:4 "falls within a larger context that describes the characteristics of the coming Messiah, a passage that Jesus himself cites and applies to his own person and work in the first century (see Luke 4:16ff.)!"[33] But in Luke 4:18–19, the prophecy which Jesus cites as being fulfilled in the ministry of His first coming is Isaiah 61:1–2a, not Isaiah 11:4. The fact that Jesus applies Isaiah 61:1–2a to His first-century ministry provides no evidence whatsoever that Isaiah 11:4 is fulfilled in the present age.

According to amillennialist Dean Davis, the description of Messiah coming to the aid of the poor and afflicted in Isaiah 11:4a is fulfilled in the present age as He grants eternal life to all who recognize their poverty of spirit, and the slaying of the wicked in Isaiah 11:4b will be fulfilled at the Second Coming when He judges the world in righteousness.[34] This view that the judgment in verse 4 coincides with the Second Coming is strengthened by the use of similar terminology in 2 Thessalonians 2:8 and Revelation 19:15a, but it simply does not fit the immediate context of Isaiah 11:

1. The Divine Endowment of the Messiah (vv. 1–3a)
2. The Righteous Rule of the Messiah (vv. 3b–5)
3. The Peaceful Conditions of the Kingdom (vv. 6–9)
4. The Prerequisite Gathering of the Nations (vv. 10–16)

---

31 Blaising and Bock, *Progressive Dispensationalism*, 274.
32 Storms, *Kingdom Come*, 169.
33 Ibid.
34 Davis, *The High King of Heaven*, 288–89. This fits with Davis's overall interpretation of Isa 11:1–9 in which verses 1–4a refer to the present age, verses 4b–5 refer to the Second Coming, and verses 6–9 refer to the eternal state.

In Isaiah 11:3b–5, the prophet portrays the reign of the Messiah in a series of descriptions of what He will do as He rules over His kingdom with justice and righteousness:

> He will not judge by what His eyes see, nor make a decision by what His ears hear; but with righteousness He will judge the poor, and decide with fairness for the afflicted of the earth; and He will strike the earth with the rod of His mouth, and with the breath of His lips He will slay the wicked. Also righteousness will be the belt about His loins, and faithfulness the belt about His waist (Isa 11:3b–5).

In light of the cohesive flow of thought in Isaiah 11 in general—and within verses 3b–5 in particular—it is unwarranted to insist on such a radical break in verse 4 in which the first half of the verse describes the Messiah's activity throughout the present age and the second half describes His judgment of the wicked at the Second Coming. For this reason, "While it is possible that the reference to the rod in Isaiah 11:4 refers to the definitive final judgment, more likely it is to be understood as a general feature within the overall description of the messianic reign."[35] In other words, the judgment in Isaiah 11:4 "does not consist of simply a brief final court, but refers to the nature of the Messiah's rule,"[36] a rule best indentified as an intermediate kingdom between the present age and eternal state.

---

35 Blaising, "The Kingdom that Comes with Jesus," 144.
36 Saucy, *Progressive Dispensationalism*, 239.

Chapter 3

The Intermediate Kingdom in Isaiah 65:17–25

Introduction

One of the most difficult prophetic passages for the two-age model of amillennialism is Isaiah 65:17–25. In this prophecy, Yahweh looks ahead to the coming eschatological kingdom and describes a time of joy and prosperity when He will bless His people and make all things new:

> "For behold, I create new heavens and a new earth; and the former things will not be remembered or come to mind. But be glad and rejoice forever in what I create; for behold, I create Jerusalem for rejoicing and her people for gladness. I will also rejoice in Jerusalem and be glad in My people; and there will no longer be heard in her the voice of weeping and the sound of crying. No longer will there be in it an infant who lives but a few days, or an old man who does not live out his days; for the youth will die at the age of one hundred and the one who does not reach the age of one hundred will be thought accursed. They will build houses and inhabit them; they will also plant vineyards and eat their fruit. They will not build and another inhabit, they will not plant and another eat; for as the lifetime of a tree, so will be the days of My people, and My chosen ones will wear out the work of their hands. They will not labor in vain, or bear children for calamity; for they are the offspring of those blessed by the Lord,

and their descendants with them. It will also come to pass that before they call, I will answer; and while they are still speaking, I will hear. The wolf and the lamb will graze together, and the lion will eat straw like the ox; and dust will be the serpent's food. They will do no evil or harm in all My holy mountain," says the Lord (Isa 65:17–25).

In this description of the new heavens and new earth, verse 20 promises longevity of life to those who inhabit the coming kingdom: "No longer will there be in it an infant who lives but a few days, or an old man who does not live out his days; for the youth will die at the age of one hundred and the one who does not reach the age of one hundred will be thought accursed" (Isa 65:20). In this verse, the longevity-of-life characteristic of the kingdom is illustrated in two ways. First, the death of newborn infants will no longer be a possibility (v. 20a). The cultural context of Isaiah's prophecy highlights the significance of this promise:

> In most ancient Near Eastern societies, the medical profession was able to offer only very limited assistance when people were sick or injured. If there was any trouble in giving childbirth, there was little that could be done to save a premature child. Once born, many children still died of diseases that today are easily cured by basic modern medicines. But at that time an infected wound, a bowel blockage, diarrhea, pneumonia, cold, appendicitis, or a broken bone could lead to death.[1]

In the coming kingdom, however, the constant threat of infant death—so common in ancient Israel—will not be a concern, because "no longer will there be in it an infant who lives but a few days" (Isa 65:20a).

Second, neither will the old man fail to "live out his days, for the youth will die at the age of one hundred and the one who does not reach the age of one hundred will be thought accursed" (Isa 65:20b). In other words, life will be so long and death so unexpected that anyone who dies at age 100 will be regarded a youth, and anyone who dies earlier will be considered accursed.[2] According to Isaiah 65:20, then, no one will

---

1 Gary V. Smith, *Isaiah 40–66*, NAC vol. 15B (Nashville: Broadman & Holman, 2009), 721.
2 Walter C. Kaiser, Jr., Peter H. Davids, F. F. Bruce, and Manfred T. Brauch, *Hard Sayings*

experience an untimely or premature death, for just as in the days of Adam and his descendants, the normal lifespan will consist of hundreds of years (Gen 5).[3] Death will continue to exist, but its power over mankind will be greatly weakened.[4]

This promise of longevity of life is reinforced in verse 22: "For as the lifetime of a tree, so will be the days of My people, and My chosen ones will wear out the work of their hands" (Isa 65:22b). With the most prominent trees in that culture reaching hundreds of years in age,[5] the promise of Isaiah 65:22 confirms that the lifespan of God's people in the coming kingdom will indeed far outlast what is currently experienced in the present age. No longer will people die either in infancy or even at the age of 100—lest they be considered accursed—for the inhabitants of the kingdom will enjoy longevity of life.

---

of the Bible (Downers Grove, IL: InterVarsity Press, 1996), 308; Smith, *Isaiah 40-66*, 721. According to Michael Vlach, "When this prophecy is fulfilled people will be living so long that if they die at age 100, something must be wrong since people will live much longer than that. In fact, it will be assumed that a person dying at the age of 100 must have done something wrong. They must be 'accursed'" (Michael J. Vlach, "The Kingdom of God and the Millennium," *MSJ* 23, no. 2 [Fall 2012] 237). As Claus Westermann explains, "If a person happens not to attain to a hundred years, there must be some exceptional reason for this" (Claus Westermann, *Isaiah 40-66: A Commentary* [Philadelphia: The Westminster Press, 1969], 409).

3 Herbert M. Wolf, *Interpreting Isaiah: The Suffering and Glory of the Messiah* (Grand Rapids: Zondervan Publishing, 1985), 250; John Oswalt, *The Book of Isaiah: Chapters 40-66*, NICOT (Grand Rapids: Eerdmans Publishing, 1998), 658; A. Gardner, "Isaiah 65, 20: Centenarians or Millenarians?," *Biblica* 86, no. 1 (2005), 89, 94-96; Alva McClain, *The Greatness of the Kingdom: An Inductive Study of the Kingdom of God* (Winona Lake, IN: BMH Books, 1959), 493. In this way, Isa 65:20 promises the reversal of the limitation placed on the human lifespan because of sin (Gen 6:3). As R. N. Whybray writes, "For the Israelite long life was one of the signs of God's blessing, and early death was often attributed to sin. In Gen. 6:3 the shortness of human life in general was also attributed to sin. A restoration of what would now be regarded as exceptional longevity would therefore be a characteristic of life in the newly created Jerusalem" (R. N. Whybray, *Isaiah 40-66*, NCBC [Grand Rapids: Eerdmans Publishing, 1975], 277).

4 Robert B. Chisholm, Jr., *Handbook on the Prophets* (Grand Rapids: Baker Books, 2002), 135. As Franz Delitzsch notes, unlike Isa 25:8—which describes the ultimate *destruction* of death—Isa 65:20 refers only to the limitation of its power (F. Delitzsch, *Isaiah*, trans. James Martin, Commentary on the Old Testament [repr., Peabody, MA: Hendrickson, 1996], 7:623). According to McClain, Isaiah 65 suggests that long life will once again become the rule and physical death will be experienced "only by those incorrigible individualists who rebel against the laws of the Kingdom" (*The Greatness of the Kingdom*, 240).

5 According to Gardner, some of the trees mentioned in the Old Testament were renowned for the length of their life span, including the oak (1,600 years) and the cedar (2,000 years) ("Isaiah 65, 20: Centenarians or Millenarians?," 94).

The Premillennial Argument from Isaiah 65:17–25

Because the average human life span is currently 70–80 years (Ps 90:10; cf. Gen 6:3), the conditions described in Isaiah 65:20 and 22 cannot be fulfilled in the present age.[6] At the same time, however, the ongoing presence of physical death in these verses also renders them incompatible with the eternal state, where sin and death will no longer exist (Isa 25:8; Rev 21:4; 22:3).[7] The impossibility of locating the fulfillment of Isaiah 65:20 in either the present age or the eternal state points to the existence of an intermediate kingdom in which sin and death still persist, and yet the longevity of life far exceeds current conditions.[8] Premillennialists identify this intermediate kingdom with the thousand-year reign of Christ in Revelation 20, also known as the millennial kingdom. As Geoffrey Grogan writes, "When a promise is made of conditions that fall short of perfection—as, for instance, when life is lengthened but death is not abolished (65:20)—this does not apply to the perfected church but is best related to millennial conditions."[9] In this way, Isaiah 65:20 provides evidence for an intermediate kingdom between the present age and the eternal state.

---

6 Vlach, "The Kingdom of God and the Millennium," 237. As Vlach writes, "If a person dies today at age 100 we say he lived a long life, not a short one." According to Wayne Grudem, "This single element (the infants and old men who live long, the child dying one hundred years old, and the sinner being accursed) indicates a specific time in the future that is different from the present age" (Wayne Grudem, *Systematic Theology: An Introduction to Biblical Doctrine* [Grand Rapids: Zondervan Publishing, 1994], 1127–28).

7 As Grudem writes, "Death and sin will still be present, for the child who is one hundred years old shall die, and the sinner who is one hundred years old 'shall be accursed'" (*Systematic Theology*, 1127).

8 Vlach, "The Kingdom of God and the Millennium," 237–38. As Vlach explains, Isa 65:20 "must be fulfilled in an era that is different from our current period yet distinct from the eternal state" ("The Kingdom of God and the Millennium," 237; cf. Robert L. Saucy, *The Case for Progressive Dispensationalism: The Interface Between Dispensational and Non-Dispensational Theology* [Grand Rapids: Zondervan Publishing, 1993], 240). According to Vlach, several second-century Christians, including Justin Martyr, appealed to Isaiah 65 as support for premillennialism ("The Kingdom of God and the Millennium," 238).

9 Geoffrey W. Grogan, "Isaiah," in *EBC*, rev. ed., eds. Tremper Longman III and David E. Garland (Grand Rapids: Zondervan, 2008), 6:452. According to David Allen, "This passage cannot be referring to the heavenly reign of Christ for one obvious reason: there is no death in heaven. The text says that people who die at the age of 100 will be considered to have died young. This is a prophecy not about heaven or the eternal state but about the millennial reign of Christ on earth" (David Allen, "The Millennial Reign of Christ," in *The Return of Christ: A Premillennial Perspective*, eds. David L. Allen and Steve W. Lemke [Nashville: Broadman & Holman, 2011], 81).

The Amillennial View of Isaiah 65:17–25

Many amillennialists recognize the problem that this passage seems to present for their view. Samuel Waldron refers to Isaiah 65:17–25 as "problematic;"[10] Cornelis Venema describes it as "a difficult passage"[11] and "difficult to interpret;"[12] Sam Storms acknowledges that it portrays a period of time "in which death appears to be present"[13] and says that it poses a problem "for all Christians, regardless of their millennial beliefs;"[14] and Anthony Hoekema simply refers to it as "a difficult text to interpret."[15] Venema even concedes that the premillennial view of Isaiah 65:17–25 "has some plausibility, because verse 20 describes a time when infants will not be cut off after having lived only a few days, and when those who are older will not die prematurely."[16] In a similar way, Waldron acknowledges that Isaiah 65:20–23 seems "to apply the language of 'a new heaven and a new earth' to a period in which death is still a reality. It speaks of great longevity and remarkable freedom from early death for the people of God, but this language seems to assume that in the end death is still a reality."[17]

Despite the difficulty of verse 20, most amillennialists believe that Isaiah 65:17–25 refers exclusively to the eternal state.[18] A number of arguments have been made to support this interpretation. First, because all the other biblical uses of the phrase "new heavens and new earth" refer to the eternal state (Isa 66:22–24; 2 Pet 3:13; Rev 21:1), the new heavens and new earth in Isaiah 65 must refer to the eternal state as well.[19] According

---

10 Samuel E. Waldron, *The End Times Made Simple: How Could Everyone Be So Wrong About Biblical Prophecy?* (Amityville, NY: Calvary Press, 2003), 236.
11 Cornelis P. Venema, *The Promise of the Future* (Carlisle, PA: Banner of Truth, 2000), 293.
12 Ibid., 292.
13 Sam Storms, *Kingdom Come: The Amillennial Alternative* (Ross-shire, Scotland: Mentor, 2013), 167.
14 Ibid., 34.
15 Anthony Hoekema, *The Bible and the Future* (Grand Rapids: Eerdmans Publishing, 1979), 202.
16 Venema, *The Promise of the Future*, 292.
17 Waldron, *The End Times Made Simple*, 236–37.
18 One notable exception is amillennialist E. J. Young, who sees Isa 65:17–25 as encompassing the entire reign of Christ, including both the present age and the eternal state (Edward J. Young, *The Book of Isaiah* [Grand Rapids: Eerdmans Publishing, 1965], 3:514).
19 Waldron, *The End Times Made Simple*, 237. According to amillennialist Anthony Hoekema, Isa 65:17 clearly refers to the new heavens and the new earth, which Rev 21:1 idèntifies as the start of the eternal state (*The Bible and the Future*, 202).

to Robert Strimple, "Peter (in 2 Peter 3:13) and John (in Rev. 21:1) give us the authoritative apostolic interpretation of Isaiah's vision of the new heavens and the new earth (Isa. 65:17 and 66:22) as the *eternal* dwelling place of God's people."[20] For this reason, it is said, the entirety of Isaiah 65:17–25—including verse 20—must portray the eternal state in which physical death no longer exists.

Second, according to amillennialists, the statement in Isaiah 65:19—that there will no longer be any weeping and crying—indicates that Isaiah 65:17–25 must refer to the eternal state.[21] This is said to be obvious for two reasons: (a) the promise to wipe away all tears is connected to the abolishment of death in Isaiah 25:8,[22] and (b) the very language of Isaiah 65:19 is used in Revelation 21:4 to designate the eternal state.[23] Therefore, Isaiah 65:17–25 must describe the perfection of the eternal state where all weeping and crying have ceased and death no longer exists.[24]

Third, according to amillennialists, the conditions described in Isaiah 65 are clearly permanent and eternal, rather than lasting only for a millennium.[25] In verse 17b, the Lord says that "the former things will not be remembered or come to mind," and He exhorts His people in verse 18 to rejoice "forever" in the new heavens and new earth, not just

---

20 Robert B. Strimple, "An Amillennial Response to Craig A. Blaising," in *Three Views on the Millennium and Beyond*, ed. Darrell L. Bock (Grand Rapids: Zondervan Publishing), 265–66; emphasis original.
21 Venema, *The Promise of the Future*, 293; Hoekema, *The Bible and the Future*, 202; Waldron, *The End Times Made Simple*, 237.
22 Hoekema, *The Bible and the Future*, 202.
23 Venema, *The Promise of the Future*, 293; Hoekema, *The Bible and the Future*, 202; Waldron, *The End Times Made Simple*, 237.
24 According to Hoekema, the promise of no more tears in Isa 65:19 precludes the existence of death in the new heavens and new earth: "Can one imagine a death not accompanied by weeping?" (*The Bible the Future*, 202). As Waldron argues, "Only the perfectly redeemed (and not the millennial) earth brings about the cessation of weeping and crying" (*The End Times Made Simple*, 237; also see Arthur H. Lewis, *The Dark Side of the Millennium: The Problem of Evil in Revelation 20:1–10* [Grand Rapids: Baker Books, 1993], 37; Jonathan Menn, *Biblical Eschatology* [Eugene, OR: Resource Publications, 2013], 304).
25 Waldron, *The End Times Made Simple*, 237. According to amillennialist Dean Davis, "Isaiah himself says nothing of a thousand year epoch, nor does he even hint at the idea that the world he describes will be temporary. To the contrary, he clearly represents it as the *eschaton*, the final state, the *eternal* World to Come (65:18, 19)" (Dean Davis, *The High King of Heaven: Discovering the Master Keys to the Great End Time Debate* [Enumclaw, WA: WinePress Publishing, 2014], 279).

for a thousand years.²⁶ As Hoekema writes, "Isaiah is not speaking here about a new existence which will last no longer than a thousand years, but about an everlasting blessedness,"²⁷ the everlasting blessedness of the eternal state.

Fourth, according to amillennialists, the perfection of the conditions described in Isaiah 65:25 contradict the premillennial interpretation of this passage.²⁸ In verse 25, the Lord says: "The wolf and the lamb will graze together, and the lion will eat straw like the ox; and dust will be the serpent's food. They will do no evil or harm in all My holy mountain." According to Waldron, "Only the eternal state brings the end of all evil and harm in God's holy mountain."²⁹ Therefore, Isaiah 65:17–25 must have reference to eternity.³⁰

But what about the implication in Isaiah 65:20 that death will continue in the new heavens and new earth? How do amillennialists explain this apparent incongruity? Simply stated, most amillennialists believe that Isaiah 65:20 poetically describes the longevity of life to be enjoyed in the new heavens and earth, without actually implying that death will still exist at this time.³¹ According to Waldron, Isaiah 65:20 speaks "of great longevity and the absence of premature death."³² Hoekema says it figuratively portrays "the fact that the inhabitants of the new earth will live incalculably long lives."³³ And Venema sees it as an affirmation of "the incalculably long lives that the inhabitants of the new earth will live."³⁴

---

26 Hoekema, *The Bible and the Future*, 202.
27 Ibid.
28 Waldron, *The End Times Made Simple*, 237.
29 Ibid. Similarly, according to Hoekema, Isa 65:25 indicates that there will be no violence on the new earth (*The Bible and the Future*, 203).
30 As an additional argument, Riddlebarger points to the chiastic structure of Isaiah 65–66— as articulated and defended by J. Alec Motyer, *The Prophecy of Isaiah: An Introduction & Commentary* (Downers Grove, IL: InterVarsity Press, 1993), 522–23—as evidence that Isa 65:17–25 is the climax of these two chapters. According to Riddlebarger, as the climax of Isaiah 65–66, 65:17–25 must refer to the eternal state rather than "a half-way redeemed earth in which people experience life-extension, only to die later on" (Kim Riddlebarger, "Isaiah 65:17–25? Earthly Millennium? Or Eternal State?," accessed on April 4, 2014, http://kimriddlebarger.squarespace.com/the-latest-post/2006/6/27/isaiah-6517-25-earthly-millennium-or-eternal-state.html).
31 Venema, *The Promise of the Future*, 293; Hoekema, *The Bible and the Future*, 202; Davis, *The High King of Heaven*, 279.
32 Waldron, *The End Times Made Simple*, 238.
33 Hoekema, *The Bible and the Future*, 202.
34 Venema, *The Promise of the Future*, 293.

For the amillennialist, *incalculably* long life ultimately means *everlasting* life.[35] In other words, the longevity of life promised in Isaiah 65:20 is seen as a poetic way to portray the eternal state in which the people of God are *no longer* subject to physical death because its power over the whole of life, from infancy to old age, has been destroyed (cf. Isa 25:8; Rev 21:1–4).[36] Therefore, rather than affirming the existence of physical death in the new heavens and new earth, Isaiah 65:20 is viewed as a promise that the people of God will live forever in "a world where all the greatest sorrows and deepest tragedies of our world are unknown."[37]

To support this interpretation, amillennialists often appeal to what they see as a foundational principle for interpreting Old Testament prophetic literature.[38] According to this principle, "Prophecy can only depict the future in terms which make sense to its present."[39] In other words, when the prophets spoke about the future, "they could only do so meaningfully by using terms and realities that existed in their past or present experience."[40] For this reason, when biblical authors sought to describe future conditions they had *not* experienced, they often used language and imagery from the present which they *had* experienced.[41]

The rationale for this approach is the recognition that "our ideas

---

35 Davis, *The High King of Heaven*, 214. According to Davis, the great longevity of life promised in Isa 65:20 ultimately "typifies" eternal life and thereby indicates that the saints will live forever in the new heavens and new earth (279).
36 Venema, *The Promise of the Future*, 293; Hoekema, *The Bible and the Future*, 202–3; Strimple, "An Amillennial Response," 265–66; Davis, *The High King of Heaven*, 214, 279; Waldron, *The End Times Made Simple*, 237–38; Storms, *Kingdom Come*, 36; cf. Motyer, *The Prophecy of Isaiah*, 530.
37 Waldron, *The End Times Made Simple*, 237–38.
38 Storms, *Kingdom Come*, 34.
39 Richard Bauckham, *The Climax of Prophecy: Studies on the Book of Revelation* (Edinburgh: T&T Clark, 1993), 450.
40 Christopher Wright, "A Christian Approach to Old Testament Prophecy Concerning Israel," in *Jerusalem Past and Present in the Purposes of God*, ed. P. W. L. Walker (Cambridge: Cambridge University Press, 1992), 3; also see Menn, *Biblical Eschatology*, 9, 435. According to Donald Garlington, this involves recognizing that the future "is portrayed in terms of *the ideal past*, in terms both familiar and pleasing to the contemporaries of the prophet" (Donald Garlington, "Reigning with Christ: Revelation 20:1–6 and the Question of the Millennium," *R&R* 6, no. 2 [Spring 1997]: 61; emphasis original). Davis refers to this as reading Isaiah's prophecy "as a 'covenantally conditioned' revelation of the perfect world" (*The High King of Heaven*, 279).
41 Storms, *Kingdom Come*, 31–32. According to Storms, this involves the Old Testament prophet seeking to solve "the age-old problem of how to describe eschatological and heavenly concepts in human language" (32).

about things we have never experienced are largely controlled by things we have experienced."[42] Put another way, "Things we have no real capacity to understand can be expressed only through things we know and experience."[43] For this reason, because the original audience could not fully understand what it would be like to live in a world without death,[44] Isaiah 65:20 "is using the idealized language of the present to portray in terms intelligible to the people of his day the reality of future glory in the age to come."[45] As Storms summarizes:

> The best and most intelligible way that the original author of this prophecy could communicate the *realistic future* glory of the new heaven and new earth, to people who were necessarily limited by the progress of revelation to that point in time, was to portray it in the hyperbolic or exaggerated terms of an *ideal present*. What greater glory was imaginable to the original audience to whom Isaiah wrote than to speak of an age in which the all too familiar anguish of childbirth was a thing of the past? His point isn't to assert that people will actually die or that women will continue to give birth. Rather, he has taken two very concrete and painful experiences from the common life of people in his own day to illustrate what to them, then, was an almost unimaginable and inexpressible glory yet to come.[46]

According to the amillennialist, then, Isaiah 65:20 does not teach that believers will live exceedingly long lives and yet eventually die in the new heavens and new earth. Instead, this verse is said to describe "in the language of present experience, something of the joy, blessedness,

---

42 D. Brent Sandy, *Plowshares and Pruning Hooks: Rethinking the Language of Biblical Prophecy and Apocalyptic* (Downers Grove, IL: InterVarsity Press, 2002), 25.
43 Motyer, *The Prophecy of Isaiah*, 530.
44 Waldron, *The End Times Made Simple*, 237. As Riddlebarger explains in his discussion of Isa 65:17–25, "Metaphors are used of things neither we nor Isaiah can fully understand" ("Isaiah 65:17–25"). According to Sandy, "The prophets created metaphors and similes from their world to let us experience what the world of God and heaven is like—as best they could" (*Plowshares and Pruning Hooks*, 28).
45 Storms, *Kingdom Come*, 168.
46 Ibid., 35–36; emphasis original. Storms continues by quoting Motyer, who writes that Isa 65:20 "does not imply that death will still be present (contradicting 25:7-8) but rather affirms that over the whole of life, as we should now say from infancy to old age, the power of death will be destroyed" (Motyer, *The Prophecy of Isaiah*, 530).

and everlasting life that will be the circumstances of God's people in the new heavens and the new earth."[47] As Storms explains, "The prophet is seeking a way to communicate vividly and effectively to a people who were constantly burdened with the anguish of premature infant death and the sorrows that it invariably would bring."[48] Therefore, rather than saying people will actually die prematurely at age 100, the prophet Isaiah "uses aspects of present life to create impressions of the life that is yet to come."[49]

An Evaluation of the Amillennial View

The main problem with the amillennial view is that it underestimates the ability of the original audience of Isaiah's prophecy to understand the concept of death being abolished. To justify their interpretation of Isaiah 65:20, amillennialists repeatedly appeal to how Old Testament prophecy could only depict the future in a meaningful way if the prophets used terms which were already familiar to their immediate listeners. But because a world without death was completely foreign to their past or present experience, the amillennialist claims, the original audience needed to be addressed in idealized language of the present to portray the idea of everlasting life in terms that were intelligible to them. Therefore, when the prophet Isaiah spoke of a day when "the youth will die at the age of one hundred and the one who does not reach the age of one hundred will be thought accursed" (Isa 65:20b), he was simply using this

---

47 Venema, *The Promise of the Future*, 293.
48 Storms, *Kingdom Come*, 168. Storms continues, "He is, in effect, saying: 'People, can you imagine a time and place where if someone were to only live 100 years we would all lament the fact that he/she had died so young?' We need *not* insist that Isaiah is saying, 'Yes, and in literal fact, people in that time *will* die prematurely at age 100'" (emphasis original).
49 Motyer, *The Prophecy of Isaiah*, 530. Waldron summarizes well the amillennial solution to the "problem" of Isa 65:17–25: "How do we deal with the statements in this passage which assume the continuation of death in the New Heavens and New Earth? We must remember an important principle in the interpretation of Old Testament prophecy. Old Testament prophecy often predicts God's coming, glorious kingdom by things familiar to the people of God. Even we cannot understand what an earth without death would be like. This was even more true in the Old Testament shadows. Thus, the Prophets spoke of the age to come as the highest possible happiness in the world as we know it. Such happiness is pictured by a world where all the greatest sorrows and deepest tragedies of our world are unknown. Thus, this passage does not speak of the absence of death. It speaks rather of great longevity and the absence of premature death. The unknown is revealed in terms of the known and the future in terms of the past" (*The End Times Made Simple*, 237–38).

idealized language to describe a future world in which there will be no sorrow because the tragedy of death will no longer exist.

The most glaring weakness of this argument is that Isaiah 25:8 indicates that the original audience of Isaiah's prophecy could indeed understand what it means that Yahweh will abolish death in such a way that His people will no longer die. In describing the joy and glory of the eternal state, Isaiah writes, "He will swallow up death for all time, and the Lord God will wipe tears away from all faces, and He will remove the reproach of His people from all the earth; for the Lord has spoken" (Isa 25:8). How, then, can the amillennialist claim that the ultimate destruction of death could only be communicated intelligibly through the idealized language of the present? Was the original audience utterly mystified by the statement in Isaiah 25:8 that "He will swallow up death for all time"? Was not this promise intelligible to Isaiah's audience even though they had not yet experienced the future world of immortality? The amillennialist has no basis for the claim that the Old Testament prophets could only describe the future meaningfully by using realities that existed in the past or present experience of their immediate audience.

According to amillennialist Sam Storms, the reason that idealized language was the "best and most intelligible way" for Isaiah to communicate the future glory of the new heavens and earth is because his immediate audience was limited by the progress of revelation.[50] But if the limited knowledge of his original audience did not keep them from understanding the straightforward declaration of Isaiah 25:8, why did such limitations necessitate the use of idealized language in Isaiah 65:20? Storms refers to this idealized language as an attempt to solve "the age-old problem of how to describe eschatological and heavenly concepts in human language."[51] He claims that there was no greater glory imaginable to Isaiah's audience "than to speak of an age in which the all too familiar anguish of childbirth was a thing of the past."[52] But Isaiah 25:8 makes it clear that the prophet was not lacking for ways to clearly and

---

50 Storms, *Kingdom Come*, 35.
51 Ibid., 32.
52 Ibid., 35–36. Storms acknowledges that the prophet Isaiah is not "incapable of envisioning a scenario in which physical death is altogether absent," for he does so in Isa 25:8 (168). But Storms fails to recognize how this concession undermines the entirety of his hermeneutical approach to Isa 65:20.

meaningfully communicate the future glory of *death itself* being a thing of the past. Is not the best and most intelligible way to communicate the abolishment of death to say that death will no longer exist?

Furthermore, if Isaiah was able to communicate intelligibly that God "will swallow up death for all time" (Isa 25:8), why confuse the issue in Isaiah 65:20 by using language which explicitly assumes the ongoing existence of death? As John H. Sailhamer writes, "It is hard not to see in Isaiah's words an assumption that at this time death and misfortune will still be factors in man's earthly life. Even as figurative language there is a crucial difference between 'eternal life' and 'dying at a ripe old age.'"[53] Put simply, how is a description of the *continuation* of death the best and most intelligible way to express the *cessation* of death? The hermeneutical rationale for the amillennial view of Isaiah 65:20 is clearly lacking.[54]

Prophetic Conflation in Isaiah 65:17–25

But what about the amillennial argument that the various details in Isaiah 65:17–25 indicate that the passage refers to the eternal state? When the prophet refers to the creation of "new heavens and a new earth" (v. 17a), the leaving behind of former things (v. 17b), eternal joy (v. 18), the absence of weeping (v. 19), and the absence of evil (v. 25), does not this prove that Isaiah 65:17–25 will be fulfilled exclusively in the eternal state?[55] And if so, how does the premillennialist explain the ongoing existence of physical death, especially in light of passages indicating that death will no longer exist in the new heavens and new earth (Isa 25:8; Rev 21:1–4)?

---

53 John H. Sailhamer, "Evidence from Isaiah 2," in *A Case for Premillennialism: A New Consensus*, eds. Donald K. Campbell and Jeffrey L. Townsend (Chicago: Moody Press, 1992), 100.
54 A related problem with the amillennial interpretation of Isa 65:20 is its similar inability to explain the assumption of physical birth in this verse. Why promise that infants will no longer die shortly after birth if infants will no longer be born? Why the references to labor, bearing children, and physical offspring in Isa 65:23 if none of these will take place in the eternal state? Such metaphors would only confuse Isaiah's original audience by leading them to believe that physical birth will continue in the coming eschatological kingdom.
55 Incidentally, not all of these arguments are equally compelling. For example, the argument that Isa 65:25 refers to the absence of evil (Waldron, *The End Times Made Simple*, 237; Hoekema, *The Bible and the Future*, 203) fails to recognize that this verse describes the activity of animals (rather than human beings) and therefore could just as easily be describing the intermediate kingdom of the millennium (Isa 11:6–8).

The premillennial response to this argument appeals to the prophetic perspective of the Old Testament. As discussed in chapter 1, the Old Testament prophets frequently did not seek to distinguish between specific events in the future, oftentimes blending together two or more of these events so they were practically indistinguishable.[56] As Walt Kaiser writes:

> The fundamental idea here is that many prophecies begin with a word that ushers in not only a climactic fulfillment, but a series of events, all of which participate in and lead up to that climactic or ultimate event in a protracted series that belong together as a unit because of their corporate or collective solidarity. In this way, the whole set of events makes up one collective totality and constitutes *only one idea*, even though the events may be spread over a large segment of history by the deliberate plan of God. The important point to observe, however, is that all of the parts belong to a single whole. They are generically related to each other by some identifiable wholeness.[57]

In a somewhat dated illustration, this kind of prophetic perspective has been compared to multiple transparencies being laid on top of each other on an overhead projector, resulting in the projection of a unified whole

---

[56] According to George Eldon Ladd, "The modern mind is interested in chronology, in sequence, in time. The prophetic mind usually was not concerned with such questions but took its stand in the present and viewed the future as a great canvas of God's redemptive working in terms of height and breadth but lacking the clear dimension of depth" (George Eldon Ladd, *The Presence of the Future: The Eschatology of Biblical Realism* [Grand Rapids: Eerdmans Publishing, 1974], 64–65). Most amillennnialists also recognize this dynamic of "prophetic perspective" (Kim Riddlebarger, *A Case for Amillennialism: Understanding the End Times*, expanded ed. [Grand Rapids: Baker Books, 2013], 71; Hoekema, *The Bible and the Future*, 9, 12, 18, 21–22; Storms, *Kingdom Come*, 29; Garlington, "Reigning with Christ," 60–61; cf. Davis, *The High King of Heaven*, 247–48). In fact, amillennialist E. J. Young sees this dynamic specifically in Isa 65:17–25, which he views as encompassing the entire reign of Christ, including both the present age and the eternal state. According to Young, "In the concept of the prophet, time and eternity, the age of the New Testament and the eternal heaven, are not sharply distinguished" (*The Book of Isaiah*, 3:514).

[57] Walter C. Kaiser, Jr., *The Use of the Old Testament in the New* (Eugene, OR: Wipf and Stock Publishers, 1985), 67–68. Kaiser appeals to Willis J. Beecher, who referred to this as a generic prediction: "A generic prediction is one which regards an event as occurring in a series of parts, separated by intervals, and expresses itself in language that may apply indifferently to the nearest part, or to the remoter parts, or to the whole—in other words, a prediction which, in applying to the whole of a complex event, also applies to some of its parts" (Willis J. Beecher, *The Prophets and the Promise*, [1878; repr., Grand Rapids: Baker Books, 1963], 130).

even though it is made up of several layers.[58]

Because Isaiah 65:17-25 cannot be identified *exclusively* with either the millennium (see v. 17) or the eternal state (see v. 20), it must contain a prophetic conflation of these two stages of the coming kingdom.[59] The best way to resolve the tension between Isaiah 25:8 (the abolishment of death) and Isaiah 65:20 (the continuation of the death) is to understand Isaiah 65:17-25 as a mingling of elements from both the intermediate kingdom and the eternal state.[60] The only alternatives are either to deny that the new heavens and earth in Isaiah 65:17 refers to the eternal state or to deny the existence of physical death in Isaiah 65:20. Neither alternative does justice to the language of the biblical text.

According to Franz Delitzsch, this conflation of millennial and eternal conditions in Isaiah 65:17-25 results from the reality that "the Old

---

58 Robert L. Plummer, *40 Questions About Interpreting the Bible* (Grand Rapids: Kregel Academic & Professional, 2010), 210. In the words of Henry Virkler, "When the prophets looked toward the future, they also saw things that appeared to them to be side by side, yet as the time of fulfillment approaches, significant gaps become visible" (Henry A. Virkler and Karelynne Gerber Ayayo, *Hermeneutics: Principles and Processes of Biblical Interpretation*, 2nd ed. [Grand Rapids: Baker Academic, 2007], 169-70). As Näegelsbach observes, "Isaiah and the other prophets place closely together in their pictures future things which belong to different times. They do not draw the line sharply between this world and the next" (C. W. E. Näegelsbach, "Isaiah," in *Commentary on the Holy Scriptures*, eds. J. P. Lange and P. Schaff [1878; repr., Grand Rapids: Zondervan Publishing, 1960], 6:713).

59 According to Russell Moore, this passage appears "to conflate the 'new heavens and the new earth' with an intermediate stage of the Kingdom in which death and rebellion are still present" (Russell D. Moore, *The Kingdom of Christ: The New Evangelical Perspective* [Wheaton: Crossway Books, 2004], 64). Premillennialist Walt Kaiser argues that Isa 65:17-19 specifically refers to the eternal state whereas Isa 65:20-25 refers to the intermediate kingdom (Walter C. Kaiser, Jr., *Preaching and Teaching the Last Things: Old Testament Eschatology for the Life of the Church* [Grand Rapids: Baker Academic, 2011], 160-61; Kaiser, Davids, Bruce, and Brauch, *Hard Sayings of the Bible*, 308-9; also see Paul Lee Tan, *The Interpretation of Prophecy* [Winona Lake, IN: BMH Books, 1974], 92, and McClain, *The Greatness of the Kingdom*, 138). According to this interpretation—a minority view which Kaiser himself describes as "unusual"—the author arranged his material topically rather than chronologically and the "Jerusalem" of verses 17-19 is altogether different from the "Jerusalem" of verses 20-24 (Kaiser, *Preaching and Teaching the Last Things*, 160). Amillennialist Sam Storms rightfully disputes Kaiser's view, arguing that nothing in the passage suggests this "radical distinction," and that the antecedent of the pronoun "it" in verse 20 must be the Jerusalem of verse 19, which identifies the two cities as one and the same (*Kingdom Come*, 168-69). In contrast to Kaiser's view, most premillennialists see Isa 65:17-25 as a conflation of the millennium with the eternal state and do not draw such distinctions.

60 Grudem, *Systematic Theology*, 1127-28; Moore, *The Kingdom of Christ*, 64; Saucy, *Progressive Dispensationalism*, 55-56; McClain, *The Greatness of the Kingdom*, 138-39; Wolf, *Interpreting Isaiah*, 251; Delitzsch, *Isaiah*, 7:624; Oswalt, *The Book of Isaiah*, 656.

Testament prophet was not yet able to distinguish from one another the things which the author of the Apocalypse separates into distinct periods."[61] In other words, with further revelation later in redemptive history, the distinction between the two would become clear, but in Isaiah 65:17–25 the prophet "saw *together* on the screen of prophecy both the Millennial Kingdom and the Eternal Kingdom."[62]

Conclusion

If Isaiah 65:17–25 does indeed consist of a conflation of the intermediate kingdom and eternal state, the various amillennial arguments (that the passage refers exclusively to the eternal state) lose their force. The premillennial view—that the two stages of the coming kingdom are blended together on the prophetic canvas of Isaiah 65:17–25—is able to account for the entirety of the passage, including promises that must refer to the eternal state. But the amillennial view that Isaiah 65:17–25 refers exclusively to the eternal state cannot adequately explain the ongoing existence of physical birth and physical death as portrayed in this passage (vv. 20, 22–23). In the end, the two-age model of amillennialism has significant difficulty accommodating Isaiah 65:17–25, which points to an intermediate kingdom between the present age and the eternal state.

---

61 Delitzsch, *Isaiah*, 7:624. Kaiser agrees "that the prophet may not yet have distinguished and separated these into two separate periods" (*Hard Sayings of the Bible*, 309).
62 McClain, *The Greatness of the Kingdom*, 138; emphasis original. As Saucy writes, "The Old Testament prophetic picture does not draw as clear a line of chronological demarcation between the present history and the final perfect state as appears in Revelation 20–22" (*Progressive Dispensationalism*, 55–56).

Chapter 4

The Intermediate Kingdom in Zechariah

Introduction

Sometimes known as "the Apocalypse of the Old Testament," the prophecy of Zechariah came to the people of Judah during a season of great difficulty and discouragement.

Despite the Hebrews' return from Bablyonian exile, there was little evidence of the program of covenant restoration Yahweh had promised Jerusalem (e.g., Jer. 30–33 and Ezek 36–39). Selfishness crippled community spirit, and the general mood of the period was gloomy and dismal. In fact, only a small percentage of Hebrew captives had actually returned to Judah, and the city wall still lay in ruins, the temple of God remained a rubble heap, and drought and blight ravaged the land. Judah remained a Persian vassal state, and the surrounding nations continued to harass the leaders in Jerusalem and thwart their timid efforts to improve the bleak situation.[1]

To rouse them from their discouragement and spiritual indifference, the Lord raised up the prophet Zechariah to bring a message of rebuke, exhortation, and encouragement to the people of Judah. Zechariah not only called them to repentance and spiritual renewal, but he also directed their gaze to the future, speaking of a day when the feeble

---

[1] Andrew E. Hill and John H. Walton, *A Survey of the Old Testament*, 3rd ed. (Grand Rapids: Zondervan, 2009), 691.

structures of the present would give way to God's glorious eschatological kingdom.[2]

In his prophetic portrayals of this coming kingdom, Zechariah pictures a day when the Lord will reign over the world in peace and righteousness, and yet this earthly kingdom will also include temporal elements such as physical aging, human rebellion, and even divine judgment against sin (Zech 8:1–8; 14:1–21). Because these kingdom prophecies are impossible to harmonize with either the present age or the eternal state, they are incompatible with the two-age model of amillennialism. In contrast, they correspond well to the intermediate kingdom of premillennialism when Jesus will reign over a radically transformed and yet still imperfect world. This initial phase of the coming kingdom can be seen most clearly in Zechariah 8:4–5 and 14:16–19.

The Intermediate Kingdom in Zechariah 8:4–5

In Zechariah 8, the Lord speaks of returning to Zion with great wrath and jealousy and dwelling in the midst of Jerusalem, which will be called "the City of Truth" (vv. 1–3). When He returns, the capital city of God's kingdom will be characterized by sweet fellowship,[3] being a time of undisturbed peace and tranquility in which even the weakest and most defenseless members of society will live in security.[4] As the Lord Himself says in Zechariah 8:4–5:

> Old men and old women will again sit in the streets of Jerusalem, each man with his staff in his hand because of age. And the

---

2 Eugene H. Merrill, Mark F. Rooker, and Michael A. Grisanti, *The World and the Word: An Introduction to the Old Testament* (Nashville: B&H Publishing Group, 2011), 488.

3 Michael J. Vlach, "The Kingdom of God and the Millennium," *MSJ* 23, no. 2 (Fall 2012): 238. According to amillennialist Dean Davis, many premillennialists confidently assert that Zech 8:1–8 was fulfilled in 1948 when the modern-day state of Israel was established. In refuting this view, Davis points out that "even a cursory reading of this heart-warming text will persuade the reader that the happy scenes depicted therein cannot possibly speak of life in modern war-torn Israel" (Dean Davis, *The High King of Heaven: Discovering the Master Keys to the Great End Time Debate* [Enumclaw, WA: WinePress Publishing, 2014], 657). In reality, however, Davis would be hard-pressed to name a single premillennial scholar who believes that Zech 8:1–8 was fulfilled in 1948 or that it describes life in modern war-torn Israel.

4 Kenneth L. Barker, "Zechariah," in *EBC*, rev. ed., ed. Tremper Longman III and David E. Garland (Grand Rapids: Zondervan Publishing, 2008), 8:783; George L. Klein, *Zechariah*, NAC vol. 21B (Nashville: Broadman & Holman, 2008), 236.

streets of the city will be filled with boys and girls playing in its streets (Zech 8:4–5).[5]

According to this passage, "the entire population will enjoy an atmosphere of renewal and blessing."[6] As George Klein describes:

> The very young will have the freedom to enjoy the carefree play that rightly belongs to childhood. Those in their middle years will divide their time equally between their work and the leisure their labors have earned them. The aged will rest peacefully after a lifetime of toil, celebrating the riches of God's blessings.[7]

Even the use of walking sticks by the elderly does not diminish the joy and renewal of this kingdom scene but rather emphasizes the longevity of life promised in Isaiah 65:20.[8] In the coming kingdom, God's people will live to a "ripe old age" and will enjoy the blessing of seeing their descendants playing in the streets.[9]

In this description of peace and joy in the coming kingdom, however, it cannot be ignored that not only do age discrepancies still exist—"old men and old women" (v. 4) and "boys and girls" (v. 5)—but the weakness of old age makes it necessary for the elderly to lean on a cane: "each man with his staff in his hand *because of age*" (v. 4b). This physical weakness suggests some kind of intermediate era "that is different from the present evil age but different also from the eternal state in which all negative aspects of aging and death are removed."[10] As premillennialist Michael Vlach writes:

---

[5] According to George Klein, verse 4 represents a shift in focus from the spiritual health that the Lord will bring to Judah when He comes (v. 3) to the material benefits He will provide through His return, including long life, political security, and undisturbed peace (vv. 4–5) (Klein, *Zechariah*, 236).
[6] Klein, *Zechariah*, 236; cf. Alva McClain, *The Greatness of the Kingdom: An Inductive Study of the Kingdom of God* (Winona Lake, IN: BMH Books, 1959), 228.
[7] Klein, *Zechariah*, 236.
[8] Eugene H. Merrill, *Haggai, Zechariah, Malachi: An Exegetical Commentary* (Chicago: Moody Press, 1994), 222.
[9] Robert B. Chisholm, Jr., *Interpreting the Minor Prophets* (Grand Rapids: Zondervan Publishing, 1990), 256.
[10] Vlach, "The Kingdom of God and the Millennium," 238–39.

From Zechariah's time until now there has never been a time where the conditions of Zechariah 8 have happened. On the other hand, there will be no elderly who are weak in the final eternal state for all remnants of the curse have been removed (see Revelation 21 and 22). What Zechariah describes here, therefore, must take place in an initial phase of God's kingdom before the eternal state begins.[11]

In other words, there must be a preliminary stage in the coming kingdom that includes natural human processes such as procreation, birth, and aging. This initial phase of God's kingdom in Zechariah 8:4–5 coincides well with the millennial kingdom of premillennialism, but it appears to be incompatible with the two-age model of amillennialism.

The Amillennial View of Zechariah 8:4–5

According to amillennialist Dean Davis, because Jesus taught that there will be neither marriage nor procreation in the completed kingdom (Luke 20:34–36), Zechariah 8:4–5 must be using Old Testament images of divine blessing to describe the everlasting joys of God's New Testament people.[12] Amillennialist Floyd Hamilton makes this same appeal to Luke 20:34–36, raising the question of which is to be the standard—the "literal interpretation of Old Testament prophecy" or "the eschatological teaching of Christ."[13] According to Hamilton, "a literal interpretation of these prophecies brings them into contradiction with the plain teachings of Christ," and therefore Zechariah 8:4–5 must be interpreted symbolically.[14]

---

11 Ibid., 239. According to Vlach, "Such an intermediate state between the present age and the eternal state is described in Revelation 20 where a thousand-year reign of Christ is emphasized."
12 Davis, *The High King of Heaven*, 213. Later Davis says that Zech 8:1–8 "uses familiar OT imagery to speak of the blessedness of Christ's Church" (657). At the foundation of Davis's approach to this passage is his commitment to a "New Covenant Hermeneutic." As explained more fully below in the discussion of Zech 14:16–19, Davis believes that when God revealed kingdom promises through the Old Testament prophets, He chose to veil these prophecies in imagery drawn from the Old Covenant. Therefore, today's reader must use the New Testament to interpret the mystical language of the Old Testament, resulting in a figurative interpretation of the prophet's words rather than a literal one (15, 182–83).
13 Floyd E. Hamilton, *The Basis of Millennial Faith* (Grand Rapids: Eerdmans Publishing, 1942), 135–36.
14 Ibid., 136.

In the view of amillennialists, then, "Zechariah is not saying that literal old men and women will watch literal boys and girls play in the new heavens and the new earth."[15] Instead, the meaning of Zechariah 8:4–5 is found in the symbolic significance given to it by the New Testament. According to this approach, Zechariah 8:4–5 means that

> in the last days God will bless his NT people with great longevity (Exodus 20:12, Deut. 5:33, 6:2, 11:8–9), and with great fruitfulness (Gen. 1:28, 9:1, 17:6, Exodus 1:7, Lev. 26:9, Deut. 7:14). In other words, he will bless them with *eternal life*, and with all the child-like joy and *spiritual fruitfulness* that must characterize the people who receive it (John 15:8, Gal. 5:22f, 1 Peter 1:8).[16]

To summarize, then, Zechariah 8:4–5 does not describe a coming kingdom which includes natural human processes such as procreation, birth, and aging; it symbolically portrays the child-like joy, eternal life, and spiritual fruitfulness characteristic of God's people in the last days.[17]

An Evaluation of the Amillennial View

The initial problem with this interpretation is that the immediate context indicates that the scene in Zechariah 8:4–5 will be ushered in by the Second Coming of Christ (see 8:1–3 and 6–8), but Davis sees this passage fulfilled in the experience of the church in both the present age and the world to come.[18] Davis contends that Zechariah 8:4–5 is a symbolic

---

15 Davis, *The High King of Heaven*, 213.
16 Ibid.; emphasis original. In a similar way, Mitchell, Smith, and Brewer interpret the "elderly with canes" as a symbol of Yahweh blessing His people with a multitude of days, as promised in passages like Exod 20:12, Deut 4:4, Isa 65:20, and Prov 3:2 (Hinckley G. Mitchell, John Merlin Powis Smith, and Julius A. Brewer, *A Critical and Exegetical Commentary on Haggai, Zechariah, Malachi, and Jonah*, ICC [New York: Charles Scribner's Sons, 1912], 207).
17 An alternative amillennial explanation of this passage comes from Anthony Hoekema, who contends that, rather than predicting an eschatological restoration of Israel, Zechariah 8 was fulfilled literally in 458 BC when Ezra returned from Babylon to Jerusalem with a number of Jews. According to Hoekema, this passage was designed to urge even more Babylonian captives to return to Jerusalem (Anthony Hoekema, *The Bible and the Future* [Grand Rapids: Eerdmans Publishing, 1979], 208). The difficulty with Hoekema's view is two-fold: (a) there is simply no evidence that the scene described in Zech 8:4–5 was fulfilled in the return to Jerusalem under Ezra, and (b) this prophecy is connected to the return of the Lord to Jerusalem in Zech 8:1–3 and 6–8 and therefore must be eschatological.
18 Davis, *The High King of Heaven*, 657.

portrayal of how believers "bear much fruit" (John 15:8) and produce the fruit of the Spirit (Gal 5:22–23) during the present age. But the conditions in the streets of Jerusalem described in Zechariah 8:4–5 will only be possible because the Lord has returned to Zion and dwells in the midst of the city (Zech 8:3).[19] So Zechariah 8:4–5 cannot be understood as having its fulfillment prior to the Second Coming.

An additional problem with this interpretation is its inability to provide a reasonable and coherent explanation of the details of Zechariah 8:4–5, even with a symbolic approach to the passage. According to Davis, the scene of the elderly sitting with their canes in the streets while the children play alongside them symbolizes three specific blessings experienced by the church: child-like joy, eternal life, and spiritual fruitfulness.[20] If Zechariah 8:4–5 is to be understood symbolically rather than literally, it is certainly reasonable to interpret boys and girls playing in the streets as signifying child-like joy promised to the people of God.[21] But Davis's argument that this scene symbolizes *eternal life* and *spiritual fruitfulness* is far less convincing.

To support his claim that this prophetic scene promises *eternal life*, Davis cites Old Testament passages where Yahweh promises to prolong Israel's days in the land if they obey His commandments (Exod 20:12; Deut 5:33; 6:2; 11:8–9).[22] According to Davis, the elderly in Zechariah 8:4 symbolize this promise of long life, and this longevity of life typifies the gift of *eternal* life. In this way, the picture of elderly men and women sitting with their canes in the streets is said to symbolize eternal life.

The difficulty with this view comes when the interpreter examines the scene in Zechariah 8:4–5 and tries to find the concept of eternal life. How can a description of the elderly who use a cane "because of age" be interpreted as portraying the promise of eternal life in which there will be no aging, weakness, infirmity, or death? If the prophetic purpose of

---

19 This is clear from the focus on the Lord returning to Zion and restoring the nation of Israel in Zech 8:1–3 and 6–8.
20 Davis, *The High King of Heaven*, 213.
21 A symbolic approach to this passage is granted here merely for the sake of argument. In reality, it is difficult to deny the obvious implication that the presence of children in this scene also indicates the continuation of physical birth, which renders this passage incompatible with the eternal state.
22 Davis, *The High King of Heaven*, 213. A connection between Zech 8:4–5 and Exod 20:12 is also made by Mitchell, Smith, and Brewer, *A Critical and Exegetical Commentary*, 207.

Zechariah 8 is to portray a day when the saints will be immortal and no longer subject to the effects of growing old, why accentuate those very effects in the way the saints are described? Why picture them as sitting with a staff in hand because of their old age? Promising a longevity of life which includes the effects of aging—and therefore the implication of death—is an ineffective if not misleading way to communicate the promise of eternal life.

To support his claim that Zechariah 8:4–5 promises *spiritual fruitfulness*, Davis cites Old Testament passages in which (a) Yahweh exhorts His people to be fruitful and multiply (Gen 1:28; 9:1); (b) Yahweh promises that His people will be fruitful and multiply (Gen 17:6; Lev 26:9; Deut 7:14); and (c) His people actually become fruitful and multiply (Exod 1:7). According to Davis, the repopulation of Jerusalem with both young and old in Zechariah 8:4–5 is the fulfillment of this promise of physical fruitfulness, and the promise of physical fruitfulness typifies the promise of *spiritual* fruitfulness. Therefore, the repopulation of Jerusalem in Zechariah 8:4–5 is seen by Davis as a symbolic portrayal of how believers will "bear much fruit" (John 15:8), produce the fruit of the Spirit (Gal 5:22–23), and rejoice in their love for Jesus (1 Pet 1:8) in the present age.

Although it seems reasonable to interpret the repopulation of Jerusalem as the fulfillment of God's promise to multiply the physical descendants of His people, the shift from physical to spiritual fruitfulness is much more difficult to justify. Even in light of New Testament revelation, how could the objective interpreter read the description of the elderly sitting in the streets while the children play and conclude that this promise is fulfilled when God's people exhibit the fruit of the Holy Spirit in the last days? Who would read Zechariah 8:4–5 and Galatians 5:22–23 and see the latter as a fulfillment of the former? Where does Scripture itself make this connection between physical offspring and the fruit of the Holy Spirit? This explanation of Zechariah 8:4–5 effectively denies the perspicuity of the Old Testament and introduces a subjectivity and arbitrariness of interpretation characteristic of an allegorical approach to Scripture.

All of this highlights the larger issue of amillennialism's inability to explain Zechariah 8:4–5 in a way that is compatible with its two-age model. In other words, the problem is not simply with the specific symbolic interpretation proposed by Davis, but with any interpretation that sees Zechariah 8 as fulfilled either in the present age or in the eternal state. The specific challenge for the amillennialist is how to explain the existence of children and the aging of the elderly as characteristic of the eternal state.

Rather than letting the words of Luke 20:34–36 silence the promise of Zechariah 8:4–5, the systematic theologian must harmonize the two passages to account for all that Scripture teaches about the coming kingdom. Premillennialism does so by seeing Zechariah 8:4–5 as being fulfilled in an initial phase of the kingdom between the present age and the eternal state. But because of its rejection of an intermediate kingdom, amillennialism has significant difficulty explaining how and when Zechariah 8:4–5 will be fulfilled.

The Intermediate Kingdom in Zechariah 14:16–19

Zechariah 14 pictures a coming day when Jesus will return to this world,[23] arriving on the Mount of Olives (vv. 3–5) to defeat the invading enemies of Jerusalem (vv. 12–15) and to establish His messianic kingdom (vv. 8–11).[24] Once the Lord has established Himself as "king over all the earth" (v. 9), He will reign over the nations of the world (vv. 16–21). In verses 16-19, the prophet Zechariah describes the annual worship of the Lord that will take place during His reign:

> Then it will come about that any who are left of all the nations that went against Jerusalem will go up from year to year to worship the King, the Lord of hosts, and to celebrate the Feast of Booths. And it will be that whichever of the families of the earth does not go up to Jerusalem to worship the King, the Lord of

---

23 As Robert Saucy writes, "The reference to the personal presence of the Messiah (his feet stand on the Mount of Olives, v. 4) and the overwhelming triumph (cf. vv. 12–15) show that this passage relates to the triumphant coming (or in the light of the New Testament, the second coming) of the Messiah" (Robert L. Saucy, *The Case for Progressive Dispensationalism: The Interface Between Dispensational and Non-Dispensational Theology* [Grand Rapids: Zondervan Publishing, 1993], 239).

24 As Robert Chisholm explains, the temporal relationship between verses 8–11 and verses 12–15 is not sequential. Before describing the Lord's destruction of His enemies in verses 12–15, Zechariah looks ahead to the time after the battle in verses 8–11 when Yahweh makes Jerusalem the capital of His worldwide kingdom (*Interpreting the Minor Prophets*, 271).

hosts, there will be no rain on them. If the family of Egypt does not go up or enter, then no rain will fall on them; it will be the plague with which the Lord smites the nations who do not go up to celebrate the Feast of Booths. This will be the punishment of Egypt, and the punishment of all the nations who do not go up to celebrate the Feast of Booths.

The Premillennial Argument from Zechariah 14:16–19

In this prophetic picture of the coming kingdom, those among the nations who survive the battle against Jerusalem will take part in annual worship of King Jesus (v. 16).[25] This worship will consist of these survivors going up to the city of Jerusalem from year to year to celebrate the Feast of Booths.[26] Over time, however, some will refuse to make this

---

25 Regarding these survivors, some premillennialists see "any who are left of all the nations" (Zech 14:16) as unbelieving survivors of the final battle (e.g., Robert H. Gundry, *The Church and the Tribulation: A Biblical Examination of Posttribulationism* [Grand Rapids: Zondervan Publishing, 1973], 167; Merrill, *Haggai, Zechariah, Malachi*, 361; George Eldon Ladd, *A Commentary on the Revelation of John* [Grand Rapids: Eerdmans Publishing, 1972], 257). For example, according to Merrill, the survivors of these nations will of necessity come to acknowledge Jesus as King of the earth and will render signs of outward submission to Him, but inwardly they will remain unconverted (Merrill, *Haggai, Zechariah, Malachi*, 361–62). But this view appears difficult to sustain, for as Feinberg explains, "The *complete elimination* of the wicked from entrance into the kingdom rests *not just* on the destruction of the wicked at the descent of Christ at the Second Advent, *but also* on the separation of the sheep from the goats in the judgment that follows (Matt. 25:31–46). While many unbelievers will be slain at Christ's return, two judgments follow to root out all who remain" (Paul D. Feinberg, "The Case for the Pretribulation Rapture Position," in *Three Views on the Rapture: Pre-, Mid-, or Post-Tribulation?* [Grand Rapids: Zondervan Publishing, 1996], 74; emphasis original). For this reason, it is better to see these survivors as a converted remnant from the nations which went up against Jerusalem (Barker, "Zechariah," 831; Charles L. Feinberg, *The Minor Prophets* [Chicago: Moody Press, 1990], 343; Klein, *Zechariah*, 421; Harold W. Hoehner, "Evidence from Revelation 20," in *A Case for Premillennialism: A New Consensus*, eds. Donald K. Campbell and Jeffrey L. Townsend [Chicago: Moody Press, 1992], 252; Chisholm, *Interpreting the Minor Prophets*, 275; C. F. Keil, *Minor Prophets*, trans. James Martin, Commentary on the Old Testament [repr., Peabody, MA: Hendrickson, 1996], 10:624) and to see those who refuse to "go up to Jerusalem to worship the King" (Zech 14:17) as their unbelieving descendants in subsequent years.
26 As Charles Feinberg notes, "The nations will go up representatively, for even all Israel never went up to the feasts to the last man" (Lev 23:33–44; Deut 16:13–17) (*The Minor Prophets*, 343). According to Klein, the Hebrew verb translated "will go up" (עָלָה) "occurs frequently in the Old Testament to describe a pilgrimage to Jerusalem to worship. The term occurs in the headings of the Psalms of Ascent (Pss 120–34), generally understood to be psalms associated with the journey of the faithful to go to the temple to worship. Isaiah chose the same verb to signify the many peoples who will 'go up to the mountain of the

annual pilgrimage to worship the King, and consequently God will punish them by withholding rain and bringing drought upon their land.[27] This divinely imposed drought—described as "the plague with which the Lord smites the nations" (v. 18)[28] and "the punishment of all the nations" (v. 19)[29]—will serve as a fitting penalty for those who refuse to celebrate the Feast of Booths to acknowledge God's sovereignty and goodness in providing for their physical needs (Lev 23:33–43; Deut 16:13–17).[30]

According to this passage, then, the Lord Himself will rule as king over all the earth, and yet this messianic reign of peace will not immediately involve the exclusion of all sin.[31] Instead, the rebellion of nations

---

Lord, to the house of the God of Jacob' (Isa 2:3; Mic 4:2). In light of the widespread association of the verb 'go up' with the worship of God in the Old Testament, Zechariah's use of this verb for non-Israelites participating in worship at the temple is particularly emphatic" (*Zechariah*, 422).

27 In the Old Testament, shutting off rain is commonly portrayed as an act of divine judgment (1 Kgs 17:1; Hag 1:11; Amos 4:7–8) (Walter C. Kaiser, Jr., *Micah/Nahum/Habakkuk/ Zephaniah/Haggai/Zechariah/Malachi*, The Preacher's Commentary vol. 23 [Nashville: Thomas Nelson Publishers, 1992], 443; Klein, *Zechariah*, 424). Although the withholding of rain was one of the curses for covenant disobedience (Lev 26:4; 19–20; Deut 28:12, 24), Merrill's claim that it functions as a *pars pro toto* and therefore represents all the covenant curses in Leviticus 26 and Deuteronomy 28 is unwarranted (Merrill, *Haggai, Zechariah, Malachi*, 363).

28 Because the word translated "plague" (מַגֵּפָה) refers to the death of the firstborn in Exod 12:13, Eugene Merrill concludes that the plague in Zech 14:18 refers to punishment by death (*Haggai, Zechariah, Malachi*, 364). As Klein notes, this meaning is possible, but the word does not always signify capital punishment. "Moreover, the punishment meted out to the other nations for not commemorating the Feast of Tabernacles in v. 17 does not appear to be death" (Klein, *Zechariah*, 425).

29 Zechariah 14 specifically names Egypt, which historically has received so little rainfall and therefore has relied instead on irrigation water from the Nile River. Several interpreters believe Egypt is singled out to make it clear that no nation will escape divine judgment for its refusal to worship, not even those that don't seem dependent on the rain that God will withhold (Klein, *Zechariah*, 424; Merrill, *Haggai, Zechariah, Malachi*, 364; Walter C. Kaiser, Jr., *Preaching and Teaching the Last Things: Old Testament Eschatology for the Life of the Church* [Grand Rapids: Baker Academic, 2011], 140; Barker, "Zechariah," 696). Regardless of the precise reason, the passage makes it clear that this divine punishment will ultimately come upon *all* the nations "who do not go up to celebrate the Feast of Booths" (vv. 18b, 19c).

30 Klein, *Zechariah*, 422. As Mitchell, Smith, and Brewer write, "A refusal to celebrate it would argue an ingratitude which could not be more appropriately punished than by withholding rain, which began to fall soon after the feast of tabernacles, and thus preventing a normal harvest the following year" (*A Critical and Exegetical Commentary*, 354; also Chisholm, *Interpreting the Minor Prophets*, 272; Klein, *Zechariah*, 423–24).

31 Saucy, *Progressive Dispensationalism*, 234. According to Saucy, "That sin is present during the Messiah's reign is evident in his settling disputes among the nations (cf. Isa 2:4) and in the possibility of punishing the disobedient (Zech 14:16–19). But that sin will never be able to thwart the righteous, powerful reign of the Messiah." As Blaising and Bock write, the tension

refusing to worship the Messiah will be met with decisive judgment as the Lord smites the disobedient with the plague of drought.[32] The kingdom of Jesus in Zechariah 14, in other words, will take place in a radically transformed and yet imperfect world in which sin, rebellion, suffering, and death continue to exist.[33]

As premillennialists commonly argue, the sin and punishment of the nations in this post-parousia kingdom of Christ is incompatible with either the present age or the eternal state.[34] This prophetic description does not fit the present age, because the Lord is reigning as King over all the earth; but neither does it fit the eternal state, because of the rebellion against the Lord, which is so clearly present.[35] Instead, as Vlach observes, the events in Zechariah 14 fit best with the intermediate kingdom of premillennialism:

> While people from all nations are being saved in the present age, the nations themselves do not obey our Lord (see Psalm 2). In fact, they persecute those who belong to the Lord. In the millennial kingdom Jesus will rule the nations while He is physically present on the earth. The nations will obey and submit to His rule, but as Zechariah 14 points out, whenever a nation does [not] act as [it] should there is punishment. On the other hand, in the eternal state there will be absolutely no disobedience on the part of the nations. The picture of the nations in the eternal state is only positive. The kings of the nations bring their contributions to the New Jerusalem (see Rev 21:24) and the leaves of the tree of life are said to be for the healing of the nations (see Rev 22:2).[36]

---

between the King and the nations in the millennial kingdom will be "a tension which is easily suppressed (Zech. 14:9, 16–21; Isa. 11:4; cf. Ps. 2)" (*Progressive Dispensationalism*, 274).

32 Vlach, "The Kingdom of God and the Millennium," 239–40; Craig A. Blaising and Darrell L. Bock, *Progressive Dispensationalism* (Grand Rapids: Baker Books, 1993), 227; Wayne Grudem, *Systematic Theology: An Introduction to Biblical Doctrine* (Grand Rapids: Zondervan Publishing, 1994), 1129; Craig A. Blaising, "Premillennialism," in *Three Views on the Millennium and Beyond*, ed. Darrell L. Bock (Grand Rapids: Zondervan Publishing, 1999), 202. According to Feinberg, the outward conformity of unbelievers to Christ in the millennial kingdom is described in Ps 66:3b: "Because of the greatness of Your power Your enemies will give feigned obedience to you" (*The Minor Prophets*, 344).

33 Grudem, *Systematic Theology*, 1129; also Saucy, *Progressive Dispensationalism*, 239.

34 Grudem, *Systematic Theology*, 1129; Vlach, "The Kingdom of God and the Millennium," 239–40.

35 Grudem, *Systematic Theology*, 1129; also Saucy, *Progressive Dispensationalism*, 239–40.

36 Vlach, "The Kingdom of God and the Millennium," 239–40.

Because the description in Zechariah 14:16–19 is incompatible with both the present age and the eternal state, this passage provides evidence for an intermediate kingdom established at the Second Coming of Christ. As Vlach observes, a comparison between the three time periods clarifies the distinctiveness of the millennial kingdom as described in Zechariah 14:16–19: in the present age Jesus is in heaven and the nations do not yet submit to Him as King; in the millennial kingdom Jesus will rule the nations and punish nations that are rebellious; and in the eternal state the nations will be free from sin and rebellion and therefore have no need of punishment.[37]

The straightforward reading of Zechariah 14:16–19, then, fits perfectly with the eschatology of premillennialism. In contrast, the two-age model of amillennialism has signficant difficulty harmonizing this passage with its denial of an intermediate kingdom in which Jesus reigns as king over a transformed and yet imperfect world still tainted by rebellion and divine judgment.

The Amillennial View of Zechariah 14:16–19

According to amillennialism, the prophecy of Zechariah 14 portrays (a) the final battle between God and His enemies at the Second Coming of Christ (vv. 1–15) and (b) the everlasting worship of the eternal state that follows (vv. 16–21).[38] The primary difference between the two eschatological positions, then, is that premillennialists interpret verses 16–21 as fulfilled in the intermediate kingdom of the millennium, but amillennialists see this passage as fulfilled in the eternal state.

The most extensive response to the premillennial argument from Zechariah 14 comes from amillennialist Dean Davis.[39] According to Davis,

---

37 Ibid., 240.
38 Sam Storms, *Kingdom Come: The Amillennial Alternative* (Ross-shire, Scotland: Mentor, 2013), 432.
39 Davis, *The High King of Heaven*, 383–84. Many amillennialists mention Zechariah 14 and yet fail to comment on the premillennial argument made from verses 16–19 (e.g., Kim Riddlebarger, *A Case for Amillennialism: Understanding the End Times*, expanded ed. [Grand Rapids: Baker Books, 2013], 92, 119; Storms, *Kingdom Come*, 345, 432; Robert B. Strimple, "Amillennialism," in *Three Views on the Millennium and Beyond*, ed. Darrell L. Bock [Grand Rapids: Zondervan Publishing, 1999], 98; Hoekema, *The Bible and the Future*, 188), whereas others ignore it altogether (e.g., Cornelis P. Venema, *The Promise of the Future* [Carlisle, PA: Banner of Truth, 2000]). At the same time, most amillennialists address passages like Zech 14:16–19 *indirectly* by explaining their hermeneutical approach

there are five reasons why the premillennial interpretation of Zechariah 14:16–19 should be rejected, but none of these objections are compelling. First, according to Davis, the passage says nothing at all about a temporary millennial reign of Christ.[40] Davis writes:

> Anyone who reads the text objectively, refusing to import millennial presuppositions into it, will see immediately that Zechariah is speaking of the conversion of eschatological Israel, the Last Battle, the Day of the LORD, and the eternal worship of the World to Come. It is completely counterintuitive to think that an oracle so grand—so cosmic—in its scale, should have as its *terminus ad quem* a temporary millennial reign of the Messiah, rather than the ultimate glories of the perfected Kingdom of God.[41]

In response, the problem with dismissing an intermediate kingdom in Zechariah 14:16–19 because it seems "counterintuitive" is that this argument grants authority to human intuition in determining the meaning of Scripture. If the rebellion and punishment of the nations in this prophecy cannot be harmonized with the eternal state, then a temporary millennial reign of the Messiah may be the only way to understand Zechariah 14, regardless of what seems counterintuitive to a given interpreter.

Second, according to Davis, if Zechariah 14 and the other Old Testament prophecies of the final battle (Ezek 38–39; Dan 7:1–28; 9:26–27; 11:36–12:17; Joel 3:1–17; Mic 4:11–5:1; Zech 12:1–7) are interpreted *literally*, "it is impossible to reconcile the conflicting data."[42] Because of these contradictions, Davis claims, the only viable solution is to interpret each of these prophecies as a symbolic, typologically veiled revelation of the final clash between the church and the world, the nature of which is

---

to Old Testament prophecy in general (e.g., Strimple, "Amillennialism," 84–100; Riddlebarger, *A Case for Amillennialism*, 83–94; Storms, *Kingdom Come*, 15–42). Representative of the amillennial approach are the words of Riddlebarger: "The Old Testament prophecies regarding Jerusalem and the mountain of the Lord are fulfilled in Christ's church. The promise of a land, as we have seen, will be fulfilled in a new heaven and a new earth in the consummation. Likewise, the New Testament taught that Christ is the new temple and that a new order of commemoration involving the ceremonies typical of the earthly temple can only commemorate the types and shadows, not the reality" (*A Case for Amillennialism*, 93).

40 Davis, *The High King of Heaven*, 383.
41 Ibid.
42 Ibid.; see 218–20, where Davis discusses the contradictions he sees in the literal reading of these passages.

fully disclosed only in the New Testament. Otherwise, Davis argues, the divine inspiration and inerrancy of Scripture cannot be retained.[43]

In response to this argument, the discrepancies cited by Davis consist of details which are *complementary* rather than *contradictory*. For example, according to Davis, the following "contradictions" are impossible to reconcile: (a) Daniel and Ezekiel identify a specific invading and occupying power, but the other prophets do not designate one;[44] (b) Joel and Zechariah state that *all* the nations will take part in the battle, whereas Ezekiel, Daniel, and Micah simply refer to *many* nations;[45] (c) Daniel and Ezekiel speak of a single leader who spearheads the final battle, whereas Joel, Micah, and Zechariah say nothing about an individual leader;[46] (d) Micah, Daniel, and Zechariah envision God's people as fighting against His enemies, but Ezekiel and Joel depict God Himself as the One who fights victoriously;[47] and (e) Joel pictures the sun and moon growing dark, with God shaking the heavens and earth, but Micah describes no such cosmic disturbances, and Ezekiel pictures God shaking the land but not the heavens.[48]

Harmonizing these so-called contradictions, however, is no more difficult for most interpreters than harmonizing differences between parallel accounts in the New Testament gospels. If the interpreter starts with the recognition that no single prophetic or narrative account is an exhaustive description of what has happened or will happen, the supposed contradictions are easy to explain. When Joel mentions God shaking the heavens and earth while Ezekiel pictures God shaking only the earth, this is no more a contradiction than when Mark 16:1 mentions the grave of Jesus being approached by *three* women ("Mary Magdalene, Mary the mother of James, and Salome"), while Matthew 28:1 mentions only *two* ("Mary Magdalene and the other Mary"). The details mentioned in the various prophetic descriptions of the final battle *complement* one another, and a literal interpretation of these prophetic passages poses no threat to the doctrines of biblical inspiration and inerrancy.

---

43 Ibid., 383.
44 Ibid., 218.
45 Ibid., 219.
46 Ibid.
47 Ibid.
48 Ibid.

Third, according to Davis, the anachronisms in Zechariah preclude the possibility of a literal interpretation of Zechariah 14. As Davis writes: "Do we really want to say, for example, that at the end of the present (and very modern) age, the nations of the earth will come up against ethnic Israel riding horses, camels, and donkeys; or that they will bring cattle with them to serve as food (12:4, 14:15)?"[49] This, according to Davis, poses one of the "intractable problems" for the premillennial view of this passage.[50]

Although this argument raises a valid hermeneutical question, it poses no actual problem for the premillennial interpretation of Zechariah 14. Premillennialists have long recognized the need to take an "analogical approach" with some Old Testament prophecies.[51] With this approach, the interpreter recognizes that sometimes the prophets "described the armaments of future eschatological battles in terms of the implements of war known to that day,"[52] and therefore "statements are interpreted literally but then translated into their modern-day equivalents."[53]

Because it is unlikely (although certainly not impossible) that horses will be used as the primary means of advancing on Israel in the Battle of Armaggedon (Zech 12:4), the prophet may be describing the implements of future war with battle imagery familiar in his own day.[54] If so,

---

49 Ibid., 383.
50 Ibid.
51 Henry A. Virkler and Karelynne Gerber Ayayo, *Hermeneutics: Principles and Processes of Biblical Interpretation*, 2nd ed. (Grand Rapids: Baker Academic, 2007), 172. Grant Osborne describes it as seeking a "language of equivalents" (Grant R. Osborne, *The Hermeneutical Spiral: A Comprehensive Introduction to Biblical Interpretation* [Downers Grove, IL: InterVarsity Press, 1991], 218–19).
52 Walter C. Kaiser, Jr., *Toward an Old Testament Theology* (Grand Rapids: Zondervan Publishing, 1978), 244.
53 Virkler and Ayayo, *Hermeneutics*, 172.
54 Walter C. Kaiser, *Micah—Malachi*, The Preacher's Commentary vol. 23 (Nashville: Thomas Nelson Publishers, 1992), 416–17; Klein, *Zechariah*, 354; Virkler and Ayayo, *Hermeneutics*, 172; Mark F. Rooker, "Evidence from Ezekiel," in *A Case for Premillennialism: A New Consensus*, eds. Donald K. Campbell and Jeffrey L. Townsend (Chicago: Moody Press, 1992), 133. The rationale behind this approach is that if God had revealed the specific eschatological referent that will eventually fulfill the prophecy—the approach of Israel's enemies in armored tanks or F-16 fighter jets, for example—neither the prophet nor his original audience would have any understanding of what was being communicated (cf. Virkler and Ayayo, *Hermeneutics*, 172). At this point, an amillennialist might raise the objection that the premillennialist is inconsistent in taking the analogical approach with horses in Zechariah 12 and 14 but not with the prophetic description of everlasting life in Isa 65:20. The difference is that Isaiah's original audience was perfectly capable of understanding the promise that death will be abolished (Isa 25:8), but Zechariah's audience

to interpret the intended meaning of Zechariah 12:4 one must understand the role that horses played in ancient Near Eastern warfare. In that culture, the warhorse functioned as an elite military weapon, and therefore the approach of the invading nations on horses made it clear that Judah faced overwhelming odds, leaving her with no hope for deliverance but in God alone.[55]

Because of the role of the warhorse in that culture, modern analogies, although inexact, might include weapons such as armory, artillery, and advanced military aircraft.[56] But regardless of whether the modern-day interpreter is able to identify the specific referent that will fulfill this prophecy in the future, the intended meaning of the use of horses in warfare—and its implications for how this prophecy will be fulfilled—is clear to the one who understands the text literally in its original historical and cultural context. The use of anachronisms in Zechariah presents no difficulty for the premillennial interpretation of Zechariah 14.

Fourth, according to Davis, a literal reading of Zechariah 14 presents a number of theological problems. For example, according to the literal interpretation of this prophecy, Israel and the nations will revert to observing the Mosaic Law even though it was fulfilled and rendered obsolete by Christ (Matt 5:17; Rom 10:4; Heb 8:13), and they will travel to Jerusalem to observe the Feast of Booths and make animal sacrifices in the Temple (Zech 14:20–21).[57] According to Davis, the mind steeped in New Testament revelation "simply cannot bring itself to assent to such propositions," and it looks instead for the spiritual realities of which these mysterious pictures are Old Testament types, shadows, and symbols.[58]

In spite of Davis's inability to assent to the straightforward description in this prophecy, the literal reading of Zechariah 14:16–21 presents no insurmountable theological problems. As prescribed in the Old Testament, the sacrifices offered in the Feast of Booths were intended to be

---

would have no hope of comprehending a reference to 21st-century military technology. In addition, the amillennial explanation of how Isa 65:20 communicates the abolition of death is questionable at best, but the reference to the war horse as an elite military weapon in Zech 12:4 communicates with clarity.

55 Klein, *Zechariah*, 355.
56 Ibid., 354; Virkler and Ayayo, *Hermeneutics*, 172.
57 Davis, *The High King of Heaven*, 383.
58 Ibid., 384; also see Jonathan Menn, *Biblical Eschatology* (Eugene, OR: Resource Publications, 2013), 446–47.

an expression of worship in which the people of Israel rejoiced before the Lord and celebrated not only their deliverance from bondage in Egypt but also the annual harvest that God provided for the year (Lev 23:33–43; Deut 16:13–17). Known as "the Feast of the Ingathering" (Exod 23:16; 34:22), it was to be a time a great joy in which the people acknowledged the faithfulness of God and expressed their gratitude for His goodness and sovereignty in providing for their physical needs.[59] As such, the reinstitution of this celebration during the millennial kingdom will serve as an appropriate opportunity for God's people—both Jew and Gentile—to express their devotion to the Lord who reigns in Jerusalem. As Carl Friedrich Keil writes, "This feast will be kept by the heathen who have come to believe in the living God, to thank the Lord for His grace, that He has brought them out of the wanderings of this life into the blessedness of His kingdom of peace."[60] There is simply no reason why a future, eschatological celebration of this feast would require the re-establishment of anything that has been abolished or rendered obsolete by the first coming of Christ.

As some premillennialists have noted, the Feast of Booths is the only Old Testament feast without a corresponding New Testament anti-type.[61] But even if an anti-type of the Feast of Booths were identified, Jesus Himself indicates that this would not preclude the possibility of its future celebration.[62] In Luke 22, when Jesus spoke about the establishment of a New Covenant, He looked ahead to eating a Passover meal with His disciples in the coming kingdom (vv. 15–16). Consequently, even though the New Covenant has replaced the Mosaic Covenant (Jer 31:31–34; Heb 8:13)—and even though Christ is identified as the anti-type of the Passover in 1 Corinthians 5:7—Jesus and His disciples will nonetheless eat a Passover meal together. Celebrating the Feast of Booths in the messianic kingdom will no more constitute a return to the Mosaic Law than eating the Passover will.[63]

---

59 Klein, *Zechariah*, 422.
60 Keil, *Minor Prophets*, 10:625.
61 Merrill F. Unger, *Zechariah* (Grand Rapids: Zondervan Publishing, 1963), 265; Feinberg, *The Minor Prophets*, 343.
62 I am indebted to Michael Vlach for this observation in personal conversation.
63 Some premillennialists deny that the fulfillment of this prophecy will necessarily include animal sacrifices or the celebration of the Feast of Booths. According to Wayne Grudem, for example, even though Zech 14:16–21 describes these blessings in terms of Old Covenant sacrifices and an Old Covenant festival, this was the only kind of terminology and

Fifth, according to Davis, the apocalyptic genre of Zechariah indicates that this prophecy must be interpreted symbolically rather than literally.[64] In fact, the apocalyptic genre of Zechariah appears to be the most important factor for most amillennialists in their reading of this passage. For example, Vern Poythress concedes that "Zechariah 14, if read in a straightforward manner, is particularly difficult for an amillennialist," even stating that he would probably choose this prophecy as a main text if he were to defend premillennialism in a debate.[65] "On the other hand," Poythress writes, "the fact that Zechariah 14 is apocalyptic means that it presents hermeneutical challenges. I am reluctant to put much weight on it."[66]

Davis makes a similar argument:

> Was there ever an OT prophet whose writing more fully embodied the "apocalyptic" mode of divine revelation than Zechariah? Was there ever a prophet who more consistently edified and encouraged God's OT people by clothing his great eschatological revelations in vision and symbol?[67]

---

description available to the people of that day; "but the New Testament can allow for greater (spiritual) fulfillment of a number of these items" (*Systematic Theology*, 1130). The rationale for this view is that the Old Testament prophets often described the future in terms that were familiar and easily understood by the original audience even though their specific eschatological referents would not coincide with their literal meaning. This is often seen as the only effective way for the prophet to describe future realities to a people who were limited by their own immediate context. For example, in denying the existence of animal sacrifices in the millennial kingdom of Ezekiel 40–48, premillennialist Mark Rooker asks: "How else could worship have been described?" ("Evidence from Ezekiel," 133). According to this approach, the description of Israel and the nations traveling to Jerusalem to celebrate the Feast of Booths in Zechariah 14 need only be understood as the people of God worshiping the Lord in the millennial kingdom.

The problem with this view is that the prophet could have portrayed the people of God worshiping the Lord in a way that was clear and easily understood by his original audience even without using terminology that includes the celebration of the Feast of Booths. For this reason, it is difficult to understand why the prophet would unnecessarily describe millennial worship in a potentially misleading way. At the same time, it is possible that the Feast of Booths will take on additional nuances of significance in the millennial kingdom because of the historical-redemptive context of its celebration, but this recognition does not deny the literal fulfillment of Zech 14:16–21.

64 Davis, *The High King of Heaven*, 384.
65 Vern Poythress, "Response to Robert L. Saucy's Paper," *GTJ* 10, no. 2 (Fall 1989): 158.
66 Ibid.
67 Davis, *The High King of Heaven*, 384.

Because of the apocalyptic genre of this prophecy, Davis believes that Zechariah 14 must be interpreted "eschatologically, covenantally, typologically, and ecclesiologically."[68] Adopting this approach means understanding the passage as a "veiled" or "mysterious" representation of life under the New Covenant which is designed to provide wisdom, strength, and comfort for the Christian Church.[69] For Davis, the "only hope of penetrating to the deep meaning of this great oracle lies in the skillful use" of what he calls a "New Covenant Hermeneutic."[70]

The New Covenant Hermeneutic starts with recognizing that when God revealed kingdom promises through the Old Testament prophets, He chose to veil those prophecies in imagery drawn from the Old Covenant. According to Davis, this rendered the true nature of the coming kingdom a mysterious secret that would not be fully revealed until the coming of Christ.[71] For this reason, when today's interpreter comes to Old Testament prophecy, he must use the New Covenant to "translate the mystical language" of the Old Covenant, which results in a figurative interpretation of the prophet's words rather than a literal one.[72] In doing so, the interpreter's goal is "to see the blessings that Christ brought us in New Testament times mystically promised and prefigured in the Old."[73]

By applying this hermeneutic to Zechariah 14:16–19, Davis interprets the celebration of the Feast of Booths as a typological portrayal of the eternal worship of the glorified church in the eternal state.[74] According to Davis, "Zechariah's eschatological Feast of Booths will indeed be a *harvest* feast, since here, in the World to Come, all the saints will have been gathered into the barn of God's completed Kingdom (Mt. 13:30, John 4:38, Rev. 14:14–16)."[75]

---

68 Ibid., 382. According to Davis, understanding "the meaning of the mysterious prophecy" involves seeking to discern "the deep, NT meaning of Zechariah's words" (402).
69 Ibid., 382.
70 Ibid., 384; also see 15, 182–83. Davis refers to the New Covenant Hermeneutic as "one of Christ's most precious gifts to the church" (183). Apart from this hermeneutic, says Davis, the church is unable to understand the Old Testament in general and the kingdom promises in particular; but with it "the Great End Time Debate is fully resolved once and for all."
71 Ibid., 15.
72 Ibid.
73 Ibid.
74 Ibid., 402–3.
75 Ibid., 403; emphasis original. According to another amillennialist, "We cannot fully understand why the writer cites the Feast of Booths, but it is likely that this feast, which recalls

As for Egypt and the nations that refuse to celebrate the Feast of Booths, Davis believes that these typify all those "who refused to accept spiritual rescue from the Domain of Darkness, and spiritual transfer into the Kingdom of God's beloved Son (Col. 1:13)" and "who refused to walk with Christ through the wilderness of this world to the Promised Land (Heb. 11:26, Rev. 12:1f)."[76] In other words, the nations refusing to celebrate the feast are those who have rejected the gospel and refused to worship the one true God during the present age.

This interpretation raises the question of how Davis explains the existence of these unbelievers alongside the saints on earth in the eternal state. According to Davis, this puzzle is solved by looking to the description of the world to come in Revelation 22. According to Revelation 22:15, the unbelieving nations are far from Jerusalem, outside the gates of the Holy City, in the Lake of Fire (cf. Isa 66:24; Rev 19:20; 20:10, 14).[77] Davis writes:

> It is, therefore, in death (and hell) that the impenitent enemies of God will endure the very plague of drought that they chose for themselves in life, when they refused to drink of the Rock, and to follow the Rock, that God offered them in the Gospel (Mt. 12:43 NAS, Luke 16:24, John 7:37, 1 Cor. 10:4, Rev. 21:6, 22:17).[78]

According to Davis, then, the description of the Lord punishing those who refuse to worship in Zechariah 14:16–19 is fulfilled when unbelievers are tormented in the eternal Lake of Fire as described in the Book of Revelation.

The main problem with this view is that it fails to provide a feasible explanation of the judgment of the nations in Zechariah 14:16–19, even if a symbolic hermeneutic is used. The primary reason this interpretation falls short is because the divine punishment of Zechariah 14:16–19 is directed at rebellion which takes place *after the Lord returns to earth and*

---

the wilderness experience, functions as a motif for the childlike obedience that sometimes marked the Israelites' response to God in their earliest history" (Thomas Edward McComiskey, "Zechariah," in *The Minor Prophets: An Exegetical and Expository Commentary*, ed. Thomas Edward McComiskey [Grand Rapids: Baker Books, 1998], 3:1242). But exactly how this motif symbolizes childlike obedience is neither immediately clear nor explained by the one who makes this assertion.

76 Davis, *The High King of Heaven*, 403.
77 Ibid.
78 Ibid.

establishes Himself as King. As Wayne Grudem explains, an amillennialist might insist

> that this is a typical Old Testament prophecy in which distinct future events are conflated and not distinguished in the prophet's vision, though they may be separated by long ages when they actually occur. However, it is difficult to make such a distinction in this passage because it is specifically rebellion against the Lord who is King over all the earth that is punished by these plagues and lack of rain.[79]

In other words, rather than being poured out on those who reject the gospel prior to the Second Coming—as Davis asserts in his explanation of the passage[80]—the divine judgment of Zechariah 14:16–19 is poured out on those who refuse to worship the Lord *after* His Second Coming.

To clarify the incongruity of the amillennial view, it is helpful to review the sequence of events set forth in Zechariah 14:

- The nations attack Jerusalem (vv. 1–2).
- The Lord returns (2nd Coming) and intervenes on Israel's behalf (vv. 3–7).
- The Lord destroys most of Israel's enemies in the battle (vv. 12–15).
- The Lord is established in Jerusalem as king of the earth (vv. 8–11).[81]
- The survivors of battle worship the Lord annually in Jerusalem (vv. 16–19).
- Some survivors of the battle refuse to worship the Lord in Jerusalem (vv. 16–19).
- The Lord punishes those who refuse by withholding rain (vv. 16–19).
- The people of God continue to worship the Lord in holiness (vv. 20–21).

---

79 Grudem, *Systematic Theology*, 1129–30.
80 Davis, *The High King of Heaven*, 403.
81 As noted above, the temporal relationship between verses 8–11 and verses 12–15 is not sequential. Before describing the Lord's destruction of His enemies in verses 12–15, Zechariah looks ahead to the time after the battle in verses 8–11 when Yahweh makes Jerusalem the capital of His worldwide kingdom (Chisholm, *Interpreting the Minor Prophets*, 271).

Because amillennialism asserts that the eternal state begins when the nations are judged at the Second Coming, it cannot account for a subsequent judgment of some of the survivors of that battle when they refuse to worship the Lord.[82] Even its typological hermeneutic cannot explain Zechariah 14 in a way that removes the need for an intermediate kingdom prior to the eternal state. In contrast, premillennialism accounts well for this subsequent judgment by affirming the straightforward reading of Zechariah 14: The nations will be judged and destroyed at the Second Coming of Christ (vv. 12–15), and those survivors of the battle who refuse to worship the King during the millennium will be punished by the Lord (vv. 16–19).

An alternative amillennial interpretation of Zechariah 14:16–19 holds that the portrayal of nations refusing to worship God in this passage is purely hypothetical. According to this view, no such nations will exist at that time, but instead the prophet Zechariah has created a hypothetical scenario to convey the absoluteness of God's rule in the eternal state and to envision the end of all rebellion against Yahweh.[83]

The problem with this view is that this hypothetical scenario fails to accomplish the goal of conveying the absoluteness of God's rule. How does portraying the existence of rebellion against Yahweh serve to envision the end of all rebellion against Yahweh? How does a hypothetical rise of defiance against God communicate that no such defiance will ever arise, especially since it is not identified as hypothetical? How would this scenario increase the assurance of God's people that human rebellion will not exist in the eternal state? Would not a more effective way to communicate the impossibility of this scenario be to portray a kingdom where sin and rebellion no longer exist because they have already been destroyed once and for all? This view fails to provide a reasonable explanation of the passage, and the premillennial case for an intermediate kingdom in Zechariah 14 remains compelling.

---

82 The temporal sequence between verses 12–15 and 16–19 is not simply assumed but rather is required by the passage itself for two reasons: (1) those punished in verses 16–19 are described as survivors of the battle in verses 12–15, and (2) those punished in the judgment in verses 16–19 are judged for their refusal to worship the Lord who reigns because He defeated the enemies of Israel and established Himself as king over the earth in verses 1–15.

83 McComiskey, "Zechariah," 1242. Even premillennialist George Klein is open to this possibility, stating that it is unclear whether the circumstances of Zech 14:17 are real or hypothetical (*Zechariah*, 424).

Chapter 5

The Intermediate Kingdom in Isaiah 24:21–23

INTRODUCTION

The prophecy in Isaiah 24:21–23 provides evidence for the messianic kingdom of premillennialism in a unique way. In contrast to the Old Testament passages discussed in chapters 2–4, Isaiah 24:21–23 indicates the existence of an intermediate kingdom by explicitly naming a gap of time—identified as "many days" in verse 22—which takes place between the Second Coming and the final state of immortality (Isa 25:6–8). According to Isaiah 24, this intervening gap of time will occur between two stages of divine punishment—one that occurs at the Day of the Lord (v. 21) and one that occurs after "many days" of God's enemies being confined in prison (v. 22). These two phases of divine judgment, separated by a lengthy period of imprisonment, can be seen clearly in Isaiah 24:21–23:

> So it will happen in that day, that the Lord will punish the host of heaven on high, and the kings of the earth on earth. They will be gathered together like prisoners in the dungeon, and will be confined in prison; and after many days they will be punished. Then the moon will be abashed and the sun ashamed, for the Lord of hosts will reign on Mount Zion and in Jerusalem, and His glory will be before His elders (Isa 24:21–23).

According to premillennialists, this gap of time in Isaiah 24:22 represents an intermediate kingdom between the present age and the eternal state.

The Premillennial Argument from Isaiah 24:21-23

This prophecy of divine punishment is found in the immediate context of Isaiah 24–27, which is preceded by a series of judgments against the nations in Isaiah 13–23. Unlike the oracles in Isaiah 13–23, however, the divine judgment in Isaiah 24 is universal, making no reference to specific nations or historical events and eventually extending beyond the earth.[1] As Robert B. Chisholm observes, "The litany of divine judgment on the nations of Isaiah's day (chapters 13–23) forms a fitting prelude to chapters 24–27, which depict God's culminating worldwide judgment and the establishment of his earthly kingdom."[2]

Isaiah 24 begins with a thesis statement—"Behold, the Lord lays the earth waste, devastates it, distorts its surface and scatters its inhabitants" (Isa 24:1)—and the remainder of the chapter details this divine destruction of the earth and the enemies of God (Isa 24:2–20). A careful comparison between this passage and the Apocalypse demonstrates that the earthly destruction of Isaiah 24:1–20 corresponds to the global judgments of Revelation 6–19.[3] In fact, Isaiah 24–27 has often been called "The Little Apocalypse" because of its resemblance to the book of Revelation in both its literary style and its emphasis on the eschatological judgment of God and establishment of His eternal kingdom.[4]

After describing the destruction of earth in Isaiah 24:1–20, the prophet identifies this judgment as the eschatological Day of the Lord—indicated by the introductory formula "in that day" (בַּיּוֹם הַהוּא) in verse 21[5]—and broadens its scope to include both "the kings of the earth on

---

1 Geoffrey W. Grogan, "Isaiah," in *EBC*, rev. ed., eds. Tremper Longman III and David E. Garland (Grand Rapids: Zondervan, 2008), 6:616.
2 Robert B. Chisholm, Jr., *Handbook on the Prophets* (Grand Rapids: Baker Books, 2002), 64.
3 Michael J. Vlach, "The Kingdom of God and the Millennium," *MSJ* 23, no. 2 (Fall 2012): 234; Robert D. Culver, *Daniel and the Latter Days* (Chicago: Moody Press, 1954), 50. According to Craig Blaising and Darrell Bock, "The Day of the Lord in Isaiah 24 is given expanded treatment in Revelation 6–19" (Craig A. Blaising and Darrell L. Bock, *Progressive Dispensationalism* [Grand Rapids: Baker Books, 1993], 275).
4 Chisholm, *Handbook on the Prophets*, 64–65; Vlach, "The Kingdom of God and the Millennium," 227.
5 The formula "in that day" occurs seven times in Isaiah 24–27 (24:21; 25:9; 26:1; 27:1, 2, 12, 13), "each time enlarging on some aspect of the general situation sketched in 24:1–20 and

earth" and "the hosts of heaven on high" (Isa 24:21).⁶ According to Isaiah, all the enemies of Yahweh, whether earthly or heavenly powers, will be punished by God on the Day of the Lord. As Herbert Wolf explains, "To complete the judgment of the earth, God must deal with the evil forces that foment rebellion against Him, namely Satan and his army of angels."⁷

In Isaiah 24:22, the prophet describes the first part of this divine judgment as confinement in prison: "They will be gathered together like prisoners in the dungeon, and will be confined in prison" (Isa 24:22ab).⁸ According to Isaiah, this imprisonment of God's earthly and heavenly enemies will continue for "many days" (רֹב יָמִים), an indefinite expression used elsewhere in reference to a very long period of time (Jer 35:7), even hundreds of years (2 Chron 15:3; Hos 3:4–5). Then, after this lengthy confinement of "many days," they will experience the final judgment:

---

offering a balanced presentation of the theme" (J. Alec Motyer, *The Prophecy of Isaiah: An Introduction & Commentary* [Downers Grove, IL: InterVarsity Press, 1993], 205).

6 As Gary Smith notes, "The heavenly hosts could refer to the stars and planets (40:26; 45:12; Ps. 33:6), but it seems more likely that this is a reference to enemy angelic beings (2 Kgs 22:19; Job 1:6; Dan 4:32; 8:10; 10:13), not inanimate objects" (Gary V. Smith, *Isaiah 1–39*, NAC vol. 15A [Nashville: Broadman & Holman, 2007], 424). Geoffrey Grogan similarly argues that the concept of punishment implies personal beings and therefore the reference is probably to fallen angels (Grogan, "Isaiah," 623). In addition, the parallelism between the two halves of Isa 24:21 "invites the comparison between the defeat of the powerful evil rulers on earth (21b) and the powerful rulers in heaven (21a)" (Smith, *Isaiah 1–39*, 424; also see F. Delitzsch, *Isaiah*, trans. James Martin, Commentary on the Old Testament [repr., Peabody, MA: Hendrickson, 1996], 7:282).

7 Herbert M. Wolf, *Interpreting Isaiah: The Suffering and Glory of the Messiah* (Grand Rapids: Zondervan Publishing, 1985), 139–40. According to Robert Chisholm, "In the progress of biblical revelation, one discovers that the driving force behind this coalition is none other than Satan, whose defeat and imprisonment the Apostle John describes (see Rev. 20:2–3)" (*Handbook on the Prophets*, 67).

8 The word translated "dungeon" (בּוֹר) in verse 22 literally refers to a cistern, but it is often used metaphorically to signify the place of the dead (Ps 28:1; 30:3; 40:2; 88:4; 143:7; Prov 1:12; Isa 14:15; 38:18; Ezek 26:20; 31:14, 16) (Bryan E. Beyer and Eugene H. Merrill, "בּוֹר," in *NIDOTTE*, 1:620–21; William L. Holladay, *A Concise Hebrew and Aramaic Lexicon of the Old Testament: Based upon the Lexical Work of Ludwig Koehler and Walter Baumgartner* [Grand Rapids: Eerdmans Publishing, 1972], 36; Ludwig Koehler and Walter Baumgartner, *HALOT*, 1:116). The word translated "prison" (מַסְגֵּר) refers to a prison or dungeon (Isa 42:7; Ps 142:8) (Holladay, *A Concise Hebrew and Aramaic Lexicon*, 203; Koehler and Baumgartner, *HALOT*, 1:604), and in Isa 24:22 it refers to the subterranean prison into which the rebellious human leaders and the superterrestrial evil powers will be confined (A. H. Konkel, "מִסְגֶּרֶת," in *NIDOTTE*, 2:996). According to Craig Blaising, "A parallel can be found in 1 Enoch 10, where Azazel is bound and imprisoned for a period of time prior to the final, eternal judgment and new earth conditions" (Craig A. Blaising, "Premillennialism," in *Three Views on the Millennium and Beyond*, ed. Darrell L. Bock [Grand Rapids: Zondervan Publishing], 203; also see Konkel, "מִסְגֶּרֶת," 2:996).

"and after many days they will be punished" (Isa 24:22c). With the defeat of this evil cosmic alliance completed, the Lord will now reign supreme: "Then the moon will be abashed and the sun ashamed, for the Lord of hosts will reign on Mount Zion and in Jerusalem, and His glory will be before His elders" (Isa 24:23).

The eschatological judgment of God's enemies, then, will take place in two stages separated by a lengthy period of confinement in prison. According to premillennialists, the "many days" of this imprisonment coincides with the "thousand years" of Revelation 20:1–6, and therefore Isaiah 24:22 necessitates an intermediate kingdom between the Day of the Lord (Isa 24:1–22b) and the final state of immortality where sin and death have been abolished (Isa 25:6–8).[9] In this way, the "many days" of Isaiah 24:22 and "thousand years" of Revelation 20:1–6 begin with the defeat and imprisonment of earthly and heavenly rulers, and they end with the final judgment upon them after this intervening period of incarceration.[10] As Craig Blaising writes:

> The many days of imprisonment between the coming of God in the Day of the Lord and the punishment after which the Lord

---

9 Culver, *Daniel and the Latter Days*, 31–32, 50–52; Blaising, "Premillennialism," 203–4; Vlach, "The Kingdom of God and the Millennium," 234–36; Craig A. Blaising, "The Kingdom that Comes with Jesus: Premillennialism and the Harmony of Scripture," in *The Return of Christ: A Premillennial Perspective*, eds. David L. Allen and Steve W. Lemke (Nashville: Broadman & Holman, 2011), 145–46, 158; Alva J. McClain, *The Greatness of the Kingdom: An Inductive Study of the Kingdom of God* (Winona Lake, IN: BMH Books, 1959), 215–16, 494; Blaising and Bock, *Progressive Dispensationalism*, 274–75; Walter C. Kaiser, Jr., *The Christian and the "Old" Testament* (Pasadena: William Carey Library, 1998), 138; Nathaniel West, *The Thousand Years in Both Testaments* (Fincastle, VA: Scripture Truth Book Company, 1889), 35–49; Chisholm, *Handbook on the Prophets*, 67. According to Blaising, "The first stage of this judgment is described in Isaiah 24 as the coming Day of the Lord. While that judgment is catastrophic, it results in an 'imprisonment' of some who will subsequently be 'punished' after 'many days' (Isa 24:21–22). After this latter punishment death will be abolished (Isa 25:6–8).... The latter punishment, then, separates two phases of the coming rule. Since the removal of death is relegated to the latter phase, death is still present during the earlier phase, the time of the imprisonment" ("The Kingdom that Comes with Jesus," 145–46).

10 McClain, *The Greatness of the Kingdom*, 215–16, 494. According to Blaising, because this final judgment separates two phases of the coming kingdom—and because the removal of death is relegated to the latter phase (Isa 25:6–8)—death must still be present during the earlier phase of "many days" when the enemies of God are imprisoned ("The Kingdom that Comes with Jesus," 145–46). This coincides well with Isa 65:20 which indicates the existence of death in the intermediate kingdom (see chapter 3).

reigns in glory greater than sun or moon bear a correspondence to the millennial period in Revelation 20, which also follows the coming of the Lord in the Day of the Lord (Rev. 6–19) and transpires between the imprisonment of the devil (20:1–3) and his future punishment (20:7–10).[11]

To support this argument, Michael Vlach highlights several key parallels between Isaiah 24:21–23 and Revelation 19 and 20:[12]

Isaiah 24:21–23	Revelation 19–20
"kings of the earth" who are opposed to God (v. 21)	"kings of the earth" who are opposed to God (19:19)
kings of earth and host of heaven are incarcerated (v. 21)	kings of earth are defeated (19:21) Satan is bound and incarcerated (20:1–3)
imprisonment in a dungeon which is called a "prison" (v. 22)	imprisonment in the abyss which is called a "prison" (20:1–3, 7)
final punishment takes place "after many days" (v. 22)	unbelievers and Satan sentenced to the lake of fire after a "thousand years" (20:7–15)
the Lord will reign as king (v. 23)	the Lord will reign for a thousand years (20:6)

Harmonizing the prophetic details in Isaiah 24 and Revelation 6–22 yields the following chronology of eschatological events:

- The Divine Judgment of the Earth (Isa 24:1–20; Rev 6–19)
- The Second Coming of Christ (Rev 19:11–18)
- The Defeat of the Kings of the Earth (Isa 24:21a; Rev 19:19–21)
- The Imprisonment of the Kings of the Earth (Isa 24:22ab; cf. Luke 16:19–31)
- The Imprisonment of Satan and His Demons (Isa 24:22ab; Rev 20:1–3)
- The Intermediate Kingdom of "Many Days"/"1,000 Years" (Isa 24:22c; Rev 20:1-6)

---

11 Blaising, "Premillennialism," 203.
12 Vlach, "The Kingdom of God and the Millennium," 235.

- The Final Judgment of Satan and His Demons (Isa 24:22d; Rev 20:7–10)
- The Final Judgment of the Kings of the Earth (Isa 24:22d; Rev 20:11–15)
- The Eternal State of the New Heavens and Earth (Isa 24:23; Rev 21–22)

The reason that the "many days" of Isaiah 24:22 requires an intermediate kingdom is because it represents a lengthy period of time which separates the Second Coming of Christ from the final judgment and eternal state.[13] This intermediate confinement of "many days" corresponds to the millennial kingdom of premillennialism, coinciding with the thousand-year incarceration of Satan and reign of Jesus Christ in Revelation 20.

In contrast, this intervening period of time cannot be harmonized with the two-age model of amillennialism, which sees the final judgment taking place at the Second Coming rather than after a gap of "many days" in which the enemies of God are imprisoned. Isaiah 24:21–23 not only suggests the existence of an intermediate kingdom between the present age and the eternal state, but it poses a seemingly insurmountable problem for amillennial eschatology.

The Amillennial Response

Unfortunately, most amillennialists neither discuss Isaiah 24:21–23 nor respond to the premillennial argument above.[14] Craig Blaising specifically faults amillennialist Kim Riddlebarger for his failure to discuss Isaiah 24:21–23 and its eschatological implications:

---

13 According to amillennialist Meredith Kline, the repetition of the verb "punish" in Isa 24:21–22 forms an inclusio and therefore indicates not only that the same punishment is in view in both verses, but also that "after many days" in verse 22 is equivalent to "in that day" in verse 21 (Meredith G. Kline, "Death, Leviathan, and Martyrs: Isaiah 24:1–27:1," in *A Tribute to Gleason Archer*, ed. Walter C. Kaiser, Jr. and Ronald R. Youngblood [Chicago: Moody Press, 1986], 246). The problem with Kline's interpretation is that the phrase "after many days" simply does not mean the same thing as the phrase "in that day," and insisting that the two are equivalent effectively strips the former phrase of its unambiguous meaning. Kline's attempt to eliminate the concept of a lengthy period of time from the designation "many days" should be rejected as an obvious departure from the actual words of the prophet.

14 For example, neither this passage nor the premillennial argument from it are discussed by Oswald T. Allis (*Prophecy and the Church* [Philadelphia: Presbyterian and Reformed Publishing, 1945], Floyd E. Hamilton (*The Basis of Millennial Faith* [Grand Rapids: Eerdmans Publishing, 1942]), Anthony Hoekema (Anthony Hoekema, *The Bible and the Future* [Grand Rapids: Eerdmans Publishing, 1979]), Cornelis Venema (*The Promise of the Future*), Kim Riddlebarger (*A Case for Amillennialism: Understanding the End Times*, expanded ed. [Grand Rapids: Baker Books, 2013]), or Sam Storms (*Kingdom Come: The Amillennial Alternative* [Ross-shire, Scotland: Mentor, 2013]).

> Riddlebarger makes no reference to Isaiah 24 in his brief discussion of the Day of the Lord ... and only mentions Isaiah 25 in relation to resurrection.... So, he fails to note not only the structure of imprisonment and future punishment for Isaiah's teaching on the coming kingdom but also the important intertextual bearing this passage has for Revelation 19–21.[15]

One of the few amillennial responses comes from Dean Davis, who raises three objections to the premillennial interpretation of this passage. First, according to Davis, Isaiah 24:21–23 says nothing whatsoever about the Messiah, much less His coming in glory.[16] The implication of this objection is that the imprisonment of the earthly and heavenly powers in Isaiah 24:21–22 does not take place at the Second Coming, and therefore the "many days" of their incarceration does not coincide with the intermediate kingdom of premillennialism.[17]

The problem with this objection is that even though Isaiah 24 does not explicitly mention the return of Messiah, it does indeed describe the eschatological Day of the Lord, which obviously includes the Second Coming of Christ.[18] This is clear from (a) the emphasis on the eschatological judgment of God and establishment of His kingdom in Isaiah 24–27;[19] (b) the description of the worldwide judgment of the earth in Isaiah 24:1–20; (c) the introductory formula "in that day" in Isaiah

---

15 Blaising, "The Kingdom that Comes with Jesus," 146.
16 Dean Davis, *The High King of Heaven: Discovering the Master Keys to the Great End Time Debate* (Enumclaw, WA: WinePress Publishing, 2014), 292.
17 Davis does not spell out this implication in his objection, but this appears to be his argument. If not, it is difficult to understand the point he is trying to make with this observation.
18 Davis appears to acknowledge this, noting that Isa 24:21–23 (a) is found "in the midst [of] a long string of prophecies devoted to the end-time judgments of God (Isaiah 24:1–27:13)"; (b) is immediately preceded by a description of "the final destruction of the earth" in verses 17–20; and (c) is introduced "by the telltale phrase 'In that Day'" in verse 21 (*The High King of Heaven*, 291). Elsewhere Davis states that "the Day of the LORD will occur at the Parousia of the High King of Heaven ... when he *descends from heaven* in power and great glory to consummate Salvation History" (136; emphasis original; also see 250). For this reason, it is difficult to understand why Davis would suggest that Isa 24:21–23 is separated from the Second Coming of Christ. In fact, one of the two interpretations of this passage proposed by Davis sees Isa 24:21–22 as a reference to the final judgment, which takes place at the Second Coming of Christ according to his amillennial view (292).
19 See Wolf, *Interpreting Isaiah*, 137–46; Chisholm, *Handbook on the Prophets*, 64–70.

24:21;[20] and (d) the reign of the Lord of hosts in Jerusalem in Isaiah 24:23. For this reason, the attempt to separate Isaiah 24:21–22 from the Second Coming of Christ falls short, and this first objection fails to undermine the argument for an intermediate kingdom.

Second, according to Davis, Isaiah 24:21–22a speaks of the incarceration of the evil hosts of heaven and the impenitent kings of earth, but Revelation 20 refers only to the imprisonment of Satan and "says nothing at all about a divine judgment of men, let alone kings."[21] But this objection is simply untrue. In Revelation 20:11–15, after the thousand-year reign of Christ, the unbelieving dead are raised to stand before the Great White Throne, being judged according to their deeds and cast into the Lake of Fire. This divine judgment of human beings coincides with the final punishment of the kings of the earth as described in Isaiah 24:22. For this reason, it is difficult to understand how one could assert that Revelation 20 "says nothing at all about a divine judgment of men."

Perhaps Davis means that Revelation 20 makes no explicit reference to the *incarceration* of human kings as described in Isaiah 24:22. But even so, it is not necessary for Isaiah 24 and Revelation 20 to include all of the same details in their respective eschatological accounts for the premillennial interpretation to remain valid. As demonstrated in the harmonized chronology above, the differences between the two passages are complementary rather than contradictory. In fact, the details in Isaiah and Revelation are not only compatible, but together they provide a fuller picture of the divine judgment of "the host of heaven on high" and "the kings of the earth on earth." The premillennial interpretation introduces no contradiction between Isaiah and Revelation, and therefore this objection fails to weaken the argument for an intermediate kingdom in Isaiah 24:22.

Third, according to Davis, Isaiah 24 teaches that the Lord's reign on Zion in verse 23 will take place *after* the judgments of verses 21–22, and therefore verse 23 must describe the eternal state rather than the alleged

---

20 See the six other uses of the same phrase "in that day" in the immediate context (Isa 25:9; 26:1; 27:1, 2, 12, 13). According to Wolf, this phrase is "a strong indication that the end times are in view" (*Interpreting Isaiah*, 139).
21 Davis, *The High King of Heaven*, 292.

intermediate kingdom of premillennialism.²² Davis highlights this as a problem for premillennialists because they interpret Isaiah 24:23 as the millennial reign in Jerusalem (Rev 20) rather than the eternal reign in the New Jerusalem (Rev 21–22).²³

In response, the premillennial argument for an intermediate kingdom in Isaiah 24:22 does not depend on interpreting verse 23 as a reference to the millennial reign of Christ. Some premillennialists see Isaiah 24:23 as a reference to the millennial kingdom;²⁴ others see it as a reference to the eternal state;²⁵ and still others believe it encompasses both the millennial kingdom and the eternal state.²⁶ All three of these views are compatible

---

22 Ibid. According to Davis, this is clear from the conjunction "then" at the beginning of verse 23.
23 Ibid., 291.
24 McClain, *The Greatness of the Kingdom*, 215–16; Vlach, "The Kingdom of God and the Millennium," 235; West, *The Thousand Years in Both Testaments*, 35–49. If Isa 24:23 refers to the millennial kingdom, it recapitulates and describes the reign which takes place during the "many days" of imprisonment in verse 22. In this view, the imprisonment of verse 22 is part of what makes the reign of verse 23 possible, similar to how the binding of Satan in Rev 20:1–3 enables the millennial reign of Christ in Rev 20:4–6. The strongest argument for this view is the parallel between Isa 24:23 and Isa 27:12–13. Isa 24:23 pictures the Lord of hosts reigning "on Mount Zion and in Jerusalem," and Isa 27:12–13 describes the previously exiled sons of Israel worshipping the Lord "in the holy mountain at Jerusalem" after being gathered from foreign nations and reestablished in their own land. Because Isa 27:12–13 describes a scene of millennial worship (also see Isa 25:6, 7, 10), the parallels between the two passages suggest that Isa 24:23 also describes the millennial kingdom. An additional argument for this view is that unless verse 23 refers to the millennial kingdom, Isa 24:21–23 makes no direct reference to the millennial reign of Christ whatsoever, even though the "many days" of verse 22 still requires an intermediate period of time between the Second Coming and eternal state.
25 Blaising, "Premillennialism," 197–98, 203; Blaising and Bock, *Progressive Dispensationalism*, 275; and Smith, *Isaiah 1–39*, 426, who interprets Isa 24:23 as "a separate thought describing what will happen after the powers in heaven and earth are defeated" in verses 21–22. The strongest argument for this view is the parallel between Isa 24:23 and Rev 21:23. The former speaks of the sun and the moon being darkened as they pale in comparison to the light of the glorious reign of the Lord, and the latter describes how there will be no need for light from the sun or moon in the New Jerusalem because of the illumination of God's glory during His eternal reign (see Blaising and Block, *Progressive Dispensationalism*, 275; Grogan, "Isaiah," 623; Vlach, "The Kingdom of God and the Millennium," 235). If these two verses describe the same time period, then Isa 24:23 must refer to the eternal state. In addition, this view enjoys the simplicity of interpreting the entirety of Isa 24:21–23 in chronological order, with the reign of verse 23 taking place after the punishment at the end of verse 22 rather than before it. At the same time, despite the common translation "then," the use of the *wᵉqatal* at the start of verse 23 does not demand chronological sequence between verse 22 and verse 23 as Davis seems to imply (*The High King of Heaven*, 292).
26 Blaising, "The Kingdom that Comes with Jesus," 145–46. Although Blaising identifies the reign of Isa 24:23 with the eternal state in his earlier writings ("Premillennialism," 197–98,

with the premillennial argument from Isaiah 24, because none of them undermines the primary point that the gap of "many days" in verse 22 can only be explained as an intermediate period of time between the present age and the eternal state.

THE AMILLENNIAL VIEW OF ISAIAH 24:21–23

Amillennialist Dean Davis refers to Isaiah 24:21–23 as a "short but challenging" prophecy, conceding that "it is indeed difficult to be dogmatic about the exact meaning" of this passage, which he calls "mysterious."[27] At the same time, Davis asserts that applying the New Covenant Hermeneutic to Isaiah 24:21–23 gets the interpreter "in the ballpark" and opens up "viable interpretations that harmonize well with NT teaching about the nature and structure of the Kingdom of God."[28] In his discussion of Isaiah 24:21–23, Davis suggests two such interpretations of this passage, both of which see the "many days" in verse 22 as a reference to the present age.[29]

First, according to Davis, one could argue that Isaiah 24:21–22 speaks of the punishment meted out by God through the long "day" of His heavenly reign in the present age. This punishment consists of God casting impenitent kings and evil spirits into Hades where they are reserved for final judgment (Luke 8:31; Col 2:15; 1 Pet 3:18–20; 2 Pet 2:4).[30] With this

---

203; Blaising and Bock, *Progressive Dispensationalism*, 275), his most recent treatment of Isaiah 24 asserts that the imprisonment for many days in verse 22 "must be included in the 'reign' in verse 23" ("The Kingdom that Comes with Jesus," 146). Thus it appears that Blaising interprets the reign of Isa 24:23 as encompassing both the millennial kingdom and the eternal state. Isaiah 25–27 appears to contain a great deal of prophetic conflation of the millennial kingdom and eternal state, making it difficult to distinguish one from the other in many of its descriptions. For this reason, perhaps it is best to leave open the possibility that Isa 24:23 encompasses both the millennial reign and final state, or at least that it does not attempt to specify which phase of the coming reign is in view.

27 Davis, *The High King of Heaven*, 292.
28 Ibid. According to Davis, the New Covenant Hermeneutic "enables us to think clearly about the true sphere of fulfillment of this prophecy."
29 Beale and McDonough do not fully explain their interpretation of Isa 24:21–22, but they agree that the "many days" of verse 22 refers to the present age. More specifically, they believe that the fulfillment of Isa 24:21–22 "was inaugurated at Christ's death and resurrection and will be culminated when Christ returns at the climax of history" (G. K. Beale and Sean M. McDonough "Revelation," in *Commentary on the New Testament Use of the Old Testament*, eds. G. K. Beale and D. A. Carson [Grand Rapids: Baker Academic, 2007], 1145).
30 Davis, *The High King of Heaven*, 292.

view, the final punishment in verse 22b occurs when Christ casts Death and Hades into the Lake of Fire in Revelation 20:14, which leads to the advent of the new heavens and new earth as typologically depicted in Isaiah 24:23.[31]

Second, according to Davis, it could be that Isaiah 24:21–22 refers exclusively to the final judgment which takes place at the Second Coming of Christ.[32] In this view, verse 22b is not describing a judgment which is different from (and subsequent to) the judgment in verse 21. Instead, verse 22b is simply affirming yet again that the final judgment will indeed occur, although not until after "many days" of divine forbearance while the kingdom advances through the preaching of the gospel during the present age.[33] According to Davis, this interpretation fits well with the remainder of the chapter because it makes verses 21–22 the natural and dramatic climax of all that precedes it.[34]

An Evaluation of the Amillennial View

The primary difficulty with Davis's explanations of the passage is that both proposals necessitate interpreting the "many days" as a reference to the present age, which is completely foreign to the immediate context. As Davis acknowledges, not only is Isaiah 24:21–23 one in a long line of prophecies devoted to the eschatological judgments of God (Isa 24–27), but it is also immediately preceded by a description of the final destruction of the earth (Isa 24:1–20).[35] Therefore, according to both interpretations suggested by Davis, the "many days" of Isaiah 24:22 refers to a period of time which takes place prior to every other event described in the entirety of Isaiah 24–27.

The weakness of Davis's view is reflected in the following chronological outlines of his two proposed interpretations of Isaiah 24:

---

31 Ibid.
32 Ibid.
33 Ibid.
34 Ibid.
35 Ibid., 291.

Amillennial Proposal #1
- Second Coming/Final Destruction of the Earth (vv. 17–20)
- *Judgment of God's Enemies in the Present Age* (vv. 21–22ab)[36]
- Final Judgment of God's Enemies (v. 22c)
- Divine Reign of the Eternal State (v. 23)

Amillennial Proposal #2
- Second Coming/Final Destruction of the Earth (vv. 17–20)
- Final Judgment of God's Enemies (v. 21)
- *Parenthetical Reference to the Present Age* (v. 22ab)
- Final Judgment of God's Enemies (v. 22c)
- Divine Reign of the Eternal State (v. 23)

There is simply nothing in the immediate or broader context indicating that verse 22 is a reference to the present age. Not only is this interpretation foreign to the context, but it is difficult to understand what contribution a parenthetical reference to the present age makes to the prophet's description of the final judgment in Isaiah 24.[37]

In contrast, the premillennial interpretation sees the incarceration of God's enemies for "many days" as the first stage of the two-phase judgment described in Isaiah 24:21–22. The premillennial view that the "many days" of Isaiah 24:22 corresponds to an intermediate kingdom fits the context perfectly:

The Premillennial View of Isaiah 24
- Second Coming/Final Destruction of the Earth (vv. 17–20)
- Initial Judgment of God's Enemies (v. 21)
- *Lengthy Incarceration During Intermediate Kingdom* (v. 22ab)
- Final Judgment of God's Enemies (v. 22c)
- Divine Reign of the Eternal State (v. 23)

---

36 An additional problem with this interpretation is that Isa 24:21 contains a clear reference to the eschatological Day of the Lord ("in that day"), but Davis connects it instead to the entirety of the present age.

37 If Isaiah were providing parenthetical background information about an imprisonment which preceded the remainder of the events in the passage, one might expect verse 22 to begin with a disjunctive clause, but it does not.

An additional problem with the first view suggested by Davis concerns the reference to "the kings of the earth" in Isaiah 24:21. According to Davis's first proposal, Isaiah 24:21–22 refers to divine punishment throughout the present age in which God casts unrepentant kings and evil spirits into Hades to await the final judgment. To support this interpretation, Davis cites Luke 8:31, Colossians 2:15, 1 Peter 3:18–20, and 2 Peter 2:4, but none of those passages refer to casting human beings—much less earthly kings—into Hades. More importantly, this interpretation provides no adequate explanation as to why "the kings of the earth" are highlighted over and above other unbelievers who die and face a similar "imprisonment" throughout the present age. In contrast, the reference to kings fits perfectly within the premillennial view of Isaiah 24:21–23 because of the parallel with Revelation 19:19, where "the kings of the earth" wage war against the returning Messiah and are decisively defeated by Him.

An additional problem with the second view concerns the imprisonment in Isaiah 24:22. According to Davis, this verse refers to the "many days" of divine forbearance while the kingdom advances through the preaching of the gospel in the present age, but he fails to explain the significance of the imprisonment which takes place during this same time period. Because Isaiah 24:22 says nothing about divine forbearance during gospel proclamation in the present age—and because the primary point of the verse is the imprisonment of God's enemies—Davis's interpretation suffers from the weakness of ignoring what Isaiah actually says and focusing instead on what he does not say. Any credible interpretation of Isaiah 24:21–23 must include an explanation of the significance of the imprisonment in verse 22, and Davis's second proposal fails to provide one.[38]

Conclusion

In the Old Testament passages considered in chapters 2–5, the prophets looked ahead to the glorious reign of the coming Messiah. During this

---

38 Davis may intend his readers to assume the same explanation of the imprisonment for the second interpretation as that which he provided in the first. If so, the second interpretation faces the same problem as the first in its inability to explain adequately the reference to "the kings of the earth" in Isa 24:21.

time, the Messiah will reign as King over the entire world (Ps 72:2–4, 7–8, 12; Zech 14:9)—all the kings of the earth will bow down before Him (Ps 72:11), all the nations of the earth will serve Him (Ps 72:11; Zech 14:16), and all the peoples of the earth will be blessed by the exercise of His rule (Ps 72:7, 16–17). Knowledge of the Lord will fill the earth (Isa 11:9), and the whole world will be filled with His glory (Ps 72:19). He will reign in peace, justice, righteousness, and faithfulness (Isa 11:3–5), resulting in longevity of life (Isa 65:20, 22) and lasting peace and harmony among the nations of the world (Zech 8:4–5; Isa 2:4; Mic 4:3; Isa 11:6–9). The kingdom reign of Messiah portrayed in these passages clearly transcends what takes place in the present age and will not be ushered in until the Second Coming of Jesus Christ (Zech 14:4, 7, 9).

But these passages also contain features of the coming kingdom which are incompatible with the perfection of the eternal state. For example, this kingdom reign of Messiah will include the existence of the poor (Ps 72:13; Isa 11:4), the wicked (Isa 11:4), the needy (Ps 72:4, 12–13), the afflicted (Ps 72:2, 4, 12; Isa 11:4), enemies of God (Ps 72:9; Isa 11:4), and victims of violence and oppression (Ps 72:4, 14). It will include physical birth and physical death (Isa 65:20), distinctions between the young and the elderly (Zech 8:4–5), and physical weakness due to old age (Zech 8:4). The nations will learn the ways of the Lord (Isa 2:3; Mic 4:2); disputes will continue to arise between them (Isa 2:4; Mic 4:3); and those who refuse to worship the King will be punished by the Lord (Zech 14:17–19).

This portrayal of the coming kingdom reveals a certain amount of tension. The reign of Messiah will be characterized by peace, righteousness, and universal blessing, and yet human sin will continue to exist, sometimes requiring divine intervention to bring deliverance to the afflicted and judgment to the rebellious. These kingdom prophecies are not being presently fulfilled, and they are not compatible with the eternal state. For this reason, they necessitate a future stage in the history of redemption which is far greater than the present age but which does not see the removal of all sin and death from the earth.[39]

---

39 Wayne Grudem, *Systematic Theology: An Introduction to Biblical Doctrine* (Grand Rapids: Zondervan Publishing, 1994), 1127. According to amillennialist Anthony Hoekema, the intermediate kingdom of premillennialism is "something of a theological anomaly" because it is "neither completely like the present age" nor "completely like the age to come" (*The Bible and the Future*, 186). Although Hoekema intends this as a criticism

In addition to these indications of an intermediate phase of the kingdom, the prophet Isaiah refers to a lengthy period of time that will separate the return of Christ from the final judgment of God's enemies (Isa 24:21–23). This intervening gap of "many days" between the Day of the Lord and the eternal state coincides perfectly with an initial phase of the kingdom between the Second Coming and the new heavens and earth. Moreover, this lengthy gap of time is impossible to accommodate apart from the existence of an intermediate kingdom.

The key that brings all of these features together is the explicit New Testament revelation of a millennial kingdom between the Second Coming and the Final Judgment.[40] In other words, what is strongly implied in the Old Testament prophets is clarified and made explicit in the Book of Revelation, where the apostle John reveals a thousand-year earthly reign of the Lord Jesus Christ (Rev 20:1–6).[41] This intermediate kingdom in Revelation 20 separates the Second Coming of Revelation 19 and the eternal state of Revelation 21–22, coinciding with the "many days" of Isaiah 24:22 and fulfilling the prophecies in Psalm 72:1–20, Isaiah 2:1–3//Micah 4:2–4, Isaiah 11:1–9, Isaiah 65:20, Zechariah 8:4–5, and Zechariah 14:16–19. In contrast to the two-age model of amillennialism, the Old Testament provides clear evidence of an intermediate kingdom in which Jesus will reign upon the earth between the present age and the eternal state.

---

of premillennialism, his words are a fitting description of the prophetic portrayal of the kingdom in the Old Testament passages discussed above.

40 Blaising, "Premillennialism," 204.

41 According to Blaising, "The millennial kingdom revealed to John, while new in its specific content, is compatible with this earlier revelation concerning the eschatological kingdom and the manner of its coming. Not only that, but now that we have the revelation of a future millennial kingdom, that revelation harmonizes with and clarifies earlier revelation that spoke of the coming eschatological kingdom in a more general manner" (ibid., 200). Ironically, this reasoning appears to coincide perfectly with the view articulated by amillennialist Kim Riddlebarger, who describes the book of Revelation as "a New Testament commentary on those redemptive-historical themes left open-ended by the Old Testament prophets, viewed in the greater light of postmessianic revelation" (*A Case for Amillennialism*, 225).

PART 2

The Two-Age Argument
in the
New Testament

Chapter 6

The Succession of the Two Ages

Introduction

As discussed in chapter 1, the two-age model has become the primary amillennial argument against the eschatology of premillennialism. More specifically, amillennialists have used this model to disprove the messianic kingdom of premillennialism in three distinct ways:

1. Because "the age to come" will immediately follow this present age (Matt 12:32; Eph 1:21), there is no gap of time between the two ages to allow for an intermediate kingdom.

2. Because the qualities ascribed to "the age to come" are all eternal in nature (Mark 10:30; Luke 18:30; 20:34–36), the temporal aspects of premillennialism's intermediate kingdom—such as sin, death, and procreation—render it incompatible with the coming age.

3. Because the Second Coming is the line of demarcation between the two ages—and because it will be accompanied by the resurrection and judgment of all mankind (Dan 12:2; John 5:28–29; Acts 24:15; Matt 25:31–46; 2 Thess 1:6–10), the destruction and renewal of the cosmos (2 Pet 3:10–13; Rom 8:18–23), and the final victory over sin and death (1 Cor 15:20–28, 50–57; Rom 8:17–23)—there is no gap of time to allow for the intermediate kingdom of premillennialism.

These three arguments will be examined carefully in chapters 6–10 to determine whether the two ages in the New Testament do indeed preclude the possibility of an intermediate kingdom. The first argument will be considered here in chapter 6, the second argument in chapter 7, and the third argument—which is the strongest and most compelling of the three—in chapters 8–10. This examination will demonstrate that the two-age argument fails to preclude the possibility of an intermediate kingdom between the present age and the eternal state.

The Amillennial Argument

The first way the two-age model is used to challenge premillennialism involves the immediate succession of the two eschatological ages. According to Geerhardus Vos, the declaration of Jesus that blasphemy against the Holy Spirit will not be forgiven "either in this age or in the age to come" (Matt 12:32) indicates that the coming age will begin immediately after the present one. "To say that a sin will not be forgiven either in this age or in the age to come," Vos writes, "could never have served as a formula for absolute unforgiveableness *ad infinitum* ... if there were conceivable a gap between the two aions."[1] Vos referred to this as the "direct successiveness" of the two ages, meaning that the age to come will immediately follow this age, with no intervening gap of time separating the two.[2]

According to some amillennialists, the immediate succession of the two ages precludes the possibility of an intermediate kingdom between the present age and the eternal state. Matthew 12:32 and Ephesians 1:21, in particular, are said to "indicate that there is no intervening or temporary time period between 'this age' and the 'age to come.'"[3] As Anthony Hoekema argues, because there is no indication in Scripture "that there will also be a third age in between the present age and the age to come,"[4] the intermediate kingdom of premillennialism is precluded as a possibility.[5] Similarly, according to Samuel Waldron, because the age to come will

---

1 Geerhardus Vos, *The Pauline Eschatology* (1930; repr., Phillipsburg, NJ: Presbyterian and Reformed Publishing, 1994), 26.
2 Ibid., 25.
3 Jonathan Menn, *Biblical Eschatology* (Eugene, OR: Resource Publications, 2013), 42.
4 Anthony Hoekema, *The Bible and the Future* (Grand Rapids: Eerdmans Publishing, 1979), 185.
5 Samuel E. Waldron, *The End Times Made Simple: How Could Everyone Be So Wrong About Biblical Prophecy?* (Amityville, NY: Calvary Press, 2003), 42.

immediately follow this age, the two ages exhaust all of human history and therefore they leave "no possibility of a state intermediate between them."[6]

Amillennialist Robert Reymond makes the same argument. According to Reymond: "Jesus envisioned two ages—this present (evil) age and the age to come—as comprehending the remainder of human existence. He said nothing about a third, intermediate period or millennial age. I find no millennial reign in Jesus' eschatology."[7] Furthermore, Reymond writes, "He envisioned these two ages as consecutive, that is, they neither overlap, nor is there any indication of a gap between them, but the age to come follows immediately upon this present age."[8] According to this argument, then, the immediate transition from this age to the age to come allows no time for an intermediate kingdom between the two:

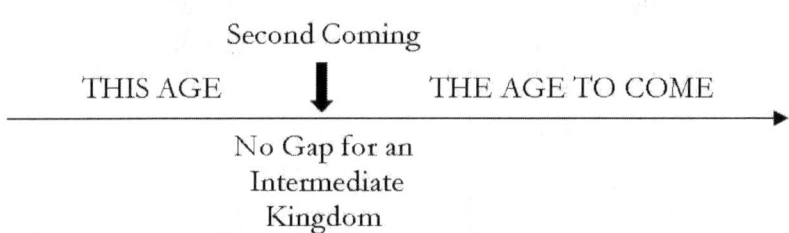

---

6 Ibid., 40. Elsewhere Waldron writes: "This age and the age to come taken together exhaust all time, including the endless time of the eternal state. This means that there is no period between or beside this age and the age to come" (42). Waldron argues for the exhaustiveness of the two ages from Matt 12:32 // Mark 3:29, Mark 10:29–30, and 1 Tim 6:17–19 (37–39). There is disagreement among amillennial two-age proponents, however, regarding the extent of the time period designated "this age." According to some, "this age" covers all of human history, extending from creation to the Second Coming of Christ (Waldron, *The End Times Made Simple*, 37–42). Others divide human history into "the past age" (from creation to the first coming) and "this age" (from the first to the Second Coming) (Hoekema, *The Bible and the Future*, 20). And still others divide human history into "the age of innocence" (from creation to fall) and "this age" (from the fall to the Second Coming) (Dean Davis, *The High King of Heaven: Discovering the Master Keys to the Great End Time Debate* [Enumclaw, WA: WinePress Publishing, 2014], 165). But this disagreement ultimately has little or no bearing on the two-age argument against premillennialism, because the amillennial consensus is that the "age to come" is a single age that begins at the Second Coming and extends into eternity.

7 Robert L. Reymond, "Response by Robert L. Reymond," in *Perspectives on Israel and the Church: 4 Views*, ed. Chad O. Brand (Nashville: B&H Publishing Group, 2015), 209.

8 Ibid.

In this way, the intermediate kingdom of premillennialism is said to be incompatible with the two-age model presented in the New Testament.

The Premillennial Response

Ironically, the premillennial response to this argument was anticipated by Vos himself. According to Vos, the immediate succession of the two ages isn't necessarily incompatible with the eschatology of premillennialists, for "under their scheme the millennium could in part be identified with the age to come as the beginning thereof."[9] In other words, as Vos recognized, the premillennialist has no need to dispute the direct succession of the two ages as implied by passages like Matthew 12:32 and Ephesians 1:21. Instead, by viewing the intermediate kingdom as an initial phase of the age to come—rather than a separate age or dispensation preceding it—premillennialism is able to harmonize its millennium with the absence of an interval between the two ages,[10] resulting in the following:

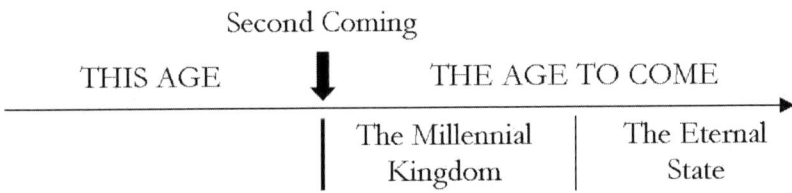

Rather a separate time period which elapses between the two ages, then, the millennium is the first thousand years of the age to come.[11]

---

9 Vos, *The Pauline Eschatology*, 25. For this reason, Vos, unlike other amillennialists, did not see the immediate succession of the two ages as necessarily excluding an intermediate kingdom between the present age and the eternal state.
10 George Eldon Ladd, *The Gospel of the Kingdom: Scriptural Studies in the Kingdom of God* (Grand Rapids: Eerdmans Publishing, 1959), 26–40.
11 For this reason, the premillennialist has no need to deny that the two ages constitute the basic structure of biblical eschatology. In fact, the "inaugurated eschatology" popularized by premillennialist George Eldon Ladd was based largely on his own understanding of two-age paradigm in the New Testament (*The Gospel of the Kingdom*, 26–51; *Crucial Questions about the Kingdom of God* [Grand Rapids: Eerdmans Publishing, 1952], 167–69). According to premillennialist Walter Kaiser, "With the use of the twin terms, 'this age' and 'the age to come,' the New Testament lays down one of the most helpful frameworks from which to view the grand spectacle of God's dramatic conclusion to the series of events that

This kind of harmonization is not foreign to amillennialists. In fact, according to its proponents, the two-age model itself consists of a modification of the Old Testament prophetic expectation, which originally understood the coming of Christ as ushering in a single glorious messianic age.[12] But when it was later revealed that the coming of Messiah would be fulfilled in two different stages—in a first and a second coming—the anticipated age to come was likewise seen to unfold in two different ages: "this age" and "the age to come."[13] According to Vos, not until the messianic appearance had unfolded in two successive stages was the age to come "perceived to bear in its womb another age to come."[14] The premillennialist appeals to this same dynamic of progressive revelation and simply asks the amillennialist to accept the possibility of further modification in light of later revelation, modification in which the age to come "bears in *its* womb" both an intermediate kingdom (Rev 20) and the eternal state (Rev 21–22).[15]

---

are already in motion" (Walter C. Kaiser, Jr., *Back Toward the Future: Hints for Interpreting Biblical Prophecy* [Eugene, OR: Wipf & Stock Publishers, 1989], 118).

[12] Vos, *The Pauline Eschatology*, 36–38; Hoekema, *The Bible and the Future*, 12, 18; Kim Riddlebarger, *A Case for Amillennialism: Understanding the End Times*, expanded ed. (Grand Rapids: Baker Books, 2013), 76, 79.

[13] Vos, *The Pauline Eschatology*, 36–38; Hoekema, *The Bible and the Future*, 12; Riddlebarger, *A Case for Amillennialism*, 76, 79. As Hoekema writes, "In the New Testament we also find the realization that what the Old Testament writers seemed to depict as one movement must now be recognized as involving two stages: the present Messianic age and the age of the future" (*The Bible and the Future*, 18).

[14] Vos, *The Pauline Eschatology*, 36.

[15] See Ladd, *The Gospel of the Kingdom*, 26–40. One amillennialist cites Paul's reference to "the *ages* to come" (τοῖς αἰῶσιν τοῖς ἐπερχομένοις) in Eph 2:7 as evidence that the age to come is composed of a plurality of "lesser ages" (Waldron, *The End Times Made Simple*, 35), but he fails to recognize how this might allow for an intermediate kingdom as the first phase of the age to come. It is difficult to determine whether Paul's intention in Eph 2:7 is indeed to imply the existence of more than one age within the age to come. In contrast to this possibility, most amillennial interpreters believe that the plural of αἰών in Eph 2:7 is simply a reference to eternity (Vos, *The Pauline Eschatology*, 316; Hoekema, *The Bible and the Future*, 18; Davis, *High King of Heaven*, 171) because of how the plural so often designates eternity elsewhere in the New Testament (Hermann Sasse, "αἰών," in *TDNT*, ed. Gerhard Kittel [Eerdmans Publishing, 1964], 1:199, 206; Oscar Cullmann, "The Significance of the New Testament Terminology for Time," in *Dimensions of Faith*, ed. William Kimmel and Geoffrey Cline [New York: Twayne, 1960], 316). But in most of these other plural uses, αἰών functions as the object of the preposition εἰς and/or in a genitive relationship with another use of αἰών which is functioning as the object of εἰς, such as: εἰς τοὺς αἰῶνας/"unto the ages" (Luke 1:33; Rom 1:25; 9:5; 11:36; 16:27; 2 Cor 11:31; Heb 13:21; 1 Pet 5:11); εἰς πάντας τοὺς αἰῶνας/"unto all the ages" (Jude 25); εἰς τοὺς αἰῶνας τῶν αἰώνων/"unto the ages of the ages" (Gal 1:5; Phil 4:20; 1 Tim 1:17; 2 Tim 4:18; 1 Pet 4:11;

The Premillennial Evidence

Three lines of evidence support this view. First, as discussed in chapters 2-4, the Old Testament prophets portray the future reign of Messiah as characterized by peace, righteousness, and a universal blessing which clearly transcends the conditions of the present age; and yet some of these same prophetic portrayals of the kingdom include the existence of physical birth, physical death, and human rebellion, all of which are incompatible with the eternal state (Ps 72:1-20; Isa 2:1-3; Mic 4:2-4; Isa 11:1-9; 65:17-25; Zech 8:4-5; 14:16-19). In addition, as discussed in chapter 5, Isaiah 24:21-23 speaks of a lengthy period of "many days" which will separate the Second Coming of Christ from the final judgment and subsequent eternal state.

As premillennialist Craig Blaising writes, "The key that puts all these features together is John's explicit revelation [in Revelation 20] of a millennial kingdom between the return of Jesus and the Final Judgment."[16] In this way, even though the Old Testament prophets do not set forth a clear distinction between the intermediate and ultimate phases of the coming kingdom, this distinction is implied in many of their prophecies, and it is later made explicit by John's prophecy in Revelation 20.[17] For this reason, the best way to account for all the biblical data, and to resolve

---

Rev 1:6, 18; 4:9, 10; 5:13; 7:12; 10:6; 11:15; 15:7; 19:3; 20:10; 22:5); εἰς αἰῶνας αἰώνων/"unto ages of ages" (Rev 14:11); and εἰς τοὺς αἰῶνας τοῦ αἰῶνος/"unto the ages of the age" (Heb 1:8). This is similar to the most common way to designate eternity, namely the singular use of αἰών as the object of εἰς—εἰς τὸν αἰῶνα/"unto the age" (Matt 21:19; Mark 3:29; 11:14; Luke 1:55; John 4:14; 6:51, 58; 8:35 [2x], 51, 52; 10:28; 11:26; 12:34; 13:8; 14:16; 1 Cor 8:13; 2 Cor 9:9; Heb 5:6; 6:20; 7:17, 21, 24, 28; 1 Pet 1:25; 1 John 2:17; 2 John 2; Jude 13).

The uniqueness of Paul's expression in Eph 2:7—in contrast to these technical formulas, which are so prevalent throughout the New Testament—undermines the argument that the plural of αἰών in Eph 2:7 must refer to eternity. At the same time, the uniqueness of Paul's expression also makes it difficult to affirm with certainty that it envisions the existence of more than one age within the age to come. Although it may indeed reflect this reality, it appears more likely that the plural "ages to come" in Eph 2:7 is Paul's way to describe eternity by referring to "one age supervening upon another like successive waves of the sea, as far into the future as thought can reach" (F. F. Bruce, *The Epistles to the Colossians, to Philemon, and to the Ephesians*, NICNT [Grand Rapids: Eerdmans Publishing, 1984], 288; also see Peter T. O'Brien, *The Letter to the Ephesians*, PNTC [Grand Rapids: Eerdmans Publishing, 1999], 173; Andrew T. Lincoln, *Ephesians*, WBC [Dallas: Word Books, 1990], 110-11).

16 Craig A. Blaising, "Premillennialism," in *Three Views on the Millennium and Beyond*, ed. Darrell L. Bock (Grand Rapids: Zondervan Publishing, 1999), 204.
17 Ibid., 200-4.

the aforementioned tension in the prophetic picture, is to recognize the existence of two stages of the coming kingdom—the millennium (Rev 20) and the eternal state (Rev 21–22).

Second, the original context of the two-age terminology in the New Testament supports the idea of a temporary phase of the kingdom between the present age and the eternal state. When Jesus and the New Testament writers referred to "this age" and "the age to come" (e.g., Matt 12:32; Mark 10:30; Luke 18:30; 20:34–35; Eph 1:21), they were using existing terminology and thereby appealing to an already well-established eschatological framework.[18] As explained in the appendix of this book—"The Intermediate Kingdom in Intertestamental Judaism"—the two-age model ultimately had its roots in the Jewish apocalyptic writings in the late second and early first century BC, when these terms were first used.[19] By 100 BC this two-age framework in Jewish eschatology came to include a distinction between a temporary kingdom on earth and the final state of eternity, resulting in a three-fold division of redemptive history: the present age, an intermediate kingdom, and the eternal state.[20]

---

18 Larry R. Helyer, "The Necessity, Problems, and Promise of Second Temple Judaism for Discussions of New Testament Eschatology," *JETS* 47, no. 4 (Dec 2004), 598; J. Julius Scott, Jr., *Jewish Backgrounds of the New Testament* (Grand Rapids: Baker Books, 1995), 271, 286; W. D. Davies, *The Setting of the Sermon on the Mount* (London: Cambridge University Press, 1963), 182–83; Vos, *The Pauline Eschatology*, 14, 16, 28. As Walter Kaiser writes, "Just as intertestamental Judaism expressed a divine division in time between 'this age' and the 'age to come,' so the New Testament follows suit and uses the same terms and similar concepts" (Walter C. Kaiser, Jr., *Preaching and Teaching the Last Things: Old Testament Eschatology for the Life of the Church* [Grand Rapids: Baker Academic, 2011], xv). Kaiser refers to this as the New Testament writers using "the traditional Jewish concept of the 'two ages.'" According to Vos, "There is no escape from the conclusion that a piece of Jewish theology has been … incorporated into the Apostle's teaching. Paul had none less than Jesus Himself as a predecessor in this. The main structure of the Jewish Apocalyptic is embodied in our Lord's teaching as well as in Paul's" (*The Pauline Eschatology*, 28). At the same time, Vos contends that Paul's eschatology differed from the Jewish writings in certain fundamental features, claiming, for example, that there was no place in the apostle's eschatology "for an earthly, provisional kingdom of the Messiah."
19 Helyer, "Second Temple Judaism and New Testament Eschatology," 598; Sasse, "αἰών, αἰώνιος," 206–7; Haïm Zʾew Hirschberg, "Eschatology," in *Encyclopaedia Judaica* (New York: The MacMillan Company, 1971), 6:874. See the appendix, "The Intermediate Kingdom in Intertestamental Judaism," for an explanation (and documentation) of how this two-age model emerged and developed in the Jewish writings.
20 R. H. Charles, *Eschatology, the Doctrine of a Future Life in Israel, Judaism, and Christianity: A Critical History* (New York, Schocken Books, 1963), 167–361; R. H. Charles, *A Critical and Exegetical Commentary on the Revelation of St. John*, vol. 2, ICC (Edinburgh: T. & T. Clark, 1970), 142; D. S. Russell, *The Method and Message of Jewish Apocalyptic: 200 BC*

This was the clear consensus of Jewish thought between 100 BC and AD 100.[21]

Therefore, when Jesus and the New Testament writers referred to "this age" and "the age to come," this terminology and the framework it represented were understood by their original audience to include the existence of an intermediate kingdom. For this reason, the original cultural and historical context of these two-age passages places the burden of proof on those who believe that Jesus and the New Testament writers departed from the commonly understood two-age framework when they referred to "this age" and "the age to come." If the two-age model of first-century Judaism included an intermediate kingdom between the present age and the eternal state, one should be slow to conclude that the New Testament's use of the very same terminology precludes the

---

– AD 100 (Philadephia: The Westminster Press, 1964), 291, 297; Scott, *Jewish Backgrounds of the New Testament*, 292; Philip Schaff, *History of the Christian Church*, 3rd ed. (Peabody, MA: Hendrickson Publishers, 2006), 2:614; J. W. Bailey, "The Temporary Messianic Reign in the Literature of Early Judaism," *JBL* 53, no. 1 (1934): 187; George Foot Moore, *Judaism in the First Centuries of the Christian Era: The Age of Tannaim*, vols. 2 and 3 (Peabody: MA, Hendrickson Publishers, 1960), 2:378.

21 In spite of this consensus, some confusion existed regarding the precise relationship between this temporary kingdom and the terminology "the age/world to come." Sometimes the intermediate kingdom and the "age to come" are clearly distinguished—with the former being portrayed as a transitional stage between this world and the world to come—and other times the two cannot be separated, being either conflated or referred to interchangeably (Scott, *Backgrounds of the New Testament*, 292–93; also see Russell, *The Method and Message of Jewish Apocalyptic*, 296–97; Jacob Neusner and William Scott Green, eds., *The Dictionary of Judaism in the Biblical Period: 450 B.C.E. to 600 C.E.* [New York: Simon & Schuster Macmillan, 1996], 1:203; Joseph Klausner, *The Messianic Idea in Israel from Its Beginning to the Completion of the Mishnah*, trans. W. F. Stinespring [London: George Allen and Unwin Ltd, 1956], 408–19; W. D. Davies, *Paul and Rabbinic Judaism: Some Rabbinic Elements in Pauline Theology* [Mifflintown, PA: Sigler Press, 1998], 316; A. Cohen, *Everyman's Talmud* [New York: E.P. Dutton and Co., 1949], 356; Joseph Bonsirven, *Palestinian Judaism in the Time of Jesus*, trans. William Wolf [New York: Holt, Rinehart and Winston, 1964], 205–6; Davies, *The Setting of the Sermon on the Mount*, 182; George Eldon Ladd, *The Presence of the Future: The Eschatology of Biblical Realism* [Grand Rapids: Eerdmans Publishing, 1974], 92; Robert H. Gundry, *The Church and the Tribulation: A Biblical Examination of Posttribulationism* [Grand Rapids: Eerdmans Publishing, 1999], 142). Because of this ambiguity, it is difficult to identify with certainty the precise referent of "the age to come" in Jewish thought at the time of the New Testament. But regardless of whether (a) the age to come = the intermediate kingdom, (b) the age to come = the eternal state (with the intermediate kingdom viewed as a transitional phase between the present age and the eternal state), or (c) the age to come = the intermediate kingdom and the eternal state, one thing is clear: The two-age model of first-century Judaism included a belief in a temporary kingdom of Messiah between the present age and the eternal state.

possibility of such a kingdom, and one should require clear and compelling evidence before reaching this conclusion. Passages indicating the direct succession of the two ages—such as Matthew 12:32 and Ephesians 1:21—do not meet this burden of proof.

Third, as discussed above and demonstrated later in chapters 11–14, Revelation 20 clearly sets forth an intermediate kingdom between the present age and the eternal state. As George Eldon Ladd explains, embracing the unique contribution of Revelation 20 to the Bible's teaching on the coming kingdom involves recognizing that divine revelation in Scripture is progressive rather than static:

> The implications of progressive revelation are always applied in the study of the relationship between the New Testament and the Old and within the movement from Moses to the post-exilic prophets in the Old Testament writings. There is no reason why there might not be a further application of progress in revelation in the New Testament books. It might well be that in the Apocalypse, elements of a new revelation were imparted to John by the Lord, to the effect that there should be a millennial interregnum.[22]

According to Blaising, recognizing this progress of revelation—and harmonizing all that Scripture teaches about the coming kingdom, including Revelation 20—is at the heart of the biblical case for premillennialism:

> My argument for premillennialism is that the millennial kingdom revealed to John, while new in its specific content, is compatible with this earlier revelation concerning the eschatological kingdom and the manner of its coming. Not only that, but now that we have the revelation of a future millennial kingdom, that revelation harmonizes with and clarifies earlier revelation that spoke of the coming eschatological kingdom in a more general manner.[23]

At the foundation of this approach is the recognition that later revelation often brings additional detail and therefore greater clarity to earlier revelation. Because of the divine authorship (and therefore perfect unity) of

---

22 Ladd, *Crucial Questions About the Kingdom of God*, 181–82.
23 Blaising, "Premillennialism," 200.

Scripture, this subsequent revelation will never contradict or reinterpret previous revelation in a way that departs from its original meaning, but later prophecies may supplement or clarify earlier revelation by providing more context or detail.

In the case of Revelation 20, this passage clarifies that the coming eschatological kingdom will consist of two phases which follow the return of Christ—an intermediate kingdom of a thousand years (Rev 20) and the eternal state of the new heavens and new earth (Rev 21–22). In this way, just as the two mountain ranges of Christ's two comings were not clearly distinguished until the New Testament, so the two future stages of the kingdom (and the age to come) are not clearly distinguished until the last book of the Bible.[24]

---

24 Daniel B. Wallace, "New Testament Eschatology in the Light of Progressive Revelation," accessed on August 7, 2014, https://bible.org/article/new-testament-eschatology-light-progressive-revelation.

Chapter 7

The Characteristics of the Two Ages

Introduction

The second way that the two-age model is used as an argument against premillennialism involves the characteristics ascribed to these two ages in the New Testament. According to amillennialist Kim Riddlebarger, "The qualities assigned by the biblical writers to 'this age' are always temporal in nature and represent the fallen world and its sinful inhabitants awaiting the judgment to come at our Lord's return."[1] In this way, "this age" is always used in reference to things which are destined to perish.[2] In contrast, says Riddlebarger, "The qualities assigned to the age to come are all eternal (or nontemporal) in nature."[3] Consequently, the age to come is an age of eternal life and immortality,[4] an age "in which there are no marriages or sexual relationships,"[5] an age

---

1 Kim Riddlebarger, *A Case for Amillennialism: Understanding the End Times*, expanded ed. (Grand Rapids: Baker Books, 2013), 97. In support of his description of the present age, Riddlebarger cites Matt 24:3; 28:20; Luke 18:30; 20:34; Mark 10:30; Rom 12:2; Gal 1:4; 1 Cor 1:20; 2:6–8; 2 Cor 4:4; Eph 2:2; 1 Tim 6:17; and Titus 2:12–13.
2 Riddlebarger, *A Case for Amillennialism*, 97.
3 Ibid., 104. As amillennialist Jonathan Menn summarizes, "This age is temporal; the age to come is eternal. This age is characterized by sin, death, marriage, and all that accompanies life in this body; the age to come is characterized by holiness and new, resurrected life" (Jonathan Menn, *Biblical Eschatology* [Eugene, OR: Resource Publications, 2013], 342; see ibid., 370).
4 Riddlebarger, *A Case for Amillennialism*, 96.
5 Ibid., 97.

"characterized by the realization of all the blessings of the resurrection and consummation."[6] Put simply, the age to come is the eternal state.[7]

According to the two-age argument, the intermediate kingdom of premillennialism "belongs neither to the present age nor to the age to come,"[8] rendering it incompatible with the eschatological framework of the New Testament. For this reason, the two-age model is said to confront premillennialism with what Samuel Waldron calls "an impossible dilemma":

> Where will premillennialism put the millennium within the scheme of the two ages? In *this age* or in *the age to come*? It cannot put it into this age. Why not? Because according to premillennialism the millennium occurs after Christ's second coming, and this age concludes with Christ's second coming. Neither, however, can it put the millennium in the age to come. Again, why not? Because no wicked men in an un-resurrected condition remain in that age.... Since there is no intermediate or other period beside the two ages, premillennialism cannot be reconciled with the biblical, two-age scheme.[9]

Amillennialist Robert Strimple appeals to the two-age model and summarizes the premillennial dilemma in a similar way:

---

[6] Ibid., 98. In support of his description of the age to come, Riddlebarger cites Matt 12:32; 13:40; Mark 10:30; Luke 18:30; 1 Tim 6:19; 1 Cor 6:9–10; 15:50; Gal 5:21; and Eph 5:5.

[7] According to amillennialist Dean Davis, passages like Matt 12:32, Mark 10:30, and Luke 20:35–36 make it "quite clear that the Age (or World) to Come is the final state, the ultimate goal towards which Salvation History is tending" (Dean Davis, *The High King of Heaven: Discovering the Master Keys to the Great End Time Debate* [Enumclaw, WA: WinePress Publishing, 2014], 166). Menn lists 17 qualitative differences between "this age" and "the age to come" as evidence of this same conclusion (*Biblical Eschatology*, 41–42).

[8] Anthony Hoekema, *The Bible and the Future* (Grand Rapids: Eerdmans Publishing, 1979), 185. According to Hoekema: "The millennium of the premillennialists ... is something of a theological anomaly. It is neither completely like the present age, nor is it completely like the age to come. It is, to be sure, better than the present age, but it falls far short of being the final state of perfection. For the resurrected and glorified saints, the millennium is an agonizing postponement of the final state of glory to which they look forward so eagerly. For the rebellious nations, the millennium is a continuation of the ambiguity of the present age, in which God allows evil to exist while postponing his final judgment upon it" (186).

[9] Samuel E. Waldron, *The End Times Made Simple: How Could Everyone Be So Wrong About Biblical Prophecy?* (Amityville, NY: Calvary Press, 2003), 44; emphasis original.

Where does the Millennium fit into this fundamental structure of New Testament eschatology? Will it be the final phase of "this age" or the initial phase of "the age to come"? Will it take place on this present sin-cursed earth or on the renewed earth of the consummation?[10]

Because the intermediate kingdom of premillennialism includes temporal aspects of human existence such as sin, death, and procreation, amillennial proponents of the two-age model insist it is impossible to view this millennial reign as part of the coming age. As William Cox writes: "The Scriptures outline but two ages: the present age and the age to come. The age to come is everywhere said to be eternal, and would therefore be in complete contradistinction to an interregnum of one thousand years."[11] For this reason, the millennial kingdom of premillennialism is said to be incompatible with the two-age model presented in the New Testament.

THE PREMILLENNIAL RESPONSE

In response to this argument, it should first be noted that the amillennial description of "this age" is perfectly compatible with premillennialism. In other words, premillennialists completely agree that the various New Testament descriptions of the present age characterize this time period as sinful, temporal, and destined to perish (Rom 12:2; 1 Cor 1:20; 2:6, 8; 3:18; 2 Cor 4:4; Gal 1:4; Eph 2:2; 1 Tim 6:17–19; Titus 2:12).[12] Premillennialists also agree with two-age advocates that this present age will come to an end at the Second Coming of Christ (Matt 13:39, 40, 49; 24:3; 28:20). Because of this consensus—and because 16 of the 22 "two-age" texts cited

---

10 Robert B. Strimple, "An Amillennial Response to Craig A. Blaising," in *Three Views on the Millennium and Beyond*, ed. Darrell L. Bock (Grand Rapids: Zondervan Publishing, 1999), 268–69.
11 William E. Cox, *Amillennialism Today* (Phillipsburg, NJ: Presbyterian and Reformed Publishing Co., 1966), 65.
12 E.g., premillennialist George Eldon Ladd describes this age as "dominated by evil, wickedness, and rebellion against the will of God" (George Eldon Ladd, *The Gospel of the Kingdom: Scriptural Studies in the Kingdom of God* [Grand Rapids: Eerdmans Publishing, 1959], 28).

by amillennialists refer only to this age[13]—there is much agreement on the meaning of most of the relevant passages.

This narrows the scope of disagreement to how the age to come is characterized in the New Testament. But even here there is considerable harmony. For example, when Riddlebarger describes the age to come as that time in the future when "all redemptive-historical loose ends will be tied up and the final consummation of all things, such as the resurrection of the dead, the final judgment, and the re-creation of all things, will take place,"[14] the premillennialist fully agrees. In the premillennial view, all of these events will indeed take place in the age to come, whether in the intermediate kingdom as the initial phase of this coming age, in the new heavens and new earth as the eternal state, or in a combination of the two.

In light of this agreement, then, the only remaining question is whether the New Testament describes the age to come in such a way that precludes the existence of an intermediate kingdom as the initial phase of this coming age. Of the six passages explicitly referring to the age to come (Matt 12:32; Mark 10:30; Luke 18:30; 20:34–35; Eph 1:21; Heb 6:5), three of them are clearly compatible with a temporary millennial kingdom. Matthew 12:32 says that blasphemy against the Holy Spirit shall not be forgiven "either in this age or in the age to come;" Ephesians 1:21 teaches that Jesus has been exalted above every authority and every name "not only in this age but also in the one to come;" and Hebrews 6:5 refers to those who have tasted the powers of the age to come and yet have fallen way. There is nothing in these three references to the coming age that excludes the millennial kingdom of premillennialism. This leaves Mark 10:30, Luke 18:30, and Luke 20:34–36 as the only remaining passages to argue against an intermediate kingdom.

The Argument from Mark 10:30 and Luke 18:30

In Mark 10:30 and Luke 18:30, which are parallel accounts of the same interaction, Jesus is speaking to His disciples after the rich young ruler's

---

13 Of the various New Testament references to the two ages, 16 of them refer only to this age (Matt 13:39, 40, 49; 24:3; 28:20; Rom 12:2; 1 Cor 1:20; 2:6 [2x], 8; 3:18; 2 Cor 4:4; Gal 1:4; Eph 2:2; 1 Tim 6:17–19; Titus 2:12), five of them refer to both ages (Matt 12:32; Mark 10:30; Luke 18:30; 20:34–35; Eph 1:21), and one of them refers only to the age to come (Heb 6:5).
14 Riddlebarger, *A Case for Amillennialism*, 80.

refusal to forsake his possessions and follow Christ (Mark 10:22; Luke 18:23). After this man's departure, Peter declares to Jesus that he and his fellow disciples have left everything to follow Him (Mark 10:28; Luke 18:28). In response, Jesus tells Peter and the disciples that whoever has forsaken everything for the sake of the gospel will receive a hundred times as much in the present age, and eternal life in the age to come (Mark 10:29–30; Luke 18:29–30).

According to the amillennial argument, because Jesus promised eternal life for His disciples in the age to come, Mark 10:30 and Luke 18:30 indicate that the coming age is the "age of eternal life,"[15] an age in which "there will be no death,"[16] an age that "is characterized by resurrection life and immortality."[17] For this reason, this description of the coming age is said to exclude the possibility of an intermediate kingdom in which death continues to exist.

The amillennial interpretation of Mark 10:30 and Luke 18:30 is correct to a degree: Even though eternal life is both a present possession (John 3:36; 17:3; 1 John 5:11–13) and a future inheritance (Matt 25:46; Rom 2:7), these verses clearly emphasize eternal life as a future inheritance. For this reason, the promise of eternal life in Mark 10:30 and Luke 18:30 most likely includes the believer's resurrection and glorification as rewards to be received in the age to come (cf. Rom 2:7), just as the amillennialist says. Every disciple of Christ will indeed receive eternal life, including physical resurrection and glorification, in the age to come.

But the problem with the amillennial argument is that this understanding of Mark 10:30 and Luke 18:30 is perfectly compatible with the eschatology of premillennialism. In other words, when the amillennialist points to Mark 10:30 and Luke 18:30 as evidence that every disciple of Christ will be resurrected and glorified in the age to come, the premillennialist fully agrees. Within the various tribulational positions among premillennialists, there is some disagreement regarding when different groups of believers will be resurrected and glorified; but regardless

---

15 Menn, *Biblical Eschatology*, 41; Riddlebarger, *A Case for Amillennialism*, 98. Riddlebarger also describes this promise as indicating that "eternal life is a reward" (104), but he says nothing about the implications of these two verses.
16 Menn, *Biblical Eschatology*, 41.
17 Riddlebarger, *A Case for Amillennialism*, 96.

of whether a given group of believers is resurrected and glorified at a pre-tribulational rapture, at a mid-tribulational rapture, at the Second Coming, during the millennial kingdom, or at the end of the millennial kingdom, all premillennialists agree that every disciple of Christ will indeed receive the inheritance of eternal life in the age to come.

The unproven assumption in the amillennial argument is that if every believer will be resurrected and glorified in the age to come, then the resurrection and glorification of every believer must take place at the very beginning of the age to come, so that there is no possibility of physical death at any point during this time period. But this goes beyond what Jesus actually says in Mark 10:30 and Luke 18:30. Jesus does not say that there will be no death in the age to come—He simply says that all of His followers will inherit eternal life in the age to come.[18] Because this promise of eternal life is compatible with the view that the millennium of Revelation 20 is the initial phase of the coming kingdom, this argument fails to disprove the eschatology of premillennialism.

The Argument from Luke 20:34–36

The primary amillennial argument concerning the characteristics of the coming age is found in Luke 20:34–36, where Jesus says:

> The sons of this age [τοῦ αἰῶνος τούτου] marry and are given in marriage, but those who are considered worthy to attain to that age [τοῦ αἰῶνος ἐκείνου] and the resurrection from the dead, neither marry nor are given in marriage; for they cannot even die anymore, because they are like angels, and are sons of God, being sons of the resurrection.

According to Riddebarger, this passage has significant implications for the two-age model:

> The contrast Jesus set forth between the two ages was not strictly chronological but a contrast between two successive redemptive ages that differ from one another qualitatively, as temporal life

---

18 In contrast to the way it is portrayed by amillennialists, the statement of Jesus in Mark 10:30 and Luke 18:30 is not so much a description of the age to come as it is a promise of the reward to be received in the age to come.

differs from eternal. People marry and have families in this age. They will not in the age to come because they will be children of the resurrection (Luke 20:34–36).[19]

In other words, those who attain to the age to come will be sons of the resurrection, and therefore neither marriage nor physical birth or death will exist during this time, for they will be like angels.[20]

According to this argument, it is impossible for premillennialists to explain the existence of unresurrected, non-glorifed individuals in the millennium.[21] As Riddlebarger writes:

> How do they account for people who are not judged or raised from the dead at the time of our Lord's second advent? This is especially problematic since Jesus himself taught that in the age to come his people will all be children of the resurrection (Luke 20:34–36).[22]

Because the intermediate kingdom of premillennialism includes temporal aspects of human existence like sin, death, and procreation, amillennialists insist that Luke 20:34–36 makes it impossible to view this millennial kingdom as part of the age to come.

The key to evaluating this argument is found in the immediate context. In Luke 20:27–28a, a group of Sadducees—who categorically deny a future resurrection (v. 27)—comes to Jesus and begins to question Him (v. 28a). Appealing to the law of levirate marriage in Deuteronomy 25:5, these Sadducees raise the hypothetical example of a woman who marries seven brothers, one at a time, as each of those brothers fulfills his Mosaic duty:

> Teacher, Moses wrote for us that if a man's brother dies, having a wife, and he is childless, his brother should marry the wife and raise up children to his brother. Now there were seven brothers;

---

19 Riddlebarger, *A Case for Amillennialism*, 108.
20 As Waldron writes, "Luke 20:35 teaches that attaining to that age is equivalent to attaining to the resurrection of the dead. The resurrection is the door out of this age, and into the age to come" (*The End Times Made Simple*, 41).
21 Riddlebarger, *A Case for Amillennialism*, 276, 315; Waldron, *The End Times Made Simple*, 40–41; Floyd E. Hamilton, *The Basis of Millennial Faith* (Grand Rapids: Eerdmans Publishing, 1955), 135.
22 Riddlebarger, *A Case for Amillennialism*, 276.

and the first took a wife and died childless; and the second and the third married her; and in the same way all seven died, leaving no children. Finally the woman died also. In the resurrection therefore, which one's wife will she be? For all seven had married her (Luke 20:28b–33).

Even though the Sadducees asked Jesus a question—"which one's wife will she be?" (v. 33)—it is clear that this is not a sincere inquiry. Instead, it is a deliberate attempt to disprove the future resurrection by highlighting what they believe to be the absurdity of its implications. Their question, in other words, is not really a question—it is an argument against the resurrection. In response to their argument, Jesus exposes the absurdity of the question itself by informing the Sadducees that marriage will no longer exist among those who are resurrected (vv. 34–36), and then He provides clear biblical support for a future resurrection from the teaching of Moses (vv. 37–38), leaving His listeners with nothing more to say (vv. 39–40).

According to the immediate context, then, the words of Jesus in Luke 20:34–36 are not simply a general description of the age to come—they are designed to answer the Sadducees' argument against the future resurrection. The hypothetical example of the Sadducees specifically concerned those who had experienced the future resurrection, as indicated by the phrase "in the resurrection" (ἐν τῇ ἀναστάσει) at the beginning of their question (Luke 20:33). Therefore, when Jesus responded by describing the nature of God's people in the age to come, His focus is on the implications of the future resurrection for the question of marriage.

More specifically, Jesus corrected the premise of the question by stating that marriage will no longer exist among those who are resurrected, which nullified the argument of the Sadducees by exposing the irrelevance of their hypothetical example. The main point of Luke 20:34–36, then, is that marriage will no longer exist among those who have been resurrected, for they will be like angels, being neither married nor subject to death. In other words, the focus of Jesus is not on everyone who attains to the age to come, but on everyone who attains to "that age *and* the resurrection from the dead" (Luke 20:35).[23]

---

23 The genitives τοῦ αἰῶνος ἐκείνου ("that age") and τῆς ἀναστάσεως τῆς ἐκ νεκρῶν ("the resurrection from the dead") are joined by the conjunction καὶ as compound objects

The key, once again, is the immediate context. Because the question of the Sadducees focused exclusively on those who were resurrected, this was also the exclusive focus of the response of Jesus. Explaining that some people in the initial phase of the coming kingdom will not be resurrected would not have served His purpose in refuting the error of the Sadducees or defending the doctrine of the resurrection. Therefore, to make distinctions irrelevant to the argument of the Sadducees would not only fail to bring clarity to the issue, but it might also distract or confuse His listeners in the process. Luke 20:34–36 neither contemplates nor comments on the possibility of non-glorified individuals in the first part of the age to come, not because Jesus denies this possibility but because it was not germane to the point He was making.

If this were the only passage in Scripture describing the age to come, one might understandably conclude that there could be no physical birth or death at any point during this period of time. But with the testimony of the Old Testament prophets regarding the existence of sin, death, and procreation in the coming kingdom (Ps 72:1–20; Isa 2:1–3; Micah 4:2–4; Isa 11:1–9; 65:17–25; Zech 14:16–19)—along with the clear teaching of Revelation 19–21 that an intermediate kingdom will precede the eternal state (cf. Isa 24:21–23)—the need to harmonize the entirety of biblical teaching leads to the conclusion that Luke 20:34–36 is compatible with the millennial kingdom of premillennialism.

Conclusion

The characteristics ascribed to the two ages in the New Testament are consistent with the eschatology of amillennialisn, but they do not require it. In addition, these characteristics do not preclude the possibility of an intermediate kingdom between the present age and the eternal state. Amillennialists deny that the temporal aspects of human existence—such as sin, death, and procreation—can be present at any point in the age to come, but these passages fail to make a clear and compelling argument for this claim, and, therefore, they fail to disprove the messianic kingdom of premillennialism.

---

of the infinitive τυχεῖν ("to attain"). As such, they describe those who neither marry nor die as those who have attained both the age to come *and* the resurrection of the dead.

Chapter 8

The Resurrection and Judgment of All Mankind

INTRODUCTION

The third way that the two-age model is used to refute premillennialism involves the dividing line between the two ages. According to this argument, several New Testament passages describe the line of demarcation between this age and the age to come in a way that precludes the possibility of an intermediate kingdom between the two. These passages are said to indicate not only that the dividing line between the two ages is the Second Coming of Christ (Matt 13:39) but also that each of the following events will take place at the Second Coming:

- The Resurrection of All Mankind (Dan 12:2; John 5:28–29; Acts 24:15)
- The Judgment of All Mankind (Matt 25:31–46; 2 Thess 1:6–10)
- The Destruction of the Cosmos (2 Pet 3:10–13)
- The Renewal of the Cosmos (2 Pet 3:10–13; Rom 8:18–23)
- The Final Victory over Sin (Rom 8:18–23)
- The Final Victory over Death (1 Cor 15:20–28, 50–57)

According to this argument, because each of these will take place at the return of Christ, there is no room for a thousand-year gap between the Second Coming and these other events, and therefore the possibility of the intermediate kingdom of premillennialism is precluded.

```
                    Second Coming
    THIS AGE            ↓        THE AGE TO COME
——————————————————————————————————————————————▶
              Resurrection of All Mankind
              Judgment of All Mankind
              Destruction of the Cosmos
              Renewal of the Cosmos
              Final Victory over Sin
              Final Victory over Death
```

As amillennialist Sam Storms writes, "When we examine what the New Testament says will occur at the time of the second coming/advent of Jesus Christ, there is no place for a 1,000 year earthly reign to follow."[1] These six eschatological events will be examined in chapters 8–10 to determine not only their exact timing but also whether the corresponding biblical passages actually preclude the possibility of an intermediate kingdom. In the end, it will be demonstrated that they do not.

The Resurrection of All Mankind

According to amillennialism, the Bible presents the resurrection of all mankind—both believers and unbelievers—as occurring at the same time (Dan 12:2; John 5:28–29; Acts 24:15).[2] Although the doctrine of the future resurrection is not fully developed in the Old Testament, Daniel 12:2 says: "And many of those who sleep in the dust of the ground will awake, these to everlasting life, but the others to disgrace and everlast-

---

1 Sam Storms, *Kingdom Come: The Amillennial Alternative* (Ross-shire, Scotland: Mentor, 2013), 165; also see Jonathan Menn, *Biblical Eschatology* (Eugene, OR: Resource Publications, 2013), 344–45. According to Storms, "At the time of the second coming there will occur the final resurrection, the final judgment, the end of sin, the end of death, and the creation of the new heavens and new earth" (*Kingdom Come*, 165).
2 Cornelis P. Venema, *The Promise of the Future* (Carlisle, PA: Banner of Truth, 2000), 248; Anthony Hoekema, *The Bible and the Future* (Grand Rapids: Eerdmans Publishing, 1979), 240; William E. Cox, *Amillennialism Today* (Phillipsburg, NJ: Presbyterian and Reformed Publishing Co., 1966), 103. Menn also cites Matt 12:39–42//Luke 11:29–32 as a clear indication that there is but one resurrection of both the righteous and the wicked (*Biblical Eschatology*, 344).

ing contempt." According to amillennialist Anthony Hoekema, this verse "mentions the resurrection of the godly and that of the wicked in the same breath, with no indication that the resurrection of these two groups shall be separated by a long period of time."[3]

The simultaneous timing of the resurrection of the righteous and the wicked is also said to be taught in John 5:28–29, where Jesus says: "Do not marvel at this; for an hour is coming, in which all who are in the tombs shall hear His voice, and shall come forth; those who did the good deeds to a resurrection of life, those who committed the evil deeds to a resurrection of judgment." According to Hoekema, the clear implication of John 5:28–29 is that

> at a certain specific time, here called the coming "hour," *all* who are in their graves will hear the voice of Christ and be raised from the dead. There is no indication here that Jesus intends to teach that an extremely long period of time will separate the resurrection of life from the resurrection of judgment.[4]

Amillennialist Sam Storms claims that the premillennialist is unable to accept the straightforward declaration of John 5:28–29.[5] Instead, says Storms, the premillennialist "insists that a 1,000-year earthly reign of Christ must intervene between the resurrection of believers and the resurrection of unbelievers."[6] In contrast, amillennialism affirms that "the resurrection of believers and unbelievers will occur concurrently at the end of the age."[7] In the words of Kim Riddlebarger, "It is beyond question that the resurrection of the righteous and unrighteous both occur at the sound of the final trumpet, the last day, when Christ returns in great glory."[8]

---

3   Hoekema, *The Bible and the Future*, 240.
4   Ibid.; emphasis original.
5   Storms, *Kingdom Come*, 164.
6   Ibid. According to Kim Riddlebarger, "Both Daniel and Jesus spoke of one resurrection in which the two distinct groups simultaneously participate—believers and unbelievers—each receiving the appropriate recompense. There is no hint anywhere in these two texts, implied or otherwise, that the resurrection of the righteous and unrighteous are separated by a period of one thousand years, an essential feature of premillennialism" (Kim Riddlebarger, *A Case for Amillennialism: Understanding the End Times*, expanded ed. [Grand Rapids: Baker Books, 2013], 161).
7   Venema, *The Promise of the Future*, 333.
8   Riddlebarger, *A Case for Amillennialism*, 163.

In a similar way, amillennialists also believe that Acts 24:15—which speaks of "a resurrection of both the righteous and the wicked"—indicates a single resurrection encompassing both groups of people. Amillennialists often note that the word "resurrection" in Acts 24:15 is singular, not plural.[9] As Hoekema asks, "Can two resurrections a thousand years apart properly be called *a resurrection*?"[10]

According to amillennialists, because the righteous and the wicked will be raised at the Second Coming of Christ, a thousand-year kingdom between the resurrection of the righteous and the resurrection of the wicked is precluded. As Riddlebarger writes, "Scripture clearly teaches that the resurrection and judgment of the righteous and unrighteous will occur at the same time, thus eliminating the possibility of an earthly millennial age to dawn after the Lord's return."[11]

The Premillennial Response

In response to this objection, Daniel 12:2, John 5:28–29, and Acts 24:15 do not actually eliminate the possibility of two distinct resurrections separated by a period of time. In fact, all three passages speak of a resurrection of the righteous and a resurrection of the wicked—and always in the same order as in Revelation 20[12]—and they neither state nor require that the two resurrections happen simultaneously. They simply do not specify one way or the other.[13] As premillennialist Wayne Grudem explains:

> All of these verses, in the absence of Revelation 20:5–6, might or might not be speaking of a single future time of resurrection. But

---

9 Hoekema, *The Bible and the Future*, 241; Robert B. Strimple, "Amillennialism," in *Three Views on the Millennium and Beyond*, ed. Darrell L. Bock (Grand Rapids: Zondervan Publishing, 1999), 101.
10 Hoekema, *The Bible and the Future*, 241; emphasis original.
11 Riddlebarger, *A Case for Amillennialism*, 166.
12 This is especially clear in John 5:29 where Jesus speaks of two different physical resurrections: "a resurrection of life" (ἀνάστασιν ζωῆς) and "a resurrection of judgment" (ἀνάστασιν κρίσεως).
13 Wayne Grudem, *Systematic Theology: An Introduction to Biblical Doctrine* (Grand Rapids: Zondervan Publishing, 1994), 1119; Herman A. Hoyt, "A Dispensational Premillennial Response," in *The Meaning of the Millennium: Four Views*, ed. Robert G. Clouse (Downers Grove, IL: InterVarsity Press, 1979), 195. According to Feinberg, Dan 12:2 "does not reveal, and it should not be made to teach, exactly what period of time elapses between the resurrection of the first group and that of the second" (Charles L. Feinberg, *Millennialism: The Two Major Views*, 3rd ed. [Chicago: Moody Press, 1980], 347).

with the explicit teaching of Revelation 20:5–6 about two resurrections, these verses must be understood to refer to the future certainty of a resurrection for each type of person, without specifying that those resurrections will be separated in time.[14]

Even John 5:28–29, which speaks of "an hour" in which these two resurrections will occur, does not require that both resurrections take place at the same time. John frequently uses the word "hour" (ὥρα) in reference to an extended period of time (John 16:2), sometimes as long as the entire present age (John 4:21, 23; 1 John 2:18). In fact, this is how the apostle uses the word just three verses earlier in John 5:25.[15] As Craig Blaising argues, "If the eschatological hour can be extended over two thousand years, it is not impossible that a thousand years might transpire between the resurrection of the just and the resurrection of the unjust."[16]

As discussed in chapter 1, sometimes a given biblical prophecy will predict two or more future events and present them in such a way that it appears they will occur simultaneously, but later revelation indicates a significant gap of time which separates their fulfillment. Henry Virkler explains that this kind of prophetic telescoping can be likened to one's perception of a mountain range on the horizon:

> When one views a mountain range from a distance, the peaks appear to be quite near to one another. However, on closer examination it becomes evident that wide valleys and many miles separate the individual peaks. When the prophets looked toward the future, they also saw things that appeared to them to be side by side, yet as the time of fulfillment approaches, significant gaps become visible.[17]

---

14 Grudem, *Systematic Theology*, 1120.
15 Ibid., 1119.
16 Craig A. Blaising, "A Premillennial Response to Robert B. Strimple," in *Three Views on the Millennium and Beyond*, ed. Darrell L. Bock (Grand Rapids: Zondervan Publishing, 1999), 150.
17 Henry A. Virkler and Karelynne Gerber Ayayo, *Hermeneutics: Principles and Processes of Biblical Interpretation*, 2nd ed. (Grand Rapids: Baker Academic, 2007), 169–70. Also see William W. Klein, Craig L. Blomberg, and Robert L. Hubbard, *Introduction to Biblical Interpretation* (Nashville: W Publishing Group, 1993), 304–5; Walter C. Kaiser and Moisés Silva, *An Introduction to Biblical Hermeneutics: The Search for Meaning* (Grand Rapids: Zondervan Publishing, 1994), 144; Walter C. Kaiser, Jr., *The Use of the Old Testament in the New* (Eugene, OR: Wipf and Stock Publishers, 1985), 63.

As J. Barton Payne observes, "Biblical prophecy may leap from one prominent peak in predictive topography to another, without notice of the valley between, which may involve no inconsiderable lapse in chronology."[18]

For example, there is no clear evidence in Isaiah 9:6–7 alone that a lengthy interval of time would separate the birth of Christ at His first coming (Isa 9:6a) from the reign of Christ at His second coming (Isa 9:6b–7), and yet later revelation clarifies the existence of this temporal gap between them. Likewise, the interval between the first coming in Zechariah 9:9 and the second coming in Zechariah 9:10 could not be perceived in that passage alone, and yet subsequent revelation clarified that what the prophet depicted as a single event must now be recognized as involving two.

In the same way, when it comes to the future resurrection, what the earlier writers of Scripture seemed to depict as a single resurrection of both the righteous and the wicked (Dan 12:2; John 5:28–29; Acts 24:15) must now be recognized as involving two resurrections, a resurrection of the righteous and a resurrection of the wicked a thousand years later (Rev 20). In other words, while these other passages do not specify the timing of the two resurrections, in Revelation 20:4–5 this time element *is* specified: "They came to life and reigned with Christ for a thousand years. The rest of the dead did not come to life until the thousand years were completed" (Rev 20:4b–5a). As Robert Saucy writes:

> There is no unambiguous evidence for a so-called general resurrection at the end of the age in which both the saved and the unsaved will participate. There are references to the resurrection of both, but none explicitly demonstrates that there is only one such resurrection or that the saved and unsaved are resurrected at the same time (e.g., Da 12:2; Jn 5:28–29). There is, therefore, nothing preventing us from viewing these as general statements about the resurrection of all people that will occur at different

---

18 J. Barton Payne, *The Encyclopedia of Biblical Prophecy* (Grand Rapids: Baker Books, 1980), 137; cf. Fee and Stuart, *How to Read the Bible*, 201. According to Kaiser, "As a result of prophetic foreshortening, the prophet may have seen only events A, B, and Z, and have had no idea of what intervened" (Walter C. Kaiser, Jr., *Back Toward the Future: Hints for Interpreting Biblical Prophecy* [Eugene, OR: Wipf & Stock Publishers, 1989], 122).

times in accord with the rather plain teaching of Revelation 20:4–5.[19]

An additional argument for a gap between the resurrection of the righteous and the resurrection of the wicked comes from Philippians 3:11. In this verse, the apostle Paul looks ahead to the day when he will attain to "the resurrection from the dead" (τὴν ἐξανάστασιν τὴν ἐκ νεκρῶν). As several premillennialists have noted, Paul's reference to "the resurrection *from* the dead"—rather than "the resurrection *of* the dead"—implies a partial resurrection in which some are raised from the dead while others are left in a state of death.[20] In fact, the designation "resurrection *from* the dead" is consistently used either of Jesus (Acts 4:2; Rom 1:4; 1 Pet 1:3; cf. Acts 17:31) or of believers (Luke 20:35; Phil 3:11) as those who are raised out from among others who remain dead, but never of all the dead in general.[21]

When the biblical writers refer to the resurrection of the dead in general (Acts 17:32; 23:6; 24:21; 1 Cor 15:12, 13, 21; Heb 6:2), they use the genitive νεκρῶν—"resurrection *of the dead*"—a subjective genitive which simply indicates that the dead are raised to life. In contrast, the use of the prepositional phrase ἐκ νεκρῶν in Luke 20:35 and Phil 3:11—"resurrection *from the dead*"—indicates being resurrected out from among the dead. The prepositional phrase ἐκ νεκρῶν is used the same way in combination with various verbs to refer to the resurrection of Lazarus (John 12:1, 9, 17), Jesus (Acts 3:15; 4:10; 10:41; 13:30), and people in general (Heb 11:19) as those who are raised out from among those who remain dead. Therefore, when Philippians 3:11 (and Luke 20:35) describe believers as experiencing a "resurrection *from* the dead" (τὴν ἐξανάστασιν τὴν ἐκ νεκρῶν), this implies an initial resurrection of those who are

---

19 Robert L. Saucy, *The Case for Progressive Dispensationalism: The Interface Between Dispensational and Non-Dispensational Theology* (Grand Rapids: Zondervan Publishing, 1993), 288.
20 Craig A. Blaising, "The Kingdom that Comes with Jesus: Premillennialism and the Harmony of Scripture," in *The Return of Christ: A Premillennial Perspective*, ed. David L. Allen and Steve W. Lemke (Nashville: Broadman & Holman, 2011), 148; Blaising, "A Premillennial Response," 151; Saucy, *Progressive Dispensationalism*, 286; Feinberg, *Millennialism*, 347–48, 351; Robert D. Culver, *Systematic Theology: Biblical and Historical* (Great Britain: Christian Focus Publications, 2005), 1057–58.
21 Saucy, *Progressive Dispensationalism*, 286; Feinberg, *Millennialism*, 348.

in Christ as separate and distinct from a later resurrection of those who are not.²² This resurrection of the righteous is singled out elsewhere in Scripture, being labeled "a better resurrection" (Heb 11:35) and "the resurrection of the righteous" (Luke 14:14).

However, even though this argument makes a strong case for a distinction between the two resurrections, it falls short of actually proving a significant interval of time separating them,²³ because the amillennialist could simply argue that the resurrection of the wicked occurs immediately after the resurrection of the righteous despite the distinction between the two.²⁴ And yet the distinction that Luke 20:35 and Philippians 3:11 make between the resurrection of the righteous and the resurrection of the wicked—with the former occurring prior to the latter—does supplement the clear testimony in Revelation 20 of two resurrections separated by one thousand years and thereby provide additional support for the premillennial view.²⁵

---

22 Saucy, *Progressive Dispensationalism*, 286. In fact, as Blaising notes, Paul coins a new word for resurrection in Phil 3:11 by adding the prefix ἐκ to ἀνάστασις, resulting in ἐξανάστασις and thereby doubling the use of the preposition in the phrase ἐξανάστασιν τὴν ἐκ νεκρῶν ("resurrection out from the dead") ("The Kingdom that Comes with Jesus," 148). BDAG defines ἐξανάστασις as referring to "the state or condition of coming up from among the dead" (345).

23 Feinberg overstates the premillennial argument from Phil 3:11 in saying that this verse "teaches as clearly as any that there will be more than one general resurrection" (*Millennialism*, 351).

24 In doing so, however, amillennialists would have to slightly modify their view that there will be "one resurrection in which the two distinct groups simultaneously participate" (Riddlebarger, *A Case for Amillennialism*, 161), asserting instead that the resurrection of the righteous will take place first and be immediately followed by the resurrection of the wicked.

25 As additional evidence that "the resurrection from the dead" in Phil 3:11 does not refer to a general resurrection of both the righteous and the wicked, Saucy points out that this resurrection is something that Paul aspires to attain to. According to Saucy: "If Paul believed in one general resurrection at the end in which all people, the saved and the lost, would participate, it is difficult to understand his use of this language in relation to his personal participation. There would be no question of his being a part of such a resurrection. If his desire was to be part of those resurrected to life as opposed to those destined for judgment (and if the latter were raised at the same time), we would have expected Paul to add this qualifier. But he says simply that he hopes to attain to 'the resurrection from the dead,' apparently with reference to a distinct resurrection of the righteous—John's 'first' resurrection. Only such an understanding appears to do justice to his concern to be part of it" (*Progressive Dispensationalism*, 287).

The Judgment of All Mankind

According to amillennialism, not only will the *resurrection* of all mankind take place at the Second Coming, but so will the *judgment* of all mankind, both the righteous and the wicked. Because this universal judgment will occur at the return of Christ and usher in the eternal state, amillennialists argue that there is no room for a thousand-year gap between the Second Coming and the final judgment, thus eliminating the possibility of an intermediate kingdom. To prove that the judgment of all mankind will occur at the Second Coming and initiate the eternal state, amillennialists point to Matthew 25:31–46 and 2 Thessalonians 1:6–10.[26]

The Argument from Matthew 25:31–46

The passage most commonly cited by amillennialists is Matthew 25:31–46, where Jesus prophesies of separating the sheep and the goats at His Second Coming.[27] Matthew 25 indicates that when Jesus returns in glory, He will welcome the righteous into eternal life (vv. 34, 46) and disperse the wicked into eternal punishment (vv. 41, 46). According to amillennialists, the judgment in this passage is equivalent to the judgment of Revelation 20:11–15, and therefore Matthew 25:31–46 explicitly teaches "that the final judgment occurs when our Lord returns."[28] Riddlebarger argues that this presents an insurmountable problem for premillennialism:

> Where is the one-thousand-year gap between Christ's return and the final judgment taught in the Scriptures? It is not there. The gap must be inserted even though doing so violates the plain

---

26 As additional evidence that the final judgment takes place at the Second Coming—and not a thousand years later—amillennialists also cite Matt 13:39–40 and 49–50, which make a connection between the judgment of unbelievers and the end of the age (Riddlebarger, *A Case for Amillennialism*, 99; Storms, *Kingdom Come*, 161; Cox, *Amillennialism Today*, 115–16).

27 Riddlebarger, *A Case for Amillennialism*, 164; Hoekema, *The Bible and the Future*, 185; Samuel E. Waldron, *The End Times Made Simple: How Could Everyone Be So Wrong About Biblical Prophecy?* (Amityville, NY: Calvary Press, 2003), 55–57; Cox, *Amillennialism Today*, 116–17.

28 Riddlebarger, *A Case for Amillennialism*, 276. According to Riddlebarger, "When Jesus returns in glory with all his angels, he assigns the final outcome to both righteous and unrighteous. There is no evidence [in Matt 25:31–46] of the linchpin of premillennialism, a one-thousand-year gap between the resurrection of the righteous and unrighteous" (164).

sense of the passage and the premillennial insistence on a literal interpretation.[29]

In contrast to the amillennial view, premillennialists generally believe that Matthew 25:31–46 describes not the final judgment of all mankind, but rather the judgment of the nations which exist when Jesus returns, specifically concerning either their entrance into the millennial kingdom or their consignment to eternal fire.[30] For this reason, most premillennialists believe that the judgments in Matthew 25:31–46 and Revelation 20:11–15 should be distinguished, the former taking place when Jesus returns to establish His earthly kingdom and the latter occurring when the wicked are resurrected after His millennial reign.

Several differences between the two judgments demonstrate that Matthew 25:31–46 and Revelation 20:11–15 do not describe the same event. The first and most obvious difference is that the judgment of Matthew 25 involves both believers and unbelievers—the sheep and the goats—whereas only unbelievers are judged in Revelation 20.[31] Amillennialists dispute this claim that the judgement of Revelation 20:11–15 is restricted to unbelievers,[32] but at least four reasons lead to the conclusion that the final judgment of Revelation 20 must include only unbelievers: (a) the most obvious antecedent of "the dead" in verse 12 is "the rest of the dead" in Revelation 20:5, unbelievers who do not take part in the first resurrection; (b) the only stated outcome of the judgment in Revelation

---

29 Riddlebarger, *A Case for Amillennialism*, 277.
30 Eugene W. Pond, "Who Are the Sheep and Goats in Matthew 25:31–46?" *BibSac* 159, no. 3 (July–Sept 2002): 299–300; John F. Walvoord, *Matthew: Thy Kingdom Come* (Chicago: Moody Press, 1974), 200. In contrast, a few premillennialists have argued that the judgment of Matt 25:31–46 will occur after the millennial kingdom and should be identified with the judgment of Rev 20:11–15 (Robert H. Gundry, *The Church and the Tribulation: A Biblical Examination of Posttribulationism* [Grand Rapids: Zondervan Publishing, 1973], 168–69; George E. Ladd, "The Parable of the Sheep and the Goats in Recent Interpretation," in *New Dimensions in New Testament Study*, eds. Richard N. Longenecker and Merrill C. Tenney [Grand Rapids: Zondervan, 1974], 196), but this is clearly a minority position. For a helpful response to this view, see Eugene W. Pond, "The Background and Timing of the Judgment of the Sheep and Goats," *BibSac* 159, no. 2 (April–June 2002): 215–18.
31 Pond, "The Background and Timing of the Judgment," 219; J. T. Cooper, "The Judgment, or Judgments," in *Premillennial Essays*, ed. Nathaniel West (Minneapolis: Bryant Baptist Publications, 1981), 261–62.
32 Hoekema, *The Bible and the Future*, 242–43.

20 is the lake of fire (Rev 20:15), with the Book of Life being mentioned "only to show that the names of these dead are not written there;"[33] (c) there is no emphasis in Revelation 20:11–15 on the future resurrection as an object of the believer's hope;[34] and (d) this view fits the broader context of Revelation 19–20, which sets forth God's ultimate victory over everything corrupted by sin—the beast and the false prophet (19:19–21), Satan (20:1–10), heaven and earth (20:11; cf. 21:1), and now His unbelieving human enemies (20:12–15). For these reasons, the judgment of Revelation 20 has reference only to unbelievers, and therefore the passages must not describe the same event.

A second difference between the judgments in Matthew 25:31–46 and Revelation 20:11–15 concerns the identity of those who are judged. Unlike in Revelation 20:12–13, where "the dead" are resurrected to stand before the great white throne,[35] the objects of judgment in Matthew 25:31–46 are the nations of the world who are alive when Jesus returns and who are gathered from all over the earth (cf. Matt 24:31).[36] Not only is there no mention of any physical resurrection in Matthew 25,[37] but Jesus identifies the objects of judgment as "the nations," a designation which is never applied either directly or indirectly to those who have died.[38] In contrast, the objects of judgment in Revelation 20 are gathered not from the four corners of the earth where they live, but from the grave and the sea where their dead bodies were buried (vv. 12–13).[39]

---

33 Robert L. Thomas, *Revelation 8–22: An Exegetical Commentary* (Chicago: Moody Press, 1995), 431; cf. Feinberg, *Millennialism*, 360.
34 J. Ramsey Michaels, "The First Resurrection: A Response," *WTJ* 39, no. 1 (Fall 1976): 105.
35 The resurrection of the dead in verse 13—"the sea gave up the dead which were in it, and death and Hades gave up the dead which were in them"—is a parenthetical explanation of how the dead came to be standing before the throne in verse 12 to be judged. This resurrection of unbelievers was alluded to previously in Rev 20:5: "The rest of the dead did not come to life until the thousand years were completed."
36 Blaising, "The Kingdom that Comes with Jesus," 158; Pond, "The Background and Timing of the Judgment," 214; Pond, "Who Are the Sheep and Goats?," 299; Cooper, "The Judgment, or Judgments," 260–61.
37 Cooper, "The Judgment, or Judgments," 253; Feinberg, *Millennialism*, 362.
38 Cooper, "The Judgment, or Judgments," 253; John F. Walvoord, *The Millennial Kingdom* (Grand Rapids: Zondervan Publishing, 1959), 287; Stanley D. Toussaint, *Behold the King: A Study of Matthew* (Portland: Multnomah Press, 1980), 288.
39 As Craig Blaising writes, "The 'sheep' in that passage are nowhere said to be raised from the dead, but are gathered from the peoples alive at that time and received by the descended Lord into His kingdom" ("The Kingdom that Comes with Jesus," 158).

A third difference concerns the location of the two judgments.[40] In Matthew 25:31–46, the judgment takes place on earth, for when the Son of Man returns in glory He comes from heaven to earth and gathers the nations from the ends of the world (cf. Matt 24:31). In contrast, at the time of the judgment in Revelation 20:11–15, heaven and earth have fled away from God's presence, "and no place was found for them" because they have been destroyed (v. 11; cf. Rev 21:1). This poses a problem for the amillennial view that these are the same judgment, but it corresponds well to the premillennial view that (a) the judgment of Matthew 25 occurs when Jesus returns to establish his earthly kingdom, and (b) the judgment of Revelation 20 takes place after His millennial reign, just before the creation of the new heavens and earth. However, it may be possible for the amillennialist to harmonize this discrepancy by saying that when Jesus returns to earth, He separates the sheep and the goats, destroys the heavens and the earth so that "no place was found for them" (Rev 20:11), and then judges all mankind at the great white throne. For this reason, this third difference fails to demonstrate conclusively that the two judgments must be distinguished.

A fourth difference concerns the basis on which the people are judged in Matthew 25, which is the way the sheep and the goats have treated "the least" of Jesus' brothers (Matt 25:40, 45).[41] Some believe that the least of His brothers refers to all who are hungry, distressed, and needy, and therefore that the basis of acceptance into the kingdom is established by deeds of mercy and compassion in general. The weakness of this view is that there is no parallel in the New Testament in which the least of Jesus' "brothers" are identified with the poor and needy without distinction.[42] In addition, even though there may be a secondary sense in which all humans

---

40 Pond, "Who Are the Sheep and Goats?," 299; Cooper, "The Judgment, or Judgments," 261; Walvoord, *The Millennial Kingdom*, 285; Feinberg, *Millennialism*, 362.
41 Pond argues that the two judgments should be distinguished because "in Matthew 25 the criterion of judgment is whether a person has done acts of mercy ... whereas in Revelation 20:12–13, 15 the basis of judgment will be a person's works" ("The Background and Timing of the Judgment," 219). But this alone is insufficient to demonstrate that the two judgments must be distinguished, because acts of mercy and a person's works could be viewed as complementary descriptions of the basis of the same judgment, with the former being a subcategory of the latter. The key in Matt 25:31–46 is that Jesus refers not simply to the treatment of the needy in general but to the treatment of the least of His brothers.
42 D. A. Carson, "Matthew," in *EBC*, ed. Frank E. Gaebelein (Grand Rapids: Zondervan Publishing, 1981), 8:519.

are "brothers" and God's children, Jesus does not use the word "brothers" this way in Matthew's gospel.[43] This is not a plausible interpretation.

For this reason, most interpret the least of Jesus' brothers as having a narrower referent. Some say it refers to Christian brothers in general, followers of Christ who often face hunger, thirst, illness, and imprisonment as they seek to spread the gospel.[44] Others say it refers to the apostles and other Christian missionaries, the treatment of whom determines the fate of all men (those who receive them receive Christ, and those who reject them reject Christ).[45] Still others see it as a reference to the Jewish brothers of Jesus who are converted during the Tribulation[46] and who either (a) are alive when He returns[47] or (b) return with Him because they were previously martyred.[48]

---

43 James Montgomery Boice, *The Gospel of Matthew* (Grand Rapids: Baker Books, 2001), 541; Craig L. Blomberg, *Matthew*, NAC vol. 22 (Nashville: Broadman & Holman Publishers, 1992), 378.
44 Carson, "Matthew," 8:520; Robert H. Gundry, *Matthew: A Commentary on His Handbook for a Mixed Church Under Persecution*, 2nd ed. (Grand Rapids: Eerdmans Publishing, 1994), 514; John A. Broadus, *Commentary on Matthew* (Grand Rapids: Kregel Publications, 1990), 510-11; Heinrich August Meyer, *Critical and Exegetical Handbook to the Gospel of Matthew*, 6th ed., trans. and ed. Peter Christie and William Stewart (Edinburgh: T. & T. Clark, 1879), 181. This view fails to preserve an adequate distinction between the sheep and the least of Jesus' brothers. As Robert Thomas writes, "The brothers differ from the sheep and the sheep must be Christ's spiritual brothers, so the brothers cannot refer to the same group" (Robert L. Thomas, "Jesus' View of Eternal Punishment," MSJ 9, no. 2 [Fall 1998]: 155; also see Toussaint, *Behold the King*, 291).
45 Blomberg, *Matthew*, 378. Not only does this view fail to preserve an adequate distinction between the sheep and the least of Jesus' brothers, but because the proclamation of the gospel to the nations (Matt 24:14; 28:18-20) and the suffering that Jesus envisages for His disciples (Matt 24:9-13) are not restricted to the apostles and missionaries, this definition is not inclusive enough (Carson, "Matthew," 8:519). In addition, this view has difficulty explaining why Jesus would refer to apostles and missionaries as "the least" of His brethren (Thomas, "Jesus' View of Eternal Punishment," 155; Meyer, *Gospel of Matthew*, 181).
46 The primary strength of this view is that it preserves the distinction between the three groups of individuals mentioned in this passage by seeing the least of Jesus' brothers as Jews converted and persecuted (and perhaps even martyred) during the Tribulation, and the sheep and the goats as Gentile believers and unbelievers, respectively, from among the nations of the world. It also affirms the standard New Testament use of τὰ ἔθνη as a reference to Gentiles as distinct from Jews.
47 Thomas, "Jesus' View of Eternal Punishment," 155–56.
48 Eugene W. Pond, "Who Are 'the Least' of Jesus' Brothers in Matthew 25:40?" *BibSac* 159, no. 4 (Oct-Dec 2002): 436-48. According to Pond: "It seems best to recognize that Jesus' 'brothers,' who are called 'the least,' are believers who will be slain for their faith during the Tribulation and who will return with the risen Lord at His second coming. The judgment of the sheep and goats will be a judgment of all non-Jews who will be alive at the end of the Tribulation period. Their eternal destinies—inheriting the kingdom or departing to fiery

Regardless of which of these three views is correct, because the treatment of the least of the brothers of Jesus is the basis of this separation of the sheep and the goats, Matthew 25:31–46 cannot refer to the universal judgment of all mankind. As J. T. Cooper observes, "There are millions upon millions who have died to whom these reasons would have been *wholly inapplicable*. What multitudes, in the ages of the past, have passed away who never heard of the name of Jesus or his brethren!"[49] For this reason, a judgment based on how people have treated the least of the brothers of Jesus cannot be understood as a universal judgment of all mankind throughout history, as amillennialism teaches.

The fifth and most compelling reason to distinguish between the two judgments is that the separation of the sheep and the goats in Matthew 25 takes place at the Second Coming of Christ—"when the Son of Man comes in His glory" (v. 31)—whereas the judgment in Revelation 20:11–15 occurs a thousand years later, after the millennial reign of Christ (Rev 19–20). According to the book of Revelation, the Second Coming of Christ (Rev 19:11–21) and the final judgment of unbelievers (Rev 20:11–15) will be separated by the thousand-year reign of Christ (Rev 20:1–10), and therefore these two judgments cannot take place at the same time.[50] For this reason, premillennialists believe that when the sheep are invited to inherit the kingdom in Matthew 25:34, they enter the millennial kingdom as the initial phase of the age to come.[51]

It is more difficult, however, for premillennialism to account for the judgment of the goats. In Matthew 25:41, when Jesus says to those on His left, "Depart from Me, accursed ones, into the eternal fire which has been prepared for the devil and for his angels," this appears to match the description in Revelation 20:15: "And if anyone's name was not found written in the book of life, he was thrown into the lake of fire."[52] For this

---

punishment—will be based on their actions that reflect whether they believe or reject the message of witnesses for the Son of Man as Savior and King. These witnesses are called the 'brothers' of Jesus Christ because they will be His devoted disciples, and they are called 'the least' of Jesus' brothers because many of them will have been put to death for their faith" (448).

49 Cooper, "The Judgment, or Judgments," 255.
50 See chapters 11–14 for a thorough defense of this interpretation of Revelation 20.
51 Pond, "The Background and Timing of the Judgment," 220.
52 This is further supported by the description in Matt 25:46 of the wicked going away "into eternal punishment."

reason, amillennialists argue that the judgment of Matthew 25:31–46 must be the final judgment of Revelation 20:11–15, which ushers in the new heavens and new earth of Revelation 21, thereby eliminating the possibility of an intermediate kingdom between the Second Coming and the eternal state.

There are three different ways that premillennialists have responded to this argument. The first response is that Matthew 25 contains an example of prophetic foreshortening, a compression of future events in which the divine sentence of eternal punishment is rendered at the Second Coming, but the actual consignment to eternal fire does not occur until a thousand years later.[53] According to this view, the righteous enter the millennial kingdom at the Second Coming, but the wicked are not immediately thrown into the lake of fire, even though this eternal sentence is rendered at the return of Christ. In this way, at the judgment of Matthew 25 the eternal fire prepared for the devil becomes the immutable and ultimate destination of these unbelievers without being their immediate experience. As Robert Thomas explains, "The 'goats' of this judgment will be in a place of waiting with the rest of the lost until time for the second resurrection."[54]

This view has a number of strengths. First, the clear precedent of prophetic foreshortening elsewhere in Scripture makes this a legitimate way to harmonize Matthew 25:31–46 and Revelation 20. Second, there is a clear example of prophetic foreshortening earlier in the very same discourse, where Jesus describes the future destruction of the temple in AD 70 and His Second Coming hundreds of years later (Matt 24:1–41), with no clear indication of a lengthy gap of time in between.[55] Third, this view interprets the "eternal fire" in Matthew 25:41 as the lake of fire—rather than some kind of intermediate punishment—which corresponds to its

---

[53] Thomas, "Jesus' View of Eternal Punishment," 151. According to Thomas: "The case resembles Jesus' description of resurrection and future judgment in John 5:24–30, where He spoke of two future resurrections without referring to elapsed time between them. He likewise speaks here of an assignment to the kingdom and an assignment to eternal fire without referring to the time interval that will separate them. The final relegation of the lost to the lake of fire will not come until after the second resurrection that will follow the enjoyment of the temporal phase of the kingdom by those assigned thereto."

[54] Ibid.

[55] This view of the Olivet Discourse is affirmed by many amillennialists, including Riddlebarger, *A Case for Amillennialism*, 189–90.

description as the fire "which has been prepared for the devil" (cf. Rev 20:10, 15).

The second premillennial response is that the consignment of unbelievers to the eternal fire takes place immediately, but it is carried out in two phases. In the same way that believers first inherit the millennial kingdom (Matt 25:34) and then later the eternal state (Rev 21:1–4), unbelievers first experience the initial punishment described in Luke 16:19–31, and then after the thousand years (Rev 20:1–10) their bodies are resurrected at the great white throne and cast into the lake of fire (Rev 20:11–15).[56] According to Robert Saucy, this view takes the word "eternal" in Matthew 25:41 and 46 as a qualitative term describing the experience of believers and unbelievers:

> A person may presently enter into life that has the quality of "eternal life" and still have a fuller experience of that life in the future. So these unbelievers at the judgment of the sheep and goats may be cast into "eternal fire," a qualitative judgment of the lost, and already begin to experience that judgment in the intermediate state of Hades before Hades is cast into the final "lake of fire" (Rev 20:14). Thus they may be in a punishment during the millennium that shares the same quality ("eternal") as is found more intensively later in the lake of fire of the eternal state.[57]

Premillennialist Eugene Pond claims that the phrase "inherit the kingdom" in Matthew 25:34 supports this view by establishing a parallel between the two phases of the destinies of both the sheep and the goats:

> This kingdom occurs in two phases, the millennial reign of Christ and the eternal state. The sheep are invited to inherit God's (earthly) kingdom in the millennium, when the Lord will

---

[56] To support this view, Cooper appeals to Jude 7 and Rev 14:10 as examples of unbelievers experiencing "eternal fire" and being "tormented with fire and brimstone" during the intermediate state (Cooper, "The Judgment, or Judgments," 259–60). But neither of these passages describes divine punishment in the intermediate state. The judgment of Sodom and Gomorrah in Jude 7 refers to the temporal judgment of their physical destruction (even though it is presented in Jude 7 as a typological foreshadowing of the eternal punishment of the wicked in general), and the torment in Rev 14:10 looks ahead to the future judgment of the wicked described in Rev 20:11–15.

[57] Saucy, *Progressive Dispensationalism*, 288.

subdue all His enemies (1 Cor. 15:24–28). Therefore this judgment admits at least the righteous to a temporary state before the final eternal one. It is not unreasonable to understand the fate of the goats in a similar sequence of phases. First, following the judgment in Matthew 25, they will physically die and go to hades for temporary torment (similar to that of the rich man in Luke 16:19–31). Second, at the great white throne judgment their eternal death is completed with their being consigned to the lake of fire.[58]

An additional argument comes from Isaiah 24:21–23, which sets a precedent for two phases of the divine judgment of the wicked, the first at the return of Christ and the second after an intervening period of "many days" (Isa 24:22).[59] This corresponds well to an initial judgment of the goats at the Second Coming (Matt 25:31–46) and the final judgment of the wicked after a thousand years (Rev 20:11–15).

A third and final premillennial response is that the unbelievers who are alive when Jesus returns will be consigned immediately to the lake of fire in Matthew 25 and therefore will not take part in the final judgment of Revelation 20:11–15. Although this view is not common among premillennialists,[60] it appears to be consistent with the biblical data, and several arguments can be made in its favor. First, this view is most easily harmonized with the straightforward reading of Matthew 25:41 and 46, which appears to portray unbelievers being thrown into the eternal fire at the very time that this judgment takes place. Second, the description of the goats' destiny as "the eternal fire which has been prepared for the devil and for his angels" (Matt 25:41) seems to imply that they are consigned to this fire *prior* to Satan, who is not consigned there until the end of the millennium (Rev 20:10).[61] Third, Scripture clearly teaches that at least two individuals—the beast and the false prophet—will be cast into the lake of fire at the time of the Second Coming (Rev 19:20), a thousand

---

58 Pond, "The Background and Timing of the Judgment," 220.
59 See the discussion of Isa 24:21–23 in chapter 5.
60 Pond refers to this as a "less likely alternative," but he presents no arguments against this view ("Who Are the Sheep and Goats?," 300).
61 In contrast, if they are not consigned to this fire until the final judgment of Rev 20:11–15, then Satan will have been thrown into the lake of fire prior to these unbelievers.

years before the final judgment in Revelation 20:11–15; so there is no categorical reason that these unbelievers could not also be thrown into the lake of fire when Jesus returns. Fourth, if the goats are resurrected and judged again in Revelation 20:11–15,[62] their physical death must take place at the Second Coming, but Matthew 25 says nothing about their death as part of this initial judgment.[63] It cannot be proven that Scripture requires this view, but it certainly appears to be consistent with what the Bible teaches.

It is difficult to be certain which of these premillennial responses is the most faithful way to harmonize the two judgments, but each of them provides a viable alternative to understanding the judgments in Matthew 25 and Revelation 20 as one and the same. For this reason—and in light of the clarity of John's affirmation of an intermediate kingdom in Revelation 20—Matthew 25:31–46 fails to prove that the universal judgment of all mankind will occur at the Second Coming and immediately initiate the eternal state.

The Argument from 2 Thessalonians 1:6–10

Amillennialists also cite 2 Thessalonians 1:6–10 in support of the view that the final judgment of unbelievers will take place at the Second Coming.[64] To encourage the persecuted believers in Thessalonica, the apostle Paul writes:

> For after all it is only just for God to repay with affliction those who afflict you, and to give relief to you who are afflicted and to us as well when the Lord Jesus will be revealed from heaven with His mighty angels in flaming fire, dealing out retribution to those who do not know God and to those who do not obey the gospel

---

62 According to Rev 20:11–15, the objects of the final judgment are "the dead" (vv. 12–13) who are resurrected and then cast into the lake of fire.
63 This argument is certainly not conclusive—for Scripture is rarely exhaustive in its narrative and prophetic descriptions—but this "omission" appears to be consistent with the view that these unbelievers are cast (body and soul) into the lake of fire at the time of Christ's return.
64 Hoekema, *The Bible and the Future*, 227, 255; Venema, *The Promise of the Future*, 91–92, 247; Riddlebarger, *A Case for Amillennialism*, 99, 163–64; Strimple, "Amillennialism," 103; Vern S. Poythress, "2 Thessalonians 1 Supports Amillennialism," *JETS* 37, no. 4 (Dec 1994): 529–38.

of our Lord Jesus. These will pay the penalty of eternal destruction, away from the presence of the Lord and from the glory of His power, when He comes to be glorified in His saints on that day, and to be marveled at among all who have believed—for our testimony to you was believed (2 Thess 1:6–10).

In this passage, Paul speaks of the divine judgment of the wicked as being administered "when the Lord Jesus will be revealed from heaven" (v. 7),[65] "when He comes to be glorified in His saints on that day" (v. 10). For this reason, amillennialists believe that the final judgment of unbelievers will take place not after a thousand-year intermediate kingdom but at the time of the Second Coming of Christ.[66] As Riddlebarger argues, "If judgment day and the second advent occur at the same time, all forms of premillennialism collapse."[67]

In response to this argument, there are two ways that 2 Thessalonians 1:6–10 can be harmonized with the existence of an intermediate kingdom (Rev 20:1–10) separating the Second Coming of Christ (Rev 19:11–21) and the final judgment of unbelievers (Rev 20:11–15). The first way is to appeal to the dynamic of prophetic foreshortening.[68] According to this view, 2 Thessalonians 1:6–10 presents the Second Coming and the final judgment together as if the two events will happen simultaneously, even though a lengthy gap of time—the millennial reign of Christ—will separate the two. As Richard Mayhue explains:

---

65 Paul introduces this phrase in 2 Thess 1:7 with the temporal use of the preposition ἐν, rendered "at" (ASV; HCSB) or "when" (NASB; ESV; NET; NIV; KJV; NKJV; NLT; RSV; NCV) by most translations.
66 Strimple, "Amillennialism," 103; Storms, *Kingdom Come*, 163–64. According to Storms, "Since this judgment is elsewhere said to follow the millennium (Rev. 20:11–15), the millennium itself must be coterminous with the present age" (164).
67 Riddlebarger, *A Case for Amillennialism*, 251. According to Riddlebarger, the New Testament gives "no hint of a delay in the judgment of unbelievers until after the thousand-year reign of Christ on the earth. The 'white throne judgment' (Rev. 20:11) occurs at Christ's return, not one thousand years later" (105).
68 Daniel B. Wallace, "New Testament Eschatology in the Light of Progressive Revelation," accessed on August 7, 2014, https://bible.org/article/new-testament-eschatology-light-progressive-revelation. According to Wallace, "2 Thess 1:9–10 seems to 'telescope' the eschaton (in that there is no gap between the Lord's return and the eternal destruction of the wicked)."

> Paul is not writing a detailed, chronological, or even precise prophetic treatise here, but rather is wanting to give the Thessalonians hope that, in the end, God's righteousness would prevail. Like Old Testament prophets (cf. Is. 61:1–2; 1 Pet 1:10–11), Paul has compressed the details so that the range of time is not apparent, nor are all the details. The apostle is plainly assuring the Thessalonians that there will certainly be a coming day of retribution for their persecutors.[69]

In other words, details about the interval of time between the immediate relief of the saints and the ultimate retribution of the wicked were not included because they did not serve Paul's primary purpose in writing. Paul's goal was not to set forth an exhaustive presentation of eschatological events, but rather to assure his persecuted readers that the justice of God would prevail. Therefore, the apostle focused on comforting the Thessalonian church by emphasizing the certainty of this coming relief and retribution, without clarifying the existence of an interval of time between the two.[70]

The second way that 2 Thessalonians 1:6–10 can be harmonized with an intermediate kingdom is very similar to the first. According to this view, the divine retribution of the wicked begins at the Second Coming of Christ (Rev 19:11–21; Matt 25:31–46);[71] it continues in the intermediate state as unbelievers experience conscious torment during the millennial kingdom (cf. Luke 16:19–31); and it culminates when they are resurrected at the final judgment and cast into the lake of fire (Rev 20:11–15).[72] In

---

69 Richard Mayhue, "Why a Pretribulation Rapture?" in *Christ's Prophetic Plans: A Futuristic Premillennial Primer*, eds. John MacArthur and Richard Mayhue (Chicago: Moody Publishers, 2012), 101. In this context, Mayhue is defending a pre-tribulational rapture rather than an intermediate kingdom, but his explanation applies equally to both.

70 The weakness of this view is that 2 Thessalonians 1 appears to connect this divine retribution directly to the time of the Second Coming—"when [ἐν] the Lord Jesus will be revealed from heaven" (v. 7) and "when [ὅταν] He comes to be glorified in His saints on that day" (v. 10).

71 Rev 19:11–21 describes the destruction of those unbelieving armies which battle against Christ at the Second Coming, and Matt 25:31–46 describes the judgment of the unbelievers who do not fight in (and therefore survive) that war.

72 In 2 Thessalonians 1, it is possible that the participial phrase "dealing out retribution" in verse 8 portrays the initial retribution unleashed on the day of Christ's return, whereas "the penalty of eternal destruction" in verse 9 focuses on retribution in the eternal state, but it is not clear that Paul intended this distinction.

2 Thessalonians 1:6–10, the apostle Paul compresses the stages of this divine judgment into a simplified portrayal of God bringing relief to the Thessalonians when Jesus returns by dealing out retribution to their unbelieving persecutors.[73] The strength of this view is that it affirms precisely what is taught in 2 Thessalonians 1—that the divine retribution of unbelievers will begin at the Second Coming (vv. 7, 10) and will continue into the eternal state as they "pay the penalty of eternal destruction" (v. 9).[74]

To harmonize Paul's presentation of divine retribution in 2 Thessalonians 1:6–10 with the two-stage judgment in Isaiah 24:21–23 and Revelation 19–20, it is helpful to recognize that the former can set forth the eschatological judgment of God with less precision without contradicting the more detailed presentation of the latter. In the process, it is helpful to remember that Paul's purpose in 2 Thessalonians 1 was to comfort the persecuted church in Thessalonica, not to set forth all of the future events concerning the eschatological judgment of unbelievers. Therefore, even though the judgment of God's enemies is portrayed elsewhere as taking place in two stages separated by a lengthy period of time—being described as "many days" in Isaiah 24:22 and a "thousand years" in Revelation 20:1–6—it did not serve Paul's purpose in 2 Thessalonians 1 to make those same distinctions. There is nothing in 2 Thessalonians 1 which precludes the existence of an intermediate kingdom or the straightforward reading of Revelation 19–21.

---

73 According to Craig Blaising, even though 2 Thessalonians 1 speaks of several events that will happen "in that day," Scripture does not depict the Day of the Lord as an instantaneous event ("A Premillennial Response," 150), which allows for the kind of compression of eschatological judgments described here.

74 After all, one does not pay the *entirety* of "the penalty of eternal destruction" (2 Thess 1:9) on the very day that Christ returns—it is an ongoing punishment that begins at a point in time and continues endlessly. For this reason, not even the amillennialist believes that 2 Thess 1:6–10 is completely fulfilled at the Second Coming, affirming instead that this divine retribution begins at the Second Coming and continues into the eternal state, which is precisely the view articulated here.

Chapter 9

The Destruction and Renewal of the Cosmos

Introduction

According to the two-age model of amillennialism, the New Testament teaches that the destruction and renewal of the cosmos will take place at the Second Coming of Christ. This is said to have significant implications for the intermediate kingdom of premillennialism. As amillennialist Cornelis Venema writes:

> Rather than teaching that the return of Christ will bring a provisional phase of God's kingdom, the millennium, which itself will be surpassed in the final state of God's eternal kingdom, the New Testament teaches that Christ's return will introduce the final state of new heavens and a new earth.[1]

For this reason, amillennialists argue that the eschatology of the New Testament does not allow for a millennial kingdom between the Second Coming of Christ and the eternal state. To demonstrate that the destruction and renewal of the cosmos will occur at the Second Coming, amillennialists point to 2 Peter 3:10–13 and Romans 8:16–23.

The Argument from 2 Peter 3:10–13

In 2 Peter 3:10–13, the apostle Peter looks ahead to the Day of the Lord and the judgment of God that will come upon the earth:

---

1 Cornelis P. Venema, *The Promise of the Future* (Carlisle, PA: Banner of Truth, 2000), 247–48.

> But the day of the Lord will come like a thief, in which the heavens will pass away with a roar and the elements will be destroyed with intense heat, and the earth and its works will be burned up. Since all these things are to be destroyed in this way, what sort of people ought you to be in holy conduct and godliness, looking for and hastening the coming of the day of God, because of which the heavens will be destroyed by burning, and the elements will melt with intense heat! But according to His promise we are looking for new heavens and a new earth, in which righteousness dwells.

According to the straightforward reading of this passage, when Jesus returns on the Day of the Lord, the heavens will pass away, the elements will be destroyed, the earth and its works will be burned up (vv. 10–12), and these will be replaced with a new heavens and new earth (v. 13).[2] Because the Day of the Lord will be accompanied by the destruction and re-creation of the universe, amillennialists argue that 2 Peter 3:10–13 "does not allow for a thousand years intervening between the second coming of Christ and the coming of the day of divine judgment and cosmic renewal."[3] According to Sam Storms, there is no room in Peter's scenario for the millennial kingdom of premillennialism: "On the contrary, the present heavens and earth will be judged at Christ's return, at which time the new heavens and new earth (not a millennium) shall emerge as an eternal dwelling for God's people."[4] As Kim Riddlebarger asks, where exactly is the "millennial gap" in this passage?[5]

---

2 According to Anthony Hoekema, "Peter states with unmistakable clarity that the Second Coming will be followed at once by the dissolution of the old earth and the creation of the new earth (2 Peter 3:10-13)" (*The Bible and the Future* [Grand Rapids: Eerdmans Publishing, 1979], 185–86).

3 Robert B. Strimple, "Amillennialism," in *Three Views on the Millennium and Beyond*, ed. Darrell L. Bock (Grand Rapids: Zondervan Publishing, 1999), 107. Also see Venema, *The Promise of the Future*, 247–48; Kim Riddlebarger, *A Case for Amillennialism: Understanding the End Times*, expanded ed. (Grand Rapids: Baker Books, 2013), 99, 166–67; Samuel E. Waldron, *The End Times Made Simple: How Could Everyone Be So Wrong About Biblical Prophecy?* (Amityville, NY: Calvary Press, 2003), 63; Sam Storms, *Kingdom Come: The Amillennial Alternative* (Ross-shire, Scotland: Mentor, 2013), 154, 159–60, 551; Hoekema, *The Bible and the Future*, 185–86.

4 Storms, *Kingdom Come*, 159. In a similar way, Sam Waldron writes, "The natural significance of 2 Peter 3:10 is, however, that when Christ comes the world is immediately (not 1000 years later) destroyed" (*The End Times Made Simple*, 63).

5 Riddlebarger, *A Case for Amillennialism*, 99. As Storms argues, "If the new heavens and new earth come at the time of Christ's second advent, there can be no earthly millennial reign intervening between the two" (*Kingdom Come*, 159–60).

The Premillennial Response

There are three primary ways that premillennialists have responded to this argument. The first and most common response is that the Day of the Lord is an extended period of time that includes the coming of Christ, His millennial reign, the final judgment, and the creation of the new heavens and new earth.[6] Because this extensive period of divine intervention encompasses all of these eschatological events, the destruction of the earth described in 2 Peter 3:10 will occur not at the Second Coming but at the close of the Day of the Lord, at the end of the millennium when all wickedness in the earth will be judged in a final way.[7] Therefore, even though Peter does not mention a gap of time between the Second Coming and the eternal state, 2 Peter 3:10–13 will be fulfilled at the conclusion of the future millennium, and this prophecy presents no difficulty for the existence of an intermediate kingdom.[8]

---

6   Robert L. Saucy, *The Case for Progressive Dispensationalism: The Interface Between Dispensational and Non-Dispensational Theology* (Grand Rapids: Zondervan Publishing, 1993), 288. According to Richard Mayhue ("The Bible's Watchword: Day of the Lord," *MSJ* 22, no. 1 [Spring 2011]: 74) and Craig Blaising ("The Day of the Lord: Theme and Pattern in Biblical Theology," *BibSac* 169, no. 673 [Jan 2012]: 8), this is the most popular view among dispensationalists, e.g., J. Dwight Pentecost, *Things to Come: A Study in Biblical Eschatology* (Grand Rapids: Zondervan Publishing, 1978), 174, 230–32; Lewis Sperry Chafer, *Systematic Theology* (Dallas: Dallas Seminary Press, 1948), 7:110; J. T. Cooper, "The Judgment, or Judgments," in *Premillennial Essays*, ed. Nathaniel West (Minneapolis: Bryant Baptist Publications, 1981), 247; R. Larry Overstreet, "A Study of 2 Peter 3:10–13," *BibSac* 137, No. 548 (Oct 1980): 358–59; D. Edmond Hiebert, *Second Peter and Jude: An Expositional Commentary* (Greenville, SC: Unusual Publications, 1989), 158. This also appears to be the view of Blaising, who writes that the syntax in 2 Pet 3:10 and 12 does not require "that everything happens at the inception of the Day of the Lord" (Craig A. Blaising, "A Premillennial Response to Robert B. Strimple," in *Three Views on the Millennium and Beyond*, ed. Darrell L. Bock [Grand Rapids: Zondervan Publishing, 1999],150). But elsewhere Blaising declines to take a position on the relationship of the millennium to the Day of the Lord ("The Day of the Lord: Theme and Pattern in Biblical Theology," 8).
7   John F. Walvoord, *The Millennial Kingdom* (Grand Rapids: Zondervan Publishing, 1959), 273. According to Dwight Pentecost, "2 Peter 3:10 gives authority for including the entire millennial age within this period" (*Things to Come*, 230).
8   This view is not, however, without difficulties. According to Mayhue, because the Day of the Lord is chiefly a time of judgment, "there is minimal biblical evidence to warrant extending [it] into the Millennium" ("The Bible's Watchword," 75). Blaising summarizes this objection by asking the question: "How can the day of the Lord be a day of judgment if it is mostly the millennial reign of Christ?" ("The Day of the Lord: Theme and Pattern in Biblical Theology," 5). Cooper responds to this objection by insisting that the entire millennial period consists of divine judgment: "It opens with judgment; it has judgment running through it, and it closes with the judgment of the Great White Throne" ("The Judgment, or Judgments," 247). According to Lewis Sperry Chafer, this ongoing millennial judgment

This first view is supported by Isaiah 24, which appears to describe the Day of the Lord as encompassing not only an initial judgment at the Second Coming of Christ (vv. 1–22a) but also an ultimate judgment after an extended period of "many days" (v. 22b):

> So it will happen in that day, that the Lord will punish the host of heaven on high, and the kings of the earth on earth. They will be gathered together like prisoners in the dungeon, and will be confined in prison; and after many days they will be punished (Isa 24:21–22).

If the "many days" of Isaiah 24:22 can be equated with the thousand years of Revelation 20—and if the subsequent judgment after these "many days" also takes place "in that day" (Isa 24:21)—Isaiah 24:21–22 provides evidence that the Day of the Lord extends throughout the millennial reign of Christ and includes the final judgment afterward.[9]

The second premillennial response is very similar to the first, especially with regard to the timing of the judgment described in 2 Peter 3:10–13. According to this view, biblical prophecies concerning the Day of the Lord can be fulfilled either at the Second Coming or at the end of the millennium. Because the specific destruction and renewal prophesied

---

is described in 1 Cor 15:25–26, where Paul characterizes the millennial kingdom as a time of protracted judgment in which Christ is subduing His enemies throughout the entire period (Chafer, *Systematic Theology*, 4:398). It should also be noted that prophecies like Joel 3 describe God not only judging the nations (vv. 1–17) but also blessing His people (vv. 18–21) as part of the Day of the Lord. Therefore, even though the dominant feature of the Day of the Lord is divine judgment, this does not exclude the presence of divine blessing, which may allow for the inclusion of the millennial kingdom in this time period.

9 According to Craig Blaising: "The description of the coming of the Day of the Lord in Isaiah 24–25 indicates a two-stage judgment process preceding the final elimination of death. This two-stage judgment overlaps the beginning of the future kingdom, thereby yielding a temporary phase of that kingdom before eternal conditions are fully realized. The first stage of this judgment is described in Isaiah 24 as the coming Day of the Lord. While that judgment is catastrophic, it results in an 'imprisonment' of some who will subsequently be 'punished' after 'many days' (Isa 24:21–22). After this latter punishment death will be abolished (Isa 25:6–8). The imprisonment for many days must be included in the 'reign' of verse 23, under whose authority the imprisonment will take place. The latter punishment, then, separates two phases of the coming rule. Since the removal of death is relegated to the latter phase, death is still present during the earlier phase, the time of the imprisonment" (Craig A. Blaising, "The Kingdom that Comes with Jesus: Premillennialism and the Harmony of Scripture," in *The Return of Christ: A Premillennial Perspective*, eds. David L. Allen and Steve W. Lemke [Nashville: Broadman & Holman, 2011], 145–46).

in 2 Peter 3:10–13 will occur at the end of the millennium, it is said to pose no threat to the existence of a future messianic kingdom in the way that amillennialists claim.[10]

This appeal to multiple fulfillments is defended by premillennialist Richard Mayhue, who demonstrates that the biblical phrase "Day of the Lord" is not a technical term always referring a single event in God's plan.[11] Instead, the Old Testament prophets used this designation to speak of both near historical and future eschatological events.[12] This relationship between near and far can be seen, for example, in the prophets Obadiah (near in 1–14; far in 15–21), Joel (near in 1:15; 2:1, 11; far in 2:31; 3:14), Isaiah (near in 13:6; far in 13:9), and Zephaniah (near in 1:7; far in 1:14).[13]

According to Mayhue, there are two periods of the Day of the Lord which have yet to be fulfilled on the earth: "(1) the judgment which climaxes the tribulation period (2 Thess 2:2; Rev 16–18), and (2) the consummating judgment of this earth which ushers in the new earth (2 Pet 3:10–13; Rev 20:7–21:1)."[14] In this way 2 Peter 3:10–13 can be harmonized with the intermediate kingdom of Revelation 20 by seeing Peter's prophecy fulfilled not at the time of Christ's return (as in 1 Thess 5:2 and 2 Thess 2:2),[15] but at the end of the millennium when "the termination of earth's history is marked by God's final judgment and cleansing of His creation."[16] For this reason, the amillennial argument from 2 Peter

---

10 Mayhue, "The Bible's Watchword," 74.
11 Richard Mayhue, "The Prophet's Watchword: Day of the Lord," *GTJ* 6, no. 2 (Fall 1985): 245.
12 Ibid., 231–46; Mayhue, "The Bible's Watchword," 66–69.
13 Mayhue, "The Bible's Watchword," 66.
14 Mayhue, "The Prophet's Watchword," 246. According to Mayhue, 2 Peter 3 reveals an ultimate expression of the Day of the Lord "which even the Old Testament prophets did not envision or did not separate from that which they viewed as final" ("The Bible's Watchword," 74). According to Mayhue, Day of the Lord prophecies will be fulfilled only at the end of the tribulation period, not throughout its duration, and only at the end of the millennium, not throughout its duration ("The Prophet's Watchword," 246).
15 The phrase "the time of Christ's return" is intentionally vague to allow for various views on the exact starting point of the Day of the Lord. As Mayhue observes, there are at least four different views among dispensationalists regarding when the Day of the Lord begins: with the rapture, soon after the rapture, at the mid-point of Daniel's seventieth week, and at the end of Daniel's seventieth week, i.e., the Second Coming of Christ ("The Bible's Watchword," 83–84).
16 Mayhue, "The Bible's Watchword," 74.

3:10–13 is said to present no problem for the intermediate kingdom of premillennialism.

The primary strength of these first two views is their ability to account for an intermediate kingdom between the Second Coming and the eternal state by seeing 2 Peter 3:10–13 fulfilled at the end of the millennium. If Revelation 20 does indeed teach that Jesus will reign for a thousand years after He returns to earth, then 2 Peter 3:10–13 must be harmonized with this reality, and both of these views constitute possible ways this can be done. But to be fair, both views also suffer from a common weakness, for even if the concept of the Day of the Lord is broad enough to encompass a fulfillment of this passage after the millennial kingdom, Peter's argument in this passage focuses on what occurs at the Second Coming, not what happens a thousand years later.

This emphasis on the Second Coming is very clear throughout the immediate context. The apostle begins this section in 2 Peter 3 by introducing the disturbance caused by false teachers who scoff at the idea of the Second Coming and the divine judgment associated with it: "Where is the promise of His coming?" these mockers say, "for ever since the fathers fell asleep, all continues just as it was from the beginning of creation" (vv. 3–4). He continues by rebuking them for their foolishness in denying that God will judge and destroy the present world, since He Himself created it and has brought destruction upon it once already (vv. 5–7).[17] Peter then reminds his beloved readers that God's timetable in delaying the return of Jesus cannot be interpreted by their human reckoning of time, "for with the Lord one day is like a thousand years, and a thousand years like one day" (v. 8). In fact, Peter says, in contrast to being slow about the promise of the Second Coming, God the Father delays the return of His Son because of His patient desire for all to come to repentance (v. 9). In contrast to this idea that God is slow to fulfill His promise to send Jesus, Peter insists that the Day of the Lord will indeed come—and will come unexpectedly—bringing destruction to the heavens and the earth (v. 10).[18] In light of this future judgment, Peter exhorts his readers to live

---

17 Douglas J. Moo, *2 Peter, and Jude*, The NIV Application Commentary (Grand Rapids: Zondervan Publishing, 1996), 185.

18 The adversative use of the conjunction δέ at the beginning of 2 Pet 3:10 marks a mild contrast between the idea that God is slow to fulfill His promise in verse 9 and the certainty

holy and godly lives (v. 11), eagerly awaiting (and even hastening) the coming of Christ and the fulfillment of these promises (vv. 12–13).[19]

The clear and consistent emphasis in 2 Peter 3:3–13, then, is on the Second Coming of Christ: Peter introduces "the promise of His coming" as the main topic (v. 4); he assures his readers that God is not slow to keep this promise (v. 9); he assures them that this day will indeed come, unexpectedly bringing destruction to heaven and earth (v. 10); and he exhorts them to live holy lives as they long for that day and hasten its arrival through their obedience (vv. 11–14). With such a pervasive focus on the Second Coming, a description of the divine judgment at the end of the millennium appears to be completely foreign to the immediate context.[20] For this reason, it is difficult to understand how the destruction described in this passage could occur a thousand years after the return of Christ.

At the same time, because the return of Christ is the monumental event that will set all of these eschatological events in motion, perhaps it could be argued that it is perfectly natural for Peter to move quickly from the Second Coming to the divine judgment that will take place at the end of the millennium, without explicitly noting the gap of time that will separate the two. Regardless, even though the emphasis on the Second Coming in 2 Peter 3 may not constitute an absolutely definitive objection, it remains the most significant challenge to the first two views on this passage.

In contrast, a third premillennial response is that 2 Peter 3:10 will take place at the Second Coming of Christ, at the beginning of the millennial

---

that the Day of the Lord will come in verse 10. Peter stresses this certainty by placing the verb ἥξει ("will come") in the emphatic position at the beginning of verse 10.

19 R. Larry Overstreet argues that this passage must not describe the Second Coming "since Peter mentions only 'the day of the Lord' which is an extended period of time" ("A Study of 2 Peter 3:10–13," 360), but this argument is not compelling in light of all the contextual evidence to the contrary.

20 If one denies that the divine judgment of 2 Pet 3:10–13 occurs at the Second Coming, then one must also conclude that Peter raised the issue of whether or not Jesus would return (vv. 3–4) only to focus instead on the divine judgment one thousand years after His return. As Robert Strimple argues, if the coming of Christ in verse 4 is not the same event as the "day of the Lord" in verse 10, then "Peter's affirmation in verse 10 would not be relevant as an answer to the mocking question of verse 4" ("Amillennialism," 107). According to Blaising, the "coming" (παρουσία) in verse 4 is used interchangeably with the Day of the Lord in verse 10 (Craig A. Blaising, "The Day of the Lord and the Seventieth Week of Daniel," *BibSac* 169, no. 674 [April 2012]: 141).

kingdom rather than the end of it.[21] Consequently, the new heavens and new earth ushered in by the divine judgment in 2 Peter 3:13 is understood not as the eternal state, but as the messianic kingdom which precedes the eternal state. According to this view, the destruction described in this passage refers not to the complete annihilation of the heavens and the earth so that they no longer exist, but rather to the judgment and transformation of creation so that heaven and earth are completely renewed.[22] For this reason, it is said, 2 Peter 3:10–13 does not teach that the Second Coming initiates the eternal state, and therefore this passage presents no real difficulty for the intermediate kingdom of premillennialism.

Several arguments have been presented for this view that 2 Peter 3:10 takes place at the Second Coming.[23] First, the Old Testament teaches that a judgment of fire, very similar to the one described in 2 Peter 3, will immediately precede the establishment of the messianic kingdom (Joel 2:30–31; Mal 3:1–3; 4:1; Isa 66:22; cf. Isa 66:15–16).[24] Second, the Old Testament teaches that disturbances in the material heavens, identical

---

21 George N. H. Peters, *The Theocratic Kingdom*, vol. 2 (1884; repr., Grand Rapids, Kregel Publications, 1972), 506–9; Robert D. Culver, *Daniel and the Latter Days* (Chicago: Moody Press, 1954), 177–90.

22 For a strong defense of the view that the judgment in 2 Pet 3:10–13 refers to transformation and renewal rather than complete annihilation, see Craig A. Blaising, "The Day of the Lord Will Come: An Exposition of 2 Peter 3:1–18," *BibSac* 169, no. 676 (Oct 2012): 394–401; Gale Z. Heide, "What's New About the New Heaven and the New Earth? A Theology of Creation from Revelation 21 and 2 Peter 3," *JETS* 40, no. 1 (March 1997): 46–55; Culver, *Daniel and the Latter Days*, 183–90. Also see Moo, *2 Peter and Jude*, 185–202, who provides a very helpful discussion of this passage, highlighting arguments on both sides of the annihilation/transformation debate, despite his failure to take a firm position. It should be noted that some premillennialists interpret the destruction in 2 Peter 3 as a transformation and renewal (rather than annihilation) and yet still believe that this passage will be fulfilled at the transition from the millennial kingdom to the eternal state (e.g., Alva J. McClain, *The Greatness of the Kingdom: An Inductive Study of the Kingdom of God* [Winona Lake, IN: BMH Books, 1959], 510).

23 Peters, *The Theocratic Kingdom*, 506–9; Culver, *Daniel and the Latter Days*, 177–90. For a premillennial response to this view and many of these arguments, see Overstreet, "A Study of 2 Peter 3:10–13," 359–61.

24 Culver, *Daniel and the Latter Days*, 179; Peters, *The Theocratic Kingdom*, 507. According to Culver, Peter's declaration that his readers were already looking "for these things" (2 Pet 3:14) indicates that they had been expecting a consuming fire to precede the coming kingdom of Messiah since the days of the Old Testament prophets. This, Culver believes, strengthens the connection between these Old Testament prophecies and 2 Pet 3:10–13. Premillennialist R. Larry Overstreet disputes this claim that the new heavens and new earth of Isa 66:22 refers to the millennial kingdom, asserting instead that it refers to the eternal state ("A Study of 2 Peter 3:10–13," 359).

to those described in 2 Peter 3, will occur immediately before the establishment of the messianic kingdom (Isa 34:4; Hag 2:6–7; Joel 3:16; Isa 13:13; 51:6).[25] Third, the New Testament also places a judgment of fire at the inception of the coming messianic kingdom (2 Thess 1:7–8; Rev 16:8–9).[26] Fourth, because the Bible teaches that the coming kingdom will occupy a regenerated earth from its very beginning (Isa 65:17–25; 66:22–24), the purifying effects of the prophetic dissolution in 2 Peter 3:10–13 must take place at the beginning of the millennium, not at the end.[27] Fifth, the coming kingdom promised in Scripture is characterized by a perpetual continuity (Luke 1:32–33; Dan 2:44; 7:14, 18), precluding a massive destruction at the end of the millennium which would interrupt this continuity.[28] Sixth, the immediate context of 2 Peter 3:10 indicates that Peter is describing something that will occur at the Second Coming, not a thousand years later.[29] In addition to the previously discussed focus on the Second Coming throughout 2 Peter 3:3–13, this is also supported by (a) Peter's description that this day "will come like a thief" (v. 10)—a metaphor used elsewhere to express the unexpectedness of Christ's return (Matt 24:43; Luke 12:39; 1 Thess 5:2, 4; Rev 16:15)[30]—and (b) Peter's focus

---

25 Culver, *Daniel and the Latter Days*, 179–80. According to Culver, the Old Testament "places the coming cosmic disturbances at the beginning of the coming kingdom, not at some point one thousand years along the course of it."
26 Culver, *Daniel and the Latter Days*, 180; Peters, *The Theocratic Kingdom*, 507. According to Culver, no one can read 2 Thess 1:7–8 and Rev 16:8–9 objectively "and not feel that the New Testament predicts a judgment of fire at the commencement of the coming kingdom" (*Daniel and the Latter Days*, 180–81). Overstreet disputes the claim of Culver that 2 Pet 3:10–13, 2 Thess 1:7–8, and Rev 16:8–9 all refer to the same event ("A Study of 2 Peter 3:10–13," 361).
27 Culver, *Daniel and the Latter Days*, 181. According to Overstreet, this argument is negated by the fact that Isa 65:17–25 and 66:22–24 contain conflated descriptions of both the millennial kingdom and the eternal state ("A Study of 2 Peter 3:10–13," 361).
28 Culver, *Daniel and the Latter Days*, 182. According to Culver, "Even though a change in the mediation of rulership of that kingdom is predicted (I Cor. 15:23–28), an abolition of the earthly realm is nowhere promised—unless II Peter 3:10 be the exception." Those who make this argument must be prepared to explain what it means that heaven and earth "fled away" (Rev 20:11) and "passed away" (Rev 21:1) at the end of the millennial kingdom.
29 Culver, *Daniel and the Latter Days*, 181.
30 Overstreet counters this argument by asserting that more than one aspect of the coming as a thief is possible during this extended period of time known as the Day of the Lord: "The judgments of God which fall in the tribulation period will come unexpectedly. Christ will come back suddenly at the second advent in judgment. Likewise, at the conclusion of the millennium, judgment falls unexpectedly on the earth-dwellers who are unsaved" ("A Study of 2 Peter 3:10–13," 359). Overstreet is correct in noting that the divine judgments

on the need for his readers to expectantly "look for" this day to arrive (vv. 12–14; cf. 1 Thess 1:10; 2 Tim 4:8; Titus 2:13).[31] Seventh, this view is supported by the exhortations in 2 Peter 3:11–14, which Peter issued to his readers "on the basis of this predicted dissolution as if it were something they should expect to see if they should live to the end of the present age, rather than as if it were something at least a millennium away."[32]

Despite the strength of these arguments, this third view is also not without weaknesses. The primary difficulty is this view's interpretation of the new heavens and new earth as a reference to the millennial kingdom rather than the eternal state. In Revelation 21:1, at the end of the millennial kingdom, the apostle John writes: "Then I saw a new heaven and a new earth [οὐρανὸν καινὸν καὶ γῆν καινήν]; for the first heaven and the first earth passed away, and there is no longer any sea." In light of the clear contrast John makes between (a) the "first" heaven and earth of the present age and millennial kingdom and (b) the "new" heaven and earth of the eternal state in Revelation 21:1, it difficult to understand how 2 Peter 3:13 could apply the designation "new heavens and a new earth" (καινοὺς ... οὐρανοὺς καὶ γῆν καινὴν) to the millennial kingdom.

In response, however, it is possible to see the intermediate kingdom of premillennialism as the initial phase—a kind of "first fruits"[33]—of the new heavens and new earth.[34] This view is supported by Isaiah 65:17–25,

---

during the tribulation and at the Second Coming will arrive unexpectedly, but because the judgment at the end of the millennium will come in response to an attack initiated by Satan and the unbelieving nations (Rev 20:7–9), it is difficult to see how its arrival could be described as thief-like.

31 Culver, *Daniel and the Latter Days*, 181. This focus can be seen in Peter's three uses of the verb προσδοκάω ("to look for") in 2 Pet 3:12–14. According to Culver, it is clear that Peter did not question the possibility that his original readers might live to see the inauguration of the destruction described in 2 Peter 3: "How inconsistent such statements are with the view that verse 10 describes events known to be at least a thousand years away needs only to be noted to be appreciated" (182).

32 Culver, *Daniel and the Latter Days*, 182–83. According to Culver, the same hope and the same attendant moral lessons are also set forth in Matt 24:42–51, Mark 13:32–37, and Luke 21:25–36 (183).

33 This terminology is adapted from Ralph Alexander, who describes the millennium as a "first fruits" of the eternal state (Ralph H. Alexander, "Ezekiel," in *EBC*, ed. Frank E. Gaebelein [Grand Rapids: Zondervan Publishing, 1981], 6:945). According to Alexander, "The Millennium will be like a preview of the eternal messianic kingdom that will be revealed fully in the eternal state."

34 According to Culver, "The new heavens and new earth begin at the inauguration of the kingdom," which is the millennium (*Daniel and the Latter Days*, 189).

which begins with the creation of the new heavens and new earth in verse 17, and then continues with a prophetic conflation of the two stages of the coming kingdom (the millennial kingdom and the eternal state) in verses 18–25. If Isaiah views both stages of the eschatological kingdom as part of the new heavens and new earth, this makes it more likely for Peter to use the same terminology for the millennial kingdom (2 Pet 3:13), even though John reserves it for the eternal state (Rev 21:1):

New Heavens and New Earth

	Millennium	Eternal State	Conflation
Isaiah 65:17–25			X
2 Peter 3:10–13	X		
Revelation 21:1–4		X	

This is consistent with the fact that, in the progress of divine revelation, Peter was appealing to the terminology as used by the prophet Isaiah, not by the apostle John, who had not yet written the book of Revelation. This view also gains support from the argument of Mayhue above that the biblical phrase "Day of the Lord" is not a technical term always referring to a single event in God's plan, but rather can be fulfilled at different times in reference to different eschatological events in redemptive history.[35]

These three premillennial responses possess various strengths and weaknesses, but each of them provides a plausible explanation of how the judgment in 2 Peter 3:10–13 can be harmonized with the millennial kingdom of premillennialism. In light of the clarity of John's description of an intermediate kingdom in Revelation 20, then, 2 Peter 3:10–13 fails to prove that the Second Coming will immediately usher in the eternal state, without an earthly reign of Christ separating the two.

THE ARGUMENT FROM ROMANS 8:18–23

This connection between the renewal of the cosmos and the Second Coming of Christ can also be seen in Romans 8:18–23, where Paul writes:

---

35 Mayhue, "The Prophet's Watchword," 231–46; Mayhue, "The Bible's Watchword," 66–69.

For I consider that the sufferings of this present time are not worthy to be compared with the glory that is to be revealed to us. For the anxious longing of the creation waits eagerly for the revealing of the sons of God. For the creation was subjected to futility, not willingly, but because of Him who subjected it, in hope that the creation itself also will be set free from its slavery to corruption into the freedom of the glory of the children of God. For we know that the whole creation groans and suffers the pains of childbirth together until now. And not only this, but also we ourselves, having the first fruits of the Spirit, even we ourselves groan within ourselves, waiting eagerly for our adoption as sons, the redemption of our body. For in hope we have been saved, but hope that is seen is not hope; for who hopes for what he already sees? But if we hope for what we do not see, with perseverance we wait eagerly for it (Rom 8:18–23).

According to amillennialists, because Romans 8:18–23 teaches that creation will be delivered from the curse when God's children are resurrected and glorified—and because this resurrection and glorification will occur at the Second Coming—the divine renewal of the created order must *also* occur at the return of Christ, not a thousand years later.[36] For this reason, Romans 8:18–23 is said to allow no room for an intermediate kingdom between the Second Coming and the final restoration of the universe.[37] The challenge for the premillennialist is to explain how Romans 8 allows for a millennial reign of Christ between the present age and the eternal state.

The Premillennial Response

In Romans 8:18–23, Paul describes the symmetrical relationship between the redemption of believers and the redemption of the non-human,

---

36 Strimple, "Amillennialism," 106; Venema, *The Promise of the Future*, 94, 378; Hoekema, *The Bible and the Future*, 282; Storms, *Kingdom Come*, 153, 551.

37 Riddlebarger, *A Case for Amillennialism*, 166; Storms, *Kingdom Come*, 153–54; Strimple, "Amillennialism," 106; Venema, *The Promise of the Future*, 247–48. For this reason, Storms argues that "amillennialism alone is consistent with the New Testament teaching that the natural creation will be delivered from the curse and experience its 'redemption,' in conjunction with the 'redemption' of our bodies, at the time of the second coming of Christ (Rom. 8:18–23)" (*Kingdom Come*, 551).

physical creation, for just as believers will one day be transformed and glorified, so "the creation itself also will be set free from its slavery to corruption into the freedom of the glory of the children of God" (Rom 8:21).[38] Despite the apparent challenge that Romans 8 presents for the existence of an intermediate kingdom, there are three possible ways to harmonize this passage with a millennial reign of Christ between the Second Coming and the eternal state.

First, some premillennialists believe that the glorification of creation in Romans 8 takes place *after* the millennium, just prior to the eternal state.[39] According to this view, the glorification of believers at the Second Coming and the glorification of creation after the millennial kingdom are conflated into a single description in Romans 8 even though an unstated gap of a thousand years will separate the two. The primary strength of this view is that, in spite of the parallelism between the glorification of believers and the glorification of creation, Romans 8:18–23 does not explicitly state that the two will occur at the same time. For this reason, suggesting a gap of time is a plausible way to harmonize Romans 8 with the clear teaching of an intermediate kingdom in Revelation 20. The primary weakness is that even though the temporal relationship between the two glorifications is not stated *explicitly*, Romans 8:19 in particular—where Paul says that "the anxious longing of the creation waits eagerly for the revealing of the sons of God"—links them in a way that implies their simultaneous occurrence.

---

38 Throughout Romans 8, the word "creation" (κτίσις) refers to the non-human, physical creation which was cursed at the fall of Adam (Gen 3:14, 17–19) (C.E.B. Cranfield, *A Critical and Exegetical Commentary on the Epistle to the Romans*, vol. 1, ICC [Edinburgh: T. & T. Clark, 1983], 411–12; Douglas J. Moo, *The Epistle to the Romans*, NICNT [Grand Rapids: Eerdmans Publishing, 1996], 513–14; Thomas R. Schreiner, *Romans*, BECNT [Grand Rapids: Baker Books, 1998], 435). Cranfield refers to it as "the sum-total of subhuman nature both animate and inanimate" (*Critical and Exegetical Commentary*, 411–12).

39 George Eldon Ladd, *Crucial Questions About the Kingdom of God* (Grand Rapids: Eerdmans Publishing, 1952), 84; George Eldon Ladd, *The Gospel of the Kingdom: Scriptural Studies in the Kingdom of God* (Grand Rapids: Eerdmans Publishing, 1959), 76–77; Craig A. Blaising and Darrell L. Bock, *Progressive Dispensationalism* (Grand Rapids: Baker Books, 1993), 121, 265–66, 269. According to George Eldon Ladd, "God's reign will be eventually manifested in the entire creation in the Age to Come. The final form of the kingdom must include the redemption of creation itself which is now under the curse and bondage of sin (Rom. 8:20–22)" (*Crucial Questions*, 84). Elsewhere Ladd refers to this as "the day when God's redemptive purpose will be completed and the creation will be delivered from the bondage of corruption into the glorious liberty of the sons of God" (*The Gospel of the Kingdom*, 76–77).

In the end, however, Romans 8:19 does not conclusively preclude the possibility of an interval of time separating the two glorifications. The reason that the created order longs for the revelation of God's children in verse 19 is because that same renewal will be the fate of the physical creation as well.[40] It could therefore be argued that even though creation longs to see the glorification of believers because that will be its own eventual destiny, this does not prove that the two glorifications will happen simultaneously. In Paul's use of personification,[41] it may be that creation longs to see this transformation because of how the glorification of God's people foreshadows its own transformation, even though that subsequent renewal will not occur until after the millennium.[42] So this first view remains a possible way to harmonize Romans 8 with the intermediate kingdom of Revelation 20.

Second, other premillennialists believe that the glorification of creation in Romans 8 will occur at the Second Coming and therefore at the same time that the saints are resurrected and glorified.[43] This view agrees with amillennialism regarding the *timing* of creation's redemption in

---

40 Schreiner, *Romans*, 434.
41 Paul's use of personification to communicate this truth should caution the reader against pressing for too much precision as he interprets the temporal relationship between the two glorifications.
42 In the same way, when Paul writes that "the creation itself also will be set free from its slavery to corruption into the freedom of the glory of the children of God" (Rom 8:21), it could be that the creation will be delivered into this freedom a thousand years after the children of God.
43 Culver, *Daniel and the Latter Days*, 189; R. Stanton Norman, "The Doctrine of Eschatology: Themes, Summary, and Significance," in *The Return of Christ: A Premillennial Perspective*, eds. David L. Allen and Steve W. Lemke (Nashville: Broadman & Holman, 2011), 120; Pentecost, *Things to Come*, 538; Charles L. Feinberg, *Millennialism: The Two Major Views*, 3rd ed. (Chicago: Moody Press, 1980), 186; Peters, *The Theocratic Kingdom*, 479–93. Elsewhere, however, Culver asserts that Romans 8 will be fulfilled "at the consummation" (Robert D. Culver, *Systematic Theology: Biblical and Historical* [Great Britain: Christian Focus Publications, 2005], 335). Other premillennialists are equally unclear regarding when they believe the redemption of creation in Romans 8 will occur. For example, Alva J. McClain cites Rom 8:17–23 in support of his assertion that the church "must be perfected in order to reign with Christ over the nations in the coming Kingdom" (*The Greatness of the Kingdom*, 329–30) and he therefore appears to view this prophecy as fulfilled at the Second Coming. But he says very little else about the passage—and nothing specifically on the timing of the glorification of creation—so it is difficult to be certain. Paul Benware cites Rom 8:19–23 as evidence that creation will continue to experience futility and corruption "until God finishes saving mankind" (Paul N. Benware, *Understanding End Times Prophecy: A Comprehensive Approach* [Chicago: Moody Publishers, 2006], 283), but he is not clear about when exactly he believes this will take place.

Romans 8, but it asserts that this glorification will usher in the millennial kingdom, which will take place on a divinely renewed earth prior to the eternal state (Rom 8:18–23). As premillennialist Charles Feinberg explains:

> Nature will be rejuvenated, and harmony will once more reign (Isa. 35:1; Rom. 8:19–22). The curse will be removed from the ground, and the desert and wilderness will be abundantly fruitful and productive (Zech. 14:11). Animal creation also will experience a change in which animals of rapacious appetites will become meek and tame. The age of man will be lengthened, for a man of one hundred years will be esteemed but a child (Isa. 65:20).[44]

Among the strengths of this view, (a) it affirms the simplest and most straightforward reading of Romans 8 by seeing the glorification of creation at the same time as the Second Coming and the glorification of believers; (b) it is consistent with the Bible's teaching regarding the renewal of the earth during the millennial kingdom;[45] and (c) it is able to harmonize all the relevant biblical data—including Old Testament prophecy, Romans 8, and the intermediate kingdom of Revelation 20—in a way that incorporates the unique contribution of each passage.

An obvious objection to this view comes from amillennialist Robert Strimple, who says the existence of sin in the millennial kingdom would once again subject creation to the curse, since sin brings death and destruction not only to mankind but also to the realm that mankind rules.[46] In response to this objection, even though God cursed creation because of Adam's transgression (Gen 3:14–19; Rom 8:20), sin in the millennial kingdom will not bring a new curse on earth because God will be renewing and restoring creation as Christ reigns until He has put all His enemies under His feet (1 Cor 15:25). Part of this process will involve severely disciplining those who refuse to worship the Lord, but even this divine judgment will be temporary and limited in scope (Zech

---

44 Feinberg, *Millennialism*, 186.
45 The specifics of this renewal will be discussed below under the third view.
46 Robert B. Strimple, "An Amillennial Response to Craig A. Blaising," in *Three Views on the Millennium and Beyond*, ed. Darrell L. Bock (Grand Rapids: Zondervan Publishing), 269.

14:17–19), and therefore it will not adversely affect the overall renewal of the broader created order.

At the same time, it does seem, as Strimple insists, that the deliverance of creation must be just as final, total, absolute, and everlasting as it is for the children of God.[47] This is not stated explicitly in Romans 8, but the parallelism between the glorification of believers and the glorification of creation appears to imply an absoluteness to the redemption of the created order which is not entirely realized in the millennium. For this reason, it may be preferable to see Romans 8 as only partially fulfilled in the millennium. This leads to the final way to harmonize Paul's prophecy with the existence of an intermediate kingdom.

Thirdly, other premillennialists believe that an initial fulfillment of Romans 8 will take place at the Second Coming, but that its ultimate fulfillment will not occur until the end of the millennial kingdom.[48] According to this view, because it does not fit His immediate purposes in Romans 8, Paul does not distinguish between these two stages in the redemption of creation, even though he is aware of them and even though they are taught elsewhere in Scripture. Instead, he conflates them into a single description of the created order being set free from futility and its slavery to corruption (Rom 8:19–21). In this way, the glorification of non-human creation begins at the Second Coming, but this two-stage process of renewal is not complete until the transition to the eternal state (Rev 21:1–4).

To understand this third view, it is helpful to consider the initial transformation of creation that will take place in the millennium. The Bible teaches that even though the millennial kingdom will be established on this present earth, the earth will be supernaturally renewed.[49] The curse of the ground will be lifted (Isa 30:23–25; 32:13–15; 35:1–2, 7; 41:18); the animal world will be tamed (Isa 11:6–8; 65:25); sickness and death will be greatly reduced (Isa 29:18; 33:24; 35:5–6; Ezek 34:16), leading to great longevity of life (Isa 65:20, 22); and even though sin and judgment will not yet be entirely eliminated (Ps 2:9; Zech 14:16–19; Ezek 44:25, 27; Rev 19:5; 20:7–10), it will be a time of unprecedented prosperity for humanity

---

47 Ibid.
48 Blaising, "A Premillennial Response," 150.
49 Benware, *Understanding End Times Prophecy*, 283.

(Jer 31:12; Ezek 34:25–29; Amos 9:13–14).[50] The land of Palestine, in particular, will be fertile and productive (Ezek 36:6–9; Amos 9:13–15; Zech 8:11–12), blessed by an abundance of rainfall and no longer subject to famine (Ezek 34:26–29; 36:29–30; Joel 2:21–27), being compared to the Garden of Eden by everyone who passes by (Ezek 36:35).[51]

The reversal of the curse reflected in these millennial descriptions appears to fulfill the promise in Romans 8 that creation, which was "subjected to futility" when cursed at the fall of Adam (Rom 8:20; Gen 3:14, 17–19), "will be set free from its slavery to corruption" (Rom 8:21). And yet because this initial phase of the coming kingdom falls short of the final state of absolute perfection (Rev 21:1–4; 22:1–5),[52] it is more precise to say that the prophecy of creation's redemption in Romans 8 will be fulfilled in two stages, with an initial/partial fulfillment in the millennial kingdom and an ultimate/complete fulfillment in the eternal state. As premillennialist Craig Blaising writes, "There is nothing in Romans 8 that prevents the glorification of creation from taking place in stages (cf. Isa. 25 and 65),"[53] and therefore this appears to be the best way to harmonize all that Scripture teaches about the future redemption of the created order.

---

50 Nathan Busenitz, "The Kingdom of God and the Eternal State," *MSJ* 23, no. 2 (Fall 2012): 267; also see John MacArthur, "Does the New Testament Reject Futuristic Premillennialism?," in *Christ's Prophetic Plans: A Futuristic Premillennial Primer*, eds. John MacArthur and Richard Mayhue (Chicago: Moody Publishers, 2012), 174; McClain, *The Greatness of the Kingdom*, 237–41; Benware, *Understanding End Times Prophecy*, 283–84; Walvoord, *The Millennial Kingdom*, 318.
51 As Paul Benware writes, "Much of the present earth is unproductive because it is desert, but the millennial kingdom will be characterized by an abundance of water, and the desolate, dry areas of the earth will blossom as the rose (Isa. 35:1–7)" (*Understanding End Times Prophecy*, 283).
52 According to John Walvoord, the existence of death in the millennial kingdom indicates that the curse on the earth "is only partly lifted" during the earthly reign of Christ and "will remain in some measure" until the arrival of the new heaven and the new earth (*The Millennial Kingdom*, 318).
53 Blaising, "A Premillennial Response," 150.

Chapter 10

The Final Victory over Sin and Death

INTRODUCTION

For some amillennialists, the singlemost compelling argument against premillennialism is Paul's teaching in 1 Corinthians 15 about God's final victory over sin and death. According to this argument, because God will utterly destroy sin and death when Jesus returns, the intermediate kingdom of premillennialism—in which sin and death continue to exist—is a theological impossibility. To demonstrate that this final destruction of sin and death will occur at the Second Coming, amillennialists point to two related passages: 1 Corinthians 15:20–28 and 1 Corinthians 15:50–57.

THE ARGUMENT FROM 1 CORINTHIANS 15:20–28

In 1 Corinthians 15:20–28, the apostle Paul sets forth a series of events initiated by the resurrection of Christ:

> But now Christ has been raised from the dead, the first fruits of those who are asleep. For since by a man came death, by a man also came the resurrection of the dead. For as in Adam all die, so also in Christ all shall be made alive. But each in his own order: Christ the first fruits, after that those who are Christ's at His coming, and then comes the end, when He delivers up the kingdom to the God and Father, when He has abolished all rule and all authority and power. For He must reign until He has put all His

enemies under His feet. The last enemy that will be abolished is death. For He has put all things in subjection under His feet. But when He says, "All things are put in subjection," it is evident that He is excepted who put all things in subjection to Him. And when all things are subjected to Him, then the Son Himself also will be subjected to the One who subjected all things to Him, that God may be all in all (1 Cor 15:20–28).

The Amillennial Argument

According to amillennialists, this passage indicates not only that believers will be resurrected when Jesus returns (v. 23), but also that His coming will usher in "the end" (vv. 23–24), which will be marked by the destruction of death, the final enemy of God (v. 26).[1] At the Second Coming of Christ, then, the righteous will be raised and death itself will be abolished once and for all (cf. Rev 20:14; 21:4). For this reason, amillennialists believe that "when Christ comes at the end of the age, this will mark the closure of redemptive history and commence … the final state."[2]

The problem this presents for premillennialism is obvious: If death is destroyed at the Second Coming of Christ, how can the Second Coming usher in an intermediate kingdom in which people continue to die? How can death be abolished when Jesus returns if death continues to prevail for a thousand years after His return?[3] Because of this dilemma,

---

1 Cornelis P. Venema, *The Promise of the Future* (Carlisle, PA: Banner of Truth, 2000), 250–51.
2 Ibid., 251.
3 Sam Storms, *Kingdom Come: The Amillennial Alternative* (Ross-shire, Scotland: Mentor, 2013), 151. According to amillennialists, an additional problem for premillennialism concerns the significance of death being identified as "the *last* enemy" in verse 26. If the final enemy of God is abolished at the Second Coming, how can so many of His enemies still remain a thousand years later, as the premillennial interpretation of Rev 20:1–10 requires? (Samuel E. Waldron, *The End Times Made Simple: How Could Everyone Be So Wrong About Biblical Prophecy?* [Amityville, NY: Calvary Press, 2003], 82; William E. Cox, *Amillennialism Today* [Phillipsburg, NJ: Presbyterian and Reformed Publishing Co., 1966], 105–6). For amillennialists, this indicates that the millennium of Revelation 20 "must occur prior to the destruction of the last enemy at Christ's second coming" and it renders the premillennial interpretation of Rev 20:1–10 "impossible" (Waldron, *The End Times Made Simple*, 82). According to amillenialist Robert Strimple, premillennialists must believe "that Paul speaks of *two* victories over death in this chapter: a preliminary one at Christ's coming and the resurrection of believers (vv. 54–55), and a final one after the Millennium at the resurrection and judgment of unbelievers (vv. 24–26)" ("Amillennialism," 111; emphasis original). Strimple argues that nothing in Paul's language in 1 Corinthians 15 supports this view: "In both these sections he speaks simply of 'death' absolutely, without further qualification."

amillennialists believe that 1 Corinthians 15:20–28 precludes the possibility of premillennialism.[4]

The millennial debate in this passage centers on the indefinite phrase εἶτα τὸ τέλος ("then comes the end")[5] at the beginning of verse 24, which introduces the third in a sequence of events presented in 1 Corinthians 15:23–24:

> But each in his own order:
>   [the resurrection of] Christ the first fruits,
>   after that [ἔπειτα]
>   [the resurrection of] those who are Christ's at His coming,
>   and then [εἶτα]
>   the end comes,
>   when He delivers up the kingdom to the God and Father,
>   when He has abolished all rule and all authority and power.

The key question is whether the temporal adverb εἶτα ("then") at the beginning of verse 24 allows time for an earthly reign of Messiah between "His coming" (τῇ παρουσίᾳ αὐτοῦ) and "the end" (τὸ τέλος), when the kingdom is handed over to the Father. According to amillennialists, the adverb εἶτα indicates that "the end" comes immediately at the time of "His coming," leaving no time for an intermediate kingdom before the eternal state.[6] But according to premillennialists, the adverb εἶτα allows for a lengthy interval of time between the Second Coming and the consummation, the thousand years of Revelation 20.

Amillennialist Kim Riddlebarger considers this view of an extended interval to be a departure from the premillennialist's "professed literal method of interpretation,"[7] and Cornelis Venema says it requires "an

---

[4] Waldron, *The End Times Made Simple*, 82; Jonathan Menn, *Biblical Eschatology* (Eugene, OR: Resource Publications, 2013), 354–55. According to Samuel Waldron, "In light of 1 Cor. 15:21–28 a premillennial interpretation of Rev. 20:1–10 is impossible" (*The End Times Made Simple*, 82).

[5] In the absence of a verb, the Greek literally reads, "then the end" (εἶτα τὸ τέλος), but interpreters on both sides of the debate agree that the verb "comes"—or something very similar—must be supplied in the English translation.

[6] Kim Riddlebarger, *A Case for Amillennialism: Understanding the End Times*, expanded ed. (Grand Rapids: Baker Books, 2013), 102.

[7] Ibid.

unnatural reading of this passage."[8] According to Venema, every other New Testament use of the temporal adverb εἶτα—as well as its synonym ἔπειτα, which is used in conjunction with εἶτα in 1 Corinthians 15:23-24—expresses "events in the closest temporal connection, without any protracted period of time intervening (Luke 8:12, Mark 4:17, John 20:27)."[9] Furthermore, says Venema, these same two adverbs (εἶτα and ἔπειτα) are used interchangeably in the immediate context of 1 Corinthians 15, "and there, too, they express a simple sequence of events (1 Cor. 15:5-7)."[10] Therefore, Venema claims, if the ordinary usage of this adverb is considered, "these words ought to be read as expressing a simple sequence of events—when Christ comes, the dead in Christ will be raised and the end state will ensue."[11]

The Premillennial Response

In response, Venema's appeal to the "ordinary usage" of εἶτα in the New Testament is puzzling, and his claim that it always indicates the next in a sequence of events without an interval of time is simply untrue. Outside 1 Corinthians 15:24, the adverb εἶτα is used 14 times in the New Testament, 13 of which introduce something that occurs next in a sequence of events.[12] Of these 13 temporal uses of εἶτα, five introduce an event

---

8 Venema, *The Promise of the Future*, 249.
9 Ibid., 249-50.
10 Ibid., 250. Venema also claims that εἶτα is used in 1 Thess 4:17 to express an immediate sequence of events with no intervening period of time, but the adverb used in that verse is actually ἔπειτα.
11 Ibid. In contrast, other amillennialists acknowledge that εἶτα may be used to describe a sequence of events either with or without a chronological interval (Geerhardus Vos, *The Pauline Eschatology* [1930; repr., Phillipsburg, NJ: Presbyterian and Reformed Publishing, 1994], 244; Storms, *Kingdom Come*, 144).
12 The remaining occurrence is found in Heb 12:9, where εἶτα introduces an additional stage in an argument ("furthermore"), rather than what comes next in a sequence of events (Frederick William Danker, *The Concise Greek-English Lexicon of the New Testament* [Chicago: University of Chicago Press, 2009], 113; *BDAG*, 295). For some reason, amillennialist Robert Reymond appeals to this less common use of εἶτα as evidence against the premillennial view of a temporal gap between verses 23 and 24 (Robert L. Reymond, "Response by Robert L. Reymond," in *Perspectives on Israel and the Church: 4 Views*, ed. Chad O. Brand [Nashville: B&H Publishing Group, 2015], 212). But this non-temporal use of the adverb is not relevant to the debate over 1 Cor 15:23-24, because both sides agree that the adverb introduces what comes next in a sequence of events. The disagreement is not over whether Paul's use of εἶτα is temporal (both sides agree that it is), but rather whether this next event will occur immediately or after a gap of time.

that happens immediately after the previous event (Mark 8:25; Luke 8:12; John 13:5; 19:27; 20:27); six introduce an event that occurs after a interval of time between the two events (Mark 4:17; 4:28 [2x]; 1 Cor 15:5, 7; 1 Tim 2:13); and once there may or may not be an intervening gap of time in view (1 Tim 3:10). In contrast to Venema's claim, then, εἶτα is often used to denote events separated by an interval of time—in fact, it is Paul's most common use of the temporal adverb.[13]

Similarly, its synonym ἔπειτα is also used to describe a sequence of events either with or without a chronological interval. Of the 13 times this adverb is used temporally to introduce the next in a sequence of events,[14] seven uses of ἔπειτα introduce an event that happens immediately after the previous event (Mark 7:5; Luke 16:7; John 11:7; Gal 1:21; 1 Thess 4:17; Heb 7:27; James 4:14), and six introduce an event that occurs after an interval of time between the two events (1 Cor 15:6, 7, 23, 46; Gal 1:18; 2:1). Therefore, Venema's claim that ἔπειτα always indicates a sequence of events without a chronological interval is not true, and his appeal to the ordinary usage of these two adverbs fails to support his argument.

Not only does Paul most often use these temporal adverbs to join two events with an intervening gap of time,[15] but this pattern is well established earlier in the very same chapter. In 1 Corinthians 15:5–7, the apostle lists a series of post-resurrection of appearances of Christ, writing:

> He appeared to Cephas, then [εἶτα] to the twelve. After that [ἔπειτα] He appeared to more than five hundred brethren at one time, most of whom remain until now, but some have fallen asleep; then [ἔπειτα] He appeared to James, then [εἶτα] to all the apostles (1 Cor 15:5–7).

In each of these uses of the temporal adverbs, Paul envisions an interval of time between the two events. The amount of time between each

---

[13] Outside of 1 Cor 15:24, Paul uses εἶτα this way either three or four out of four times, depending on how the use in 1 Tim 3:10 is classified.

[14] The remaining four uses of ἔπειτα (1 Cor 12:28 [2x]; Heb 7:2; Jas 3:17) are not temporal, but instead are used to describe that which is "next in position of an enumeration of items" (*BDAG*, 361).

[15] Outside of 1 Cor 15:24, Paul uses εἶτα and ἔπειτα this way either nine or 10 out of 12 times, depending on how the use in 1 Tim 3:10 is classified.

appearance of Christ varies, but none of them introduces the next appearance as something that happens immediately after the previous one.

Furthermore, when Paul sets forth the sequence of three events in 1 Corinthians 15:23–24, his use of ἔπειτα clearly encompasses a lengthy interval of time between the first two events:

> But each in his own order: Christ the first fruits, after that [ἔπειτα] those who are Christ's at His coming, and then [εἶτα] comes the end, when He delivers up the kingdom to the God and Father, when He has abolished all rule and all authority and power (1 Cor 15:23–24).

Because Paul's use of ἔπειτα in verse 23 includes a gap of time between the resurrection of Christ and the Second Coming—a gap that is currently almost 2,000 years in length—it is at least possible that Paul envisions of gap of 1,000 years between the Second Coming and "the end."[16] Contrary to Riddlebarger's claim,[17] then, seeing a gap between the Second Coming and the end (vv. 23b–24a) is no more of a departure from a literal approach to interpretation than seeing a gap between the resurrection of Christ and the Second Coming (vv. 23a–23b), provided such a gap

---

16 Craig A. Blaising, "A Premillennial Response to Kenneth L. Gentry Jr.," in *Three Views on the Millennium and Beyond*, ed. Darrell L. Bock (Grand Rapids: Zondervan Publishing), 79; Craig A. Blaising, "The Kingdom that Comes with Jesus: Premillennialism and the Harmony of Scripture," in *The Return of Christ: A Premillennial Perspective*, eds. David L. Allen and Steve W. Lemke (Nashville: Broadman & Holman, 2011), 147; Michael Vlach, "The Eschatology of the Pauline Epistles," in *The Return of Christ: A Premillennial Perspective*, eds. David L. Allen and Steve W. Lemke (Nashville: Broadman & Holman, 2011), 261. In addition, as Robert Saucy notes, "If Paul had desired to say that the 'end' occurred at the coming of Christ, he could easily have used another adverb (τότε, meaning 'at that time') for the second 'then'" (Robert L. Saucy, *The Case for Progressive Dispensationalism: The Interface Between Dispensational and Non-Dispensational Theology* [Grand Rapids: Zondervan Publishing, 1993], 281). But Godet takes this argument too far when he insists that the use of τότε is *required* if Paul intended to communicate that "the end" will take place immediately after the Second Coming (F. L. Godet, *Commentary on the First Epistle of St. Paul to the Corinthians* [reprint, Grand Rapids: Zondervan, 1957], 2:357). According to Godet, Paul's use of εἶτα instead *demands* an interval of time between the two, but as previously discussed, sometimes εἶτα does introduce an event that happens immediately after the previous one (Mark 8:25; Luke 8:12; John 13:5; 19:27; 20:27).

17 According to Riddlebarger, "Despite their professed literal method of interpretation, premillenarians must find or insert these long intervals between resurrections to support the separation of the final judgment from Christ's coming, justifying a one-thousand-year earthly millennium" (*A Case for Amillennialism*, 102).

is warranted by the immediate context and/or other biblical revelation. Premillennialists believe it is warranted by both.[18]

The Case for a Temporal Gap

The argument for a temporal gap between verses 23 and 24 begins with an examination of the two adverbial ὅταν clauses in verse 24, which specify the timing of when "the end" arrives—"then comes the end, when [ὅταν] He hands over the kingdom to the God and Father, when [ὅταν] He has abolished all rule and all authority and power" (1 Cor 15:24). As Wallis argues, the distinction in verb tense between the two clauses—the present subjunctive παραδιδῷ ("hands over") in verse 24b vs. the aorist subjunctive καταργήσῃ ("has abolished") in verse 24b—indicates a sequence of events in which the abolishment of all rule/authority/power in the second clause takes place *prior* to the handing over the of the kingdom in the first clause.[19] This sequence of events is reflected clearly in the translation of the English Standard Version: "Then comes the end, when he delivers the kingdom to God the Father after destroying every rule and every authority and power" (1 Cor 15:24).[20] This establishes the following sequence of events in verses 23–24:

The Sequence of Events in 1 Corinthians 15:23–24

1. Christ is resurrected as the first fruits (v. 23a).
2. Christ's people are resurrected at His Second Coming (v. 23b).
3. Christ abolishes all of His enemies (v. 24c).
4. Christ delivers up the kingdom to the Father (v. 24b).
5. Then comes the end (v. 24a).

---

18 According to premillennialist D. Edmond Hiebert, such a gap "is not only possible, but the most probable understanding of Paul's meaning" (D. Edmond Hiebert, "Evidence from 1 Corinthians 15," in *A Case for Premillennialism: A New Consensus*, ed. Donald K. Campbell and Jeffrey L. Townsend [Chicago: Moody Press, 1992], 230).

19 Wilbur Wallis, "The Problem of an Intermediate Kingdom in 1 Corinthians 15:20–28," *JETS* 18, no. 4 (Fall 1975): 230. For this reason, the first ὅταν clause modifies the main clause in verse 24—εἶτα τὸ τέλος ("then comes the end")—whereas the second ὅταν clause modifies the first ὅταν clause. This is recognized even by amillennialist Sam Storms, who writes that the second "when" clause "describes the conditions that must be fulfilled before the kingdom is handed over to the Father" (*Kingdom Come*, 145).

20 This same temporal relationship is expressed by several other translations (NASB, RSV, NRSV, NET, NIV, NLT, ASV), although most not as clearly as the ESV.

According to Wallis, this sequence has significant implications for the possibility of a temporal gap between (2) the Second Coming in verse 23 and (5) "the end" in verse 24:

> Therefore, since there is a sequence clearly marked, the *telos* cannot be simultaneous with the Parousia. Because the *telos* is preceded by the destruction of enemies, and the destruction of enemies cannot be put before the Parousia, the *telos* must stand beyond the Parousia and judgment.[21]

In other words, because Christ must abolish His enemies after His Second Coming and yet prior to the arrival of "the end," the Second Coming and "the end" cannot occur at the same time—there must be at least some gap of time separating the two.[22]

As evidence for the *extent* of this temporal gap, premillennialists point to verse 25, where Paul explains why Christ must first defeat His adversaries before He hands the kingdom over to the Father: "For He must reign until He has put all His enemies under His feet. The last enemy that will be abolished is death" (1 Cor 15:25–26). According to premillennialism, this reign in which Christ conquers the last of His enemies is the millennial reign of Jesus (Rev 20), extending from His Second Coming until the end of the thousand years, when He defeats death and delivers the kingdom to the Father to commence the eternal state. This further explanation in verses 25–26 results in a slight modification (note the italics below) of the previously listed sequence of events in 1 Corinthians 15:23–26:

The Premillennial View of 1 Corinthians 15:23–26

1. Christ is resurrected as the first fruits (v. 23a).
2. Christ's people are resurrected at His Second Coming (v. 23b).
3. *Christ reigns on earth and continues the process of subjugating His enemies* (vv. 24c–25).
4. Christ abolishes *His final enemy* (v. 24c), *which is death* (v. 26).

---

21 Wallis, "The Problem of an Intermediate Kingdom," 231.
22 Amillennialism is able to accommodate the sequence of events listed above, as long as (2), (3), (4), and (5) all occur in immediate succession, one right after the other, with little or no gap of time separating them. For this reason, the premillennialist must be able to show that a temporal gap exists between the Second Coming and these other events.

5. Christ delivers up the kingdom to the Father (v. 24b).
6. Then comes the end (v. 24a).

In contrast, amillennialism places the reign of Christ in verse 25 during the present age, resulting in the following sequence of events:

The Amillennial View of 1 Corinthians 15:23–26

1. Christ is resurrected as the first fruits (v. 23a).
2. *Christ reigns throughout the present age* (v. 25).
3. Christ returns to earth (v. 23b), resulting in the following:
    a. Christ's people are resurrected at His Second Coming (v. 23b).
    b. Christ abolishes His final enemy (v. 24c), which is death (v. 26).
    c. Christ delivers up the kingdom to the Father (v. 24b).
    d. Then comes the end (v. 24a).

Both millennial views affirm that the reign of Christ will result in the defeat of His enemies, culminating in the abolishment of death and the deliverance of the kingdom to the Father. But the critical difference is the timing of the reign of Christ in verse 25 and, consequently, the timing of the abolishment of death and the deliverance of the kingdom. Amillennialists believe that this reign is taking place now in the present age and will culminate at the Second Coming, whereas premillennialists believe it will take place in the future, during the intermediate kingdom between the Second Coming and the eternal state.

The Case for a Future Reign

A closer look at this passage indicates that the reign of Christ in 1 Corinthians 15:25 cannot be a present reality and therefore must refer to a future kingdom. Since Jesus concludes this reign by handing the kingdom over to the Father when "the end" arrives (1 Cor 15:24), if Jesus is reigning now and the arrival of "the end" coincides with His Second Coming (as amillennialism claims), then the present age is the only age in which Jesus will reign over the messianic kingdom.[23] This is problematic for the amillennial view because according to the New Testament, not only will the saints reign with Christ in His messianic kingdom,

---

23 Saucy, *Progressive Dispensationalism*, 282.

but this co-reign is always described as being future rather than present (2 Tim 2:12; Rev 3:21; 5:10; 20:4–5; cf. 1 Cor 4:8; 6:1–3).[24] As Robert Saucy explains, "Such a coreign of believers with Christ in his messianic kingdom … is not possible if that reign is concluded with the handing over of the kingdom to the Father at the coming of Christ."[25] There is simply no time for it to take place.[26]

In contrast, amillennialists believe that the mediatorial reign of Christ in 1 Corinthians 15:25 began when He rose from the dead and was exalted to the right hand of the Father (Acts 2:36; Heb 1:3).[27] According to this view, this reign of Christ continues throughout the present age until the Second Coming, when He abolishes death and delivers the kingdom over to the Father. As Wallis argues, however, Paul's use of the Psalms in 1 Corinthians 15 (Psa 110:1 in verse 25b and Psa 8:6 in verse 27a) demonstrates that this is not possible.[28]

Wallis' argument begins by noting that the writer of Hebrews makes similar use of the same two passages—Psalm 110:1 in Hebrews 1:13 and Psalm 8:6 in Hebrews 2:8. According to Wallis, the parallel use of these Psalms allows 1 Corinthians 15:20–28 and Hebrews 1–2 to "mutually support and explain one another."[29] Therefore, because the use of these Psalms in Hebrews indicates that the subjugation of the enemies of Christ

---

24 Ibid., 282–83.
25 Ibid., 282.
26 Ibid., 106. As Saucy explains, because the believers' co-reign with Christ is yet future, according to the amillennial view the believers' co-reign with Christ would appear to be either (a) placed in the eternal state or (b) limited to participation in the final judgment at the Second Coming. As to the former, Scripture does portray the saints reigning throughout eternity, apparently with God and Christ (Rev 22:5; cf. v. 1), but this co-reign "after the work of the Messiah is completed hardly does justice to the total biblical picture of God's historical purpose for humanity and the full redemption brought through the Messiah" (283). "As to the latter, while judging in the sense of judicial action is an essential part of reigning, it seems inadequate for the total concept of that term and the promises that we shall 'reign on the earth' (Rev 3:21) and do so for some period of time (Rev 20:4). A brief role in the final judgment hardly constitutes 'reigning' with Christ in his kingdom" (283).
27 Robert B. Strimple, "Amillennialism," in *Three Views on the Millennium and Beyond*, ed. Darrell L. Bock (Grand Rapids: Zondervan Publishing), 111. In support of this view, Strimple also cites Eph 1:20–23, Phil 2:9–11, Heb 10:12–13, and 1 Pet 3:21–22.
28 Wilbur Wallis, "The Use of Psalms 8 and 110 in 1 Corinthians 15:25-27 and Hebrews 1 and 2," *JETS* 15, no. 1 (Winter 1972): 26–29; Wallis, "The Problem of an Intermediate Kingdom," 239–42.
29 Wallis, "The Use of Psalms 8 and 110," 29; Wallis, "The Problem of an Intermediate Kingdom," 241.

is accomplished not in the present age but in the age to come, the mediatorial reign in 1 Corinthians 15 must take place in the future, after the Second Coming.[30]

Here is the essence of the argument: After Jesus rose from the dead, He was exalted to the right hand of the Father (Acts 2:36; Heb 1:3), where He was given the position of authority over all powers and authorities (Eph 1:20–23; 1 Pet 3:22). What Jesus was given in *position* (Heb 2:7–8a), however, has not yet been fully realized in *practice*, for these enemies have not yet been subjected to Him (Heb 2:8b; cf. Heb 1:13).[31] In other words, even though Jesus was granted authority over all things, "now we do *not yet* see all things subjected to him" (Heb 2:8; emphasis added), for when He sat down at the right hand of the Father, Jesus began "waiting from that time onward until His enemies be made a footstool for His feet" (Heb 10:13). This subjection of all rulers and powers and authorities, then, is yet future, being identified by the writer of Hebrews with "the world to come" (Heb 2:5).[32]

As Saucy explains, "Although Christ has been exalted to the messianic kingship, nowhere else in the New Testament is he said to be presently exercising that kingship in an actual 'reigning' over his enemies."[33] Hebrews emphasizes that His subjugation of all things is yet future (1:13; 2:5–8;

---

30 Wallis, "The Use of Psalms 8 and 110," 28; Wallis, "The Problem of an Intermediate Kingdom," 241.
31 According to Saucy, even though God has already placed all things under the feet of Christ (Eph 1:22)—and even though Christ "has already received the rulership of all things … this task remains to be accomplished as part of his messianic work" (*Progressive Dispensationalism*, 283).
32 Wallis, "The Use of Psalms 8 and 110," 28. According to Wallis: "Jesus Christ has resumed His place at the Father's right hand, and is waiting until His enemies shall be made His footstool, Hebrews 10:13. Parallel to and identical with the subjugation not yet begun nor accomplished is the subjugation of the world to come mentioned in [Heb 2:5], which in turn had its antecedent in the promise of [Heb 1:13], 'Sit at my right hand, until I make your enemies the footstool of your feet.'" To support his assertion that Heb 2:5–8 continues the argument from Heb 1:13–14, Wallis points to the resumptive γάρ in Heb 2:5 and the continuation of the discussion about angels ("The Problem of an Intermediate Kingdom," 238–39). In this way, the exhortation in Heb 2:1–4 is seen as parenthetical in the larger flow of thought.
33 Saucy, *Progressive Dispensationalism*, 282. According to Saucy: "Not only is the language of 'reign' never used for his present ministry (unless this instance [in 1 Cor 15:25] is an exception), but the prevailing teaching of the futurity of the kingdom both in the teaching of Christ and the later church, and the commencement of the actual exercising of his kingship at the parousia argue against this 'reign' during the present age."

10:12–13), in the world to come (2:5), and 1 Corinthians 15 portrays the subjugation of God's enemies taking place during the reign of Christ between the Second Coming and "the end" (vv. 23–26).[34] For this reason, it is best to understand the mediatorial reign of Christ in 1 Corinthians 15:25 as a reference to an intermediate kingdom between the present age and the eternal state. Rather than posing a problem for premillennialism, then, 1 Corinthians 15:20–28 coincides with its straightforward interpretation of the millennial kingdom in Revelation 20.

The Case for a Final Modification

Premillennialists often note that Paul refers to three stages of resurrection in 1 Corinthians 15:23–24: (1) the resurrection of Jesus, (2) the resurrection of believers at the Second Coming, and (3) the resurrection of everyone else at the conclusion of the messianic kingdom.[35] Amillennialists agree that verse 23 refers to the resurrection of Christ and the resurrection of the saints, but Paul's introductory words, "each in his own order" (ἕκαστος ... ἐν τῷ ἰδίῳ τάγματι) seem to imply a sequence of more than just two stages.[36] For this reason, most premillennialists see "the end" (τὸ τέλος) in verse 24 as "the end of the resurrection process—a resurrection of the wicked dead removed by a significant interval from the resurrection of the righteous dead at the *parousia*."[37]

According to this argument, when the apostle presents this sequence— "Christ the first fruits, after that those who are Christ's at His coming, then comes the end" (1 Cor 15:23–24a)—"*the end* is a distinguishable

---

34 Wallis, "The Use of Psalms 8 and 110," 28; Wallis, "The Problem of an Intermediate Kingdom," 240.
35 Saucy, *Progressive Dispensationalism*, 285–86; Craig A. Blaising, "A Premillennial Response to Robert B. Strimple," in *Three Views on the Millennium and Beyond*, ed. Darrell L. Bock (Grand Rapids: Zondervan Publishing, 1999), 151; Blaising, "The Kingdom that Comes with Jesus," 146; Craig A. Blaising and Darrell L. Bock, *Progressive Dispensationalism* (Grand Rapids: Baker Books, 1993), 273; Robert D. Culver, "A Neglected Millennial Passage from Saint Paul," *BibSac* 113, no. 450 (Apr 1956): 142–49; Charles L. Feinberg, *Millennialism: The Two Major Views*, 3rd ed. (Chicago: Moody Press, 1980), 349–50; Robert D. Culver, *Systematic Theology: Biblical and Historical* (Great Britain: Christian Focus Publications, 2005), 1056.
36 Saucy, *Progressive Dispensationalism*, 285. This argument is persuasive, and yet it is also possible that Paul merely intends a sequence of two resurrections, especially since the first two events are so clearly identified as resurrections, whereas the third event is simply described as the arrival of "the end" (τὸ τέλος).
37 Culver, "A Neglected Millennial Passage," 149.

stage of resurrection parallel to the resurrection of Christ Himself and then to the resurrection of those who belong to Him, who are raised at His return."[38] More specifically, this "third stage of the resurrection sequence"[39] is said to be the resurrection of the wicked at the conclusion of the millennial kingdom (Rev 20:5a, 13), a thousand years after the resurrection of the righteous (Rev 20:4–6).[40] As Robert Culver argues, if 1 Corinthians 15:23–24 specifies three groups in the resurrection of men, "then this passage clearly teaches premillennialism."[41]

---

38 Bock and Blaising, *Progressive Dispensationalism*, 273.
39 Blaising, "The Kingdom that Comes with Jesus," 146.
40 This is what the apostle John refers to in Rev 20:5a ("The rest of the dead did not come to life until the thousand years were completed") and describes in Rev 20:13 ("And the sea gave up the dead which were in it, and death and Hades gave up the dead which were in them; and they were judged, every one of them according to their deeds"). According to Craig Blaising, if "the end" in 1 Cor 15:24a does not refer to the resurrection of the wicked, then the sequence in verses 23–24 "leaves the resurrection of unbelievers unaccounted for" ("A Premillennial Response," 151). As Saucy explains: "Since Paul clearly believed in the resurrection of all people, including the unrighteous (cf. Ac 24:15), the question may be asked, why are only believers mentioned as being raised at Christ's coming?" (*Progressive Dispensationalism*, 285). At the same time, it should be noted that "the general resurrection of the dead is not Paul's concern, neither here nor elsewhere in the argument" (Gordon D. Fee, *The First Epistle to the Corinthians*, NICNT [Grand Rapids: Eerdmans Publishing, 1987], 749). Instead, Paul's concern is the resurrection of the saints, and he "mentions only those things that are germane to his argument" (David E. Garland, *1 Corinthians*, BECNT [Grand Rapids: Baker Books, 2003], 709). Furthermore, if the resurrection of the wicked had been of concern to Paul, one might expect him to have described their resurrection explicitly like he did with the others (Fee, *The First Epistle to the Corinthians*, 750).
41 Culver, "A Neglected Millennial Passage," 142. As support for this argument, some premillennialists assert that Paul's statement in verse 22 that "all will be made alive" describes the resurrection of all people, both believers and unbelievers. Therefore, because verse 23 unfolds the stages of this universal resurrection, this sequence must include not only Christ and His people, but also unbelievers as the final stage of resurrection (Blaising, "The Kingdom that Comes with Jesus," 146; Culver, *Systematic Theology*, 1056; Culver, "A Neglected Millennial Passage," 145). But the difficulty with the universal view of "all" is that both "the context and Paul's theology as a whole make it clear that in saying 'in Christ all will be made alive,' he means 'in Christ all *who are in Christ* will be made alive'" (Fee, *The First Epistle to the Corinthians*, 749–50; emphasis original). When Paul writes, "For as in Adam all die, so also in Christ all shall be made alive" (1 Cor 15:22), the first "all" refers to those related to Adam, and the second "all" refers only to those related to Christ. As David Garland explains: "The analogy assumes human solidarity with those at the beginning of a line who then become the representatives of those who follow. Adam leads the way and represents the old order; Christ leads the way and represents the new order. Paul assumes that the representative determines the fate of the group. All those bound to Adam share his banishment from Eden, his alienation, and his fate of death so that death becomes the common lot of his posterity.... All those bound to Christ receive reconciliation and will share his resurrection and heavenly blessings" (*1 Corinthians*, 707). This

In contrast, other premillennialists believe that "the end" is better understood as the consummation of redemptive history rather than a reference to the final stage in the resurrection sequence. This view is consistent with a common use of the noun τέλος—"the goal or outcome toward which a movement is being directed"[42]—and it fits the immediate context, which focuses broadly on the scope of redemptive history. But even if "the end" is not an *explicit* reference to a third resurrection, the abolishment of death as the final enemy (vv. 24–26) necessitates the resurrection of this third group of individuals at the same time,[43] for it "must logically entail a reversal of state for those who are dead at that time."[44] Because only "those who are Christ's" are said to be raised at the Second Coming (v. 23), the resurrection of everyone else must occur when death is abolished at the arrival of "the end."[45] This results in a final modification (once again, note the italics below) of the previously proposed sequence of events:

The Sequence of Events in 1 Corinthians 15:23–28

1. Christ is resurrected as the first fruits (v. 23a).
2. Christ's people are resurrected at His Second Coming (v. 23b).
3. Christ reigns on earth and continues the process of subjugating His enemies (vv. 24c–25).
4. Christ abolishes His final enemy (v. 24c), which is death (v. 26).
5. *Unbelievers are resurrected when death is abolished* (vv. 24–26).
6. Christ delivers up the kingdom to the Father (v. 24b).

---

interpretation makes the best sense of the analogy between Adam and Christ; it affirms the most common New Testament meaning of the phrase "in Christ"; and it recognizes that the future resurrection of "those who have fallen asleep in Christ" (v. 18) is the focus of this entire section. At the same time, the argument for a third resurrection in 1 Cor 15:20–28 does not depend on interpreting Paul's words, "all will be made alive," as a reference to the resurrection of all people.

42 BDAG, 998.
43 Blaising, "A Premillennial Response," 151; Blaising, "The Kingdom that Comes with Jesus," 147; Saucy, *Progressive Dispensationalism*, 285; George Eldon Ladd, *The Gospel of the Kingdom: Scriptural Studies in the Kingdom of God* (Grand Rapids: Eerdmans Publishing, 1959), 43.
44 Blaising, "A Premillennial Response," 151. As Blaising explains elsewhere: "The destruction of death logically means two things: (1) no one dies after that point, and (2) any who had been dead up to that point must be raised" ("The Kingdom that Comes with Jesus," 147).
45 This certainly entails the resurrection of the wicked (Rev 20:5a, 13) and may include the resurrection of those who are converted during the millennial kingdom as well.

7. Then comes the end (v. 24a).
8. The Father is all in all (vv. 27–28).

A Summary of the Premillennial Response

To summarize, then, the amillennial argument from 1 Corinthians 15:20–28 falls short for a number of reasons: (1) the temporal adverb εἶτα ("then") in verse 24 clearly allows for a lengthy gap of time for an intermediate kingdom between "His coming" and "the end;" (2) the two ὅταν clauses in verse 24 indicate a sequence of events in which the subjection of all things to Christ and the deliverance of the kingdom to the Father must take place between the Second Coming and "the end," which requires a gap of time; (3) the reign of Christ in verse 25 must take place in the future, between the Second Coming and "the end," because both the co-reign of believers with Christ and the subjection of all things to Christ are yet future; and (4) "the end" in verses 24–26 requires a third resurrection—the resurrection of unbelievers unto judgment—which is separate from the resurrection of Christ's people at His coming. For these reasons, 1 Corinthians 15:20–28 actually provides a much stronger argument for premillennialism than it does for amillennialism.

THE ARGUMENT FROM 1 CORINTHIANS 15:50–57

Amillennialists believe that this connection between the Second Coming, the resurrection of believers, and the final destruction of death is strengthened further by 1 Corinthians 15:50–57, where Paul writes:

> Now I say this, brethren, that flesh and blood cannot inherit the kingdom of God; nor does the perishable inherit the imperishable. Behold, I tell you a mystery; we will not all sleep, but we will all be changed, in a moment, in the twinkling of an eye, at the last trumpet; for the trumpet will sound, and the dead will be raised imperishable, and we will be changed. For this perishable must put on the imperishable, and this mortal must put on immortality. But when this perishable will have put on the imperishable, and this mortal will have put on immortality, then will come about the saying that is written, "DEATH IS SWALLOWED UP IN VICTORY. O DEATH, WHERE IS YOUR VICTORY? O DEATH, WHERE

IS YOUR STING?" The sting of death is sin, and the power of sin is the law; but thanks be to God, who gives us the victory through our Lord Jesus Christ (1 Cor 15:50–57).

The Amillennial Argument

According to amillennialists, this passage presents two insurmountable obstacles for the eschatology of premillennialism. The first obstacle is Paul's assertion that flesh and blood cannot inherit the kingdom of God (v. 50), which is said to preclude the possibility of an intermediate kingdom inhabited in part by people in their natural bodies.[46] According to this argument, premillennialism asserts that those who inherit the kingdom of Revelation 20 will include non-glorified believers, but 1 Corinthians 15:50 denies this possibility.[47] According to amillennialist Sam Storms, this leaves premillennialists with two options: "either deny these believers that inheritance of the kingdom which Christ has promised ... or recognize that 1 Corinthians 15:50 precludes the millennial age traditionally defined and defended by the premillennialist."[48]

The second obstacle is that Paul's description of death being abolished at the Second Coming (1 Cor 15:51–57) excludes the possibility of an intermediate kingdom in which people continue to die. According to this argument, at the time of the Second Coming—referred to as "the last trumpet" in verse 52—not only will the dead in Christ be resurrected and glorified (vv. 50–53), but death itself will be swallowed up in victory (vv. 54–57). The death of death, in other words, will occur at the same time as the resurrection of the righteous and the Second Advent of Jesus, ushering in the eternal state in which death is no more (Rev 21:1–4).[49]

---

46 Storms, *Kingdom Come*, 149–50, 552; Riddlebarger, *A Case for Amillennialism*, 98, 276.
47 Storms, *Kingdom Come*, 150.
48 Ibid.
49 Ibid., 151; Menn, *Biblical Eschatology*, 354–55; Cox, *Amillennialism Today*, 105–6; According to Strimple, "The adverb 'then' (*tote*) in the middle of verse 54 tells us when this victory over death will be accomplished. And that 'then' points us back to what Paul has been describing for several verses here: *the resurrection of believers*. Therefore, we must conclude that victory over death will occur at the resurrection of believers (v. 54), which occurs at the coming of Christ (v. 23), and that this victory occurs at 'the end' (vv. 24–26)" ("Amillennialism," 110–11; emphasis original).

Amillennialists believe that Paul's quotation of Isaiah 25:8 in 1 Corinthians 15:54 confirms that death will be abolished at the Second Coming. As Storms explains:

> According to Isaiah 25:8, not only will God "swallow up death forever," he will also at that time "wipe away tears from all faces." Both these events will occur ... at the time of the second coming. But according to Revelation 21:1–4, it is at the time of the creation of the new heavens and new earth that God "will wipe away every tear from their eyes, and death shall be no more" (21:4).[50]

According to Storms, this presents premillennialism with an impossible dilemma:

> How can these two prophesied events (Isa. 25:7–9) find their fulfillment at the close of a 1,000-year post-parousia millennial kingdom when Paul has so clearly stated that they find their fulfillment at the time of the second coming of Christ? Is it not obvious that at the second coming of Christ the new heavens and new earth are created and the eternal state begins? Is it not equally obvious, therefore, that there is no room or place or role in either Paul's or John's theology for an intervening millennial kingdom? Is it not obvious that death's death at the second coming and the wiping away of all tears at the second coming, both of which mark the inauguration of the new heavens and new earth, preclude the existence of any such millennial kingdom?[51]

First Corinthians 15:50–57, then, is said to present two insurmountable obstacles for premillennialism: (1) Paul's assertion that flesh and blood cannot inherit the kingdom of God (v. 50) precludes the possibility of an intermediate kingdom including people in their natural bodies; and (2) Paul's assertion that death will be abolished at the Second Coming (vv. 51–57) precludes the possibility of a post-parousia kingdom in which death continues to exist. To harmonize 1 Corinthians 15:50–57 with the earthly reign of Christ in Revelation 20, the premillennialist must overcome these obstacles.

---

50 Storms, *Kingdom Come*, 152.
51 Ibid. Also see Menn, *Biblical Eschatology*, 43, 75.

The Premillennial View of 1 Corinthians 15:50

The first obstacle concerns 1 Corinthians 15:50. When Paul refers to the inability of "flesh and blood" to inherit the kingdom of God (1 Cor 15:50), he does not mean that those who inherit the kingdom will exist in a non-physical state. Instead, the expression "flesh and blood" refers to human bodies as they now exist in their present state of mortality—in the likeness of Adam after the fall—being subject to weakness, corruption, decay, and ultimately death.[52] According to 1 Corinthians 15:50, those who have believed in Christ cannot inherit the kingdom of God in these mortal bodies (v. 50a), for the perishable cannot inherit the imperishable (v. 50b). Therefore, all believers, both the living and the dead, must first experience the radical transformation of glorification before they can inherit this kingdom (1 Cor 15:51–53).

For this reason, amillennialists are right to object to any scenario in which people are said to inherit the kingdom of 1 Corinthians 15:50 in their natural, un-glorified bodies. But in contrast to the claims of amillennialists, even though some premillennialists have understood 1 Corinthians 15:50 as a reference to the intermediate kingdom,[53] this view is not required by the premillenialism. Instead, as other premillennialists have asserted, it is better to understand the kingdom of God in 1 Corinthians 15:50 as a reference to the eternal state, the kingdom which has been handed over to the Father after the millennial reign of Jesus (1 Cor 15:24–25).[54]

---

52 Wayne Grudem, *Systematic Theology: An Introduction to Biblical Doctrine* (Grand Rapids: Zondervan Publishing, 1994), 833; Fee, *The First Epistle to the Corinthians*, 798–99; Garland, *1 Corinthians*, 741; W. Harold Mare, "1 Corinthians," in *EBC*, ed. Frank E. Gaebelein (Grand Rapids: Zondervan Publishing, 1981), 10:291. As Fee writes, "Most likely it refers simply to the body in its present form, composed of flesh and blood, to be sure, but subject to weakness, decay, and death, and as such ill-suited for the life of the future" (*The First Epistle to the Corinthians*, 799). According to Grudem, "This is the point he has made in the previous four verses (1 Cor. 15:45–49), in which he has been contrasting Adam with Christ" (*Systematic Theology*, 833).
53 J. Dwight Pentecost, *Things to Come: A Study in Biblical Eschatology* (Grand Rapids: Zondervan Publishing, 1978), 175; Alva J. McClain, *The Greatness of the Kingdom: An Inductive Study of the Kingdom of God* (Winona Lake, IN: BMH Books, 1959), 433.
54 David L. Turner, "The New Jerusalem in Revelation 21:1–22:5," in *Dispensationalism, Israel and the Church: The Search for Definition*, eds. Craig A. Blaising and Darrell L. Bock (Grand Rapids: Zondervan Publishing, 1992), 289; John MacArthur, *1 Corinthians*, MacNTC (Chicago: Moody Publishers, 1984), 443. According to MacArthur, "the kingdom of God" in 1 Cor 15:50 is used in its consummate sense as a reference to the eternal state.

In 1 Corinthians 15, premillennialism distinguishes between the millennium, during which Christ must reign on earth until all of His enemies are defeated (v. 25), and the eternal state, which begins when Jesus hands the kingdom over to the Father at "the end" (v. 24). As Saucy explains:

> In the reign of Christ and its transfer to the Father at the end, Paul portrays the completion of the Messiah's work of redemption.... The handing over of the kingdom to the Father thus signifies nothing less than the conclusion of the messianic administration of the kingdom through which Christ brings all things back under the rule or kingdom of God.[55]

In 1 Corinthians 15:50, then, when Paul writes that non-glorified people cannot inherit "the kingdom of God," he is specifically referring to the eternal state. Although premillennialism affirms the existence of non-glorified individuals in the intermediate kingdom of the Son, when the last enemy is defeated and Jesus hands the kingdom over to the Father, death will be abolished and all who enter the eternal kingdom of God will exist in a glorified state. For this reason—in contrast to the claim of amillennialists—premillennialism does not require that some will inherit this eternal kingdom in their natural bodies, and 1 Corinthians 15:50 does not preclude the possibility of an intermediate kingdom.[56]

The amillennialist cannot raise a categorical objection to a distinction between the kingdom reign of Christ in 1 Corinthians 15:25 and "the kingdom of God" in 1 Corinthians 15:50, for amillennialism also makes a distinction between the two, seeing the former as the present age and the latter as the eternal state. If the amillennialist insists that the two must be equated, then 1 Corinthians 15:50 presents an insurmountable obstacle for his own view as well, for this would require that believers today are part of the kingdom of God even though they have not yet been glorified. For this reason, 1 Corinthians 15:50 itself presents no more of a problem for premillennialism than it does for amillennialism.

---

55 Saucy, *Progressive Dispensationalism*, 282.
56 This stands in contrast to the claim of Sam Storms that "amillennialism alone can account for Paul's declaration that 'flesh and blood cannot inherit the kingdom of God' (1 Cor. 15:50–57)" (*Kingdom Come*, 552).

The Premillennial View of 1 Corinthians 15:51–57

According to the second obstacle, Paul's assertion that death will be abolished at the Second Coming (1 Cor 15:51–57) precludes the possibility of an intermediate kingdom in which death continues to exist. This is the heart of the amillennial argument from this passage, and it raises a crucial question: Does 1 Corinthians 15:51–57 indicate that death is abolished once and for all at the Second Coming of Christ? Put another way, can 1 Corinthians 15:51–57 be harmonized with an intermediate kingdom in which death continues to exist for a thousand years after the return of Christ? Amillennialists say no, but premillennialists believe it can.

The most plausible way to harmonize 1 Corinthians 15:51–57 with Revelation 20 is to see the language of victory over death in this passage as applicable to each stage of resurrection set forth in Scripture.[57] According to this view, verses 51–53 do indeed describe the glorification of believers at the return of Christ, but this transformation of God's people does not signify the final destruction of death as an enemy which is able to claim other lives. Instead, when the saints are glorified at the return of Christ, they themselves experience this victory over death as they are clothed with immortality, but the final destruction of death itself remains future, taking place when death and Hades are cast into the Lake of Fire at the end of the millennium (Rev 20:14; cf. 21:4).

The crux of the issue involves Paul's use of the Old Testament in 1 Corinthians 15:54–55. In these verses, the apostle says that when believers are glorified at the return of Christ, the words of Isaiah 25:8 and Hosea 13:14 will be fulfilled:

> But when this perishable will have put on the imperishable, and this mortal will have put on immortality, then will come about the saying that is written, "DEATH IS SWALLOWED UP IN VICTORY [ISA 25:8]. O DEATH, WHERE IS YOUR VICTORY? O DEATH, WHERE IS YOUR STING [Hos 13:14]?"[58]

---

57 Blaising, "A Premillennial Response," 151.
58 Paul's citation of Isa 25:8—"Death is swallowed up in victory" (Κατεπόθη ὁ θάνατος εἰς νῖκος)—differs significantly from the LXX, which reads, "Death, being strong, swallowed [them] up" (κατέπιεν ὁ θάνατος ἰσχύσας). At the same time, Aquila, Theodotion, and Symmachus have differing variants, some of which are very similar to Paul's citation, so the apostle may be following a preexisting Greek text (Roy E. Ciampa and Brian S.

In contrast to the amillennial interpretation, it is not necessary to see Paul's use of Isaiah 25:8 in verse 54 as a once-and-for-all fulfillment of this prophecy which signals the final defeat of death so that it no longer exists.[59] Instead, when Paul says that the words of Isaiah 25:8 "will come about" (γενήσεται) when the saints are glorified at the return of Jesus, he means that this victory will become a reality for God's people—those who are His children at the time of Christ's coming—when they undergo this radical transformation. But again, this does not rule out the possibility that others will subsequently be raised from the dead and/or experience the same victory over death described in this passage.

This view does not require a gap of time between the ὅταν clause in verse 54a and the τότε clause in verses 54b–55, for this victory will indeed take place when God's people are glorified at the return of Christ. This view is also consistent with both the larger context of 1 Corinthians 15 and the immediate context of verses 50–57.

With regard to the larger context, if the premillennial interpretation defended above is correct, 1 Corinthians 15:23–28 sets forth the following sequence of eschatological events:

- The resurrection of Christ (v. 23a)
- The resurrection of the saints at the return of Christ (v. 23b)
- The reign of Christ in which He subjugates His enemies (vv. 24c–25)
- The abolishment of death as the final enemy (vv. 24c, 26)
- The deliverance of the kingdom to the Father (v. 24b; vv. 27–28)

Rosner, *The First Letter to the Corinthians*, PNTC [Grand Rapids: Eerdmans Publishing, 2010], 832; Anthony C. Thiselton, *The First Epistle to the Corinthians: A Commentary on the Greek Text*, NIGTC [Grand Rapids: Eerdmans Publishing, 2000], 1299). According to Gordon Fee, even though the word "victory" is not found in the Septuagint, the phrase εἰς νῖκος is an idiom meaning "forever" in the LXX, and so it may render the Hebrew phrase לָנֶצַח ("forever") in Isa 25:8 (*The First Epistle to the Corinthians*, 803–4).

In his citation of Hos 13:14, Paul modifies the language and adapts a prophecy of judgment against Ephraim into a taunt against death in which he declares the victory over the grave (Fee, *The First Epistle to the Corinthians*, 804; Ciampa and Rosner, *The First Letter to the Corinthians*, 834–36; Garland, *1 Corinthians*, 745). For an explanation of Paul's modifications of Hosea, see Fee, *The First Epistle to the Corinthians*, 804.

59 For this reason, the fulfillment of Isa 25:8 in 1 Cor 15:54 should not be viewed as equivalent to the final abolition of death described in 1 Cor 15:24–26.

For this reason, when Paul describes the glorification of God's people at the return of Christ in 1 Corinthians 15:51–57, it must be understood in light of this previously established sequence of events.[60] Therefore, because the future messianic reign of Christ will take place between this glorification of God's people and the final destruction of death, death must not be completely abolished at the Second Coming. The need to harmonize both passages leads to an interpretation of verses 54–57 in which the Old Testament language of victory over death applies to this stage in the resurrection process, even though it is not the final one.

With regard to the immediate context, Paul's primary concern in verses 50–57 is not to set forth a comprehensive outline of eschatological events. As George Eldon Ladd explains, the apostle "is far more concerned with the ultimate outcome and with the immediate application of it than he is with the stages by which the consummation is realized."[61] For this reason, after Paul sets forth the universal principle in verse 50 that mere mortal human beings cannot inherit the kingdom of the eternal state, his primary purpose is to address the direct implications of this for his immediate readers. But because he does not know when Jesus will return, Paul includes both possibilities in verses 51–53—that some will still be living at this time and that others will have died:

> Behold, I tell you a mystery; we will not all sleep, but we will all be changed, in a moment, in the twinkling of an eye, at the last trumpet; for the trumpet will sound, and the dead will be raised imperishable, and we will be changed. For this perishable must put on the imperishable, and this mortal must put on immortality (1 Cor 15:51–53).[62]

---

60 See Blaising, "A Premillennial Resonse," 151.
61 George Eldon Ladd, *Crucial Questions About the Kingdom of God* (Grand Rapids: Eerdmans Publishing, 1952), 180. As Ladd explains, "The force in the line of reasoning based on 1 Corinthians 15:23–26 is that Paul is not concerned with the stages by which Christ's ultimate triumph is achieved; he is concerned with the certainty of that triumph *whose realization is assured because it has already begun*" (emphasis original).
62 The "last trumpet" in verse 52 does not refer to the last in a series, but rather to the trumpet which announces the eschatological Day of the Lord (Isa 27:13; Joel 2:1; Zeph 1:16; Zech 9:14) (Douglas J. Moo, "A Case for the Posttribulation Rapture," in *Three Views on the Rapture: Pretribulation, Prewrath, or Posttribulation*, ed. Alan Hultberg [Grand Rapids: Zondervan Publishing, 2010], 198; Alan Hultberg, "A Case for the Prewrath Rapture," in *Three Views on the Rapture: Pretribulation, Prewrath, or Posttribulation*, ed. Alan Hultberg

Even though the Corinthian believers presently exist in perishable bodies and are therefore currently unfit for the eternal kingdom of the Father, Paul says they will be transformed and glorified at the coming of Christ, whether dead or alive when this occurs. According to verses 54–55, when this transformation takes place—when God's people are clothed with immortality—they will experience the victory over death described in the Old Testament, for "then will come about the saying that is written, 'DEATH IS SWALLOWED UP IN VICTORY. O DEATH, WHERE IS YOUR VICTORY? O DEATH, WHERE IS YOUR STING?'" (1 COR 15:54–55). In other words, those who are glorified at the return of Christ will experience the victory over death which was purchased by Christ through His work of redemption (2 Tim 1:10),[63] and when they do, the victorious words of Isaiah 25:8 and Hosea 13:14 will become a reality in their lives. As Paul celebrates in verses 56–57: "The sting of death is sin, and the power of sin is the law; but thanks be to God, who gives us the victory through our Lord Jesus Christ" (1 Cor 15:56–57).

The primary concern of 1 Corinthians 15:50–57, then, is the future glorification of the saints at the time of Christ's return, which makes them fit for the eternal kingdom of God. But nothing in this passage explicitly precludes (a) the existence of death in an intermediate kingdom after the Second Coming; (b) the future glorification of any who believe in Christ during this intermediate kingdom; or (c) the resurrection of the wicked unto judgment at the end of this intermediate kingdom. Paul did not concern himself with any of these scenarios because none of them directly involved the Corinthians or other believers in the present age, and therefore he had no reason to mention them.

Returning to the two obstacles in 1 Corinthians 15, then, verse 50 does not preclude the possibility of natural bodies in the intermediate

---

[Grand Rapids: Zondervan Publishing, 2010], 152). As Blaising notes, because the Day of the Lord is an *eschatological* day, "any feature associated with it is properly 'last'" (Craig Blaising, "A Pretribulation Response," in *Three Views on the Rapture: Pretribulation, Prewrath, or Posttribulation*, ed. Alan Hultberg [Grand Rapids: Zondervan Publishing, 2010], 250; emphasis original). Vos claims that Paul's reference to the *last* trumpet "excludes the prospect of any further crisis" (*The Pauline Eschatology*, 246), but he fails to provide evidence for this assertion.

63 Through His triumph at the cross, Christ has "abolished death and brought life and immortality to light through the gospel" (2 Tim 1:10), but this positional victory has not yet been realized in the experience of God's people.

kingdom, and verses 51–57 do not preclude the possibility of physical death in the intermediate kingdom. As demonstrated above, Paul's teaching can be harmonized with the millennium of Revelation 20 in a way that honors the divine intention of both passages, and therefore 1 Corinthians 15:50–57 fails to provide any insurmountable difficulties for the eschatology of premillennialism.[64]

Conclusion

Amillennialists believe that the two-age model of the New Testament precludes the possibility of an intermediate kingdom for three specific reasons: (1) the successiveness of the two ages eliminates the possibility

---

64 Amillennialists also point to Rom 8:17–23 as an indication that sin and death will no longer exist after the Second Coming. In this passage, not only will creation itself "be set free from its slavery to corruption" (v. 21), but the children of God will be glorified with Christ, being fully delivered from sin (vv. 17–23). Paul specifically refers to being "glorified" with Christ (v. 17); "the glory that is to be revealed to us" (v. 18); "the revealing of the sons of God" (v. 19); "the glory of the children of God" (v. 21); and "our adoption as sons, the redemption of our body" (v. 23). According to amillennialists, this indicates that the Second Coming will be a time of full deliverance from sin and all of its effects, a time when the curse is lifted and every trace of wickedness will be removed from the entirety of the created order, including the children of God. Therefore, it is said, Rom 8:17–23 clearly excludes the possibility of an intermediate kingdom in which sin and death continue after the Second Coming (Venema, *The Promise of the Future*, 94; Riddlebarger, *A Case for Amillennialism*, 166; Anthony Hoekema, *The Bible and the Future* [Grand Rapids: Eerdmans Publishing, 1979], 282; Storms, *Kingdom Come*, 153–54, 551).

In response, premillennialism fully affirms the glorification of God's people at the return of Christ as taught in Romans 8, but this does mean that sin and death are abolished at the Second Coming. Not only do the Old Testament prophets speak of the existence of sin and death in the initial phase of the coming kingdom (Isa 65:20; Zech 14:17–19; see chapter 2–4 for a fuller explanation), but Rev 20:7–10 describes a revolt at the end of the millennium in which unbelievers are deceived by Satan, led into battle against Christ and the saints, and decisively judged by fire from heaven. According to premillennialists, these unbelievers will arise either from (a) unbelievers who survive the battle of Rev 19:17–19 and enter the millennial kingdom in non-glorified bodies or (b) the descendants of those who are converted during the Tribulation and enter the millennial kingdom in non-glorified bodies. Both of these premillennial views are consistent with the teaching of Romans 8. Under the first scenario, Romans 8 describes the glorification of all God's people—both dead and alive—at the return of Christ when He comes to establish His kingdom on earth, but sin and death continue among those non-glorified people who populate this kingdom. Under the second scenario, Romans 8 describes the glorification of God's people both at the rapture (1 Thess 4:13–18) and at the Second Coming (Rev 20:4–6)—conflating the two into a single description—and sin and death continue among those non-glorified people in the millennial kingdom. Because nothing in Romans 8 requires that sin and death are abolished and no longer exist, both views are consistent with the glorification of God's people at the Second Coming of Christ.

of an interval of time between this age and the age to come; (2) the qualities of the age to come are incompatible with an intermediate kingdom which includes sin and death; and (3) the dividing line between the two ages indicates that the Second Coming immediately ushers in the eternal state, leaving no room for an intermediate kingdom.

As demonstrated in chapters 6–10, however, these three arguments fail to disprove the possibility of an intermediate kingdom: (1) The millennium of Revelation 20 is best understood as the initial phase of the age to come, and therefore the biblical references to the two ages do not require an interval of time between them to accommodate an intermediate kingdom; (2) the qualities ascribed to the age to come in Scripture are compatible with the millennial kingdom as the first phase of that coming age, and therefore the characteristics of the two ages fail to provide a compelling argument against premillennialism; and (3) the Bible's description of the dividing line between the two ages fails to demonstrate that the Second Coming introduces the eternal state, and therefore the millennial kingdom can be harmonized with the remainder of the New Testament. Put simply, the two-age model fails to disprove the existence of the millennial kingdom taught so clearly in Revelation 20, and therefore it poses no compelling refutation of the eschatology of premillennialism.

PART 3

The Intermediate Kingdom *in* Revelation 20

Chapter 11

The Timing of Satan's Binding

Introduction

Revelation 20 has long been considered the clearest and most convincing argument for the eschatology of premillennialism. For this reason, any credible defense of amillennialism must be able to make a compelling case that its own interpretation of Revelation 20 accurately expresses the divinely intended meaning of the passage. If amillennialism is not able to do so—if it is unable to demonstrate how Revelation 20:1–6 is consistent with its rejection of an intermediate kingdom—the two-age model must be modified to make room for a millennial reign of Christ between the present age and the eternal state.

In recent years, an increasing number of amillennial voices have risen to embrace this challenge. Many of them have even insisted that Revelation 20 provides more compelling evidence for amillennialism than it does for premillennialism. For example, Sam Storms points to Revelation 20 as "a strong and immovable support for the amillennial perspective;"[1] Kim Riddlebarger describes it as "the weak link in any form of

---

1 Sam Storms, *Kingdom Come: The Amillennial Alternative* (Ross-shire, Scotland: Mentor, 2013), 137. In describing his journey from premillennialism to amillennialism, Storms explains that Revelation 20 served not as a hindrance to this conversion, but rather a catalyst. "Contrary to what I had been taught and long believed," Storms writes, "I came to see Revelation 20 as a strong and immovable support for the amillennial perspective" (ibid.). In fact, unlike many of his fellow amillennialists, Storms says he embraced amillennialism *because of* Revelation 20, not in spite of it (ibid.; Sam Storms, "I Am an Amillennialist 'because of' Revelation 20," accessed on August 3, 2014, http://www.samstorms.com/enjoying-god-blog/post/i-am-an-amillennialist--because-of--revelation-20.).

premillennialism;"[2] and Dean Davis argues that "the amillennial approach gives us a remarkably clear, consistent, and exegetically natural interpretation of this notoriously challenging text."[3]

This kind of confidence among amillennialists raises the question of whether premillennialists may have overstated the clarity of John's teaching in Revelation 20. The purpose of chapters 11–14 is to re-examine this monumental passage in the millennial debate, with an emphasis on the amillennial interpretation of four key exegetical issues—the timing of Satan's binding, the nature of the first resurrection, the duration of the thousand years, and the chronology of John's visions. These four chapters will demonstrate that the case for the amillennial interpretation is unconvincing and that Revelation 20 clearly teaches a millennial kingdom between the present age and the eternal state.[4]

THE BINDING OF SATAN

In Revelation 20:1–3, John's vision focuses on the status of Satan during the millennial reign of Christ:

> Then I saw an angel coming down from heaven, holding the key of the abyss and a great chain in his hand. And he laid hold of the dragon, the serpent of old, who is the devil and Satan, and bound him for a thousand years; and he threw him into the abyss, and shut it and sealed it over him, so that he would not deceive the nations any longer, until the thousand years were completed; after these things he must be released for a short time (Rev 20:1–3).

---

2 Kim Riddlebarger, *A Case for Amillennialism: Understanding the End Times*, expanded ed. (Grand Rapids: Baker Books, 2013), 235.

3 Dean Davis, *The High King of Heaven: Discovering the Master Keys to the Great End Time Debate* (Enumclaw, WA: WinePress Publishing, 2014), 475. According to Davis, "Premillennial interpretations of Revelation 20 shatter the simplicity, vitiate the power, and becloud the glory of NT eschatology, thereby plunging Christ's Church into needless confusion and controversy. Meanwhile, the amillennial interpretation achieves the exact opposite: It wonderfully opens up the meaning of the text itself, further illumines the structure and message of the book as a whole, harmonizes perfectly with the rest of NT theology ... and prepares, strengthens, and encourages Christ's pilgrim Church with a simple, powerful, and unspeakably majestic vision of the Consummation of all things at the end of the age" (501–2).

4 For a brief discussion of these four exegetical issues, see Matthew Waymeyer, "What About Revelation 20?," in *Christ's Prophetic Plans: A Futuristic Premillennial Primer*, eds. John MacArthur and Richard Mayhue (Chicago: Moody Publishers, 2012), 123–40.

The key question in this passage involves the timing of Satan's binding. Put simply, is the binding of Satan present or future? In other words, is Satan currently bound in the abyss during the present age, or will his thousand-year imprisonment take place after the Second Coming of Christ? Amillennialism sees the binding of Satan as a present reality—the millennium is *now*—whereas premillennialism sees it as future, taking place during an intermediate kingdom between the present age and the eternal state.

The Premillennial Argument

The primary reason that Satan's imprisonment cannot be considered a present reality is because Revelation 20:1–3 is incompatible with the New Testament's portrayal of his influence during the present age. According to this passage, Satan will be cut off from all earthly activity during the thousand-year reign of Christ. The imagery of Satan being bound with a great chain and cast into the abyss—which is then shut and sealed over him—provides a vivid picture of the total removal of his influence on earth.[5] In fact, if a vision were intended to teach that Satan is rendered completely inactive during the thousand years, it is difficult to imagine how this could have been portrayed more clearly.[6] As G. R. Beasley-Murray writes:

> A seal on a prison door ensured that prisoners could not escape unobserved. Only he who authorized the imprisonment could authorize release from it (see Dan. 6:17; Mt. 27:66). Thus the incarceration of the Devil is trebly circumscribed. He is bound up, locked in, and sealed over. The writer could hardly have expressed more emphatically the inability of Satan to harm the race of man.[7]

---

5 Wayne Grudem, *Systematic Theology: An Introduction to Biblical Doctrine* (Grand Rapids: Zondervan Publishing, 1994), 1117; Harold W. Hoehner, "Evidence from Revelation 20," in *A Case for Premillennialism: A New Consensus*, eds. Donald K. Campbell and Jeffrey L. Townsend (Chicago: Moody Press, 1992), 250; Robert H. Mounce, *The Book of Revelation*, NICNT (Grand Rapids: Eerdmans Publishing, 1977), 353.

6 John F. Walvoord, "The Theological Significance of Revelation 20:1–6," in *Essays in Honor of J. Dwight Pentecost*, eds. Stanley D. Toussaint and Charles H. Dyer (Chicago: Moody Press, 1986), 231.

7 G. R. Beasley-Murray, *The Book of Revelation*, NCB (Greenwood, SC: The Attic Press, 1974), 285. Even some amillennialists recognize this, for example, G. C. Berkouwer who states that those who identify the millennium as the present age are forced to relativize the

In contrast, the New Testament makes it abundantly clear that Satan—who is described as "the god of this age" (ὁ θεὸς τοῦ αἰῶνος τούτου) (2 Cor 4:4) and "the ruler of this world" (ὁ ἄρχων τοῦ κόσμου τούτου) (John 12:31; cf. John 14:30; 16:11; 1 John 4:4)—is extremely active on earth during the present age. He not only "prowls about like a roaring lion, seeking someone to devour" (1 Pet 5:8), but he is also involved in a host of other activities—he tells lies (John 8:44); he tempts believers to sin (1 Cor 7:5; Eph 4:27); he disguises himself as an angel of light (2 Cor 11:13–15); he seeks to deceive the children of God (2 Cor 11:3; cf. 2 Cor 2:11); he snatches the gospel from unbelieving hearts (Matt 13:19; Mark 4:15; Luke 8:12; cf. 1 Thess 3:5; 1 Tim 1:20; 4:1–2); he takes advantage of believers (2 Cor 2:11); he influences people to lie (Acts 5:3); he holds unbelievers under his power (1 John 5:19; Eph 2:2; Acts 26:18; 1 John 3:8–10); he torments the servants of God (2 Cor 12:7); he thwarts the progress of ministry (1 Thess 2:18; Rev 2:10); he seeks to destroy the faith of believers (Luke 22:31); he wages war against the church (Eph 6:11–17); and he traps and deceives unbelievers, holding them captive to do his will (2 Tim 2:26). It is impossible to reconcile this portrayal of Satan's activities in the present age with the view that he is currently sealed in the abyss.

The location of the devil's imprisonment makes it especially clear that the confinement of Revelation 20:1–3 will prevent any satanic activity and influence on earth during the thousand years. The "abyss" (ἄβυσσος) is a prison for evil spirits (Rev 20:7), and the New Testament indicates that when evil spirits are confined in this prison, they are prevented from participating in their normal demonic activities on earth (Luke 8:31; Rev 9:1–3). For this reason, Satan can either be locked away in the abyss, or he can be engaging in the various activities ascribed to him in the present age, but he cannot be both. The description of Satan's imprisonment in Revelation 20 is incompatible with the New Testament's portrayal of his influence during the church age, and therefore the binding of Satan cannot be understood as a present reality.

---

dimensions of Satan's binding. Berkouwer writes, "I think it is pertinent to ask whether this sort of interpretation really does justice to the radical proportions of the binding of Satan" (G. C. Berkouwer, *The Return of Christ: Studies in Dogmatics* [Grand Rapids: Eerdmans Publishing, 1972], 305).

The difficulty that this presents for amillennialism is obvious: If the binding of Satan is not a present reality, the thousand years of Revelation 20 must represent a future reign of Christ which will take place between the present age and the eternal state. This intermediate phase of the coming kingdom is a key component in the eschatology of premillennialism, but it presents a significant problem for the two-age model of amillennnialism.

The Amillennial View

Amillennialist Kim Riddlebarger recognizes the challenge that Revelation 20:1–3 presents for his eschatology, conceding that this passage initially appears to be a formidable objection to the amillennial view. But according to Riddlebarger, "once we look closely at what John actually taught about the binding of Satan, the notion of Satan being bound in the present age becomes an argument in favor of the amillennial position."[8]

According to amillennialism, the binding of Satan in Revelation 20:1–3 took place at the first coming of Christ, and his imprisonment in the abyss extends throughout the present age, concurrent with the millennial reign of Jesus.[9] Rather than describing a future event that will occur at the Second Coming, then, Satan's binding was accomplished by Christ when He conquered the devil through His death and resurrection during His earthly ministry.[10] In this way, amillennialism asserts that the thousand-year binding of Satan extends from the time of the first coming of Christ to the time of His second coming and is therefore a present reality.

In contrast to the premillennial view that the incarceration of Satan renders him completely inactive on earth, amillennialism sees the binding

---

8   Riddlebarger, *A Case for Amillennialism*, 237.
9   Samuel E. Waldron, *The End Times Made Simple: How Could Everyone Be So Wrong About Biblical Prophecy?* (Amityville, NY: Calvary Press, 2003), 94–95; William Hendriksen, *More Than Conquerors: An Interpretation of the Book of Revelation* (Grand Rapids: Baker Books, 1967), 187–88.
10 Although most amillennialists emphasize that the binding of Satan was accomplished through the death and resurrection of Christ, others believe this binding began earlier when Jesus triumphed over Satan by resisting his temptations in the wilderness (Matt 4:1–11; Luke 4:1–13) (Donald Garlington, "Reigning with Christ: Revelation 20:1–6 and the Question of the Millennium," *RefR* 6, no. 2 [Spring 1997]: 91; Anthony Hoekema, *The Bible and the Future* [Grand Rapids: Eerdmans Publishing, 1979], 229; Floyd E. Hamilton, *The Basis of Millennial Faith* [Grand Rapids: Eerdmans Publishing, 1955], 130–31; Hendriksen, *More Than Conquerors*, 187).

of Satan in Revelation 20 as "a figurative description of the way in which Satan's activities will be curbed during the thousand-year period."[11] More specifically, amillennialists believe that this binding does not eliminate the activities of Satan on earth, but merely limits them to some extent. As Riddlebarger explains:

> What this binding of Satan means is that, after the coming of the long-expected Messiah, Satan lost certain authority that he possessed prior to the life, death, burial, resurrection, and ascension of the Savior. It does not mean that all satanic operations cease during the millennial age, as many opponents of amillennialism mistakenly assume.[12]

Amillennialists describe the restriction imposed upon Satan in Revelation 20 as the limiting,[13] the curbing,[14] the curtailing,[15] the relative curtailment,[16] the partial paralyzing,[17] and the restraining[18] of the devil's influence on earth, but again, not the *elimination* of it.[19] According to amillennialist William Cox, "Satan, though bound, still goes about like a roaring lion seeking whom he may devour. The chain with which he is bound is a long one, allowing him much freedom of movement."[20] As William Hendriksen illustrates, "A dog ... bound with a long and heavy

---

11 Hoekema, *The Bible and the Future*, 228; also see Sydney H. T. Page, "Revelation 20 and Pauline Eschatology," *JETS* 23, no. 1 (March 1980): 35.
12 Riddlebarger, *A Case for Amillennialism*, 237.
13 William E. Cox, *Amillennialism Today* (Phillipsburg, NJ: Presbyterian and Reformed Publishing, 1966), 59; Page, "Revelation 20 and Pauline Eschatology," 34; Hamilton, *The Basis of Millennial Faith*, 132.
14 Page, "Revelation 20 and Pauline Eschatology," 35; Hendriksen, *More Than Conquerors*, 190; Hoekema, *The Bible and the Future*, 228–29.
15 Hendriksen, *More Than Conquerors*, 188, 190; Sam Hamstra Jr., "An Idealist View of Revelation," in *Four Views on the Book of Revelation*, ed. C. Marvin Pate (Grand Rapids: Zondervan Publishing, 1998), 120; Hoekema, *The Bible and the Future*, 229; Storms, *Kingdom Come*, 440.
16 Jonathan Menn, *Biblical Eschatology* (Eugene, OR: Resource Publications, 2013), 290.
17 Hendriksen, *More Than Conquerors*, 190.
18 Page, "Revelation 20 and Pauline Eschatology," 34; Robert B. Strimple, "An Amillennial Response to Craig A. Blaising," in *Three Views on the Millennium and Beyond*, ed. Darrell L. Bock (Grand Rapids: Zondervan Publishing, 1999), 273; Leon Morris, *Revelation*, TNTC (Grand Rapids: Eerdmans Publishing, 1987), 229; Riddlebarger, *A Case for Amillennialism*, 237, 239.
19 Hamstra, "An Idealist View of Revelation," 120; Riddlebarger, *A Case for Amillennialism*, 239; Hendriksen, *More Than Conquerors*, 190.
20 Cox, *Amillennialism Today*, 139.

chain can do great damage within the circle of his imprisonment."[21]

According to amillennialists, then, Satan is indeed bound in the present age, but his binding is partial rather than absolute.[22] This view of Revelation 20:1–3 allows the amillennialist to affirm both the binding of Satan as a current reality and the present-day activity of Satan as described in the New Testament. To argue for this view—and against the interpretation of premillennialism—amillennialists typically point to three related aspects of the binding of Satan: the significance of the abyss, the purpose of the binding, and the parallels to Revelation 20:1–3 elsewhere in the New Testament.

The Significance of the Abyss

During the thousand years of Revelation 20:1–3, Satan is said to be bound and sealed specifically in the "abyss" (ἄβυσσος). When addressing the significance of the abyss in this vision, amillennialists typically emphasize the use of symbolism throughout the passage. For example, Dennis Johnson writes:

> The multiplication of visual features—key, chain, hand, dragon, throwing, locking, and sealing—underscores the symbolic genre of the entire vision, since John's audience knows well that Satan is not a literal dragon who can be bound with a physical chain or locked away in a physical pit.[23]

For this reason, amillennialists believe that the premillennial view of the abyss as a spatial location imposes "a rigidly wooden and artificial structure on symbolism that it simply isn't designed to sustain."[24] As G. K. Beale states, understanding the abyss as an actual *location* is to interpret it "in an overly literalistic manner."[25]

---

21 Hendriksen, *More Than Conquerors*, 190.
22 Strimple, "Amillennialism," 123.
23 Dennis E. Johnson, *Triumph of the Lamb: A Commentary on Revelation* (Phillipsburg, NJ: Presbyterian and Reformed Publishing, 2001), 283.
24 Storms, *Kingdom Come*, 445.
25 G. K. Beale, *The Book of Revelation*, NIGTC (Grand Rapids: Eerdmans Publishing, 1999), 987. Storms also rejects the idea of "a localized geo-spatial place called the abyss" (*Kingdom Come*, 442), and according to Menn, the abyss in Revelation 20 is "not spatial" but rather functions as a metaphor (*Biblical Eschatology*, 18).

Accordingly, Storms argues that "if the premillennialist insists on saying that Satan's being cast into the abyss in Revelation 20 must be interpreted in a literal, spatial way," he must also affirm the following in order to be consistent: (a) the angel was physically holding a literal key that could literally lock and unlock the pit; (b) the angel was holding a literal chain with material links that could be measured; (c) the angel literally grabbed the devil and wrestled him into submission and threw him into this pit; and (d) Satan was a literal, physical serpent as he is called in verse 2.[26] In a similar way, amillennialist Jonathan Menn insists that consistency requires the premillennialist to affirm that the abyss in Revelation 20 "is an actual pit in the earth which has a physical lock and physical 'seal.'"[27]

In contrast to the literal interpretation of premillennialism, Beale says the abyss should be understood as representing a spiritual dimension which exists alongside—and in the midst of—the earthly dimension.[28] In this way, Beale sees the abyss in Revelation 20:1–3 as "one of the various metaphors representing the spiritual sphere in which the devil and his accomplices operate."[29] For this reason, he rejects the idea that the abyss is spatially removed from the earth[30] and that Satan's confinement in the abyss requires a complete abolition of his activity on earth.[31] This view

---

26 Storms, *Kingdom Come*, 442–43.
27 Menn, *Biblical Eschatology*, 18, 357.
28 Beale, *The Book of Revelation*, 987. According to Beale, "The abyss and the physical world are two different dimensions interpenetrating each other or existing alongside one another" (990); elsewhere he refers to the abyss as "the realm of demons over which Satan rules" (493). In a similar way, Venema refers to the abyss as "the dwelling place of the demons" (Cornelis P. Venema, *The Promise of the Future* [Carlisle, PA: Banner of Truth, 2000], 316), and Storms calls it "the abode of demons" (*Kingdom Come*, 429) and "the source or abode of those demonic powers that are opposed to God" (478). But none of them emphasize the fact that the abyss is a "prison" (Rev 20:7). Other amillennialists are even less precise in their explanation of the abyss. For example, Hoekema says the abyss should "be thought of as a figurative description of the way in which Satan's activities will be curbed during the thousand-year period" (*The Bible and the Future*, 228), but this explanation communicates the effect of confinement in the abyss without defining what the abyss actually is.
29 Beale, *The Book of Revelation*, 987. This same definition of the abyss is quoted and affirmed by Riddlebarger (*A Case for Amillennialism*, 237) and Menn (*Biblical Eschatology*, 357). In addition, Beale also identifies the abyss as "probably" a synonym for "death and Hades" (*The Book of Revelation*, 984, 987; also see Riddlebarger, *A Case for Amillennialism*, 237).
30 Beale, *The Book of Revelation*, 990.
31 Ibid., 985–90.

of the abyss enables the amillennialist to affirm that Satan prowls about like a roaring lion, engaged in the various activities ascribed to him in the New Testament, while simultaneously being confined to the abyss as described in Revelation 20.

The immediate problem with this argument concerns the false alternative it establishes between a literal and figurative interpretation of the abyss. According to the amillennialist, the abyss must be understood as either (a) a literal reference to a physical, bottomless pit which extends endlessly into the depths of the earth, or (b) a symbolic metaphor signifying "the spiritual sphere in which the devil and his accomplices operate."[32] But this ignores the possibility that the abyss in Revelation 20 is a spirit prison for demonic beings, an actual location which imprisons them and prevents them from functioning outside of its confines. According to this third view, the abyss is neither a physical hole in the ground (the woodenly literal view) nor the spiritual sphere of demonic activity in general (the amillennial view), but rather *an actual location in the spiritual realm where evil spirits are confined and prevented from roaming free on earth*. A careful examination of ἄβυσσος indicates that this is indeed the meaning of this word in Revelation 20.

The noun ἄβυσσος was originally an adjective meaning "bottomless" or "unfathomable," and then a noun signifying a deep place.[33] In the Septuagint, it usually translates תְּהוֹם and most often refers to "the watery depths of the earth, whether oceans or springs, in contradistinction to the land" (e.g., Pss 77:16; 78:15; 106:9; Isa 55:10; Amos 7:4).[34] In the Jewish writings, ἄβυσσος predominantly referred to a prison where evil spirits were confined and punished (e.g., 1 En 10:4–16; 18:11–19:3; 21–22; 88:1–3; 90:24–27; 108:2–6; Jub 5:6–14; Tob 8:3; cf. Isa 24:20–23).[35] In the New

---

32 Beale, *The Book of Revelation*, 987.
33 W. L. Liefeld, "Abyss," in *The Zondervan Pictorial Encyclopedia of the Bible*, ed. Merrill C. Tenney (Grand Rapids: Zondervan Publishing, 1976), 1:30; also see *BDAG*, 2; Joachim Jeremias, "ἄβυσσος," in *TDNT*, ed. Gerhard Kittel (Grand Rapids: Eerdmans Publishing, 1964), 1:9; Hans Bietenhard, "ἄβυσσος," in *NIDNTT*, ed. Colin Brown (Grand Rapids: Zondervan Publishing, 1986), 2:205.
34 Walter A. Elwell, "Abyss," in *Baker Theological Dictionary of the Bible*, ed. Walter A. Elwell (Grand Rapids: Baker Books, 1996), 9.
35 Otto, Böcher, "ἄβυσσος," in *EDNT*, eds. Horst Balz and Gerhard Schneider (Grand Rapids: Eerdmans Publishing), 1:4; Bietenhard, "ἄβυσσος," 2:205; Beale, *The Book of Revelation*, 989–90; Elwell, "Abyss," 9; William J. Webb, "Revelation 20: Exegetical Considerations," *The Baptist Review of Theology* 4, no. 2 (Fall 1994): 20. Beale acknowledges that whenever

Testament, ἄβυσσος is used only nine times and has two basic usages, referring either to (a) the realm of the dead (Rom 10:7), or (b) a prison for evil spirits (Luke 8:31; Rev 9:1–2, 11; 11:7; 17:8).[36] Its use in Revelation 20 conveys this second nuance of meaning—a prison for evil spirits—which is clear from (1) the description of Satan being thrown into the abyss and having it "sealed" (ἐσφράγισεν) over him in verse 3, and (2) the description of Satan being released from his "prison" (φυλακή) in verse 7. Put very simply, the abyss of Revelation 20 is a spirit prison.

The use of ἄβυσσος in Luke 8 and Revelation 9 demonstrates that confinement to this spirit prison entails the complete removal of demonic/satanic activity and influence upon the earth. In Luke 8, Jesus encountered a demon-possessed man and began conversing with the evil spirits indwelling him (vv. 26–30). These demons understood full well that Jesus was "Son of the Most High God" (v. 28), and recognizing His authority over them, they began "imploring Him not to command them to go away into the abyss" (v. 31). Instead, they asked if Jesus would permit them to enter a nearby herd of swine (v. 32)—which He did—and they proceeded to enter the swine and drive them into the lake where the herd drowned (v. 33).

This remarkable episode in Luke 8 reveals several significant truths about the abyss. First, the abyss in Luke 8:31 must be a specific spirit prison which was well-known to both Jesus and the demons. This is clear not merely from the articular use of ἄβυσσος,[37] but primarily from the

---

evil spirits are imprisoned in the abyss in the Jewish writings, they are always confined "in a complete way without any exception" (*The Book of Revelation*, 989). According to Beale, however, this does not necessitate that the same reality is depicted in Rev 20:1–3 because these Jewish writings refer to demons (rather than Satan) being imprisoned in the abyss (989–90). But it is difficult to understand why Beale would conclude that Satan is able to depart from the abyss if other demonic beings are not, especially in light of John's description in Rev 20:3 that the abyss is sealed over him. Beale also makes the point that "the only apparently explicit Jewish references to the binding of Satan speak of a 'binding' that is not absolute" (989). But this fails to support the amillennial view, because it is Satan's incarceration specifically in the *abyss*—not his binding *per se*—which securely eliminates his activity on earth during the thousand years of Revelation 20.

36 Jeremias, "ἄβυσσος," 1:10; Elwell, "Abyss," 9.
37 The noun ἄβυσσος is articular every time it is used in the New Testament to refer to a spirit prison (Luke 8:31; Rev 9:1, 2, 11; 11:7; 17:8, 20:1, 3). In each case, it is most likely the "celebrity" or "familiar" use of the article "to point out an object that is well known" (Daniel B. Wallace, *Greek Grammar Beyond the Basics: An Exegetical Syntax of the New Testament* [Grand Rapids: Zondervan Publishing, 1996], 225).

way the demons immediately refer to the abyss as a possible destination now that Jesus has commanded them to depart from their human victim. Here in Luke 8:31, the abyss is not some nebulous metaphor in an apocalyptic vision filled with symbolism—it is a technical term used in narrative literature to refer to a specific prison for evil spirits which was familiar to both Jesus and the demons.

Second, the spirit prison in Luke 8:31 must refer to an actual *location*. This can be seen in the way that Luke's narrative sets the abyss alongside of the herd of swine as two possible destinations for the demons. Satan and demons are spiritual beings, but they are not omnipresent—they exist and function in a specific location at any given time. When Jesus first approached the demon-possessed man, these demons resided *inside* of this man (v. 27). But once they "came *out of* [ἐξελθεῖν ἀπὸ] the man" (v. 29), two locations for their new place of residence were now possible—either they could "go away *into* [εἰς ... ἀπελθεῖν] the abyss" (v. 31), or they could "enter *into* [εἰς ... εἰσελθεῖν] the swine" (v. 32). In response to the permission of Jesus, these demons "entered *into* [εἰσῆλθον εἰς] the swine" (v. 33). The use of proper and improper spatial prepositions throughout this narrative—εἰς, ἀπὸ, and ἐκ—highlights the possible and actual movements of the demons into (or out of) specific places and therefore makes it clear that the abyss should be understood as a location.

Third, the narrative in Luke 8 indicates that confinement in the abyss involves the complete removal of demonic activity and influence upon the earth. This can be seen in the request of the demons in verse 31. The reason for the demons' request was not because of their determination to kill the swine. The reason for their request was because imprisonment in the abyss would have cut them off from having any influence in this world—at least as long as they were *in* the abyss—whereas a departure into the swine would allow them to continue to roam free and wreak havoc on the earth.[38] This indicates that either these evil spirits could be imprisoned in the abyss or they could be prowling about the earth—engaged in demonic activities—but they could not be both.[39]

---

38 If the demons' earlier request that Jesus not "torment" them (v. 28) overlaps with their request not to be sent into the abyss (v. 31), this may imply that this spirit prison is also a place of torment and therefore that avoiding its torment was an additional reason for their request.
39 In discussing the incarceration of Satan in Revelation 20, most amillennialists do not even

The various uses of ἄβυσσος in the book of Revelation leads to a similar conclusion. For example, in John's vision in Revelation 9:1–6, a multitude of demons—pictured as a swarm of "locusts"—must first be released from the abyss before it is able to cause harm on the earth. The apostle writes:

> Then the fifth angel sounded, and I saw a star from heaven which had fallen to the earth; and the key of the bottomless pit [τῆς ἀβύσσου] was given to him. He opened the bottomless pit [τῆς ἀβύσσου], and smoke went up out of the pit, like the smoke of a great furnace; and the sun and the air were darkened by the smoke of the pit. Then out of the smoke came locusts upon the earth, and power was given them, as the scorpions of the earth have power. They were told not to hurt the grass of the earth, nor any green thing, nor any tree, but only the men who do not have the seal of God on their foreheads. And they were not permitted to kill anyone, but to torment for five months; and their torment was like the torment of a scorpion when it stings a man. And in those days men will seek death and will not find it; they will long to die, and death flees from them (Rev 9:1–6).

As Craig Blaising observes, the harm caused by these demonic locusts in this vision occurs only after the abyss is opened and they are released from its confines.[40] According to Blaising:

> The necessary implication is that their influence is not experienced by anyone as long as they are locked up in the pit. The graphic language about the key, opening the pit, subsequent instructions about harming, and coming on the earth (*eis tēn gēn*, v. 3) ... all converges to make the point that these "locusts" had no influence on earthly inhabitants prior to the time of their release.[41]

---

mention—much less comment on—the implications of Luke 8:31 for an accurate understanding of the abyss (e.g., Riddlebarger, *A Case for Amillennialism*; Venema, *The Promise of the Future*; Hoekema, *The Bible and the Future*; Storms, *Kingdom Come*).

40 Craig A. Blaising, "Premillennialism," in *Three Views on the Millennium and Beyond*, 217–18.
41 Ibid., 218. According to Blaising, "This does not mean that evil was non-existent, but that these locusts themselves played no role prior to their release."

According to Revelation 9, therefore, confinement of demons in the abyss entails the complete removal of activity and influence upon the earth.[42]

The abyss, then, refers to an actual location in the spiritual realm where evil spirits are confined and prevented from roaming free on earth. As Charles Powell observes:

> In every reference to the abyss the being or beings in it must emerge from it in order to interact with humans. This suggests that the sphere of the abyss, like the realm of the dead, is separate from the realm of living humanity, and that those who dwell in the abyss have no contact with those outside that sphere.[43]

This understanding of confinement in the abyss fits perfectly with John's description of Satan's imprisonment and release in Revelation 20. Not only is Satan thrown "into the abyss" (εἰς τὴν ἄβυσσον)—which is then "shut" (ἔκλεισεν) and "sealed over him" (ἐσφράγισεν ἐπάνω αὐτοῦ)—but he must first be "released from [λυθήσεται ... ἐκ] his prison" (v. 7) before he can "come out [ἐξελεύσεται] to deceive the nations which are in the four corners of the earth" (v. 8). But as long as he is confined in the abyss, the devil is not able to depart from his prison and therefore his activity on earth is completely non-existent.[44]

---

42 Webb, "Revelation 20," 20–21. In a similar way, in Rev 11:7 the satanically inspired beast must first "come up out of the abyss" (τὸ ἀναβαῖνον ἐκ τῆς ἀβύσσου) before he is able to make war with the two witnesses on earth (cf., Rev 17:8, where the beast "is about to come up out of the abyss [ἀναβαίνειν ἐκ τῆς αβύσσου] and go to destruction"). As Webb explains, the designation "those who dwell on the earth" (τοὺς κατοικοῦντας ἐπὶ τῆς γῆς) is a key phrase for understanding the cosmology of Revelation (3:10; 6:10; 8:13; 11:10; 13:8, 14; 17:2, 8): "The whole point of locking someone (an angel or the Devil) in the abyss ... is so that they cannot bring any harm against those who dwell on the earth. The abyss is not simply a metaphorical 'reduction in influence' as amillennialists suggest. Thus an amillennial perspective breaks down when the abyss is considered more broadly throughout the book of Revelation. Also, confinement in the abyss stands in direct contrast to the outcome of Satan being thrown out of heaven to the earth. [John] declares Satan's arrival upon the earth as one of the three great 'woes' to its inhabitants: 'woe, woe, woe, to those who dwell on the earth (τοὺς κατοικοῦντας ἐπὶ τῆς γῆς)' (8:13; cf. 12:12–13). Within Revelation, demonic confinement in the abyss brings safety to the earthdwellers. In contrast, demonic beings thrown down to the earth (from heaven) or released to go up to the earth (from the abyss) brings harm to the earthdwellers" ("Revelation 20," 20–21).

43 Charles E. Powell, "Progression Versus Recapitulation in Revelation 20:1–6," *BSac* 163, no. 649 (Jan 2006): 99.

44 Some amillennialists dispute the absolute nature of Satan's confinement by appealing to Jude 6. According to this argument, in the same way that demons are still actively involved on earth even though they are "kept in eternal bonds under darkness for the judgment of

In contrast, the amillennial view that the abyss is a metaphor representing "the spiritual sphere in which the devil and his accomplices operate"[45] is essentially nonsensical when assumed in the various passages where ἄβυσσος is used. For example, what sense does it make for the demons in Luke 8:31 to plead with Jesus not to cast them into the spiritual sphere where they normally function? Weren't they already there prior to their encounter with Jesus? If the abyss is the spiritual realm in which demons operate, how is being confined in the abyss any different from indwelling the demon-possessed man or the herd of swine?

In Revelation 20, how can Satan be seized and thrown into the spiritual realm in which he normally functions (v. 3)? Wasn't he already there prior to being seized? This would be similar to seizing a dangerous shark in the Pacific Ocean and locking it in a "prison," only to then define that prison as the entirety of the Pacific Ocean. Furthermore, what does it mean that Satan is "sealed" in this realm (v. 3), and what does it mean that he is "released" from it (v. 7)? How can Satan be either sealed in or released from the realm in which he usually operates?

By equating the abyss with the spiritual sphere of Satan's activity, the amillennial definition of ἄβυσσος completely removes the idea of a

---

the great day" according to Jude 6 (cf. 2 Pet 2:4), so Satan is simultaneously bound in the abyss (Rev 20:1-3) and yet still very active on earth (Beale, *The Book of Revelation*, 990; Stanely J. Grenz, *The Millennial Maze: Sorting Out Evangelical Options* [Downers Grove, IL: InterVarsity Press, 1992], 162; Strimple, "Amillennialism," 124). As Stanley Grenz writes, "Just as the demons in chains are not totally powerless, but restricted in activity, so also the binding of Satan entails restriction rather than total incapacitation" (*The Millennial Maze*, 162). The premillennial response to this argument depends on the identity of the fallen angels in Jude 6. Some interpreters see these demons as the "sons of God" in Gen 6:2 who "took wives for themselves" and were therefore imprisoned by God as described in Jude 6. If so, this presents no support for the amillennial argument, because Jude 6 would simply be saying that only *some* of the fallen angels are in eternal bonds, not all of them, and therefore demonic activity in the present age could simply be attributed to those fallen angels who are not confined. Other interpreters see Jude 6 as a reference to the original fall of the angels who defected with Satan. If this view is correct, then Jude 6 cannot refer to confinement in the *abyss*, because the confinement of Jude 6 is *permanent* ("kept in eternal bonds under darkness for the judgment of the great day"), which would imply that every demon is permanently confined in the abyss until the final judgment. But Luke 8:31 and Rev 9:13 make it clear that not all demons are permanently confined to the abyss. Jude 6 and 2 Pet 2:4, therefore, present no support for this amillennial argument.

45 Beale, *The Book of Revelation*, 987; cf. Riddlebarger, *A Case for Amillennialism*, 237; Menn, *Biblical Eschatology*, 357.

spirit prison, in spite of the abyss being "sealed" (ἐσφράγισεν) over Satan in verse 3 and being designated his "prison" (φυλακή) in verse 7.⁴⁶ The amillennial understanding of the abyss is based on neither the consistent use of the word in the New Testament nor the immediate context of its use in Revelation 20:1–3. Rather than allowing for the kind of freedom that the amillennialist claims, imprisonment in the abyss eliminates the activity of the devil on earth and therefore the binding of Satan in Revelation 20 cannot be a present reality.⁴⁷

The Purpose of the Binding

One of the primary arguments for the amillennial view focuses on the purpose of Satan's binding in Revelation 20. In contrast to the premillennial view that this binding prevents Satan from engaging in any earthly activity whatsoever, amillennialists often point to the purpose clause in Revelation 20:3, which is said to indicate that the devil is bound in one respect

---

46 The amillennial reluctance to see the abyss as a prison is reflected not only in Beale's description of "prison" in verse 7 as "a figurative word," but also in his explanation of the seal in Rev 20:3. According to Beale, rather than connoting an absolute incarceration, the sealing of the abyss could just as easily convey the general idea of "authority over," in keeping with its primary meaning in Dan 6:17 and Matt 27:66 (*The Book of Revelation*, 985–86). But in contrast to Beale's claim, the act of sealing in these two verses was indeed designed to ensure absolute incarceration, namely by making sure that Daniel did not escape the lion's den (Dan 6:17) and that Jesus' body did not leave the tomb (Matt 27:66). As Grant Osborne writes, "This intensifies the idea of 'locking' the abyss and connotes an absolutely secure situation, guaranteed by sovereign authority. Satan is completely bound in the abyss and cannot escape" (Grant R. Osborne, *Revelation*, ECNT [Grand Rapids: Baker Academic, 2002], 701).

47 In arguing that Satan's present-day activities are compatible with his present-day imprisonment in Revelation 20, Hendriksen uses the analogy that a dog "bound with a long and heavy chain can do great damage within the circle of his imprisonment" (*More Than Conquerors*, 190; cf. Hamstra, "An Idealist View of Revelation," 120). What this illustration seems to ignore is that Satan's "circle of imprisonment" is identified in verse 3 as the *abyss*. If Satan is free to roam and do damage *only in the abyss*, then he is indeed cut off from activity on the earth. In a similar way, William Cox affirms that Satan still prowls about like a roaring lion, seeking whom he may devour, because "the chain with which he is bound is a long one, allowing him much freedom of movement" (*Amillennialism Today*, 139). And Oscar Cullman describes Satan as being "bound as to a rope, which can be more or less lengthened" (Oscar Cullman, *Christ and Time: The Primitive Christian Conception of Time and History*, trans. Floyd V. Filson [Philadelphia: The Westminster Press, 1949], 198). But rather than seeing the chain as the means by which Satan is bound (i.e., tied up), Cox and Cullman write as if the imagery were one of Satan on a leash. The length of the chain is not only unstated but irrelevant, for the imagery is one of Satan being *bound* by it and then locked and sealed in an escape-proof prison. Where in the language of Rev 20:1–3 is there any indication that Satan has "much freedom of movement"?

and one respect only: "so that [ἵνα] he should not deceive the nations any longer" (3b).[48] In the words of amillennialist William Hendriksen, "The devil can do much, indeed, during this present period of one thousand years. But there is one thing which, during this period, he cannot do. With respect to this one thing he is definitely and securely bound."[49]

For this reason, because the binding of Satan only prevents him from deceiving the nations, amillennialists believe that he is still free to prowl about the earth like a roaring lion (1 Pet 5:8), partaking in the other activities attributed to him in the New Testament.[50] As Riddlebarger explains:

> The point of John's vision was that the angel restrains Satan's evil activities. His binding does not eliminate them. Even though Satan is presently bound and cannot deceive the nations, he remains a dangerous foe, the same way in which a mortally wounded animal is far more dangerous than a healthy one.[51]

According to the amillennial view, then, the binding of Satan is a present reality which consists of a *partial* restriction of his earthly influence, leaving him free to engage in the various activities ascribed to him throughout the New Testament. Satan's activity in the present age is *limited*, but not eliminated.

The initial problem with this argument is that it mistakenly assumes that the purpose clause in verse 3 limits the degree of Satan's confinement.[52] The purpose clause can only state why the action of imprisonment is taken, not the degree of restriction portrayed, which must be discerned instead from the immediate context.[53] To illustrate, if the warden of a

---

48 Storms, *Kingdom Come*, 439–41; Cox, *Amillennialism Today*, 62; Strimple, "Amillennialism," 123; Morris, *Revelation*, 229; Hendriksen, *More Than Conquerors*, 190; James A. Hughes, "Revelation 20:4–6 and the Question of the Millennium," *WTJ* 35, no. 3 (Spring 1973): 281; Hamilton, *The Basis of Millennial Faith*, 132; Beale, *The Book of Revelation*, 985; Venema, *The Promise of the Future*, 318–19.
49 Hendriksen, *More Than Conquerors*, 190; also see Venema, *The Promise of the Future*, 319.
50 Storms, *Kingdom Come*, 439. According to Storms, "The premillennial interpretation errs in that it has attempted to universalize what John explicitly restricts."
51 Riddlebarger, *A Case for Amillennialism*, 239. The irony here is that Riddlebarger seems to imply that Satan is more dangerous while sealed in the abyss than when he is not.
52 Powell, "Progression Versus Recapitulation," 98.
53 Ibid. In addition, the use of a purpose clause does not preclude the possibility that the stated action was taken with additional purposes in mind, even though those purposes are not specifically stated in the passage itself. For example, most amillennialists link the binding

prison puts a prisoner in solitary confinement for the primary purpose of preventing him from killing other prisoners, this does not mean that he is then free to steal from them and do other such activities. After all, the location of solitary confinement completely removes him from the rest of the prison and cuts him off entirely from the other prisoners. In the same way, the degree of Satan's restriction in Revelation 20 is determined not by the purpose clause alone, but also by the location of his imprisonment, the abyss, which removes the devil from earth and cuts him off from any influence there.[54]

A second problem with this argument is that the New Testament teaches that Satan *is* in fact deceiving the nations during the present age. Therefore, even if the amillennialist were correct in his assertion that Satan is only prevented from deceiving the nations during the thousand years—remaining active on earth in every other way—the fact that he is currently engaged in such deception indicates that the millennium cannot be a present reality. This can be seen in a number of New Testament passages.

In 2 Corinthians 4:3–4, as Paul describes his apostolic ministry, he writes that "if our gospel is veiled, it is veiled to those who are perishing, in whose case the god of this world has blinded the minds of the unbelieving so that they might not see the light of the gospel of the glory of Christ, who is the image of God." According to this passage, the truth of the gospel is concealed from unbelievers because the deceptive influence of Satan has blinded their minds from understanding and embracing it.[55] In a similar way, 2 Timothy 2:26 describes unbelievers as being caught in the snare of the devil, having been deceived and held captive by Satan to do his will.[56] In addition, 1 John 5:19 highlights Satan's deceptive influ-

---

of Satan with Christ's victory over Satan at the cross (Col 2:15; Heb 2:14–15; 1 John 3:8), and yet none of them would argue that the only purpose of Christ's work of redemption was to keep Satan from deceiving the nations during the thousand years.

54 This illustration is taken from Powell, "Progression Versus Recapitulation," 98.
55 The verb τυφλόω ("has blinded") means "to blind" or "to deprive of sight" (*BDAG*, 1021), and here in 2 Cor 4:4 it refers to spiritual blindness, just as in its other two uses in the New Testament (John 12:40; 1 John 2:11).
56 Cf. Matt 13:19; 1 Tim 4:1–2. Paul says in 2 Tim 2:26 that these unbelievers are in need of repentance leading to knowledge of the truth so they can come to their senses and escape this deceptive satanic snare. As Fee observes, this metaphor "emphasizes the deceitful nature of the false teaching, which here … is depicted as ultimately demonic" (Gordon D. Fee, *1 and 2 Timothy, Titus*, NIBC [Peabody, MA: Hendrickson Publishers, 1988], 266; also see George W. Knight, *The Pastoral Epistles: A Commentary on the Greek Text*, NIGTC

ence in the hearts of unbelievers by stating that "the whole world lies in the power of the evil one." As Jeffrey Townsend writes, "The New Testament makes it clear that Satan is now very much involved in the deception of the nations, for what is the deception of the nations if it is not the deception of individuals who make up the nations?"[57]

Furthermore, the book of Revelation teaches that Satan and his demons will continue to "deceive" (πλανάω) the nations right up until the time when Jesus returns to establish His kingdom and Satan is cast into the abyss (Rev 12:9; 13:14; 18:23; 19:20).[58] Amillennialists have a particularly difficult time explaining how Satan can be described as the one "who deceives the whole world" in Revelation 12:9 while simultaneously being sealed in the abyss "so that he would not deceive the nations any longer" (Rev 20:3). How can Satan deceive the whole world (Rev 12:9) and yet be unable to deceive the nations of the world (Rev 20:3) at the same time? If Satan is prevented from deceiving the nations during the millennium, and yet he is currently deceiving the nations—and will continue to do so until the Second Coming—the thousand years of Revelation 20 cannot be equated with the present age.

Some amillennialists respond to this difficulty by insisting that Satan's inability to deceive during the thousand years is merely a matter of *degree*. According to Hendriksen, "If during the present N.T. era the devil 'blinds the minds of unbelievers,' II Cor. 4:4, that was true even *more emphatically* during the old dispensation."[59] But the purpose clause in Revelation 20:3 teaches not that Satan will deceive the nations *less emphatically* than he previously did, but that he will deceive the nations *no longer* (μὴ πλανήσῃ ἔτι). In other words, Satan's ability to deceive is not limited during the thousand years, but rather eliminated.

[Grand Rapids: Eerdmans Publishing, 1992], 425–26; William D. Mounce, *Pastoral Epistles*, WBC vol. 46 [Nashville: Thomas Nelson Publishers, 2000], 537–39).

57 Jeffrey L. Townsend, "Is the Present Age the Millennium?," *BSac* 140, no. 559 (July 1983): 217.

58 The difficulty presented by these verses from Revelation is not alleviated by the amillennial view that they describe the present age (rather than the seven-year tribulation period, as some premillennialists believe), for this would mean that Satan is actively deceiving the nations throughout the present age, the very thing the amillennialist denies according to his interpretation of Rev 20:1–3.

59 Hendriksen, *More Than Conquerors*, 186–87; emphasis added. Also see Venema, *The Promise of the Future*, 319, and Storms, *Kingdom Come*, 440.

Other amillennialists respond to this difficulty by insisting that the binding of Satan does not prevent him from engaging in any kind of deception whatsoever, but rather from deceiving the nations in two specific ways. According to this argument, the purpose clause in Revelation 20:3 means that the binding of Satan specifically precludes him from (a) deceiving the nations to gather them for an all-out assault against the people of God,[60] and (b) preventing the spread of the gospel to the nations of the world.[61]

In support of the first assertion—that Satan is restrained from gathering the nations for an all-out assault against the church—amillennialists point to the connection between verse 3 and verses 7–8.[62] In verse 3, Satan is bound so that he would not deceive the nations until after the thousand years. In verses 7–8, after the thousand years are completed, Satan comes out of the abyss to deceive the nations and thereby gather them to wage war on the people of God. If Satan's release results in an all-out effort to destroy the church, say amillennialists, this reveals something about the kind of deception he is prevented from engaging in during the thousand years—it is not simply deception *per se*, but rather "deceiving the nations in such a way as to gather them together for an all-out assault against God's saints."[63] As Storms writes:

> Although Satan may and will do much in this present age (as the New Testament epistles clearly indicate), there is one thing of which John assures us: *Satan will never be permitted to incite*

---

60 Strimple, "An Amillennial Response," 273; Hendriksen, *More Than Conquerors*, 188–90; Morris, *Revelation*, 279; Hoekema, *The Bible and the Future*, 228–29; Riddlebarger, *A Case for Amillennialism*, 238; Garlington, "Reigning with Christ," 72; Storms, *Kingdom Come*, 439–40; Beale, *The Book of Revelation*, 988; Menn, *Biblical Eschatology*, 290.

61 Garlington, "Reigning with Christ," 72; Cox, *Amillennialism Today*, 62; Hoekema, *The Bible and the Future*, 228–29; Hamstra, "An Idealist View of Revelation," 120; Hendriksen, *More Than Conquerors*, 188–90; Venema, *The Promise of the Future*, 319; Storms, *Kingdom Come*, 442; Beale, *The Book of Revelation*, 988–89; Hamilton, *The Basis of Millennial Faith*, 130; Davis, *The High King of Heaven*, 469; Menn, *Biblical Eschatology*, 290. As Anthony Hoekema summarizes, "The binding of Satan during the gospel age means that, first, he cannot prevent the spread of the gospel, and second, he cannot gather all the enemies of Christ together to attack the church" (*The Bible and the Future*, 228). For some amillennialists (a) and (b) are inextricably linked, for they say it is precisely *because* Satan is unable to destroy the church as a missionary institution that the gospel is now able to go forth to the nations (e.g., Garlington, "Reigning with Christ," 72; Hoekema, *The Bible and the Future*, 229).

62 Strimple, "An Amillennial Response," 273.

63 Ibid.

> and organize the unbelieving nations of the world in a final, catastrophic assault against the Church, until such time as God in his providence so determines.[64]

According to amillennialists, the restriction of Satan during the present age prevents him from inciting the nations to destroy the church as a missionary institution.[65]

In support of the second assertion—that Satan is restrained from preventing the spread of the gospel to the nations—amillennialists generally point to the broader landscape of redemptive history. According to this argument, the nations were left in darkness in the Old Testament era, but through His work of redemption, "Christ curtailed the forces of Satan and paved the way for the successful proclamation of the gospel throughout the world."[66] In this way,

> The binding of Satan described in Revelation 20:1–3 ... means that throughout the gospel age in which we now live the influence of Satan, though certainly not annihilated, is so curtailed that he cannot prevent the spread of the gospel to the nations of the world.[67]

As Strimple explains:

> The age of salvation for the Gentiles has arrived. Prior to Christ's ministry Israel was the one nation called out from all the nations of the world to know God's blessings and to serve him. There were exceptions, of course—those who came to know God's grace even though they were not of the children of Abraham after the flesh. But essentially all the nations on this earth were in darkness, under Satan's deception. But then, praise God! Christ came and accomplished his redemptive work.... The age of world missions had begun, and Satan's deceptive work on that grand scale over so many centuries had come to an end.[68]

---

64 Storms, *Kingdom Come*, 440; emphasis original.
65 Hendriksen, *More Than Conquerors*, 188.
66 Hamstra, "An Idealist View of Revelation," 120.
67 Hoekema, *The Bible and the Future*, 229.
68 Strimple, "Amillennialism," 123–24; also see Garlington, "Reigning with Christ," 72; Hamilton, *The Basis of Millennial Faith*, 131; Hoekema, *The Bible and the Future*, 228–29; Venema, *The Promise of the Future*, 318–19.

According to the amillennial view, then, even though Satan blinds the minds of unbelievers in the present age (2 Cor 4:4), he is unable to incite the unbelieving world to seek to destroy the church, and he is unable to prevent the spread of the gospel to the nations (Rev 20:1–3).[69]

The problem with the amillennial view of the nature of Satan's deception concerns the purpose clause in verse 3. When John says that Satan will be sealed in the abyss "so that he would not deceive the nations *any longer* [ἔτι]" (Rev 20:3), this indicates the interruption of something that is already taking place.[70] For this reason, the deception from which Satan is prevented in Revelation 20:1–3 is a deception that was already taking place prior to his incarceration in the abyss.[71] Therefore, when the amillennialist explains this deception as Satan inciting the nations into an all-out, catastrophic assault against the church, the question arises—when was this final catastrophic assault launched by Satan prior to the cross?[72] The amillennialist's inability to point to Satan leading the nations of the world in an all-out assault to destroy the people of God just prior to

---

69 Storms, *Kingdom Come*, 442; Hoekema, *The Bible and the Future*, 238; Vern S. Poythress, *The Returning King: A Guide to the Book of Revelation* (Phillipsburg, NJ: Presbyterian and Reformed Publishing, 2000), 181; R. Fowler White, "On the Hermeneutics and Interpretation of Rev 20:1–3: A Preconsummationist Perspective," *JETS* 42, no. 1 (March 1999): 65.
70 Richard A. Ostella, "The Significance of Deception in Revelation 20:3," *WTJ* 37, no. 2 (Winter 1975): 237–38. As Ostella explains, this is clear from John's temporal use of ἔτι with a negative particle (also see *BDAG*, 400).
71 It is a deception more directly identified with his deceptive activities prior to the thousand years than with what happens after his release (Ostella, "The Significance of Deception," 238). But amillennialists take just the opposite approach: To defend their understanding of this deception, they typically ignore the satanic deception which takes place prior to the thousand years and focus instead on the deception which takes place in Rev 20:7–8.
72 Sullivan, "Premillennialism and an Exegesis of Revelation 20," 21–22; accessed on July 20, 2014, http://www.pre-trib.org/data/pdf/Sullivan-PremillennialismAndA.pdf. As Sullivan asks, "If we say God prevented him from doing it then what is the difference between God's prevention of the final war of all times before the cross and the so-called binding during this age?" (21). Mathewson argues that even if the deception in Rev 20:1–3 is restricted to opposing the saints and mounting an all-out war (Rev 20:8)—as amillennialists claim—this would be no different from the deception referred to in Rev 12:9, which takes place prior to the Second Coming. According to Mathewson, "It is not clear that the deceiving in both cases is different; both have the express purpose of turning the nations from God to follow the dragon (see 13:2, 4, 7, 8, 14). The final deception of the nations in order to get them to follow the dragon ends, then, with an assault on the people of God (20:7–10). This is precisely the activity which is denied Satan for one thousand years in 20:1–3" (Dave Mathewson, "A Reexamination of the Millennium in Rev 20:1–6: Consummation and Recapitulation," *JETS* 44, no. 2 [June 2001]: 245).

the cross proves to be an insurmountable difficulty for this view.[73]

Equally problematic is the amillennial view that the binding of Satan simply restrains him from preventing the spread of the gospel to the nations. The weakness of this explanation is that the purpose clause in verse 3 concerns itself not with the freedom of the church to proclaim the Good News but with the inability of the nations to embrace it. Properly understood, satanic deception of the nations does not prevent believers from preaching the gospel to the world—satanic deception is something that takes place in the hearts of the unbelievers who make up those nations. Put another way, satanic deception does not close the mouths of believers; it deludes the hearts of unbelievers. There is no indication in Revelation 20:1–3 that the purpose of Satan's binding was to allow the gospel to go forth to Gentiles who had been previously deprived of the Good News.[74]

The New Testament Parallels

The most common amillennial argument for a present-day binding of Satan is found not in Revelation 20 itself but rather in other New Testament passages which are said to illuminate the meaning of John's vision (e.g., Matt 12:29, Luke 10:17–18, John 12:31–32, Col 2:15, Heb 2:14–15,

---

73 According to Powell, Beale (*The Book of Revelation*, 983–90) "seems to interpret the deception in terms of its degree of success and failure, not in terms of its attempt" ("Progression Versus Recapitulation," 106). As Powell explains: "While admitting that Satan will ultimately fail in his objective of destroying the covenant community of believers, nevertheless Beale views Satan as continuously attempting such a goal, and only at the end will he succeed in mounting a worldwide lethal attack. However, the imprisonment imagery shows that Satan will be *prevented* from even making an attempt at deceiving the nations, while the purpose clause makes it clear that he will not have *any* success, not simply limited success" (emphasis original).

74 An additional problem arises when one considers the question of whether Satan is currently able to keep the nations in darkness by preventing the spread of the gospel. Strimple and other amillennialists claim that Satan is no longer successful in this endeavor because he is bound during the present age (Strimple, "Amillennialism," 123–24), but the number of unreached people (and even nations) in the world would argue otherwise. In fact, as Powell explains, deception and persecution of the church have been widespread throughout the entirety of the present age: "Persecution was initiated under the reigns of Nero, Domitian, and Diocletian, the last of which was throughout the Roman Empire. The bastions of Christianity in Asia Minor and North Africa in the first six centuries have all been under Muslim control for the past several centuries. Three quarters of the earth's population are still Islamic, Buddhist, or Hindu. Communism in the twentieth century threatened to stamp out Christianity. All this suggests that in the present age Satan is 'deceiving the nations' and is having more success than failure" ("Progression Versus Recapitulation," 106–7).

1 John 3:8, and Rev 12:7–12).⁷⁵ According to amillennialists, "These passages provide the biblical context within which the vision of Revelation 20 becomes clear."⁷⁶ More specifically, these passages are said to prove that the binding of Satan occurred at the time of the first coming of Christ and therefore that the thousand years of Revelation 20 is a present reality.

In these passages, Satan is bound (Matt 12:29); he falls from heaven (Luke 10:17–18); he is cast out (John 12:31–32); he is disarmed and conquered (Col 2:15); he is rendered powerless (Heb 2:14–15); his works are destroyed (1 John 3:8); and he is thrown down from heaven to earth (Rev 12:7–11). According to amillennialists, these descriptions of the victory of Jesus over the devil in the first century are parallel to the binding of Satan in Revelation 20 and therefore indicate that this binding took place at the start of the present age. As Samuel Waldron writes, "The biblical evidence proves conclusively that any interpretation of [Revelation 20:1–3] that professes to interpret it in accord with the rest of Scripture must conclude that Satan was bound by the events of and at the time of Christ's first advent."⁷⁷

In making this argument, amillennialists appeal to the hermeneutical principle "that Scripture should interpret Scripture and that the more obscure passage should be interpreted in the light of the more clear passage."⁷⁸ In this case, amillennialists see Revelation 20:1–3 as the more obscure passage and Matthew 12:29, Luke 10:17–18, John 12:31–32, Colossians 2:15, Hebrews 2:14–15, 1 John 3:8, and Revelation 12:7–12 as those clearer passages which should be used to interpret the binding of Satan. The problem is that none of these supposed parallels actually refer to what is described in Revelation 20:1–3, and therefore this approach fails to bring clarity to the divinely intended meaning of John's vision.⁷⁹

---

75 Hendriksen, *More Than Conquerors*, 188; Hoekema, *The Bible and the Future*, 228; Venema, *The Promise of the Future*, 321–23; Waldron, *The End Times Made Simple*, 93; Davis, *The High King of Heaven*, 471; Cox, *Amillennialism Today*, 65, 107, 136–37; Hamstra, "An Idealist View of Revelation," 120.
76 Venema, *The Promise of the Future*, 321.
77 Waldron, *The End Times Made Simple*, 95.
78 Venema, *The Promise of the Future*, 323; also see Cox, *Amillennialism Today*, 65, 107, 136–37; Waldron, *The End Times Made Simple*, 93; Page, "Revelation 20 and Pauline Eschatology," 31–33.
79 For some amillennialists, consulting these cross-references actually becomes a substitute for exegeting Rev 20:1–3 itself, e.g., Cox, who writes: "Since [Rev 20] itself gives no explanation of John's meaning, its meaning must be garnered elsewhere in the Bible" (*Amillennialism Today*, 65).

Matthew 12:29

The New Testament parallel most often cited by amillennialists is Matthew 12:29. In this verse, Jesus explains to the Pharisees that His ability to cast out demons is dependent on His prior act of having bound Satan: "Or how can anyone enter the strong man's house and carry off his property, unless he first binds the strong man? And then he will plunder his house" (Matt 12:29). This verse is said to demonstrate that the binding of Satan in Revelation 20 was accomplished by Jesus during his first-century earthly ministry.[80] As many amillennialists note, the very same Greek verb "to bind" (δέω) is used with reference to Satan in both Matthew 12:29 and Revelation 20:3, strengthening the case that these passages describe the same action taken against the devil.[81]

The initial difficulty with this argument concerns the timing of this incident in the ministry of Christ. In Matthew 12:29, Jesus specifically says He is not able to exorcise the demon "unless he *first* [πρῶτον] binds the strong man." But most amillennialists believe that the binding of Satan in Revelation 20 took place through the death and resurrection of Christ. Herein lies the problem: If Jesus had not yet bound Satan through His death and resurrection (Matt 27–28), how was He able to cast out the demon in Matthew 12? The amillennial view that the binding of Satan in Revelation 20 was accomplished by the death and resurrection of Jesus precludes the possibility that this same binding is described in Matthew 12:29.[82]

---

80 Hamilton, *The Basis of Millennial Faith*, 129; Hoekema, *The Bible and the Future*, 228–29; Arthur H. Lewis, *The Dark Side of the Millennium: The Problem of Evil in Revelation 20:1–10* (Grand Rapids: Baker Books, 1993), 52; Cox, *Amillennialism Today*, 59–60; Anthony A. Hoekema, "Amillennialism," in *The Meaning of the Millennium: Four Views*, ed. Robert G. Clouse (Downers Grove, IL: InterVarsity Press, 1977), 162–63; Waldron, *The End Times Made Simple*, 94; Venema, *The Promise of the Future*, 321; Strimple, "Amillennialism," 122; Johnson, *Triumph of the Lamb*, 287; Beale, *The Book of Revelation*, 985; Poythress, *The Returning King*, 181; Garlington, "Reigning with Christ," 69–70; Hamstra, "An Idealist View of Revelation," 120; Davis, *The High King of Heaven*, 471; Menn, *Biblical Eschatology*, 288; Simon J. Kistemaker, *Exposition of the Book of Revelation*, NTC (Grand Rapids: Baker Books, 2001), 534.

81 Strimple, "Amillennialism," 122; Hoekema, *The Bible and the Future*, 229; Johnson, *Triumph of the Lamb*, 287; Venema, *The Promise of the Future*, 321; Menn, *Biblical Eschatology*, 288.

82 A few amillennialists avoid this dilemma by claiming that Christ's work of binding began earlier when the Lord triumphed over him by resisting his temptations in the wilderness back in Luke 4:1–13//Matt 4:1–11 (Garlington, "Reigning with Christ," 91; Hoekema, *The Bible and the Future*, 229; Hamilton, *The Basis of Millennial Faith*, 129; Hendriksen,

A second difficulty concerns the purpose of Satan's binding in Revelation 20. As previously discussed, amillennialists often point to the purpose clause in verse 3 as indicating that Satan is bound in one respect and one respect only: "so that he should not deceive the nations any longer" (Rev 20:3).[83] But in Matthew 12:29, the purpose of Satan's binding was to enable Jesus to heal the demon-possessed man. To the degree that amillennialists emphasize the purpose clause in Revelation 20:3 as stating the sole purpose of Satan's binding, they weaken their ability to equate that binding with the binding of the strong man in Matthew 12:29.

But the most significant problem with this argument is found in a simple comparison between the two passages. In Matthew 12:29, Jesus is continuing His response to accusations that He is casting out demons by the power Satan, and He does so with a parable. He has already shown that He is Satan's *enemy* (vv. 25–28), and now He explains that He is also Satan's *master*,[84] saying: "Or how can anyone enter the strong man's house and carry off his property, unless he first binds the strong man? And then he will plunder his house" (Matt 12:29). The point of this parable is that the very exorcism for which Jesus was condemned is a demonstration of His power and superiority over Satan. For how could Jesus have plundered the strong man's house—robbed Satan of his spiritual property by delivering the demoniac—unless He had first bound the strong man and rendered him powerless to prevent the exorcism?[85] According

---

More Than Conquerors, 187). But Luke 4 specifically indicates that Satan left the temptation scene defeated but unbound by describing the devil as departing from Jesus "until an opportune time" (Luke 4:13) (Townsend, "Is the Present Age the Millennium?," 217). In addition, there is no indication in Revelation 20 that the binding and incarceration of Satan is something that took place progressively, over the course of nearly two years.

83 Storms, *Kingdom Come*, 439–41; Cox, *Amillennialism Today*, 62; Strimple, "Amillennialism," 123; Morris, *Revelation*, 229; Hendriksen, *More Than Conquerors*, 190; Hughes, "Revelation 20:4–6 and the Question of the Millennium," 281; Hamilton, *The Basis of Millennial Faith*, 132; Beale, *The Book of Revelation*, 985; Venema, *The Promise of the Future*, 318–19.

84 Alexander Balmain Bruce, "The Synoptic Gospels," in *The Expositor's Greek Testament*, vol. 1, ed. W. Robertson Nicoll (Grand Rapids: Eerdmans Publishing, 1974), 188.

85 John A. Broadus, *Commentary on the Gospel of Matthew* (Philadelphia: American Baptist Publication Society, 1886), 270; Louis A. Barbieri, "Matthew," in *The Bible Knowledge Commentary*, eds. John F. Walvoord and Roy B. Zuck (Wheaton, IL: Victor Books, 1983), 46; Craig Blomberg, *Matthew*, NAC vol. 23 (Nashville: Broadman Press, 1992), 203. As Broadus writes, "Jesus was taking away from Satan a part of his property in delivering the demoniac, and this could not be unless he were at variance with Satan, and strong enough to bind him" (*Commentary on the Gospel of Matthew*, 270).

to Jesus, rather than casting out demons by Satan's power, He was demonstrating His own power over the devil when He performed exorcisms.[86]

In Matthew 12:29, then, the binding of Satan broke the power he had to possess specific individuals and thereby enabled Jesus to deliver those people from Satan's control. In contrast, the binding of Satan in Revelation 20 involved sealing him in the abyss and preventing him from deceiving the nations.[87] The two passages have more differences than similarities. In Matthew 12 Satan is bound in his own domain—his own "house," according to the parable—but in Revelation 20 he is removed from that domain and cast into the abyss.[88] The binding in Matthew 12 is a local reference to Satan's inability to control a single individual through demon possession,[89] but the binding in Revelation 20 is a universal reference to Satan's inability to deceive the nations of the world. As one amillennialist acknowledges:

> The binding of the strong man in the Synoptic Gospels ... bears no recognizable relationship to the thrust of the amillennial view. That thrust is that the binding of Satan applies only to his ability to deceive the nations. But where are the nations in the pericopes that refer to the binding of the strong man? They are not to be seen. What is very much in view is the local sufferers from demon possession and Satan's inability to prevent Jesus from healing them; what is not at all in view is the now blessedly undeceived nations.[90]

---

86 As Louis Barbieri writes, "By driving out demons, He was proving He was greater than Satan. He was able to go into Satan's realm (the strong man's house), the demonic world, and come away with the spoils of the victory (12:29). Since He could do this, He was able to institute the kingdom of God among them (v. 28). If He were driving out demons by Satan's power, He certainly could not be offering the people God's kingdom. That would be contradictory. The fact that He was coming to establish the kingdom clearly showed that He worked by the power of the Spirit of God, not by Satan's power" ("Matthew," 46).
87 George Eldon Ladd, "An Historic Premillennial Response," in *The Meaning of the Millennium*, 189.
88 Powell, "Progression Versus Recapitulation," 100.
89 As Robert Gromacki explains, the episode in Matthew 12 involved one demon being cast out of one person: "If Satan had been bound completely at that event, then all demon possessed individuals should have been delivered simultaneously. However, many remained demon possessed in the Gospel period, the time of apostolic ministry, and in our present day. Christ used that analogy to justify his miraculous action upon one man at one point of time" (Robert Gromacki, "Revelation 20: A Premillennial Analysis," 14; accessed on July 20, 2014, http://www.pre-trib.org/data/pdf/Gromacki-Revelation20APremille.pdf).
90 Harry R. Boer, "What About the Millennium?" *RefJ* 25, no. 1 (Jan 1975): 29.

The inability of Satan to prevent Jesus from delivering demoniacs (Matt 12:29) is simply not the same as his inability to deceive the nations of the world (Rev 20:1–3).[91] The two passages are not describing the same event, and therefore Matthew 12:29 provides no support for the amillennial view of the binding of Satan.

Luke 10:17–18

A second passage often cited by amillennialists is Luke 10:17–20, which describes the return of the missionaries sent out by Jesus:

> The seventy returned with joy, saying, "Lord, even the demons are subject to us in Your name." And He said to them, "I was watching Satan fall from heaven like lightning. Behold, I have given you authority to tread on serpents and scorpions, and over all the power of the enemy, and nothing will injure you. Nevertheless do not rejoice in this, that the spirits are subject to you, but rejoice that your names are recorded in heaven."

The key is verse 18, where Jesus says, "I was watching Satan fall from heaven like lightning." According to amillennialists, Satan's fall from heaven coincides with the binding of Satan in Revelation 20, and therefore Luke 10:18 provides evidence that Satan's binding took place in the first century.[92] To use this verse as an argument, however, the amillennialist must be able to prove not only that the fall of Satan in Luke 10:18 took place during the first-century ministry of Jesus, but also that it can be equated with the binding of Satan in Revelation 20.

Because of the ambiguity of Jesus's statement in Luke 10:18, commentators are divided on the timing and nature of Satan's fall. According to most interpreters, the fall of Satan refers to either (1) the original fall of

---

91 As Townsend writes, "When [Matt 12:29] is compared with the absolute terms used of Satan's imprisonment in the abyss, it becomes apparent that any restriction on Satan in the Gospels is not to be equated with his binding in Revelation" ("Is the Present Age the Millennium?," 217).

92 Riddlebarger, *A Case for Amillennialism*, 122; Hoekema, *The Bible and the Future*, 229; Lewis, *The Dark Side of the Millennium*, 52; Cox, *Amillennialism Today*, 61; Waldron, *The End Times Made Simple*, 94; Hoekema, "Amillennialism," 163; Venema, *The Promise of the Future*, 322; Hamstra, "An Idealist View of Revelation," 120; Beale, *The Book of Revelation*, 985; Hendriksen, *More Than Conquerors*, 187; Garlington, "Reigning with Christ," 70; Davis, *The High King of Heaven*, 471; Kistemaker, *Revelation*, 534.

Satan (Isa 14:12), (2) the defeat of Satan when Jesus resisted his temptations (Luke 4:1–13), (3) the defeat of Satan evidenced by the exorcism of demons (cf. Luke 11:17–23), or (4) the ultimate judgment of Satan in the future (Rev 20:10).[93] A fifth possibility combines views (3) and (4) and asserts that the victory of Jesus over the devil—as evidenced by demons being cast out in His name—served as a preview of the final judgment of Satan, ultimately pointing ahead to his eventual demise in the lake of fire (Rev 20:10).[94]

But regardless of which view is correct, Jesus simply does not define the fall of Satan clearly enough for the amillennialist to make his case. In fact, each of these five interpretations is consistent with the premillennial view and none of them requires the amillennial view. It is certainly possible to argue that the description of Satan in Luke 10:18 took place when Jesus spoke these words—that Satan fell from heaven when demons were cast out in the first century—but this does not demonstrate that the binding of Satan in Revelation 20 occurred at the same time.

To prove that it did, amillennialists point out that the fall of Satan in Luke 10 is associated with the missionary activity of the seventy.[95] For this reason, it is argued that the fall of Satan curtailed the devil's power and paved the way for the successful proclamation of the gospel throughout

---

93 For a survey of these views and others, see David E. Garland, *Luke*, ECNT, vol. 3 (Grand Rapids: Zondervan Publishing, 2011), 428–29; Darrell L. Bock, *Luke 9:51–24:53*, ECNT (Grand Rapids: Baker Academic, 1996), 1006–7; Alfred Plummer, *The Gospel According to S. Luke*, ICC (Edinburgh: T. & T. Clark, 1975), 277–78; Joel B. Green, *The Gospel of Luke*, NICNT (Grand Rapids: Eerdmans Publishing, 1997), 417–19; John Nolland, *Luke 9:21–18:34*, WBC, vol. 35B (Dallas: Word Books, 1993), 562–64; Norman Crawford, *Luke, What the Bible Teaches*, vol. 7 (Kilmarnock, Scotland: John Ritchie Ltd., 1989), 185–86; Leon Morris, *Luke*, TNTC, rev. ed. (Grand Rapids: Eerdmans Publishing, 1999), 202; William Hendriksen, *Exposition of the Gospel According to Luke*, NTC (Grand Rapids: Baker Books, 1978), 580–81; Robert H. Stein, *Luke*, NAC vol. 24 (Nashville: Broadman & Holman, 1992), 309–10.

94 This appears to be the most likely view. In this way, the success of the seventy was viewed by Jesus as "a symbol and earnest" of the complete and future overthrow of Satan (Plummer, *The Gospel According to S. Luke*, 278). As Green notes, "The decisive fall of Satan is anticipated in the future, but it is already becoming manifest through the mission of Jesus and, by extension, through the ministry of his envoys" (*The Gospel of Luke*, 419).

95 Hoekema, *The Bible and the Future*, 229; Waldron, *The End Times Made Simple*, 94; Venema, *The Promise of the Future*, 322; Hamstra, "An Idealist View of Revelation," 120; Hendriksen, *More Than Conquerors*, 187; Garlington, "Reigning with Christ," 70; Davis, *The High King of Heaven*, 471.

the world, just like the binding of Satan in Revelation 20.[96] Therefore, it is said, both actions must have occurred in the first century. As noted above, however, Revelation 20:3 does not say that the binding of Satan paved the way for the church to proclaim the gospel to the nations. Furthermore, the fall of Satan in Luke 10:18 is presented as evidence that the seventy were given authority to cast out demons, not that the church was now able to preach the Good News throughout the world. For this reason, even if the authority of Jesus over demons indicated that Satan was defeated in some way during the first century (Luke 10:18), this does not mean that Satan was sealed in the abyss, unable to deceive the nations (Rev 20:1–3).[97] In the absence of any clear parallels between the two passages, Luke 10:18 falls short as an argument that the binding of Satan in Revelation 20 is a present reality.[98]

John 12:31–32 / Colossians 2:15 / Hebrews 2:14–15 / 1 John 3:8

Several passages cited by amillennialists specifically refer to the victory that Jesus accomplished through His death and resurrection as He triumphed over Satan and redeemed from his control those who repent and believe in Christ:

- John 12:31–32: "Now judgment is upon this world; now the ruler of this world shall be cast out. And I, if I be lifted up from the earth, will draw all men to Myself."[99]

---

96 Hamstra, "An Idealist View of Revelation," 120.
97 According to Michael Vlach, the cosmic war between God and Satan includes several battles which progressively lead to the devil's ultimate defeat: (1) Satan is judged and cast down from heaven before the fall of man (Isa 14:12–15; Ezek 28:11–19); (2) Jesus demonstrates His power over Satan's realm by casting out demons (Matt 12:28); (3) Jesus is victorious over Satan at the cross (Col 2:15); (4) Satan is thrown down to the earth for a short time before the Second Coming (Rev 12); (5) Satan is sealed in the abyss for one thousand years at the Second Coming (Rev 20:1–3); and (6) Satan is thrown into the lake of fire forever after the millennial reign of Christ (Rev 20:7–10) (Michael J. Vlach, "The Kingdom of God and the Millennium," *MSJ* 23, no. 2 [Fall 2012]: 248–49). As Vlach explains, "These events above are separate but interrelated events in the cosmic war" (249).
98 In fact, unlike Matt 12:29—which at least refers to Satan being bound in some manner—there are no obvious similarities whatsoever between Luke 10:18 and Rev 20:1–3. Furthermore, Luke 10:18 presumably pictures Satan falling from heaven to *earth*, whereas Satan is sealed in the abyss in Rev 20:1–3 (Webb, "Revelation 20," 20).
99 Cited by Lewis, *The Dark Side of the Millennium*, 52; Hoekema, *The Bible and the Future*, 229; Cox, *Amillennialism Today*, 61; Hoekema, "Amillennialism," 163; Waldron, *The End Times Made Simple*, 94; Venema, *The Promise of the Future*, 322–23; Strimple,

- Colossians 2:15: "When He had disarmed the rulers and authorities, He made a public display of them, having triumphed over them through Him."[100]

- Hebrews 2:14–15: "Since then the children share in flesh and blood, He Himself likewise also partook of the same, that through death He might render powerless him who had the power of death, that is, the devil; and might deliver those who through fear of death were subject to slavery all their lives."[101]

- 1 John 3:8b: "The Son of God appeared for this purpose, that He might destroy the works of the devil."[102]

According to the amillennialist, these descriptions of the victory of Jesus over Satan are parallel to the binding of Satan in Revelation 20 and therefore locate the timing of that binding in the first-century ministry of Christ.

The main problem with this argument is its inability to account for the release of Satan in Revelation 20, for whatever is accomplished in

---

"Amillennialism," 122; Hamilton, *The Basis of Millennial Faith*, 132; Beale, *The Book of Revelation*, 985; Hendriksen, *More Than Conquerors*, 188; Poythress, *The Returning King*, 181; Garlington, "Reigning with Christ," 70; Davis, *The High King of Heaven*, 471–72; Menn, *Biblical Eschatology*, 288. In arguing for the connection between John 12:31–32 and Rev 20:1–3, amillennialists point out that the verb "cast out" (ἐκβάλλω) in John 12:31–32 is from the same root as the verb "threw" (βάλλω) in Rev 20:1–3 (Hoekema, *The Bible and the Future*, 229; Garlington, "Reigning with Christ," 70; Venema, *The Promise of the Future*, 323; Strimple, "Amillennialism," 122; Menn, *Biblical Eschatology*, 288). But the mere use of similar words is insufficient to equate the events described in these two passages. In addition, as used in their own contexts, the two words are less similar than amillennialists seem to imply. John 12:31 pictures Satan being "cast *out*" [ἐκβληθήσεται] in some way, whereas Rev 20:3 pictures him being "cast ... *into* [ἔβαλεν ... εἰς] the abyss." The difference between being "cast out" and "cast into" does not preclude the possibility that the two passages are describing the same event from different perspectives, but it should silence the claim that the equation can be made on the basis of the use of similar verbs.

100 Cited by Cox, *Amillennialism Today*, 61; Waldron, *The End Times Made Simple*, 95; Strimple, "Amillennialism," 122; Riddlebarger, *A Case for Amillennialism*, 238; Page, "Revelation 20 and Pauline Eschatology," 33; Hamilton, *The Basis of Millennial Faith*, 132; Beale, *The Book of Revelation*, 985; Poythress, *The Returning King*, 181.

101 Cited by Riddlebarger, *A Case for Amillennialism*, 286; Lewis, *The Dark Side of the Millennium*, 52; Cox, *Amillennialism Today*, 61; Strimple, "Amillennialism," 122–23; Hamilton, *The Basis of Millennial Faith*, 132–33; Beale, *The Book of Revelation*, 985.

102 Cited by Cox, *Amillennialism Today*, 61; Waldron, *The End Times Made Simple*, 95; Strimple, "Amillennialism," 123.

the incarceration of verses 1–3 is undone in the release of verse 7.[103] As George Eldon Ladd explains, the release of Satan is difficult to understand if it is applied to the Lord's binding of Satan in His earthly ministry: "The victory he won over Satan was won once and for all. Satan will never be loosed from bondage to Christ won by his death and resurrection."[104] In other words, if the binding of Satan in Revelation 20 refers to Christ's work of redemption on the cross (John 12:31–32; Col 2:15; Heb 2:14–15; 1 John 3:8), the finished work of Christ turns out to be the unfinished work of Christ when Satan is released.[105]

For example, according to 1 John 3:8 Jesus came to break the dominating power of sin in the lives of those who believe in Him. But if the victory over the devil in this verse is equated with the binding of Satan in Revelation 20:3, what does it mean that Satan is released in Revelation 20:7? How can the effects of this redemptive victory be reversed? Similarly, the victory of Christ over the devil in Hebrews 2:14–15 consists of Jesus redeeming sinners from the power of Satan and the fear of death. But if this victory is identified as the binding of Satan in Revelation 20, how can this act of deliverance be nullified when the devil is set free? Likewise, how can the casting out of Satan in John 12:31–32 be reversed, and how can Christ's triumph over the rulers of darkness in Colossians 2:15 be overturned? These passages must not describe the same act of divine judgment against Satan as what John describes in Revelation 20:1–3.

None of these New Testament passages, then, are truly parallel to the binding of Satan because none of them portray the kind of absolute confinement described in Revelation 20:1–3.[106] For this reason, these cross-references fail to bring any clarity to the meaning of John's vision and therefore fail to provide evidence that the millennium began with the first-century ministry of Christ.

---

103 As Robert Thomas asks, "What restrictions currently placed on him will be removed at the end of this age? No credible answer to this question has ever been advanced" (Robert L. Thomas, *Revelation 8–22: An Exegetical Commentary* [Chicago: Moody Press, 1995], 404).
104 George Eldon Ladd, *A Commentary on the Revelation of John* (Grand Rapids: Eerdmans Publishing, 1972), 263.
105 Sullivan, "Premillennialism," 21.
106 It will be demonstrated in chapter 14 that Revelation 12:7–11 and Revelation 20:1–3 do not describe the same casting down of Satan.

Conclusion

Hundreds of years before the first coming of Christ, Satan was "roaming about on the earth and walking around on it" (Job 1:7), and now, hundreds of years after the death and resurrection of Jesus, Satan still "prowls about like a roaring lion, seeking someone to devour" (1 Pet 5:8). His ultimate fate is sealed, but the devil is not currently bound and sealed in the abyss as described in Revelation 20:1–3. As Robert Saucy explains:

> All attempts to apply this picture to the present period, either as a limitation of Satan's deceptive power on believers or his inability to prevent the spread of the gospel in the world, are difficult to harmonize with the language of the passage and other teaching of the New Testament. The text gives no indication that the limitation on Satan is one of degree.[107]

To the contrary, the confinement of Revelation 20 is absolute and therefore the binding of Satan is not a present reality. Instead, the thousand years in John's vision represents a millennial kingdom which will take place between the present age and the eternal state (cf. Isa 24:21–23), just as premillennialism teaches.

---

[107] Robert L. Saucy, *The Case for Progressive Dispensationalism: The Interface Between Dispensational and Non-Dispensational Theology* (Grand Rapids: Zondervan Publishing, 1993), 276.

Chapter 12

The Nature of the First Resurrection

Introduction

One of the most significant issues in Revelation 20 involves the nature of the "first resurrection" in verses 4–6. This resurrection has been labeled one of the most hotly disputed issues in all of Scripture[1] and "the focal point of the eschatological hostilities which divide premillennialists from amillennialists."[2] Because this resurrection is described as "first"—and because John depicts the rest of the dead coming to life after the thousand years (v. 5a)—premillennialists believe Revelation 20 foresees two physical resurrections separated by the millennial reign of Christ. These two resurrections are often considered not only a "major exegetical problem for amillennialism,"[3] but also "the linchpin of the premillennial position."[4]

In response, amillennialists reject this idea of two physical resurrections separated by a thousand years, insisting instead that the first resurrection is a *spiritual* resurrection that takes place throughout the present age. More specifically, amillennialists interpret the first resurrection as either (a) the regeneration of believers at the point of conversion

---

1 Kim Riddlebarger, *A Case for Amillennialism: Understanding the End Times*, expanded ed. (Grand Rapids: Baker Books, 2013), 242.
2 Sam Storms, *Kingdom Come: The Amillennial Alternative* (Ross-shire, Scotland: Mentor, 2013), 451.
3 Millard J. Erickson, *Christian Theology* (Grand Rapids: Baker Books, 1985), 1214.
4 Millard J. Erickson, *A Basic Guide to Eschatology: Making Sense of the Millennium* (Grand Rapids: Baker Books, 1998), 97.

or (b) the entrance of believers into life in heaven at the point of death. In doing so, amillennialists argue for a single, physical resurrection of both the righteous and the wicked when Jesus returns at the end of the age.

The purpose of this chapter is to reexamine this key passage in the millennial debate, with a focus on the amillennial interpretation of the first resurrection. After setting forth the premillennial argument from Revelation 20:4–6, it will carefully evaluate the amillennial view that the first resurrection is spiritual in nature. It will then examine the two specific amillennial views on the identity of this spiritual resurrection. In the process, this chapter will demonstrate that the amillennial arguments for a spiritual resurrection in Revelation 20:4–6 fall short, and therefore that this passage provides compelling evidence for the eschatology of premillennialism.

The Premillennial View of the First Resurrection

In Revelation 20:4–6, the apostle John continues his description of the thousand years, focusing on the resurrection and millennial reign of those who are martyred for their faith in Christ:

> Then I saw thrones, and they sat on them, and judgment was given to them. And I saw the souls of those who had been beheaded because of their testimony of Jesus and because of the word of God, and those who had not worshiped the beast or his image, and had not received the mark on their forehead and on their hand; and they came to life and reigned with Christ for a thousand years. The rest of the dead did not come to life until the thousand years were completed. This is the first resurrection. Blessed and holy is the one who has a part in the first resurrection; over these the second death has no power, but they will be priests of God and of Christ and will reign with Him for a thousand years.

The most highly debated part of this passage concerns the meaning of the phrase "they came to life" (ἔζησαν) in verse 4[5] and the nature of the

---

5 The common translation "they came to life" in verse 4 interprets ἔζησαν as an ingressive aorist. Hughes argues that the aorist tense of ζάω (ἔζησαν) is *constative* ("they lived") rather than *ingressive* ("they came to life") (James A. Hughes, "Revelation 20:4–6 and the

"first resurrection" (ἡ ἀνάστασις ἡ πρώτη) in verse 5.[6] According to premillennialism, this "first resurrection" is the first of two physical resurrections in Revelation 20 which are separated by a thousand years. The first is a resurrection of the righteous, the faithful believers who are martyred during the Tribulation (v. 4), whereas the second is a resurrection of the wicked, "the rest of the dead" who "did not come to life until the thousand years were completed" (v. 5). Those raised in the first resurrection reign with Christ for a thousand years (v. 4), and those raised in the second resurrection come before the throne of final judgment after the millennium (vv. 11–15). As premillennialist John Walvoord writes:

> The sharp contrast in the passage is between those who are raised at the beginning of the thousand years and those who are raised at the end. Both are physical resurrections, but those who are raised at the beginning of the Millennium, designated as the "first resurrection," are contrasted to those who "come to life" at the end of the Millennium, who face judgment according to Revelation 20:11–15.[7]

As Robert Saucy explains, this contrast between the two physical resurrections has significant implications for the millennial debate:

> The mention of two resurrections separated by a period of a thousand years, along with the reference to the participants in the first resurrection as reigning with Christ, clearly points to a

---

Question of the Millennium," *WTJ* 35, no. 3 [Spring 1973]: 290–92), but his arguments were sufficiently refuted by Jack S. Deere ("Premillennialism in Revelation 20:4–6," *BSac* 135, no. 537 [Jan 1978]: 66–67). Most amillennialists now agree with Deere, including G. K. Beale, who writes that "it is better to view it as ingressive on analogy with [Rev] 2:8 and 13:14, as well as Luke 15:32 and Rom. 14:9" (G. K. Beale, *The Book of Revelation*, NIGTC [Grand Rapids: Eerdmans Publishing, 1999], 1000).

6 The first part of Rev 20:5 ("The rest of the dead did not come to life until the thousand years were completed") is parenthetical. Therefore, when John refers to the "first resurrection" in the next part of verse 5, he is pointing back to the coming to life described at the end of verse 4. This appears to be the general consensus on both sides of the millennial debate.

7 John F. Walvoord, "The Theological Significance of Revelation 20:1–6," in *Essays in Honor of J. Dwight Pentecost*, eds. Stanley D. Toussaint and Charles H. Dyer (Chicago: Moody Press, 1986), 236.

millennial period after the coming of Christ, when the first resurrection occurs.[8]

In this way, the physical nature of the "first resurrection" provides convincing support for the concept of a millennial kingdom between the present age and the eternal state and therefore presents a difficult problem for amillennialism.

The Premillennial Argument

The primary reason the "first resurrection" in Revelation 20 must refer to a physical resurrection concerns the terminology itself. The word "resurrection" (ἀνάστασις) is used almost exclusively in the New Testament to refer to "the elimination of the condition of physical death through bodily resurrection."[9] The word is used 41 times in the New Testament, and in 38 out of its 39 uses outside of Revelation 20, it refers to a physical resurrection. The lone exception is its metaphorical use in Luke 2:34 where it cannot refer to bodily resurrection because physical death is absent from the immediate context.[10]

This alone does not prove that ἀνάστασις refers to a physical resurrection in Revelation 20—for it is possible that John is using this word in a unique way—but it does place a heavy burden of proof on those who say otherwise. Physical resurrection is clearly the concept that would

---

8 Robert L. Saucy, *The Case for Progressive Dispensationalism: The Interface Between Dispensational and Non-Dispensational Theology* (Grand Rapids: Zondervan Publishing, 1993), 276. The closest and most reasonable antecedent of "they" in the verb "they sat" (ἐκάθισαν) in Rev 20:4 is "the armies which are in heaven, clothed in fine linen, white and clean" from Rev 19:14, that is, the people of God who accompany Christ at His return (David J. MacLeod, "The Fourth 'Last Thing': The Millennial Kingdom of Christ (Rev. 20:4–6)," *BSac* 157, no. 625 [Jan 2000]: 55; Robert L. Thomas, *Revelation 8–22: An Exegetical Commentary* [Chicago: Moody Press, 1995], 414). But as Craig Blaising observes, "The identity of the occupants of these thrones is not crucial to resolving the millennial question" (Craig A. Blaising, "Premillennialism," in *Three Views on the Millennium and Beyond*, ed. Darrell L. Bock [Grand Rapids: Zondervan Publishing], 221).
9 Blaising, "Premillennialism," 224.
10 BDAG, 71–72; Frederick William Danker, *The Concise Greek-English Lexicon of the New Testament* (Chicago: University of Chicago Press, 2009), 28; Deere, "Premillennialism in Revelation 20:4–6," 71; Blaising, "Premillennialism," 224; William J. Webb, "Revelation 20: Exegetical Considerations," *The Baptist Review of Theology* 4, no. 2 (Fall 1994): 36; A. J. Gordon, "The First Resurrection," in *Premillennial Essays*, ed. Nathaniel West (Minneapolis: Bryant Baptist Publications, 1981), 82. In Luke 2:34, ἐκάθισαν is used in its etymological sense of "rising" (MacLeod, "The Fourth 'Last Thing,'" 59).

have immediately arisen in the minds of John's original readers upon seeing the word ἀνάστασις, and therefore, if it refers to anything else in Revelation 20, this must be obvious from the immediate context.

In contrast, the immediate context confirms that John is indeed describing a physical resurrection. Because the apostle describes the subjects of this resurrection as those who were *martyred*—and follows this with the statement that "they came to life and reigned" (Rev 20:4)—this strongly implies that this new life is physical.[11] In other words, interpreting the first resurrection as a bodily resurrection fits the context in which John sees those who were killed in the physical realm coming back to life in the physical realm. As Alva J. McClain notes, "If the people involved were beheaded physically, and then lived again, common sense would suggest that they received back the same category of life that had been lost."[12] This confirms the standard meaning of ἀνάστασις in Revelation 20:5 as a physical resurrection.

In addition, since the physical resurrection of "the rest of the dead" in verse 5a is described with the word ἔζησαν ("they came to life"), and the identical form of the same verb ἔζησαν ("they came to life") is used to describe the resurrection of the saints at the end of verse 4, this resurrection must also be physical.[13] The issue here is not merely the repetition of the same form of the same verb, but also the way in which these two verbs are connected. When John writes, in effect, "Some of the dead ἔζησαν (v.

---

11 Saucy, *Progressive Dispensationalism*, 275.
12 Alva J. McClain, *The Greatness of the Kingdom: An Inductive Study of the Kingdom of God* (Winona Lake, IN: BMH Books, 1959), 488. As Gordon explains, when Paul describes those who were made alive in Eph 2:4–7 as having previously been "dead in [their] trespasses and sins" (Eph 2:1), one can "infer immediately and rightly that a spiritual revivification has taken place, because the condition on which the change took effect was spiritual. And so here [in Rev 20:4], the condition of literal death having been so unmistakably pointed out, the inference is immediate and inevitable that the quickening is a literal and corporeal quickening" ("The First Resurrection," 80).
13 Harold W. Hoehner, "Evidence from Revelation 20," in *A Case for Premillennialism: A New Consensus*, eds. Donald K. Campbell and Jeffrey L. Townsend (Chicago: Moody Press, 1992), 254; Jeffrey L. Townsend, "Is the Present Age the Millennium?," *BSac* 140, no. 559 (July 1983): 219; MacLeod, "The Fourth 'Last Thing,'" 59; George Eldon Ladd, *Crucial Questions About the Kingdom of God* (Grand Rapids: Eerdmans Publishing, 1952), 148–49; C. Marvin Pate, "A Progressive Dispensationalist View of Revelation," in *Four Views on the Book of Revelation*, ed. C. Marvin Pate (Grand Rapids: Zondervan Publishing, 1998), 171. In addition, as Thomas notes, whenever the verb ζάω ("to live") is used in the context of bodily death in the New Testament, it always speaks of bodily resurrection (e.g., John 11:25; Acts 1:3; 9:41) (*Revelation 8–22*, 417).

4b), but the rest of the dead did not ἔζησαν until later (v. 5a)," he makes it clear that the verb refers to the same act or experience in both uses. Therefore, whatever happened to one group also happened to the other—if one resurrection is physical, the other must be physical as well.[14]

These two physical resurrections—believers prior to the thousand years and unbelievers afterward—could hardly be stated more clearly:

First Resurrection: "they *came to life* [ἔζησαν] and reigned with Christ for a thousand years" (Rev 20:4)

Second Resurrection: "the rest of the dead did not *come to life* [ἔζησαν] until the thousand years were completed" (Rev 20:5a)

Subsequently, in a vision of events taking place after the thousand years, the apostle John describes the resurrection of the wicked unto judgment: "And the sea *gave up the dead* which were in it, and death and Hades *gave up the dead* which were in them; and they were judged, every one of them according to their deeds" (Rev 20:13; emphasis added). This is John's description of the rest of the dead coming to life after the thousand years, a clear reference to the second of two physical resurrections separated by the millennial reign of Christ. For this reason, the use of the word ἀνάστασις, in combination with these other clear indications in the immediate context, support the premillennial view that the first resurrection is physical in nature.

The Amillennial Objection

The most common objection to this view is that the Bible elsewhere teaches a single, general resurrection in which the righteous and the wicked will be raised at the same time (Dan 12:2; John 5:28-29; Acts 24:15).[15] As Kenneth Gentry explains:

---

14 As Ladd writes, "The same experience overtook both groups: one at the beginning, one at the end of the millennial period" (George Eldon Ladd, "Revelation 20 and the Millennium," *RevExp* 57, no. 2 [April 1960]: 169).

15 Louis Berkhof, *Systematic Theology* (Grand Rapids: Eerdmans Publshing, 1939), 715; Hamilton, *The Basis of Millennial Faith*, 121; Anthony Hoekema, *The Bible and the Future* (Grand Rapids: Eerdmans Publishing, 1979), 232.

Why should we believe that the New Testament everywhere teaches a general, singular resurrection on the last day, only to discover later in the most difficult book of the Bible that there are actually two specific, distantly separated resurrections for different classes of people?[16]

According to amillennialists, because both the righteous and the wicked will be raised at the same time when Jesus returns, Revelation 20 cannot teach two physical resurrections separated by a thousand years. As amillennialist Kim Riddlebarger writes, "Scripture clearly teaches that the resurrection and judgment of the righteous and unrighteous will occur at the same time, thus eliminating the possibility of an earthly millennial age to dawn after the Lord's return."[17]

In response to this objection, Daniel 12:2, John 5:28-29, and Acts 24:15 do not actually preclude the possibility of two distinct resurrections separated by a period of time. In fact, all three passages speak of a resurrection of the righteous and a resurrection of the wicked—and always in that same order (the same as in Revelation 20)[18]—and they neither state nor require that the two resurrections happen simultaneously. They simply do not specify one way or the other.[19] As Wayne Grudem explains:

> All of these verses, in the absence of Revelation 20:5-6, might or might not be speaking of a single future time of resurrection. But with the explicit teaching of Revelation 20:5-6 about two resurrections, these verses must be understood to refer to the future

---

16 Kenneth L. Gentry, Jr., "A Postmillennial Response to Craig A. Blaising," in *Three Views on the Millennium and Beyond*, ed. Darrell L. Bock (Grand Rapids: Zondervan Publishing), 243. Gentry is postmillennial, but this objection is raised by amillennialists and postmillennialists alike.

17 Riddlebarger, *A Case for Amillennialism*, 166.

18 This is especially clear in John 5:29 where Jesus speaks of two different physical resurrections: "a resurrection of life" and "a resurrection of judgment." According to McClain, this passage lays an exegetical foundation for the two resurrections in Revelation 20 (*The Greatness of the Kingdom*, 489).

19 Wayne Grudem, *Systematic Theology: An Introduction to Biblical Doctrine* (Grand Rapids: Zondervan Publishing, 1994), 1119; Herman A. Hoyt, "A Dispensational Premillennial Response," in *The Meaning of the Millennium*, ed. Robert G. Clouse (Downers Grove, IL: InterVarsity Press, 1977), 195.

certainty of a resurrection for each type of person, without specifying that those resurrections will be separated in time.[20]

Even John 5:28–29, which speaks of "an hour" in which these two resurrections will occur, does not require that both resurrections take place at the same time. John frequently uses the word "hour" (ὥρα) in reference to an extended period of time (John 16:2), sometimes as long as the entire present age (John 4:21, 23; 1 John 2:18). In fact, this is how he uses the word "hour" just three verses earlier in John 5:25.[21] As Craig Blaising explains, "If the eschatological hour can be extended over two thousand years, it is not impossible that a thousand years might transpire between the resurrection of the just and the resurrection of the unjust."[22]

As discussed in chapter 1, sometimes a given biblical prophecy will predict two or more future events and present them in such a way that it appears they will occur simultaneously, but later revelation indicates a significant gap of time separating them.[23] Often referred to as "telescoping," "prophetic perspective," or "prophetic foreshortening," it can be likened to seeing two mountain peaks off in the distance—initially they appear to be right next to each other, but a closer look reveals that they are separated by a valley. For example, there is no clear evidence in the Old Testament alone that there would be two distinct comings of the Messiah separated by a significant period of time. But once the later revelation of the New Testament arrives, it becomes clear that what the Old Testament writers seemed to depict as a single event must now be recognized as involving two events.

In the same way, when it comes to the future resurrection, what the earlier writers of Scripture seemed to depict as a single resurrection of both the righteous and the wicked (Dan 12:2; John 5:28–29; Acts 24:15) must now be recognized as involving two resurrections, a resurrection of the righteous and a resurrection of the wicked a thousand years later (Rev 20:1–15). In other words, while these other passages do not specify the timing of the two

---

20 Grudem, *Systematic Theology*, 1120.
21 Ibid., 1119.
22 Craig A. Blaising, "A Premillennial Response to Robert B. Strimple," in *Three Views on the Millennium and Beyond*, ed. Darrell L. Bock (Grand Rapids: Zondervan Publishing), 150.
23 See, for example, Isa 9:6–7; 40:1–5; 61:1–2 (cf. Luke 4:16–21); Jer 29:10–14; Zech 9:9–10; and Joel 2:28–32.

resurrections, in Revelation 20:5 this time element *is* specified—one thousand years will separate these two physical resurrections. Recognizing this development in the progress of revelation is the only way to harmonize all of what Scripture teaches on the subject of the future resurrection.[24]

The Amillennial View of the First Resurrection

Amillennialists reject the idea of two physical resurrections separated by a thousand years, claiming instead that the "first resurrection" is a *spiritual* resurrection that takes place throughout the present age, to be followed by a physical resurrection at the end of this age. More specifically, amillennialists interpret the first resurrection as either (a) the regeneration of believers at the point of conversion or (b) the entrance of believers into life in heaven at the point of death. But before these two specific views can be evaluated, the amillennial argument for the spiritual nature of the first resurrection in general must be considered.

The Case for a Spiritual Resurrection

In making the case for the spiritual nature of the first resurrection, most amillennialists appeal to an argument first articulated by Meredith G. Kline in 1975[25] and subsequently adopted and developed by several leading proponents of amillennialism.[26] It now appears to be the primary argument for the spiritual nature of the first resurrection in Revelation 20, but most premillennialists have largely ignored it in their critiques of the amillennial view.[27]

---

24 An additional argument against the premillennial view of the first resurrection comes from Sydney Page, who points out that there is no explicit mention of the return of Christ in Rev 20:4–6, which "would be a surprising omission if the coming to life refers to the resurrection that occurs at that time" (Page, "Revelation 20 and Pauline Eschatology," 36). But according to the premillennial view, the Second Coming is explicitly described in Rev 19:11–21, which takes place at the very beginning of the thousand years of Rev 20:1–6, so this objection carries no weight.
25 Meredith G. Kline, "The First Resurrection," *WTJ* 37, no. 3 (Spring 1975): 366–75; and Meredith G. Kline, "The First Resurrection: A Reaffirmation," *WTJ* 39, no. 1 (Fall 1976): 110–19.
26 E.g., Beale, *The Book of Revelation*, 1002–7; Vern S. Poythress, *The Returning King: A Guide to the Book of Revelation* (Phillipsburg, NJ: Presbyterian and Reformed Publishing, 2000), 179–81; Dennis E. Johnson, *Triumph of the Lamb: A Commentary on Revelation* (Phillipsburg, NJ: Presbyterian and Reformed Publishing, 2001), 291–94; Riddlebarger, *A Case for Amillennialism*, 244–49; Storms, *Kingdom Come*, 462–66.
27 The most obvious exception is found in the immediate response to Kline's original article

The Amillennial Argument

As amillennialists observe, even though the word "resurrection" (ἀνάστασις) almost always refers to physical resurrection elsewhere in the New Testament, it occurs only here in the Apocalypse, and Revelation 20:5-6 is the only place in Scripture where ἀνάστασις is modified by the ordinal "first" (πρῶτος).[28] Amillennialists consider the uniqueness of this expression "first resurrection"—rather than simply the use of "resurrection" itself—to be the decisive factor in determining the intended meaning of John's designation.[29]

According to amillennialists, by calling it the "first" resurrection, the apostle was not simply designating it the first in a series of resurrections of the *same kind*—he was indicating that this resurrection was of a *different quality* than the resurrection that follows. In other words, the modifier "first" indicates a qualitative difference between two resurrections rather than merely establishing a numerical sequence between two events.[30] According to this view, the qualitative difference is that the "first" resurrection is *spiritual* whereas the second resurrection is *physical*.

To justify this distinction, amillennialists point to the contrast between the first and second deaths in Revelation 20. The first death of believers is physical/temporal and therefore different in nature from the second death of unbelievers, which is spiritual/eternal (Rev 20:10, 14-15). As G. K. Beale reasons, "If there are thus two different kinds of deaths, it is plausible that the corresponding resurrections would also differ. The resurrection of believers is spiritual, whereas the resurrection

---

by J. Ramsey Michaels ("The First Resurrection: A Response," *WTJ* 39, no. 1 [Fall 1976]: 100-9). In subsequent years, however, most premillennialists have either ignored this argument altogether or addressed it only briefly. For example, Deere ("Premillennialism in Revelation 20:4-6," 72) and Blaising ("Premillennialism," 224) relegate their responses to a single footnote, and Hoehner ("Evidence from Revelation 20," 255) summarizes the responses of Michaels and Deere in a single paragraph. Most others don't even mention it.

28 Beale, *The Book of Revelation*, 1004; Riddlebarger, *A Case for Amillennialism*, 243-44; Storms, *Kingdom Come*, 462; Jonathan Menn, *Biblical Eschatology* (Eugene, OR: Resource Publications, 2013), 359-60.

29 Riddlebarger, *A Case for Amillennialism*, 243-44; Storms, *Kingdom Come*, 462; Beale, *The Book of Revelation*, 1004; R. Fowler White, "Death and the First Resurrection in Revelation 20: A Response to Meredith G. Kline," unpublished paper presented at ETS, 1992, 2, 19.

30 Kline, "The First Resurrection," 366; Riddlebarger, *A Case for Amillennialism*, 244-45; Beale, *The Book of Revelation*, 1002-15; Menn, *Biblical Eschatology*, 359-63. As Riddlebarger summarizes, "The terms do not indicate sequence but contrast" (*A Case for Amillennialism*, 245).

of unbelievers is physical."[31] In this way, the passage is said to reflect the following chiastic arrangement:

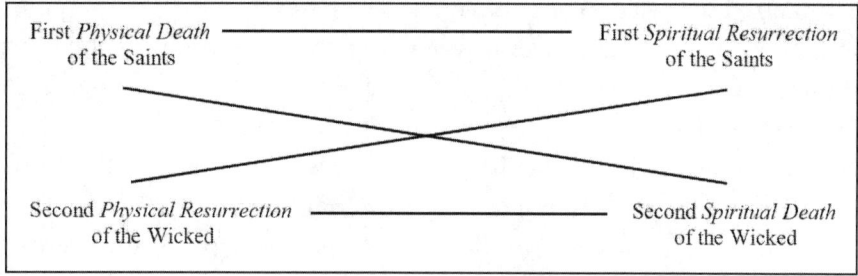

Figure 1. Beale, *The Book of Revelation*, 1005.

According to amillennialist Sam Storms, this double binary pattern reflects a beautiful irony in John's language: The believer dies physically but experiences spiritual resurrection, whereas the unbeliever is resurrected physically but experiences spiritual death.[32]

The key to understanding this expression "first resurrection" is said to be found in those New Testament passages which contain a similar antithesis between "first/old" and "second/new" (Rev 21:1; 1 Cor 15:22, 42–49; Heb 8:6–10:9). According to amillennialists, in these passages the modifier πρῶτος designates not that which is first in a sequence, but rather that which pertains to the present world order, in contrast to that which pertains to the world to come. In Revelation 21:1, for example, the modifier "first/old" refers to those pre-consummate and incomplete elements belonging to the present, sin-cursed creation order, whereas the modifier "second/new" refers to those consummate and complete elements belonging to the eternal state.[33] In Revelation 21:1, then, the adjective "first"

> does not merely mark the present world as first in a series of worlds and certainly not as first in a series of worlds of the same kind. On the contrary, it characterizes this world as different in kind from the "new" world. It signifies that the present world

---

31 Beale, *The Book of Revelation*, 1005.
32 Storms, *Kingdom Come*, 465.
33 Johnson, *Triumph of the Lamb*, 291; Beale, *The Book of Revelation*, 1005–6.

stands in contrast to the new world order of the consummation which will abide forever.³⁴

This antithesis is said to be confirmed later in Revelation 21, where physical death in the present age in verse 4 is considered part of the *"first* things," and the *"second* death" in the lake of fire in verse 8 takes place in the age to come.³⁵

According to amillennialists, then, whatever is "first" in the Book of Revelation pertains to the present world and whatever is "second" or "new" pertains to the world to come.³⁶ For this reason, because the *second* resurrection is physical and pertains to the eternal order of the age to come, the *first* resurrection must be spiritual and pertain to the temporary order of the present age.³⁷ Therefore, the first resurrection must refer to a spiritual resurrection which takes place during the present age rather than a physical resurrection in the age to come.³⁸

This same distinction is also seen in the antithesis between the "first man" (Adam) and the "second man" (Jesus) in 1 Corinthians 15 and the "old/first covenant" vs. "new/second covenant" in Hebrews 8–10.³⁹ As Beale observes:

> The first Adam had a perishable body and brought death, whereas the last Adam had an imperishable and glorious body and brought eternal life. The first covenant was temporary and led to death (e.g., Heb. 8:13), while the second was eternal and led to life.⁴⁰

---

34 Kline, "The First Resurrection," 366–67. Later Kline writes, "To be called 'first' within that pattern is to be assigned a place in this present world with its transient order. That which is 'first' does not participate in the quality of consummate finality and permanence which is distinctive of the new kingdom order of the world to come" (369).
35 Riddlebarger, *A Case for Amillennialism*, 245; Beale, *The Book of Revelation*, 1006.
36 Storms, *Kingdom Come*, 463.
37 Ibid., 464. In other words, the first resurrection of Rev 20:5 is "first" in the sense that it belongs "to the order of the present world which is passing away" (Donald Garlington, "Reigning with Christ: Revelation 20:1–6 and the Question of the Millennium," *R&R* 6, no. 2 [Spring 1997]: 75).
38 As Dennis Johnson writes, "The 'first resurrection' granted to deceased saints in Revelation 20:4–6, since it belongs to the present, preconsummation order, is not their reception of the bodies made like Christ's glorious body, fitted for immortal residence in the curse-free new earth (Phil. 3:21)" (*Triumph of the Lamb*, 291–92).
39 Beale, *The Book of Revelation*, 1007; Riddlebarger, *A Case for Amillennialism*, 246.
40 Beale, *The Book of Revelation*, 1007. According to Riddlebarger, "If two major redemptive

Therefore, in none of these passages—Revelation 21, 1 Corinthians 15, or Hebrews 8–10—"does 'first' (πρῶτος) function as an ordinal in a counting of things that are *identical in kind*."[41] Amillennialists believe that this supports the view that the "first resurrection" of Revelation 20 must be different in kind from the second resurrection (which is physical) and therefore that it must be spiritual in nature.

The Premillennial Response

In response, there are five significant problems with this argument. The initial difficulty with this view of the "first resurrection" is that the operative term in this designation is not the adjective "first" but rather the noun "resurrection."[42] As previously noted, the noun ἀνάστασις is a well-attested technical term that almost always refers to bodily resurrection in the New Testament. In the very rare instances where this word means anything else, this is instantly clear from the immediate context (e.g., Luke 2:34). In addition, the chronological use of the adjective πρῶτος—in which it refers to the first in a sequence—is extremely common in the New Testament, and especially in the Apocalypse.[43] This, in combination with the clear contextual indicators of two physical resurrections in Revelation 20 (see discussion above), identifies the most obvious meaning of the "first resurrection" as *the first in a sequence of two bodily resurrections*. Put more simply, πρῶτος means "first" and ἀνάστασις means "resurrection."

This does not mean that the two physical resurrections in Revelation 20 are identical in kind—for the first is "a resurrection of *life*" (John 5:29a) while the second is "a resurrection of *judgment*" (John 5:29b)—but it does

---

covenants—the Mosaic covenant and the new covenant—can be contrasted with the same terms, [*first*] and *new*, this certainly strengthens the case that John did the same thing in Revelation 20 and 21, contrasting two kinds of resurrection" (*A Case for Amillennialism*, 246).

41 Beale, *The Book of Revelation*, 1007.

42 Deere, "Premillennialism in Revelation 20:4–6," 72; As Blaising writes, "It seems incredible that Meredith Kline could devote two articles attempting to defend a traditional amillennial view of 'the first resurrection' by means of an argument on the word 'first,' completely ignoring the operative term 'resurrection'" ("Premillennialism," 224).

43 Steve Sullivan, "Premillennialism and an Exegesis of Revelation 20," 35; accessed on July 20, 2014, http://www.pre-trib.org/data/pdf/Sullivan-PremillennialismAndA.pdf. The adjective πρῶτος is used in two basic ways in the New Testament: It can refer either to *that which is first in a sequence* or *that which is most prominent or important* (*BDAG*, 892–94; Danker, *The Concise Greek-English Lexicon*, 309). In all of its 19 uses in Revelation, πρῶτος appears to describe being first in a sequence.

mean that both are actual resurrections. This illustrates why the appeal to Revelation 21, 1 Corinthians 15, and Hebrews 8–10 actually undermines the case for a spiritual resurrection in Revelation 20. There is a qualitative distinction in Revelation 21 between the "first" heaven and earth and the "new" heaven and earth, *but both are physical creations*; there is a qualitative distinction in 1 Corinthians 15 between the "first man" (Adam) and the "second man" (Jesus), *but both are actual men*; and there is a qualitative distinction in Hebrews 8–10 between the "first" covenant and the "second" covenant, *but both are actual covenants*.[44] In contrast, the amillennialist emphasizes the qualitative distinction between the two resurrections in Revelation 20 in such a way that the "first resurrection" is *no longer an actual resurrection*, at least not in terms of what the word ἀνάστασις means in the New Testament.

Secondly, if the "first resurrection" does not consist of a physical resurrection, then Revelation 20 contains no explicit mention of the future resurrection as the consummation of the believer's hope.[45] As J. Ramsey Michaels argues:

> It would be strange indeed if a work emphasizing so strongly at the outset the resurrection of Jesus (1:5, 18), and with such a pervasive concern to offer consolation to Christians facing persecution and martyrdom, were to overlook the very heart of the church's eschatological expectation.[46]

Although some assert that the future resurrection of believers is described in Revelation 20:11–15, this passage describes only the resurrection of judgment which awaits unbelievers.[47]

---

44 This qualitative distinction is indicated not by the terms "first/old" and "second/new" themselves but rather by the contexts in which they occur.
45 Michaels, "The First Resurrection," 105.
46 Ibid.
47 That only unbelievers are in view in Rev 20:11–15 is clear for a number of reasons: (1) "The rest of the dead" in Rev 20:5—which refers to unbelievers as those who do not take part in the "first resurrection"—is the obvious antecedent of "the dead" in verse 12. (2) The resurrection of "the dead" in Rev 20:11–13 is the second resurrection implied in verse 5b, and this resurrection leads to the "second death" in verse 6a, of which believers are said to have no part (Thomas, *Revelation 8–22*, 431). (3) The only stated outcome of this judgment is the lake of fire (Rev 20:15). (4) "The Book of Life comes into the discussion only to show that the names of these dead are not written there" (Thomas, *Revelation 8–22*, 431). (5) This fits the broader context of Revelation 19–20, which sets forth God's ultimate

The third difficulty with this argument relates to the perspicuity of Scripture. Simply stated, it is difficult to imagine that any interpreter would have ever taken this approach to the "first resurrection" prior to its discovery in the second half of the 20th century.[48] How could even the most diligent of Bible students be expected to connect all the dots necessary to arrive at this conclusion? Why would the apostle John use such obscure language, demanding such a convoluted interpretive process? How could John be sure his readers would identify this double binary pattern, much less think to consult these other three passages, to determine the meaning of the "first resurrection"? And why would the fact that "first" never modifies "resurrection" outside of Revelation 20 send his readers on this complicated interpretive journey in the first place?[49] Isn't it more likely that "first resurrection" simply means "first resurrection"? As Harold Hoehner observes, "The complexity of this view makes it suspect."[50]

Fourthly, the technical meaning ascribed to the adjective πρῶτος is highly questionable. Apart from the fact that this use of the adjective has gone almost completely unnoticed by the major lexicons,[51] it does not

---

victory over everything corrupted by sin—the beast, the false prophet, Satan, heaven and earth, and now His unbelieving human enemies. At the very least one would have to agree with the observation of Michaels that "in these verses there is no emphasis at all upon this future resurrection as positive object of Christian hope" (Michaels, "The First Resurrection," 105).

48 Even though this argument was first articulated in 1975 by Meredith Kline, the chiastic relationship between the two deaths and two resurrections was identified in 1960 by Summers (Ray Summers, "Revelation 20: An Interpretation," *RevExp* 57, no. 2 [April 1960]: 182). Jonathan Menn appears to trace Kline's view/argument back to Alexander Fraser's *Key to the Prophecies of the Old and New Testaments Which Are Not Yet Accomplished* in 1802 (Menn, *Biblical Eschatology*, 360–61), but a comparison shows that the similarities between Fraser and Kline have been exaggerated.

49 The fact that a given adjective modifies a given noun only once in the entire New Testament should not lead the interpreter to expect a specialized meaning of the adjective-noun combination which ascribes an unprecedented meaning to the noun. But the amillennial approach does just that.

50 Hoehner, "Evidence from Revelation 20," 255.

51 *BDAG*, 892–94; Danker, *The Concise Greek-English Lexicon*, 309; G. Abbott-Smith, *A Manual Greek Lexicon of the New Testament*, 3rd ed. (Edinburgh: T. & T. Clark, 1986), 389–90; J. H. Moulton and G. Milligan, *Vocabulary of the Greek Testament* (Grand Rapids: Baker Academic, 1995), 557; Wilhelm Michaelis, "πρῶτος," in *TDNT*, ed. Gerhard Kittel (Grand Rapids: Eerdmans Publishing, 1964), 6:865–68; Karl Heinz Bartels, "πρῶτος," in *NIDNTT*, ed. Colin Brown (Grand Rapids: Zondervan Publishing, 1986), 1:664–67; Johannes P. Louw and Eugene A. Nida, eds. *Greek-English Lexicon of the New Testament*

appear to be demanded by its use in 1 Corinthians 15, Hebrews 8–10, or Revelation 21. In each of these passages, the sequential use of πρῶτος—in reference to the first of two Adams, the first of two covenants, and the first of two heavens/earths—is sufficient to communicate the intended meaning of the biblical writers. Even though the first Adam, first covenant, and first creation all possess other qualities in addition to being first in a sequence—even some qualities common to all three—this does not mean that these additional qualities are inherent in the meaning of the adjective itself.[52] The amillennial argument uses a questionable meaning of the adjective "first" to reinterpret the well-attested meaning of "resurrection" and thereby ascribes to ἀνάστασις a meaning in Revelation 20 which it possesses nowhere else in the New Testament.[53]

Fifthly, and most importantly, even if the amillennial view of πρῶτος is granted for the sake of argument, an insurmountable problem arises because of the definitions given to πρῶτος and ἀνάστασις. To review, in light of the perceived antithesis between "first/old" and "second/new," amillennialists insist that πρῶτος in Revelation 20 means "to belong to the present state of affairs which is passing away."[54] As the qualitative and polar opposite of "new,"[55] πρῶτος is said to describe that which is merely provisional, transient, and temporary, in contrast to what is consummate, final, and enduring.[56] In other words, whatever is "first"

Based on Semantic Domains, 2nd ed. (New York: United Bible Societies, 1989), 2:214. One possible exception is *EDNT*, which states that John's use of πρῶτος in Rev 21:1 refers to "what was and is transitory" (Hugolinus Langkammer, "πρῶτος," in *EDNT*, 3:189). It is not clear, however, whether Langkammer believes that the concept of transitoriness is communicated by the greater context of Rev 21:1, or by the word in and of itself.

52 Put another way, the adjective πρῶτος can be used to describe several things which are first in a series without communicating other attributes which are also true of the nouns it modifies. To illustrate, if someone were to use the adjective "blue" to describe a chair, a table, and a cabinet, the fact that all three are also made of wood does not prove that the adjective "blue" is a technical term for something consisting of wood.

53 Both amillennial views of the "first resurrection" require a meaning for ἀνάστασις which is unprecedented in the New Testament, a point to be discussed more fully when these views are considered below.

54 Storms, *Kingdom Come*, 462; also see Kline, "The First Resurrection," 366–67, 369–71; Garlington, "Reigning with Christ," 75.

55 Kline, "The First Resurrection," 366, 368–70; Riddlebarger, *A Case for Amillennialism*, 245.

56 Kline, "The First Resurrection," 368; Storms, *Kingdom Come*, 463–64.

is antithetical to permanence⁵⁷ and will eventually be superseded and replaced by what is "new" when it passes away.⁵⁸ For this reason, amillennialists believe the adjective πρῶτος "is used to designate elements that belong ... to the present, sin-cursed creation order, in contrast to the new heaven and new earth."⁵⁹ As the diametrical opposite of that which characterizes eternity and resurrection life,⁶⁰ "Whatever is *first* does not participate in the quality of finality and permanence which is distinctive of the age to come."⁶¹

The difficulty arises when the amillennialist takes this definition of πρῶτος and applies it to ἀνάστασις in Revelation 20 as a reference to a spiritual resurrection. For those amillennialists who believe that the "first resurrection" refers to *regeneration*,⁶² the contradiction is obvious. In what way does the believer's regeneration belong to the present state of affairs which is passing away? How can the new life received at conversion be described as provisional, transient, and temporary, in contrast to what endures? How can the new birth be considered the qualitative and

---

57 Kline, "The First Resurrection," 370.
58 Ibid., 366, 368; Riddlebarger, *A Case for Amillennialism*, 245–46; Storms, *Kingdom Come*, 462. In explaining the antithesis between the two adjectives, Kline describes the first Adam in 1 Corinthians 15 as "earthy and physical" and the second Adam as "heavenly and spiritual" ("The First Resurrection," 368). Likewise, Riddlebarger explains, "Adam was from earth; Christ is from heaven. Adam stands at the head of the human race; Christ stands at the head of the redeemed. Death, sin, and weakness characterize Adam and his descendants, while Christ stands at the head of those raised from the dead" (*A Case for Amillennialism*, 246). Beale makes similar observations, applying them also to the antithesis between the "first/old" covenant and the "second/new" covenant in Hebrews 8–10: "The first Adam had a perishable, inglorious body and brought death, whereas the last Adam had an imperishable and glorious body and brought eternal life. The first covenant was temporary and led to death (e.g., Heb. 8:13), while the second was eternal and led to life" (*The Book of Revelation*, 1007).
59 Johnson, *Triumph of the Lamb*, 291.
60 Riddlebarger, *A Case for Amillennialism*, 246–47.
61 Storms, *Kingdom Come*, 463. As Kline writes, "That which is 'first' does not participate in the quality of consummate finality and permanence which is distinctive of the new kingdom order of the world to come" ("The First Resurrection," 369).
62 Riddlebarger, *A Case for Amillennialism*, 240–49; Sam Hamstra Jr., "An Idealist View of Revelation," in *Four Views on the Book of Revelation*, ed. C. Marvin Pate (Grand Rapids: Zondervan Publishing, 1998), 120–21; Page, "Revelation 20 and Pauline Eschatology," 37–40; Floyd E. Hamilton, *The Basis of Millennial Faith* (Grand Rapids: Eerdmans Publishing, 1942), 119–23; William E. Cox, *Amillennialism Today* (Phillipsburg, NJ: Presbyterian and Reformed Publishing Co., 1966), 4–5. This view was also held by postmillennialist Norman Shepherd ("Resurrections of Revelation 20," *WTJ* 37, no. 1 [Fall 1974]: 34–43).

polar opposite of the future resurrection? Is the believer's regeneration antithetical to permanence? Will the new life received at conversion pass away and be replaced by his bodily resurrection? Can it really be said that the spiritual birth of believers belongs to the present, sin-cursed creation and therefore that the spiritual life of regeneration does not participate in the age to come?[63] As Michaels observes:

> The point of the few New Testament passages that speak of Christians as already in some sense resurrected (e.g., Rom. 6:4, 11; Eph. 2:5ff; Col. 3:1ff.) is that, to the extent that this resurrection is a present reality, the believer is set free from the transitory present world and ushered into the age to come.[64]

For those amillennialists who believe that the "first resurrection" refers to the believer being ushered into the presence of Christ at the point of death,[65] the dilemma is similar. In what sense does the believer's entrance into the blessings of heaven belong to the present state of affairs which is passing away? How can being ushered into the presence of Christ be described as transitory or diametrically opposed to the

---

63 Most amillennialists would likely affirm that regeneration is the means by which believers *partake* of the age to come, even now in the present age. In contrast, they see the "first man" (1 Cor 15:47) and the "first covenant" (Heb 8–10) as that which leads to death (Riddlebarger, *A Case for Amillennialism*, 246; Beale, *The Book of Revelation*, 1007). This alone demonstrates the inconsistency of the amillennial position, at least for those who see the "first resurrection" as regeneration.

64 Michaels, "The First Resurrection," 104–5. As Michaels explains, "It is hard to deny that [the new birth] partakes of the very nature of consummation" (105).

65 Storms, *Kingdom Come*, 451, 462–65; Kline, "The First Resurrection," 366–75; Hoekema, *The Bible and the Future*, 232–37; William Hendriksen, *More Than Conquerors: An Interpretation of the Book of Revelation* (Grand Rapids: Baker Books, 1967), 191–93; Johnson, *Triumph of the Lamb*, 291–94; Poythress, *The Returning King*, 182; Vern Sheridan Poythress, "Genre and Hermeneutics in Rev 20:1–6," *JETS* 36, no. 1 (March 1993): 41–54; Robert B. Strimple, "Amillennialism," in *Three Views on the Millennium and Beyond*, ed. Darrell L. Bock (Grand Rapids: Zondervan Publishing, 1999), 127; Beale, *The Book of Revelation*, 991–1011; Dean Davis, *The High King of Heaven: Discovering the Master Keys to the Great End Time Debate* (Enumclaw, WA: WinePress Publishing, 2014), 475–82.

future resurrection?⁶⁶ How can a "resurrection to heavenly glories"⁶⁷—including the blessings it brings to those who are resurrected—be considered part of the present, sin-cursed creation order?⁶⁸ As Michaels explains:

> The first resurrection *as resurrection* can hardly be described as temporary or transitory. It does not "pass away," like death or the sea or the old heaven and earth. The Christian who dies ... begins to participate then and there in the blessings of the age to come. His death as death is indeed transitory, but his death *as resurrection* ... belongs to the new age. Is that not the whole point in referring to it as a resurrection?⁶⁹

---

66 Beale responds to this argument by insisting that the inconsistency is resolved "by understanding that the intermediate state of the soul's resurrection is, indeed, an incomplete state, since these souls await the final, consummated physical resurrection in the new heavens and earth" (*The Book of Revelation*, 1007; also see Kline, "The First Resurrection," 371). But as demonstrated above, the amillennialist ascribes far more to the meaning of πρῶτος than simply "incomplete." The amillennial antithesis between "first/old" and "second/new" presents the two as polar opposites in which πρῶτος describes that which belongs to the order of this sin-cursed world, being transitory and destined to pass away when it is replaced by what is "new." So the inconsistency remains.

Kline seeks to resolve the tension in a similar way, noting that this resurrection "is still not the ultimate glory of the Christian" because it "stands on this side of the consummation" ("The First Resurrection," 371). But this too significantly dilutes the amillennial view of the antithesis between the two terms. According to amillennialists, "first" does not mean pre-consummative in the chronological sense of existing or taking place prior to the consummation. (If it did, the New Covenant itself could not be considered "new" since it was inaugurated and became operative prior to the consummation.) Amillennialists present πρῶτος not as a *chronological* modifier describing what exists (or takes place) during the present world, but as a *qualitative* modifier describing what *belongs* to the present world order. For this reason, Kline's appeal to the timing of the "first resurrection"—as that which "stands on this side of the consummation"—fails to offer any substantial response to the objection.

67 Kline, "The First Resurrection," 371.

68 One amillennialist who takes this view of the "first resurrection" defines it as "the deliverance of their souls from all that threatened them on earth" (Johnson, *Triumph of the Lamb*, 294), and another describes it as an "extension" and "intensification" of the blessedness of regeneration (Garlington, "Reigning with Christ," 96). Again, how can this understanding of the first resurrection in Revelation 20 be reconciled with the amillennialist's definition of the modifier "first"?

69 Michaels, "The First Resurrection," 104. As Michaels continues, "The strangeness of [Kline's] proposal becomes clear as soon as we press the interpretation of 'first' so as to speak of the 'old' resurrection. The difficulty is not so much that Kline includes the intermediate state in the present passing order of existence, but that he does so while at the

For these five reasons, even though the amillennial argument is certainly sophisticated, it fails to provide any convincing evidence that the "first resurrection" in Revelation 20 is spiritual in nature.

Amillennial Views of the First Resurrection

Although amillennialists all agree that the first resurrection is spiritual in nature, they disagree regarding the specific kind of spiritual resurrection portrayed in Revelation 20. Some amillennialists interpret the first resurrection as the regeneration of believers at the point of conversion, while others view it as the entrance of believers into life in heaven at the point of death. Both of these amillennial views must be considered.

View 1: The Regeneration of the Believer

The first amillennial view is that the first resurrection of Revelation 20 refers to the regeneration of believers at the point of conversion.[70] This spiritual resurrection is said to take place throughout the current age as those who were previously dead in their sins are made alive in Christ and live to reign with Him in the present millennial kingdom.[71] As William Cox writes, "We believe entrance to the on-going millennium is gained solely through the new birth, and that John refers to this as the first resurrection."[72] This view is common among amillennialists. Riddlebarger

---

same time calling it a resurrection." Kline dismisses this objection as Kantian and Barthian rather than biblical, and he faults Michaels for denying "that there is a difference in kind between the 'resurrection' which the Christian experiences when he passes into the intermediate state at death ... and the resurrection he experiences at the day of redemption of his body and glorification" ("A Reaffirmation," 114–15). But Kline's argument is not simply that the two resurrections are *different in kind*—something Michaels does not deny, despite Kline's claim to the contrary—but rather that they are *qualitatively antithetical to each other*. It is this qualitative antithesis, in which "first" belongs to this present world order and "new" belongs to the age to come, that presents such a problem for Kline's view. Kline's failure to address this dilemma leaves Michaels's objection unanswered.

70 This view was held by Augustine and Calvin and has been defended more recently by Riddlebarger (*A Case for Amillennialism*, 240–49), Shepherd ("Resurrections of Revelation 20," 34–43), Hamstra ("An Idealist View of Revelation," 120–21), Page ("Revelation 20 and Pauline Eschatology," 37–40), Hamilton (*The Basis of Millennial Faith*, 117–21), Cox (*Amillennialism Today*, 4–5), and White ("Death and the First Resurrection," 17–23).

71 As Hamstra clarifies, "This reign begins for the believer while on earth but continues in heaven, since the believer's soul, on his or her death, is raised to heaven while the body waits for Christ's return" ("An Idealist View of Revelation," 121).

72 Cox, *Amillennialism Today*, 4.

identifies the first resurrection as "the believers' regeneration;"[73] Hamstra calls it "the first resurrection of regeneration;"[74] Hamilton refers to it as "the new birth of the believer;"[75] Page describes it as "initiation into the Christian life in the present age;"[76] and Shepherd simply labels it "conversion."[77]

To support this view, amillennialists note that the new birth is depicted throughout the New Testament as a rising from the dead in the spiritual realm (Mark 12:26–27; John 5:25–29; 11:25; Rom 6:4–6; 8:10–11; Eph 2:1–7; Col 2:12–13; 3:1; 1 John 3:14; 5:11–13).[78] Those regenerated by the Holy Spirit are described as having "passed out of death into life" (1 John 3:14), having been "made ... alive together with Christ" (Eph 2:5). This abundant use of resurrection terminology in reference to the new birth is said to provide clear evidence that the first resurrection of Revelation 20 is spiritual regeneration.[79]

A second argument for the regeneration view is that the apostle John describes the first resurrection as "souls" coming to life (Rev 20:4). As Floyd Hamilton writes:

> The deliberate choice of the word "soul," which almost universally means soul as distinct from body, as applying to the believers now reigning with Christ in glory, seems to make it perfectly plain that the first resurrection is [the new birth]. If it were a literal

---

73 Riddlebarger, *A Case for Amillennialism*, 249.
74 Hamstra, "An Idealist View of Revelation," 120.
75 Hamilton, *The Basis of Millennial Faith*, 117.
76 Page, "Revelation 20 and Pauline Eschatology," 37.
77 Shepherd, "The Resurrections of Revelation 20," 36. As previously noted, Shepherd was postmillennial, but his view and argumentation here coincides with that of many amillennialists.
78 Cox, *Amillennialism Today*, 4; Hamilton, *The Basis of Millennial Faith*, 118–20; Page, "Revelation 20 and Pauline Eschatology," 37–39; Shepherd, "The Resurrections of Revelation 20," 36; Hamstra, "An Idealist View of Revelation," 120; Menn, *Biblical Eschatology*, 367.
79 Hamilton, *The Basis of Millennial Faith*, 117–20. According to Cox, this view is based on the many places in the New Testament where the new birth is referred to as a resurrection (*Amillennialism Today*, 4), and Page states that "there is excellent NT precedent for describing Christian initiation as a resurrection" ("Revelation 20 and Pauline Eschatology," 37). After examining several Pauline passages, Page concludes: "If the original readers of Revelation 20 were familiar with the sort of resurrection theology that we find in Paul, they might well have interpreted 'they came to life' in v 4, and 'the first resurrection' in v 5, as referring to regeneration" (39).

resurrection of the body, why should the author choose a word which almost always does *not* mean body?[80]

A third argument for this view is found in John 5:25–29.[81] In this passage, when Jesus refers to a spiritual resurrection of believers in the present (vv. 25–27)—in contrast to a physical resurrection of believers in the future (vv. 28–29)—the spiritual resurrection in view is the new birth of the one who believes in Christ. Because of the parallel between this passage and Revelation 20, John 5:25–29 is said to support the idea not merely that the "first resurrection" is spiritual in general, but that it is the regeneration of the believer in particular.

In response, there are several significant difficulties with this view of the first resurrection in Revelation 20. First, the word "resurrection" (ἀνάστασις) is used 39 times in the New Testament outside of Revelation 20 and never is it used to refer to regeneration.[82] This objection is not conclusive, because it is possible that Revelation 20 uses this word in a unique way, especially since a metaphorical use of ἀνάστασις would be a fitting way to signify being "made alive" in the spiritual realm. But nonetheless, the lack of precedent for this use of ἀνάστασις places the burden of proof on those who claim that the "first resurrection" is the believer's regeneration.

A second problem concerns the coming to life of "the rest of the dead" at the beginning of verse 5. When John says that these individuals "came to life" (ἔζησαν), most interpreters agree that this verb refers to a physical resurrection. Because John uses the same form of the same Greek word (ἔζησαν) to refer to the coming to life of the individuals in verse 4, it stands to reason that this "first resurrection" must be a physical resurrection as well. Otherwise, "we are faced with the problem of the same word being used in the same context with two entirely different meanings, with no indication whatsoever as to the change of meaning."[83] The premillen-

---

80 Hamilton, *The Basis of Millennial Faith*, 132. Amillennialist Dennis Johnson cites the use of "souls" as an argument *against* the regeneration view, but he does not explain why he thinks it presents a problem for this interpretation (*Triumph of the Lamb*, 293).
81 Riddlebarger, *A Case for Amillennialism*, 247–48; Hamilton, *The Basis of Millennial Faith*, 118; Page, "Revelation 20 and Pauline Eschatology," 37–38; White, "Death and the First Resurrection," 22, 25–27.
82 Gordon, "The First Resurrection," 82.
83 George Eldon Ladd, *A Commentary on the Revelation of John* (Grand Rapids: Eerdmans Publishing, 1972), 266; Gordon, "The First Resurrection," 82–83. The common amillennial response to this argument cites John 5:25–29 as an example where the very same passage

nial view does not have this problem, because it sees the verb ἔζησαν as referring to a physical resurrection in both verses—a resurrection of the righteous in verse 4 and a resurrection of the wicked in verse 5.

Regarding the amillennial argument that John's use of the word "souls" in Revelation 20:4 supports this view, ψυχή is often used as a reference to the whole person (Mark 3:4; Luke 6:9; 9:56; Acts 2:41, 43; 3:23; 7:14; 15:26; 27:37; Rom 2:9; 13:1; 1 Cor 15:45; 1 Pet 3:20)[84] and therefore it need not refer to the resurrection of merely the spiritual component of man. In fact, as amillennialist G. C. Berkouwer recognizes, there seems to be no soul-body dichotomy in view in Revelation 20:4–6, for John simply sees that those who had been beheaded come to life again and sit on thrones.[85] For this reason, the use of ψυχή in Revelation 20:4 is compatible with the premillennial view of the "first resurrection" and therefore fails to provide compelling evidence that it refers to the regeneration of believers.

A third problem with this view concerns the duration of the reign of the saints. In Revelation 20:4 and 6, the apostle John describes the saints reigning "for a thousand years" (χίλια ἔτη). In doing so, he uses an *accusative of time*, which indicates that the saints will reign for the entire thousand-year period.[86] This can be illustrated by John's use of

---

refers to both the spiritual resurrection of regeneration (vv. 25–27) and the physical resurrection of the righteous and the wicked at the end of the age (vv. 28–29) (Riddlebarger, *A Case for Amillennialism*, 247–48; Hamilton, *The Basis of Millennial Faith*, 118; Page, "Revelation 20 and Pauline Eschatology," 37–38; White, "Death and the First Resurrection," 22, 25–27). But as discussed earlier, the way the two uses of ἔζησαν are connected to each other in Revelation 20—"Some of the dead ἔζησαν (v. 4b), but the rest of the dead did not ἔζησαν until later (v. 5a)"—makes it clear that they refer to the same kind of coming to life.

84 BDAG, 1099–1100; Danker, *The Concise Greek-English Lexicon*, 388; Deere, "Premillennialism in Revelation 20:4–6," 67. Furthermore, as Deere notes, "John has previously used ψυχή with a qualifying genitive to refer to the whole person (ψυχὰς ἀνθρώπων in 18:13)." Amillennialist G. K. Beale makes the same observation, noting that ψυχή is used as a substitute for "living body" elsewhere in Revelation (8:9; 12:11; 16:3; cf. 18:13) (*The Book of Revelation*, 998).

85 G. C. Berkouwer, *The Return of Christ: Studies in Dogmatics* (Grand Rapids: Eerdmans Publishing, 1972), 304.

86 See Daniel B. Wallace, *Greek Grammar Beyond the Basics: An Exegetical Syntax of the New Testament* (Grand Rapids: Zondervan Publishing, 1996), 201–3; cf. F. Blass, F. and A. Debrunner, *A Greek Grammar of the New Testament and Other Early Christian Literature*, trans. and rev. by Robert W. Funk (Chicago: University of Chicago Press, 1961), 88–89; A. T. Robertson, *A Grammar of the Greek New Testament in the Light of Historical Research* (Nashville: Broadman Press, 1934), 469–71.

the same accusative of time in Revelation 20:2—"for a thousand years" (χίλια ἔτη)—where Satan is bound and incarcerated for the entirety of the thousand years. According to John's portrayal of the vision, then, the individuals who come to life in the first resurrection will begin their reign at the same time—at the very beginning of the thousand years—and they will reign together with Christ for the entirety of that time period (Rev 20:4–6).[87]

In contrast, according to the amillennial view that the first resurrection equals regeneration, believers are regenerated *throughout* the thousand years (i.e., the present age) so that the entrance of these saints into this millennial reign is distributed throughout the millennium.[88] In this scenario, those saints who are saved during the church age do not reign for the entirety of the thousand years—as John says they will—and some of them do not begin their reign until the millennium is almost over.

If John had intended to communicate that the saints would reign *during* the thousand years (which would correspond to the amillennial view) instead of *throughout the extent* of the thousand years, a *genitive of time* would have been more appropriate.[89] As it stands, the apostle's use of the accusative χίλια ἔτη ("for a thousand years") not only presents a problem for the amillennial regeneration view, but it also fits perfectly with premillennial view of believers coming to life in the first resurrection and reigning with Christ for the entirety of the thousand years.[90]

Fourthly, and most significantly, according to the view that the "first resurrection" in Revelation 20 is regeneration, the people in verse 4 are not regenerated by the Holy Spirit *until after they are martyred for their*

---

87 Charles E. Powell, "Progression Versus Recapitulation in Revelation 20:1–6," *BSac* 163, no. 649 (Jan 2006): 109.
88 Ibid.
89 See Wallace, *Greek Grammar Beyond the Basics*, 122–24.
90 The amillennialist cannot escape this difficulty by appealing to the symbolic nature of the book of Revelation, for John's use of the accusative of time is not imagery but rather a grammatically precise explanation of the significance of what he saw in his vision. If the first resurrection refers to the regeneration of believers throughout the thousand years, why would John portray them as coming to life at the beginning of the millennium and reigning together with Christ throughout the entirety of the millennium? No satisfactory answer to this question has been proposed by proponents of amillennialism.

faith in Christ. In the second part of John's vision in Revelation 20:4, the apostle John writes:

> And I saw the souls of those who had been beheaded because of their testimony of Jesus and because of the word of God, and those who had not worshiped the beast or his image, and had not received the mark on their forehead and on their hand; and they came to life and reigned with Christ for a thousand years (Rev 20:4).

According to the straightforward reading of Revelation 20:4, this view introduces "the absurdity of having souls being regenerated *after* they've been beheaded for their faithfulness to Christ!"[91] Because this is theologically impossible, this view of the first resurrection must be rejected.[92]

---

91 McClain, *The Greatness of the Kingdom*, 488; emphasis original; also see MacLeod, "The Fourth 'Last Thing,'" 57; Walvoord, "Theological Significance," 235; Hoehner, "Evidence from Revelation 20," 253; Blaising, "Premillennialism," 223.

92 Most amillennialists who interpret the "first resurrection" as regeneration neither acknowledge nor respond to this argument. A rare exception is R. Fowler White, who argues that the apostle John does not recount the martyrs' experiences in chronological order in Rev 20:4. According to White: "He speaks first of beheading, then of refusal to worship or bear the name of the beast, then of resurrection and reign. Whatever our understanding of the first resurrection, we must all concede that, though refusal to worship or bear the name of the beast *follows* beheading *in John's presentation*, that refusal actually *preceded* beheading *in history*" ("Death and the First Resurrection," 18; emphasis original). This allows to White to argue that the first resurrection "actually precedes and ironically leads the saints into martyrdom rather than delivering them from it" (23). But White has subtly misrepresented John's presentation and thereby complicated an otherwise simple progression of events in Rev 20:4. In the second part of verse 4, the apostle uses only three independent clauses (each connected by καὶ) to describe the unfolding of his vision—"I saw the souls [[εἶδον] τὰς ψυχὰς] ... they came to life [ἔζησαν] ... they reigned with Christ [ἐβασίλευσαν μετὰ τοῦ Χριστοῦ]"—and these events are presented in chronological order. When White describes John's presentation as departing from chronological order, he is referring to the clauses which are subordinate to the first independent clause. Rather than advancing the action of the actual vision, however, these subordinate clauses supply background information by explaining how and why the souls seen by John were killed in the first place. Condensing this subordinate description into a concise paraphrase results in the following rendering of verse 4: "I saw the souls of those [who were martyred] and they came to life and reigned with Christ for a thousand years." The fact that John does not relay this background information in sequential order does not undermine the simplicity of the chronology of events portrayed by the three main clauses. Contrary to White's claim, the first resurrection does indeed remedy the death of the martyrs described in Rev 20:4 and it is therefore a physical resurrection. An additional problem with White's view (that the saints' resurrection preceded their martyrdom) is found in the very next verse. By referring to "the *rest* of the dead" (οἱ λοιποὶ τῶν νεκρῶν) not coming to life until after the thousand years (v. 5a), John makes it clear that those who came to life in verse 4 were indeed physically dead when they experienced the first resurrection.

View 2: The Death of the Believer

Other amillennialists interpret the "first resurrection" of Revelation 20 as the believer's entrance into the intermediate state at the point of death and the blessings of life that it brings.[93] William Hendriksen describes the first resurrection as "the translation of the soul from this sinful earth to God's holy heaven;"[94] Anthony Hoekema calls it "the transition from physical death to life in heaven with Christ during the time between death and the resurrection;"[95] and James Hughes defines it as "the soul's being raised from earth to heaven."[96]

According to this view, when the believer dies physically, his soul is raised and it ascends from earth to heaven where he lives and reigns with Christ for a thousand years.[97] This ascension—in which the soul enters the intermediate state of life with Christ—is called the "first resurrection."[98] In the words of Robert Strimple, "The first resurrection occurs when [the believer] departs this life and is immediately ushered into the presence of Christ to reign with him."[99]

According to this view, the first resurrection of Revelation 20 is considered a paradoxical reference to the physical death of the believer.[100] As

---

93 Storms, *Kingdom Come*, 451. This view is defended by Kline ("The First Resurrection," 366–75), Hoekema (*The Bible and the Future*, 232–37), Hendriksen (*More than Conquerors*, 191–93), Johnson (*Triumph of the Lamb*, 291–94), Poythress (*The Returning King*, 182, and "Genre and Hermeneutics in Rev 20:1–6," 53), Strimple ("Amillennialism," 127), Beale (*The Book of Revelation*, 991–1011), Storms (*Kingdom Come*, 462–65), and Davis (*The High King of Heaven*, 475–82). According to Riddlebarger (*A Case for Amillennialism*, 249) and Beale (*The Book of Revelation*, 1011–12), the two amillennial views of the "first resurrection" are not necessarily incompatible with each other, because believers are both raised spiritually from death to life at the moment of regeneration and raised spiritually from earth to heaven at the time of death.
94 Hendriksen, *More than Conquerors*, 192.
95 Anthony A. Hoekema "An Amillennial Response," in *The Meaning of the Millennium: Four Views*, ed. Robert G. Clouse (Downers Grove, IL: InterVarsity Press, 1977), 57.
96 Hughes, "The Question of the Millennium," 291.
97 Ibid., 290–91. According to Hughes, this is an example of metonymy in which the "first resurrection" is "the entrance of the soul into a glorified state of life with Christ at physical death" even though "John uses the term to refer to the soul's living with Christ a thousand years (in heaven)" (291).
98 Hoekema, *The Bible and the Future*, 237; Hughes, "The Question of the Millennium," 291. For this reason, Johnson refers to the martyrs' first resurrection as "the deliverance of their souls from all that threatened them on earth" (*Triumph of the Lamb*, 294).
99 Strimple, "Amillennialism," 127.
100 Johnson, *Triumph of the Lamb*, 293; Garlington, "Reigning with Christ," 77. As Garlington explains: "To the non-Christian onlooker, the death of the believer is the end of existence,

Meredith Kline explains, "Just as the resurrection of the unjust is paradoxically identified as 'the second death' so the death of the Christian is paradoxically identified as 'the first resurrection'.... What for others is the first death is for the Christian a veritable resurrection!"[101] In other words, even though these believers have died, "John sees them as alive, not in the bodily sense, but in the sense that they are enjoying life in heaven in fellowship with Christ."[102]

According to amillennialist Sam Storms, if the apostle John's purpose in Revelation 20:4–6 was to encourage believers who were facing persecution and possible martyrdom,

> what better, more appropriate, or even more biblical way could he have done so than by assuring them that though they may *die physically* at the hands of the beast they will *live spiritually* in the presence of the Lamb? I can think of no more vivid way of making this point than that of *life* beyond and in spite of *death*.[103]

In fact, Storms argues that the terminology John uses to describe his vision fits perfectly with the view that the first resurrection refers to entrance into the intermediate state:

> If John were attempting to describe the blessings of the intermediate state for those facing martyrdom, what terminology could he possibly have used, other than what he does use, and still

---

which compels him to draw the conclusion that there is no difference between the Christian and himself. John, however, comforts his readers by informing them that instead of being the termination of life, physical death is the portal through which the believing person enters into a new phase of that resurrection which began when he first heard the voice of the Son of Man" (74). According to Johnson: "Paradox is no stranger to those familiar with John's visions. The lion who has conquered is the lamb who has been slain. The carefully counted Israelite army of 144,000 celibate males is an innumerable multitude from every nation and people. The church is safe from destruction, yet exposed to persecution, even to the death. The beast overcomes Jesus's witnesses and kills them, yet in so doing the beast inadvertently forfeits to them the real victory, for in their fidelity to the death they overcome the dragon-accuser who animates the beast (Rev. 12:11). From one perspective the martyrs of heaven can be viewed as sacrificial victims, awaiting just vindication; but from another—even now, while the 'first things' (death, mourning, pain) exist—they have experienced a 'first resurrection,' the deliverance of their souls from all that threatened them on earth (cf. 7:15–17)" (*Triumph of the Lamb*, 293–94).

101 Kline, "The First Resurrection," 371.
102 Hoekema, *The Bible and the Future*, 233; cf. Leon Morris, *Revelation*, TNTC (Grand Rapids: Eerdmans Publishing, 1987), 231.
103 Storms, *Kingdom Come*, 453; emphasis original.

maintain the desired emphasis? There simply is no other Greek noun besides *anastasis* ["resurrection"] that would adequately make the point.[104]

As evidence that Revelation 20:4–6 refers to the experience of martyrs in the intermediate state—and therefore that the first resurrection must refer to entrance *into* the intermediate state—amillennialists point to John's use of the word "thrones" in verse 4.[105] According to Storms, because the Greek word for "throne" (θρόνος) consistently refers to heavenly thrones throughout the book of Revelation, it must refer to thrones in heaven in Revelation 20:4 as well.[106] For this reason, because the resurrected martyrs are described as sitting upon these heavenly thrones, the millennial reign of these saints must refer to life in heaven in the intermediate state.

As further evidence for this view, it is also noted that John specifically refers to "souls" (ψυχή) being resurrected and reigning with Christ (Rev 20:4).[107] According to this argument, the reason John refers to the experience of disembodied *souls* who are martyred is because he is describing the blessedness of the intermediate state of those who are now living and reigning with Christ during the thousand years.[108] Amillennialists also point to other uses of the verb "to live" (ζάω) in the New Testament.[109]

---

[104] Ibid.
[105] Johnson, *Triumph of the Lamb*, 291; Hoekema, *The Bible and the Future*, 232–33; Strimple, "Amillennialism," 125; Beale, *The Book of Revelation*, 998; Hendriksen, *More than Conquerors*, 191.
[106] According to Storms, "The word *thronos* appears sixty-two times in the New Testament, forty-seven of which are in the book of Revelation. Twice (2:13; 13:2) it refers to Satan's throne (being synonymous with his authority or power) and once to the throne of the beast (16:10). On four occasions it refers to God's throne on the *new* earth in consequence of its having *come down from heaven* (21:3, 5; 22:1, 3). In every other instance (forty times) *thronos* refers to a throne in *heaven*, either that of God the Father, of Christ, of the twenty-four elders, etc." (*Kingdom Come*, 461; cf. Cornelis P. Venema, *The Promise of the Future* [Carlisle, PA: Banner of Truth, 2000], 328).
[107] Johnson, *Triumph of the Lamb*, 293; Strimple, "Amillennialism," 125; Venema, *The Promise of the Future*, 329; Beale, *The Book of Revelation*, 998; Hendriksen, *More than Conquerors*, 191–92.
[108] Storms, *Kingdom Come*, 458.
[109] According to Beale, "In the Apocalypse [ζάω] sometimes refers to physical resurrection (1:18; 2:8) or more generally to some form of physical existence (16:3; 19:20), but more often it has figurative connotation of spiritual existence, especially with respect to God's attribute of timeless existence (six occurrences). In 3:1 the verb refers to spiritual life (and the uses in 7:17 and 13:14 are probably also figurative)" (*The Book of Revelation*, 1004).

According to this argument, because ζάω is used to describe the life and existence of souls after the death of the body in passages such as Matthew 22:32,[110] Luke 20:38,[111] and 1 Peter 4:6,[112] there is a clear precedent of this word being used to describe life in the intermediate state. This argument is said to support this specific use of the verb in Revelation 20:4.

As a final argument for this view, amillennialists point to other passages in the book of Revelation which highlight spiritual life in the intermediate state after physical death. For example, Revelation 2:10–11 promises "the crown of life" to those believers who are faithful until death;[113] Revelation 6:9–11 "is a vision of the heavenly bliss of those who have suffered martyrdom for Christ;"[114] and Revelation 14:13 emphasizes "the blessedness of Christian death."[115] These parallels are said to confirm that Revelation 20:4–6 "is concerned with the bliss of the intermediate state"[116] and therefore that the "first resurrection" refers to entrance into the intermediate state.

In response, the primary difficulty with this view concerns the term ἀνάστασις. As even amillennialist Sydney Page observes, "Like all attempts to relate the first resurrection to the intermediate state, it faces the objection that the translation of the soul of the believer to heaven at death is not spoken of as a resurrection anywhere else in the NT."[117] But not only does this view insist on a use of ἀνάστασις which is unprecedented in the New Testament, it also argues for an interpretation of the "first resurrection" that is inconsistent with the very concept of a "resurrection."[118] According

---

110 Storms, *Kingdom Come*, 455.
111 Hoekema, *The Bible and the Future*, 233–34; Beale, *The Book of Revelation*, 1008–9.
112 Garlington, "Reigning with Christ," 74, 94; Beale, *The Book of Revelation*, 1009.
113 Storms, *Kingdom Come*, 455. According to Storms, the parallels between Rev 2:10–11 and Rev 20:4–6 are "unmistakable."
114 Storms, *Kingdom Come*, 457; also see Hoekema, *The Bible and the Future*, 234–35; Beale, *The Book of Revelation*, 998, 1010; Poythress, *The Returning King*, 180; Menn, *Biblical Eschatology*, 294.
115 Storms, *Kingdom Come*, 458; also see Hoekema, *The Bible and the Future*, 235; Johnson, *Triumph of the Lamb*, 294.
116 Storms, *Kingdom Come*, 458.
117 Page, "Revelation 20 and Pauline Eschatology," 37.
118 In the words of N.T. Wright, "to use the word 'resurrection' to *refer to* death in an attempt to invest it with a new meaning seems … to strain usage well beyond the breaking point" (N. T. Wright, *The Resurrection of the Son of God* [Minneapolis: Fortress Press, 2003], 474; emphasis original). The amillennial view that the first resurrection equals regeneration does not have this problem, because being made alive in the spiritual realm certainly fits the concept of a "resurrection," even though ἀνάστασις never refers to the new birth in the New Testament.

to this view, the word "resurrection" refers to those who *live spiritually* even though they have *died physically*. In this way, the term "resurrection" refers to "the Christian's entrance into non-bodily life after bodily death" or "the Christian's passage from bodily death into non-bodily life."[119] The problem is that "resurrection" does not imply life *after* death but rather life *from* death.[120] In other words, "When the Bible and its interpreters invoke resurrection as a term or concept, life and death are understood to be either *both spiritual* (non-bodily) or *both physical* (bodily)."[121]

Therefore, when someone who is physically dead is made alive in the physical realm, this is often referred to as a "resurrection." Likewise, when someone who is spiritually dead is made alive in the spiritual realm, this could also be described as a "resurrection."[122] But when someone who is already spiritually alive continues to live spiritually even after his physical death, no coming to life—and therefore no "resurrection"—has actually taken place. For this reason, "We may rightly call such life 'the intermediate state' or 'the Christian's afterlife,' but not 'resurrection.'"[123] The word ἀνάστασις is completely ill suited to convey the believer's entrance into the intermediate state at death, and therefore this view should be rejected.[124]

A second problem with this view concerns the repetition of the identical form of the same verb ἔζησαν ("they came to life") in verses 4 and 5. If one resurrection is spiritual, then the other must also be spiritual,

---

119 These definitions are provided by White ("Death and the First Resurrection," 8–9), who is critiquing this view rather than defending it, but they summarize it accurately.
120 White, "Death and the First Resurrection," 8.
121 Ibid.; emphasis original.
122 This is acknowledged even though the New Testament itself does not use the term ἀνάστασις as a reference to regeneration (see above for discussion).
123 White, "Death and the First Resurrection," 8. White states, "I do not see that such notions are consistent with the meaning of resurrection as a term or concept in the Bible or elsewhere" (9). Along these same lines, White objects that while the Bible clearly teaches two categories of resurrection outside of Revelation 20 (e.g., in John 5), this view creates a third category of resurrection otherwise unknown in the Bible.
124 According to Storms, "If John wished to describe entrance into the intermediate state in terms of a resurrection ... with what Greek noun other than *anastasis* could he have done it?" (*Kingdom Come*, 453). The problem with this argument is that it assumes what Storms is trying to prove: that John does indeed intend to describe the believer's entrance into the immediate state as a *resurrection*. Nobody disputes that the word ἀνάστασις is the best word to express the idea of a *resurrection*—what is disputed is whether John is describing *entrance into the intermediate state* as a resurrection. One could equally argue, "If John wished to describe prayers to God in terms of a *resurrection*, with what Greek noun other than ἀνάστασις could he have done it?," but this does not prove that the word "resurrection" refers to prayers.

and if one is physical, the other must be physical as well. As A. J. Gordon writes, "The meaning of the one fixes the meaning of the other."[125] This has significant implications:

> If ἔζησαν in both verses refers to a physical resurrection, there is no problem. But if ἔζησαν refers to a spiritual resurrection in both verses, then the exegete is confronted with an insurmountable problem. For this would imply that the unbelieving dead of verse 5 live spiritually in heaven like the martyrs of verse 4 after the thousand years is completed.[126]

---

125 Gordon, "The First Resurrection," 83.
126 Deere, "Premillennialism in Revelation 20:4–6," 68. Because the same word ἔζησαν is used, amillennialist Anthony Hoekema agrees that both resurrections must be of the same nature, but he argues that neither of them are bodily resurrections. According to Hoekema, when John says "they came to life [ἔζησαν] and reigned with Christ for a thousand years" (v. 4), this refers to a spiritual resurrection of the saints during the present age. But when John continues by writing that "the rest of the dead did not come to life [ἔζησαν] until the thousand years were completed" (v. 5a), he means that the wicked never did come to life spiritually (*The Bible and the Future*, 235–36; also Augustine, *City of God*, 20.9; Strimple, "Amillennialism," 126; Hughes, "The Question of the Millennium," 301–2). Hoekema defends this interpretation by arguing that the conjunction ἄχρι in verse 5—"until [ἄχρι] the thousand years were completed"—means "up to a certain point" but does not indicate a change in the state of affairs after the time period has ended. For this reason, says Hoekema, "The use of the word *until* does not imply that these unbelieving dead will live and reign with Christ after this period has ended," for they will *never* live and reign with Christ (*The Bible and the Future*, 236). But this interpretation is highly unlikely for several reasons: (1) Every time that ἄχρι is used in the New Testament as a conjunction (as in Rev 20:5) rather than a preposition, it refers to a period of time that will come to an end and be followed by a reversal of the condition just described (e.g., Rev 7:3; 15:18; 20:3) (Deere, "Premillennialism in Revelation 20:4–6," 68–69; Blaising, "Premillennialism," 225–26; MacLeod, "The Fourth 'Last Thing,'" 58). Therefore, the use of the conjunction ἄχρι in Rev 20:5 implies that the "rest of the dead" will indeed "come to life" (ἔζησαν) and experience a physical resurrection like the saints in verse 4. (2) The exact same expression is used in Rev 20:3 ("until the thousand years were completed"—ἄχρι τελεσθῇ τὰ χίλια ἔτη) where it clearly contemplates a change after the thousand years (since Satan will be released once the millennium is completed) (Rev 20:7–8). This implies that the rest of dead will indeed "come to life" (ἔζησαν) after the thousand-year period. (3) If John wanted to deny a resurrection to the others, he could have simply written, "The rest of the dead did not come to life." The addition of "until the thousand years were ended" clearly suggests subsequent action, whereas the clause is entirely superfluous if subsequent action is not intended (Saucy, *Progressive Dispensationalism*, 276). (4) If neither use of ἔζησαν refers to a bodily resurrection, then there is no mention of the future resurrection of the believer in Revelation 20. (5) This interpretation raises the question of why John would have deemed it necessary to inform or assure his readers that unbelievers will not experience the spiritual resurrection promised only to believers. (6) A "*first* resurrection" simply implies a second one. As Saucy states, "The immediate identification of the coming to life of the first group as the 'first' resurrection seems clearly to suggest a second resurrection involving those remaining" (Saucy, *Progressive Dispensationalism*, 276). Amillennialists G. K. Beale (*The Book of Revelation*, 1015–16) and Sam Storms (*Kingdom Come*, 468–69)

This is a theological and exegetical impossibility, and for this reason, the use of the word ἔζησαν as a description of the "first resurrection" weighs heavily against this view.

A third problem with this view concerns the designation χίλια ἔτη ("for a thousand years") at the end of Revelation 20:4. As explained above, John's use of the accusative of time indicates that the individuals who come to life in the first resurrection will begin their reign at the same time—at the very beginning of the thousand years—and they will reign together with Christ for the entirety of the millennium (Rev 20:4–6).[127] In contrast, according to the view that the first resurrection refers to believers entering the intermediate state at the point of death, the entrance of these saints into their reign is distributed throughout the millennial period as they die.[128] In this scenario, believers do not live in heaven and reign with Christ for the entirety the thousand years—as John says they will—and some of them do not begin their reign until the millennium is almost over. A genitive of time would have been compatible with this view, but the accusative of time is not.

Furthermore, the various arguments in favor of this view are less than compelling. First, the claim of a clear precedent of the word ζάω ("to live") being used as a reference to life in the intermediate state is true, but also a bit misleading. The verb is used 139 times in the New Testament, but only three times is it used in this way (Matt 22:32; Luke 20:38; 1 Pet 4:6). Therefore, a clear precedent does exist, but the rarity of its use undermines the strength of this argument, especially in the absence of clear contextual indicators for this uncommon usage.[129] The verb can certainly be used to describe life in the intermediate state, but John's use of this specific word in Revelation 20:4 provides no compelling evidence that it does.

Second, John's use of the word "throne" (θρόνος) in verse 4 is not a decisive argument in favor of this view either. According to some

---

argue against Hoekema's view, insisting that Rev 20:5 refers to the physical resurrection of unbelievers after the thousand years, which leaves them with no adequate response to the premillennial objection of the two uses of ἔζησαν having different meanings.

127 Powell, "Progression Versus Recapitulation," 109.
128 Ibid.
129 In addition, the verb ζάω is used elsewhere in Revelation to refer to bodily resurrection (Rev 1:18; 2:8; 13:14; cf. Rom 14:9). Furthermore, as Thomas notes, whenever ζάω is used in the context of bodily death in the New Testament, it always speaks of bodily resurrection (e.g., John 11:25; Acts 1:3; 9:41) (*Revelation 8–22*, 417).

amillennialists, because θρόνος refers to heavenly thrones throughout Revelation, it must refer to heavenly thrones in Revelation 20:4 as well. This is said to place the scene of Revelation 20:4–6 in heaven and therefore during the intermediate state. But the word θρόνος simply refers to a *throne*, without specifying the actual location of the throne. Instead, the location of the throne mentioned in any given passage must be determined from the immediate context of its use. In Revelation 20, the context indicates that the saints who reign from these thrones are "on the broad plain of the earth" (Rev 20:9). Furthermore, the promise in Revelation 5:10 that the saints "will reign upon the earth" also argues for earthly thrones in Revelation 20:4–6 since the former is fulfilled in the latter. This amillennial argument is less than compelling, for *if John had intended to refer to thrones on earth, what other word was available to him to do so?*

Thirdly, John's reference to "souls" (ψυχή) being resurrected and reigning with Christ (Rev 20:4) fails to provide compelling evidence for this view either. As noted previously, the use of ψυχή to refer to the whole person is well attested in the New Testament (e.g., Mark 3:4; Luke 6:9; 9:56; Acts 2:41, 43; 3:23; 7:14; 15:26; 27:37; Rom 2:9; 13:1; 1 Cor 15:45; 1 Pet 3:20).[130] In addition, there seems to be no soul-body dichotomy in view in Revelation 20:4–6, for John sees simply that those who had been beheaded come to life again and sit on thrones.[131] For this reason, the use of ψυχή in Revelation 20:4 is compatible with the premillennial view of the "first resurrection" and therefore fails to prove the amillennial view.

In addition, the amillennial argument for interpreting ψυχή in Revelation 20:4 as a reference to man's soul (as distinguished from his physical body) actually highlights the primary problem with this view, for in what sense does the believer's soul experience a "resurrection" at the point of physical death? Again, when someone who is already spiritually alive continues to live spiritually even after his physical death, no *coming to life* has actually taken place.

Fourthly, none of the parallel passages cited by amillennialists confirm that Revelation 20:4–6 describes life in the intermediate state and therefore that the "first resurrection" refers to entrance into the intermediate

---

[130] *BDAG*, 1099–1100; Danker, *The Concise Greek-English Lexicon*, 388; Deere, "Premillennialism in Revelation 20:4–6," 67.
[131] Berkouwer, *The Return of Christ*, 304.

state. The strongest amillennial argument in this regard is the appeal to Revelation 6:9–11.[132] According to amillennialist Sam Storms, a careful comparison between Revelation 6:9–11 and Revelation 20:4 reveals that they are clearly describing the same experience of martyred saints in the intermediate state:[133]

Revelation 6:9	Revelation 20:4a
"And … I saw"	"And I saw"
"the souls of those who had been slain"	"the souls of those who had been beheaded"
"because of the word of God"	"because of the word of God"
"and because of the testimony which they had maintained"	"because of the testimony of Jesus"

Figure 2. Storms, *Kingdom Come*, 458.[134]

Because of these parallels, Storms says it "seems beyond reasonable doubt" that these two visions are describing the same experience of the

---

132 Amillennialists also cite Rev 2:10–11 and 13:14 as evidence that Rev 20:4–6 portrays life in the intermediate state. According to Storms, Rev 2:10–11 is parallel to Rev 20:4–6 in three specific ways: (1) "it speaks of *martyrdom* as the result of steadfast faith;" (2) "the faithful are promised 'the crown of *life*;'" and (3) "the faithful martyrs are exempt from the *second death*" (*Kingdom Come*, 459; emphasis original). But these parallels do not prove that Rev 20:4–6 describes life in the intermediate state. To use Rev 2:10–11 as a compelling argument, the amillennialist must be able to demonstrate (a) that receiving the crown of life takes place during the intermediate state rather than in the eternal state and (b) that it can be equated with the millennial reign portrayed in Rev 20:4–6. But this cannot be done. According to Kline, the "crown of life" in Rev 2:10 "might … be the royal crown," in which case it should be considered "the nominal equivalent of the verbal 'they lived and reign' … in Revelation 20:4ff" ("The First Resurrection," 374). But this has merely been asserted rather than proven.

Regarding Rev 14:13, Kline argues that the blessing of "rest from their labors" promised in this verse "is very much the same as the millennial blessings of Revelation 20:6" ("The First Resurrection," 373). According to Kline, "The biblical concept of sabbath rest includes enthronement after the completion of labors by which royal dominion is manifested or secured (cf., e.g., Isa. 66:1).… To live and reign with Christ is to participate in his royal sabbath rest." For this reason, Kline cites Rev 14:13 as evidence that Rev 20:4–6 describes life in the intermediate state. The simple problem with this argument is its inability to demonstrate that the rest of Rev 14:13 can indeed be equated with the reign of Rev 20:6. If a case can be made from Isa 66:1 that the two verses describe the same experience, then this needs to be demonstrated clearly. Until then, interpreters not already inclined to connect these dots may have a difficult time seeing the connection.

133 Storms, *Kingdom Come*, 457.

134 Storms appears to have borrowed his chart from Michel Gourgues, "The Thousand-Year Reign (Rev. 20:1–6): Terrestrial or Celestial?," *CBQ* 47, no. 4 (Oct 1985): 680.

martyrs and therefore that Revelation 20:4–6 must portray life in the intermediate state.[135]

But the problem with this argument is that the similarities listed by Storms merely prove that both visions refer to the same group of individuals, not that both visions describe the same *experience* of those individuals. In fact, John identifies the martyrs and what led to their deaths in Revelation 6:9 and 20:4a, but he does not describe the *experience* of these martyrs until Revelation 6:10–11 and 20:4b. For this reason, if Storms wants to demonstrate that Revelation 6:9–11 and 20:4 describe the same experience of these martyrs in the intermediate state, he must show clear parallels between Revelation 6:10–11 and 20:4b.[136] But these are the very parts of the passages he ignores in his comparison.

The two visions are obviously related to one another, but their relationship is one of progression rather than simple identity.[137] More specifically, the progression from Revelation 6:9–11 to 20:4–6 is such that if the former refers to the intermediate state (as it clearly does), then the latter must refer to a subsequent stage in the experience of the martyred saints.[138] In Revelation 6:10–11 the martyrs cry out to the Lord to avenge their blood because of the ongoing martyrdom of the saints (v. 10). In response to their anguished pleas, they are given a white robe and told to wait until the full number of martyrs has been slain (v. 11), with the implied promise that vindication will come when this number has been reached. This is indeed the intermediate state.

In Revelation 20:4b, however, their number is now complete (cf. Rev 13:15; 18:24) and their prayers for vindication have been answered, for the Lord has returned in judgment (Rev 19:11–21).[139] The wait for divine vengeance is over, and the entire group of martyrs comes to life and reigns with Christ for a thousand years (Rev 20:4). This distinction between the

---

135 Storms, *Kingdom Come*, 458.
136 The only similarity in experience noted by Hoekema is that in both passages "the souls of deceased believers are said to be living between death and resurrection" (*The Bible and the Future*, 235). But this simply assumes that Rev 20:4–6 describes the intermediate state (i.e., the experience of saints between death and resurrection), which is precisely what Hoekema is trying to prove.
137 Michaels, "The First Resurrection," 107; also see Blaising, "Premillennialism," 221–22.
138 Michaels, "The First Resurrection," 107–8.
139 As Michaels states, the prayer of Rev 6:9–11 is answered in Rev 20:4–6 ("The First Resurrection," 108).

two is reflected in the fact that the experience of the martyred saints in Revelation 6:9–11 lasts for a short time ("a little while longer" in v. 11), whereas the experience of the martyred saints in Revelation 20:4–6 lasts for a long time ("a thousand years" in v. 4).[140] The two passages are clearly not describing the same experience or period of time.

Storms and other amillennialists may disagree with the futuristic reading of the book of Revelation, but the consistency of this progression between the two passages demonstrates the compatibility of Revelation 6:9–11 with the premillennial view of Revelation 20:4–6. In doing so, it also demonstrates that Revelation 6:9–11 fails to provide compelling evidence that Revelation 20:4–6 describes life in the intermediate state.[141]

Conclusion

In the words of George Eldon Ladd, "It is difficult to see how this 'first resurrection' can be anything but literal bodily resurrection."[142] For this reason, the first resurrection in Revelation 20 must be the first of two physical resurrections which are separated by a thousand years. The first is a resurrection of the righteous, who will be raised at the Second Coming of Christ (Rev 20:4–6), and the second is a resurrection of the wicked (Rev 20:5a), who will be raised after the millennium to stand before the judgment of the great white throne (Rev 20:11–15). And between these two physical resurrections, King Jesus will reign upon the earth for a thousand years, just as premillennialism teaches.

---

140 Webb, "Revelation 20," 32. Rev 6:9–11 takes place during the intermediate state, but it does not cover the entirety of the present age. In fact, the event described in this passage is yet future, not yet having taken place. More specifically, it will take place during the seven-year tribulation and it describes the pleas of those who will be martyred earlier in that period. So the "little while longer" in verse 11 is less than seven years in length, in contrast to the millennial reign of Christ, which will last a thousand years.

141 In response to Michaels's argument, Kline insists that Rev 20:4–6 views the entire period of the church in the intermediate state as a whole, whereas Rev 6:9–11 sees it at a particular point early on ("A Reaffirmation," 116–17). But in his argument, Kline simply assumes that Rev 20:4–6 describes the intermediate state without actually proving it through a comparison of the two passages.

142 Ladd, "Revelation 20 and the Millennium," 169.

Chapter 13

The Duration of the Thousand Years

Introduction

The reign of Christ in Revelation 20 is often called His *millennial* reign because it is described as a thousand years in length. In fact, John uses the designation "thousand years" (τὰ χίλια ἔτη) a total of six times to refer to the duration of this time period (Rev 20:2, 3, 4, 5, 6, 7). Although the millennial controversy is not primarily a debate over the duration of the millennium,[1] this question has significant implications for the plausibility of the amillennial view.

Amillennialism teaches that the thousand years of Revelation 20 represents the time between the first and second comings of Christ.[2] But this raises an obvious question: *If the millennium is the present age, how can the thousand years of Revelation 20 refer to a period of time that is nearly two thousand years and counting?* Put simply, if the apostle John intended the thousand years to be understood literally, the millennium cannot be equated with the present age and amillennialism is confronted with an insurmountable problem. The purpose of this chapter is to determine the duration of the "thousand years" in Revelation 20.

---

1 Darrell L. Bock, "Summary Essay," in *Three Views on the Millennium and Beyond*, ed. Darrell L. Bock (Grand Rapids: Zondervan Publishing, 1999), 304–5.
2 Anthony Hoekema, *The Bible and the Future* (Grand Rapids: Eerdmans Publishing, 1979), 227; Cornelis P. Venema, *The Promise of the Future* (Carlisle, PA: Banner of Truth, 2000), 327. As Kim Riddlebarger states, "The period of time between the first and second advent of Jesus Christ ... is the same period described in Revelation 20 as a 'thousand years'" (Kim Riddlebarger, *A Case for Amillennialism: Understanding the End Times*, expanded ed. [Grand Rapids: Baker Books, 2013], 95).

The Amillennial View

Amillennialists reject the literal interpretation of the thousand years in Revelation 20, insisting instead that it must be "a symbolic number, spanning the entire church age."[3] More specifically, the designation is seen as a figurative way to describe "an indefinitely long period of time,"[4] "not a literal period of one thousand years, but the entire period, perfect, complete and extensive, between the first and second comings of Christ."[5] Put most simply, amillennialists believe the thousand years should be interpreted *symbolically*.

The Case for the Symbolic View

The primary argument for the symbolic view is that the book of Revelation is full of symbolism.[6] As Cornelis Venema writes, "A book like Revelation, with its rich symbolism and use of biblical types and figures, gives no obvious reason to take literally the term of one thousand years."[7] In addition to the symbolic nature of Revelation in general, amillennialists insist that numbers in particular are used symbolically.[8] As Robert Strimple states, "We may readily assume that the number is symbolic, for numbers are used symbolically throughout Revelation."[9] Therefore, in keeping with the symbolic nature of Revelation as a whole and its

---

3 Riddlebarger, *A Case for Amillennialism*, 236.
4 William E. Cox, *Amillennialism Today* (Phillipsburg, NJ: Presbyterian and Reformed Publishing Co., 1966), 4.
5 Venema, *The Promise of the Future*, 327.
6 G. K. Beale, *The Book of Revelation*, NIGTC (Grand Rapids: Eerdmans Publishing, 1999), 995; Samuel E. Waldron, *The End Times Made Simple: How Could Everyone Be So Wrong About Biblical Prophecy?* (Amityville, NY: Calvary Press, 2003), 96.
7 Venema, *The Promise of the Future*, 324. In fact, some amillennialists insist that the symbolic nature of Revelation is *opposed* to a literal understanding of the thousand years (e.g., Henry Barclay Swete, *Commentary on Revelation* [Grand Rapids: Kregel Publications, 1977], 266; Dean Davis, *The High King of Heaven: Discovering the Master Keys to the Great End Time Debate* [Enumclaw, WA: WinePress Publishing, 2014], 474; Jonathan Menn, *Biblical Eschatology* [Eugene, OR: Resource Publications, 2013], 355–56).
8 Riddlebarger, *A Case for Amillennialism*, 237; Sam Hamstra Jr., "An Idealist View of Revelation," in *Four Views on the Book of Revelation*, ed. C. Marvin Pate (Grand Rapids: Zondervan Publishing, 1998), 121; Sydney H. T. Page, "Revelation 20 and Pauline Eschatology," *JETS* 23, no. 1 (March 1980): 32.
9 Robert B. Strimple, "Amillennialism," in *Three Views on the Millennium and Beyond*, ed. Darrell L. Bock (Grand Rapids: Zondervan Publishing), 127.

use of numbers in particular, amillennialists argue that the number one thousand in Revelation 20 must be symbolic as well.[10]

A second argument for the symbolic view involves the immediate context. As Stanley Grenz notes, like the Apocalypse as a whole, Revelation 20 itself is a highly symbolic chapter:

> It speaks of Satan being bound with a chain and cast into a bottomless pit, and it anticipates a second death that lasts forever. The author obviously intended that none of these be interpreted in a purely literal manner, as such an interpretation would be nonsensical—that is, a spiritual being bound with a physical chain and confined in a physical pit with no bottom. Consequently, it is possible that other figures in these verses, including the thousand years, are likewise to be understood symbolically.[11]

As Kim Riddlebarger writes, "The immediate context and the figurative nature of many words used by John, such as *chain, abyss, serpent, beast*, and so on, should remind us that numbers are also symbolic of something else."[12]

A third argument for the symbolic view is that the number one thousand is rarely if ever meant to be taken with arithmetical precision elsewhere in Scripture.[13] According to amillennialist Sam Storms:

> This is true whether the context is *non-temporal* (Ps. 50:10; Song 4:4; Josh. 23:10; Isa. 60:22; Deut. 1:11; Job 9:3; Eccles. 7:28), in which case the usage is always figurative, indeed hyperbolical, or *temporal* (Deut. 7:9; 1 Chron. 16:15; Pss. 84:10; 90:4; 105:8; 2 Pet. 3:8).[14]

Venema specifically points to Exodus 20:5–6, Deuteronomy 7:9, Psalm 50:10–11, Psalm 84:10, Psalm 90:4, and 2 Peter 3:8 as evidence "that the

---

10 Beale, *The Book of Revelation*, 995. As Sydney Page summarizes, "Since symbolism is used extensively throughout the Apocalypse and numbers are used in a nonliteral sense frequently, it would be facile to insist that the number 'one thousand' be taken literally in this context" ("Revelation 20 and Pauline Eschatology," 32).
11 Stanely J. Grenz, *The Millennial Maze: Sorting Out Evangelical Options* (Downers Grove, IL: InterVarsity Press, 1992), 167.
12 Riddlebarger, *A Case for Amillennialism*, 237; cf. Beale, *The Book of Revelation*, 995; Menn, *Biblical Eschatology*, 356–57; Waldron, *The End Times Made Simple*, 96.
13 Sam Storms, *Kingdom Come: The Amillennial Alternative* (Ross-shire, Scotland: Mentor, 2013), 456.
14 Ibid.; emphasis original.

number one thousand is often used in the Scriptures to refer to an extensive period of time."[15] Of these passages, amillennialists most often cite Psalm 90:4 and 2 Peter 3:8 as evidence for the symbolic view of the "thousand years" in Revelation 20.[16]

As a final argument for the symbolic view, amillennialists cite the use of the number one thousand in Jewish and early Christian writings "as a figure for the eternal blessing of the redeemed."[17] G. K. Beale specifically points to the thousand-year period in Jubilees 23:27–30 as "clearly figurative for the complete perfection of the eternal time of blessing of God's people."[18] This, it is said, provides support for the symbolic view of the thousand years in Revelation 20.

The Significance of the Symbolism

When explaining the signficance of the symbolism, amillennialists usually tie the number one thousand back to the number ten. Anthony Hoekema writes, "Since the number ten signifies completeness, and since a thousand is ten to the third power, we may think of the expression 'a thousand years' as standing for a complete period, a very long period of indeterminate length."[19] In similar way, B. B. Warfield states: "The sacred number seven in combination with the equally sacred number three forms the number of holy perfection, and when this ten is cubed into a thousand the seer has said all he could say to convey to our minds the idea of absolute completeness."[20]

---

15 Venema, *The Promise of the Future*, 325–26; see Beale, *The Book of Revelation*, 1018, who also cites Eccl 6:6 as a temporal figurative use of the number one thousand.
16 Paul A. Rainbow, "Millennium as Metaphor in John's Apocalypse," *WTJ* 58, no. 2 (Fall 1996): 220; Donald Garlington, "Reigning with Christ: Revelation 20:1–6 and the Question of the Millennium," *R&R* 6, no. 2 (Spring 1997): 80; Venema, *The Promise of the Future*, 326. According to Hamstra, "Amillennialists typically list three reasons in support of their conviction: No other passage of Scripture mentions a thousand-year period; a symbolic interpretation is consistent with the apocalyptic nature of the text; and the historic creeds of Christendom do not mention a literal period between this age and the eternal kingdom" ("An Idealist View of Revelation," 121).
17 Beale, *The Book of Revelation*, 995.
18 Ibid., 1019.
19 Hoekema, *The Bible and the Future*, 227; also see Riddlebarger, *A Case for Amillennialism*, 237; Beale, *The Book of Revelation*, 995; Leon Morris, *Revelation*, TNTC (Grand Rapids: Eerdmans Publishing, 1987), 229.
20 B. B. Warfield, *Biblical Doctrines* (New York: Oxford University, 1929), 654. According to Warfield, "When the saints are said to live and reign with Christ a thousand years the idea

This same basic idea is articulated in various ways by amillennialists. For example, the thousand years in Revelation 20 is said to signify "a long era,"[21] "a long period of time,"[22] "an indefinitely long period of time,"[23] "an age-long, but definitely limited period of time,"[24] "an extensive period of time,"[25] "an extended, but indefinite, period of time,"[26] "an ideal period of time,"[27] "an ideal epoch,"[28] "a great epoch in human history,"[29] "a time of completion,"[30] "the complete time that God has determined,"[31] "a complete period of time, the length of which is known only by God,"[32] "the exceeding fullness of the divine action,"[33] and "the designated space of time within which the triune God will complete his redemptive purpose."[34] As Venema summarizes: "The use of one thousand years in Revelation is, when interpreted against the background of this usage of the symbolism of one thousand, likely a reference to a

---

    intended is that of inconceivable exaltation, security and blessedness as beyond expression by ordinary language" (655). Although Warfield was postmillennial, his symbolic view of the thousand years in Revelation 20 coincides with the amillennial interpretation.

21 Beale, *The Book of Revelation*, 995. At the same time, Beale argues that the "primary point of the thousand years is probably not a figurative reference to a long time but the thematic idea of the ultimate victory of Christians who have suffered" (1018).
22 Henry Barclay Swete, *Commentary on Revelation* (Grand Rapids: Kregel Publications, 1977), 260.
23 Cox, *Amillennialism Today*, 4.
24 Waldron, *The End Times Made Simple*, 96.
25 Venema, *The Promise of the Future*, 326.
26 Arthur H. Lewis, *The Dark Side of the Millennium: The Problem of Evil in Revelation 20:1–10* (Grand Rapids: Baker Books, 1993), 50.
27 Riddlebarger, *A Case for Amillennialism*, 237.
28 Beale, *The Book of Revelation*, 995, who points to Rev 2:10 as providing insight into the significance of the number one thousand in Revelation 20. According to Beale, because the saints are promised the reward of a millennial reign in Rev 2:10 if they endure a trial of ten days, the intensifying of ten to a thousand—along with the lengthening of days to years—may indicate "that present momentary affliction results in greater glory even in the intermediate state prior to eternal glory."
29 Swete, *Commentary on Revelation*, 260.
30 Riddlebarger, *A Case for Amillennialism*, 237.
31 Morris, *Revelation*, 229.
32 Cox, *Amillennialism Today*, 4.
33 Abraham Kuyper, *The Revelation of St. John*, trans. J. Hendrik Vries (Grand Rapids: Eerdmans Publishing, 1935), 277.
34 Davis, *The High King of Heaven*, 474. According to Davis, the "mystical meaning" of the number is discovered by recognizing that ten is the number of completeness and has been raised to the power of three, which is the number of the triune God (473–74).

period of fullness, completion and perfection so far as God's redemptive plan is concerned."[35]

The Premillennial View

Premillennialists are divided on the duration of the thousand years in Revelation 20. Some interpret it literally,[36] others interpret it symbolically,[37] and still others do not appear to commit one way or the other.[38] But all premillennialists believe that the thousand years represents "a real period of time, however long or short it may be,"[39] which takes place between the present age and the eternal state.

---

35 Venema, *The Promise of the Future*, 326, who continues: "Just as God's faithfulness is perfect and never failing (unto one thousand generations), so the times within his redemptive purposes are perfect and never failing. The most that can be concluded, then, from the use of the number one thousand in Revelation 20 is that the period of Satan's binding will be great and full, not small and empty, of years. That this is the sense of the vision is only reinforced by the contrasting language that describes Satan's season of rebellion as a little season, suggesting that it is a meager and limited period of time within the will of God" (326–27).

36 Harold W. Hoehner, "Evidence from Revelation 20," in *A Case for Premillennialism: A New Consensus*, eds. Donald K. Campbell and Jeffrey L. Townsend (Chicago: Moody Press, 1992), 248–50; Robert L. Thomas, *Revelation 8–22: An Exegetical Commentary* (Chicago: Moody Press, 1995), 407–9; John F. Walvoord, "The Theological Significance of Revelation 20:1–6," in *Essays in Honor of J. Dwight Pentecost*, eds. Stanley D. Toussaint and Charles H. Dyer (Chicago: Moody Press, 1986), 231; Paige Patterson, *Revelation*, NAC vol. 39 (Nashville: Broadman & Holman, 2012), 353; David J. MacLeod, "The Fourth 'Last Thing': The Millennial Kingdom of Christ (Rev. 20:4–6)," *BSac* 157, no. 625 (Jan 2000): 62–63; Robert Gromacki, "Revelation 20: A Premillennial Analysis," 9–13; accessed on July 20, 2014, http://www.pre-trib.org/data/pdf/Gromacki-Revelation20A-Premille.pdf; Steve Sullivan, "Premillennialism and an Exegesis of Revelation 20," 37–41; accessed on July 20, 2014, http://www.pre-trib.org/data/pdf/Sullivan-PremillennialismAndA.pdf; Jack S. Deere, "Premillennialism in Revelation 20:4–6," *BSac* 135, no. 537 (Jan 1978): 70–71; Jeffrey L. Townsend, "Is the Present Age the Millennium?," *BSac* 140, no. 559 (July 1983): 213–14.

37 Grant R. Osborne, *Revelation*, ECNT (Grand Rapids: Baker Academic, 2002), 701; George Eldon Ladd, *A Commentary on the Revelation of John* (Grand Rapids: Eerdmans Publishing, 1972), 262; James M. Hamilton, Jr., *Revelation: The Spirit Speaks to the Churches* (Wheaton, IL: Crossway, 2012), 368; Alan Johnson, "Revelation," in *EBC*, ed. Frank E. Gaebelein (Grand Rapids: Zondervan Publishing, 1981), 12:585–86; Bock, "Summary Essay," 304–5.

38 Wayne Grudem, *Systematic Theology: An Introduction to Biblical Doctrine* (Grand Rapids: Baker Books, 1994), 1131; Robert H. Mounce, *The Book of Revelation*, NICNT (Grand Rapids: Eerdmans Publishing, 1977), 362; Craig A. Blaising, "Premillennialism," in *Three Views on the Millennium and Beyond*, ed. Darrell L. Bock (Grand Rapids: Zondervan Publishing), 227. According to Robert Mounce, "Nothing in the immediate context favors either interpretation" (*The Book of Revelation*, 362).

39 Ladd, *A Commentary on the Revelation of John*, 262.

Premillennialists who interpret the thousand years *figuratively* argue in very much the same way as amillennialists, seeing the designation as symbolizing a lengthy period of unknown length.[40] However, because premillennialism is consistent with both the literal and symbolic views, the duration of the millennium is not consequential for premillennialism like it is for amillennialism. For this reason, some premillennialists view the length of the millennium as an incidental question in light of the more fundamental debate over the existence of an intermediate kingdom between the present age and the eternal state.[41]

The Case for the Literal View

For premillennialists who interpret the thousand years *literally*, the primary argument concerns the use of numbers elsewhere in the book of Revelation. Some insist that all the numbers in Revelation are literal;[42] others are less dogmatic, asserting that "no number in Revelation is verifiably a symbolic number;"[43] and yet other premillennialists are open to

---

40 Premillennialist James Hamilton writes, "I am happy to grant that this is symbolic. One thousand is a perfectly round number and symbolizes a very long time" (*Revelation*, 368). Likewise, George Eldon Ladd states, "It is difficult to understand the thousand years for which he was bound with strict literalness in view of the obvious symbolic use of numbers in the Revelation. A thousand equals the third power of ten—an ideal time" (*A Commentary on the Revelation of John*, 262). Similarly, Grant Osborne writes, "It is likely that this refers to an indefinite but perfect period of time, obviously much longer than the period the Antichrist 'reigns' (forty-two months) but still a symbolic period" (*Revelation*, 701).

41 Bock, "Summary Essay," 304–5. According to Wayne Grudem, "If we are convinced of [premillennialism], it really is an incidental question whether the thousand-year period is thought to be a literal thousand years or simply a long period of time of indeterminate duration" (*Systematic Theology*, 1131). Likewise, Alan Johnson believes "it is not of primary importance whether the years are actual 365-day years or symbolic of a shorter or longer period of bliss enjoyed by believers as they reign with Christ on earth (cf. 5:10 with 11:15; 22:15)" ("Revelation," 585–86). In a similar way, Darrell Bock writes, "Is it not possible to see the thousand years as symbolic of, yet still referring to, an intermediate period that would be an earthly, 'millennial,' intermediate kingdom? In other words, the issue of the potential symbolism of the number does not really answer the question whether the deliverance portrayed in Revelation 20:4–6 precludes an intermediate kingdom. If one has resurrection bracketing the beginning and end of what is described here, then it is possible to have an intermediate stage regardless of how long it lasts" ("Summary Essay," 304).

42 Walvoord, "Theological Significance," 231; cf. John F. Walvoord, *Revelation*, rev. and ed. Philip E. Rawley and Mark Hitchcock (Chicago: Moody Publishers, 2011), 28–30; MacLeod, "The Fourth 'Last Thing,'" 63.

43 Thomas, *Revelation 8–22*, 408. Later Thomas writes that "nonsymbolic usage of numbers is the rule" and that "confirmation of a single number in Revelation as symbolic is impossible" (408–9).

seeing several exceptions to what they believe is the general rule of literal numbers in the Apocalypse.[44] But regardless of how many exceptions exist, the vast majority of the 254 numerical references in Revelation do appear to communicate the conventional use of a literal number.[45] As Steve Sullivan explains:

> John demonstrates the conventional use not only by telling us totals in number, but he also counts out the number of churches, seals, trumpets, bowls, woes and living creatures. Notice John tells us the total number of elders is 24, but he also talks to one of the elders (4:4; 5:5; 7:3). In Revelation 7 he correlates the four angels, the four corners of the earth and the four winds. Addition or multiplication is indicated in Revelation 7:4–8 with the 144,000 for they are broken up into 12 groups of 12,000 each. The mentioning of 42 months (11:2; 13:5) as 1260 days (11:3; 12:6) is the conventional use of time. In addition, one could add ½ an hour (8:1), 10 days (2:10), and 5 months (9:5, 10).[46]

Furthermore, whenever a number is used with a time indicator in Revelation—such as days (1:10; 2:10, 13; 4:8; 6:17; 7:15; 8:12; 9:6, 15; 10:7; 11:3, 6, 9, 11; 12:6, 10; 14:11; 16:14; 18:8; 20:10; 21:25) or months (9:5, 10, 15; 11:2; 13:5; 22:2)—there is no clear indication that it is symbolic.[47] As Harold Hoehner argues, "There is no reason for not making the same application for years."[48]

But aside from the use of numbers elsewhere in the Apocalypse—an

---

44 Sullivan, "Premillennialism," 37–39, who sees 13 such exceptions.
45 Ibid., 37–40.
46 Ibid., 38. For further discussion of these and other numbers in Revelation, see Hoehner, "Evidence from Revelation 20," 249; Thomas, *Revelation 8–22*, 408–9; MacLeod, "The Fourth 'Last Thing,'" 63.
47 Hoehner, "Evidence from Revelation 20," 249; MacLeod, "The Fourth 'Last Thing,'" 63; Sullivan, "Premillennialism," 39–40; Gromacki, "Revelation 20," 13. According to Sullivan, in each of these verses "one finds nothing in the text which would compel the reader to understand this to be anything other than a conventional use of numbers" ("Premillennialism," 40).
48 Hoehner, "Evidence from Revelation 20," 249. In addition, premillennialists often point out that whenever the word "year" is used with a number in Scripture, the designation always refers to literal years (Deere, "Premillennialism in Revelation 20:4–6," 70; MacLeod, "The Fourth 'Last Thing,'" 63; Sullivan, "Premillennialism," 39; Gromacki, "Revelation 20," 13). This, of course, is disputed by amillennialists.

area in which there is little agreement and therefore little opportunity for one side to convince the other—there are several reasons to affirm a literal understanding of the thousand years in Revelation 20.⁴⁹ First, in contrast to the claims of some amillennialists, there is indeed a clear biblical precedent of the number "one thousand" being used literally in Scripture.⁵⁰ When amillennialist Sam Storms argues that the number "one thousand" is rarely if ever intended "with arithmetical precision,"⁵¹ he seems to imply that the only alternative is that such uses of "one thousand" be understood symbolically. But the biblical writers often use round numbers—neither with "arithmetical precision" nor as a figurative way to symbolize an undefined spiritual reality—but as a way to estimate how many persons or units of something are in view.⁵²

For example, when the Bible refers to "a thousand pieces of silver" (Gen 20:16), "a thousand men" (Judg 15:15–16), "1,000 bulls" (1 Chron 29:21), "1,000 rams" (1 Chron 29:21), "1,000 lambs" (1 Chron 29:21), "a 1,000 silver dishes" (Ezra 1:9), and "a 1,000 other articles" (Ezra 1:10),

---

49 At the same time, some premillennial arguments have been less than compelling. For example, according to some premillennialists, the fact that John repeats the number six times (vv. 2, 3, 4, 5, 6, 7) argues in favor of a literal interpretation of the thousand years (Hoehner, "Evidence from Revelation 20," 249; Thomas, *Revelation 8–22*, 409; Charles L. Feinberg, *Millennialism: The Two Major Views*, 3rd ed. [Chicago: Moody Press, 1980], 333). But if John intended the designation to be understood symbolically, it would make sense for him to repeat it several times to refer to the same period of time. An additional less-than-compelling argument comes from premillennialist John Walvoord, who says the duration of the millennial reign must be literal because John mentions the thousand years in both the vision (vv. 4–5) and his *interpretation* of the vision (v. 6) ("Theological Significance," 232). But as G. K. Beale counters, this argument "assumes that figures of speech cannot be used in interpretive comments" (*The Book of Revelation*, 1017).
50 According to Philip Jenson, the word אֶלֶף "*often* refers to a thousand, understood either as a precise or round number" (Philip P. Jenson, "אֶלֶף," in *NIDOTTE*, ed. Willem A. Van-Gemeren [Grand Rapids: Zondervan Publishing, 1997], 1:416; emphasis added).
51 Storms, *Kingdom Come*, 456.
52 When Storms claims that all non-temporal uses of the number "one thousand" in Scripture are *figurative* (*Kingdom Come*, 456), he is misclassifying round numbers as symbolic. In his thorough study of biblical numerology, John Davis refers to the "conventional use" of numbers as "that which is concerned primarily with the mathematical value of the number." According to Davis, "Numbers used in this manner are designed to denote either a specific or a general mathematical quantity" (John J. Davis, *Biblical Numerology* [Grand Rapids: Baker Books, 1968], 49). When the biblical writer believed it was unnecessary to provide the reader with exact detailed enumerations or sums, sometimes he used a general mathematical quantity, a rounded estimate of the total number (ibid., 51–52). But this use of round numbers falls in the broader category of the conventional use of numbers, which is not symbolic but rather is primarily concerned with the mathematical value of the number (ibid.).

some of these may be round numbers and therefore not intended "with arithmetical precision."[53] But this does not mean that these uses of the number are symbolic and therefore should not be taken literally, as Storms seems to imply.[54] For this reason, the observation that the number "one thousand" is rarely intended with mathematical precision may be accurate, but it is irrelevant to the question of whether a given use of the number "one thousand"—whether in Revelation 20 or elsewhere—should be understood symbolically.

The second reason to embrace the literal view is the absence of any clear precedent of the designation "a thousand years" being used symbolically in Scripture. This specific designation is used only three times outside of Revelation 20—in Ecclesiastes 6:6 (אֶלֶף שָׁנִים), Psalm 90:4 (שָׁנִים אֶלֶף), and 2 Peter 3:8 (χίλια ἔτη)—and each of these three uses is best understood literally rather than symbolically.

In Ecclesiastes 6:1–6, Solomon emphasizes how the three traditional conditions for human happiness—great wealth (vv. 1–2), an abundance of children (vv. 3–5), and longevity of life (v. 6)[55]—bring no ultimate joy and satisfaction to the one who has not been granted by God the ability to delight in such gifts (cf. Eccl 5:18–20). In the process, Solomon raises the hypothetical scenario of a man who lives to the incredibly old age of 2,000 years: "Even if the other man lives a thousand years twice and does not enjoy good things—do not all go to one place?" (Eccl 6:6). In other words, even if someone were so blessed as to live more than twice the age of Methuselah, what advantage would there be if this long life eventually terminated having yielded no enjoyment?[56] Such a life would be meaningless. In the course of this argument, Solomon uses the designation

---

53 At the same time, because the "1,000 silver dishes" in Ezra 1:9 and "1,000 other articles" in Ezra 1:10 were specifically counted out by Mithredath the treasurer (Ezra 1:8), one can only assume that these two uses of the number were indeed intended with arithmetical precision.
54 Similarly, when Mark writes that "five thousand men" were fed by Jesus (Mark 6:44), the fact that this number is not intended "with arithmetical precision" hardly means that the number five thousand is symbolic of some spiritual reality and therefore should not be taken "literally."
55 Duane A. Garrett, *Proverbs, Ecclesiastes, Song of Solomon*, NAC vol. 14 (Nashville: Broadman Press, 1993), 315.
56 Tremper Longman, *The Book of Ecclesiastes*, NICOT (Grand Rapids: Eerdmans Publishing, 1997), 172; Walter C. Kaiser, Jr., *Ecclesiastes: Total Life* (Chicago: Moody Press, 1979), 81; F. Delitzsch, *The Book of Ecclesiastes*, trans. M. G. Easton, Commentary on the Old Testament (repr., Peabody, MA: Hendrickson, 1996), 6:720.

"thousand years" literally, doubling it to pose a hypothetical scenario in which a man lived to the unthinkable age of 2,000 years.[57]

In Psalm 90, as Moses highlights the contrast between the eternity of God and the transitoriness of man, he says to Yahweh: "For a thousand years in Your sight are like yesterday when it passes by, or as a watch in the night" (Ps 90:4). As Steven Lawson explains, the meaning of Psalm 90:4 is clear:

> From the perspective of God's infinite eternality, a thousand years of human history is a mere twenty-four hour day, quickly passing away. A thousand years for man is like a short three-hour watch in the night. This is how temporal mortal man's days are. Man is transitory, but God is eternal.[58]

To emphasize this contrast between God and man, then, Moses says that a thousand years passes by like a single day—or even just three hours—in the sight of the Lord. The "thousand years" is clearly intended literally in this comparison in Psalm 90:4.

In 2 Peter 3, the apostle Peter refers to those who will mock the people of God and insist that their Savior will never return (vv. 3–7). In response, he takes the insight of Psalm 90:4 and comforts his readers by applying it to the coming of the Lord: "But do not let this one fact escape your notice, beloved, that with the Lord one day is like a thousand years, and a thousand years like one day" (2 Pet 3:8). As Thomas Schreiner explains:

> If the passing of time does not diminish God in any way and if he transcends time so that its passing does not affect his being, then believers should not be concerned about the so-called delay of Christ's coming. The passing of a thousand years, after all, is like the passing of a single day to him.[59]

---

57 Garrett refers to the hundred children (Eccl 6:3) and the two thousand years of life (Eccl 6:6) as "oriental exaggerations" (*Proverbs, Ecclesiastes, Song of Solomon*, 315) and Longman considers them "hyperbole" (*The Book of Ecclesiastes*, 172), but the references are clearly hypothetical and yet literal. In contrast, hyperbole would exist if Solomon referred to a man who *did* live to the age of 2,000 years (as a deliberate and obvious exaggeration of the man's very old age).
58 Steven J. Lawson, *Psalms 76–150*, HOTC (Nashville: Broadman & Holman Publishers, 2006), 82–83.
59 Thomas R. Schreiner, *1, 2 Peter, Jude*, NAC vol. 37 (Nashville: Broadman & Holman, 2003), 379.

The meaning of both Psalm 90:4 and 2 Peter 3:8, then, is dependent on a literal interpretation of the thousand years and a literal interpretation of the single day.[60] Consequently, there is no clear, unambiguous precedent for the symbolic use of "thousand years" in the Bible.[61] This does not mean that a symbolic use is impossible, but it does eliminate one of the primary amillennial arguments for a figurative interpretation of the number in Revelation 20.

Third, Beale's claim that the "thousand years" in Jubilees 23:27–30 is a figurative reference to "the complete perfection of the eternal time of blessing of God's people"[62] fails to provide evidence for the symbolic view of the millennium's duration. A closer look at this passage, in fact, demonstrates that the "thousand years" in Jubilees 23:27 was actually intended *literally*. The angelic address in Jubilees 23 begins with an explanation of why Abraham lived to be only 175 years of age while his ancestors had lived far longer (vv. 1–10). According to the angel, the increase of wickedness leads to a steady decrease in life spans (vv. 11–25). In the midst of this, God's people will lament the reality that the lives of Abraham's

---

[60] In a similar way, the psalmist's point in Ps 84:10 is that one (literal) day in God's courts is better than a (literal) thousand days in any other place. There is nothing in any of these verses—Ps 90:4, 2 Pet 3:8, or Ps 84:10—that compels the interpreter to seek a meaning other than the literal one. In his discussion of the duration of the millennium, Venema cites Exod 20:5–6, Deut 7:9, Ps 50:10–11, Ps 84:10, Ps 90:4, and 2 Pet 3:8 as evidence "that the number one thousand is often used in the Scriptures to refer to an extensive period of time" (*The Promise of the Future*, 326). But only three of these passages refer to periods of time—Ps 84:10, Ps 90:4, and 2 Pet 3:8—and the number is literal in all three passages (as discussed above). Of the three remaining passages, Exod 20:5–6 can be dismissed because it uses the indefinite plural "thousands" rather than the specific number "one thousand." Therefore, only in Deut 7:9 and Ps 50:10 is the number used to indicate an indefinite amount, although the figure could be understood literally in Ps 50:10.

[61] To argue for a figurative interpretation of the "thousand years" in Ps 90:4 and 2 Pet 3:8, amillennialist G. K. Beale says that early Jewish texts such as Sir 18:9–11 and 2 Bar 48:12–13 interpret the use of the number in Ps 90:4 symbolically (*The Book of Revelation*, 1018). However, even though Sir 18:9–11 and 2 Bar 48:12–13 set forth the same basic truth as Ps 90:4, neither of these passages provides an actual interpretation of Ps 90:4, so Beale's argument is not compelling. In addition, even if these passages allude to Ps 90:4, Sir 18:9–11 and 2 Bar 48:12–13 use indefinite terms rather than the specific designation "thousand years." The basic truth taught in these three passages can be communicated either with specific terms (Ps 90:4) or with general terms (Sir 18:9–11; 2 Bar 48:12–13), without the latter cancelling out the former. The use of general terms in Sir 18:9–11 and 2 Bar 48:12–13 does not constitute a figurative interpretation of the "thousand years" in Ps 90:4, and therefore Beale's argument carries no weight.

[62] Beale, *The Book of Revelation*, 1019.

forefathers extended as long as a "thousand years," but their life spans were limited to only 70 or 80 years (v. 15). But the turning point will eventually come when the children begin to seek the commandments of God and return to the path of righteousness (v. 26). As a result of this repentance, "The days will begin to become numerous and increase, and mankind as well—generation by generation and day by day until their lifetimes approach *one thousand years* and to more years than the number of days [had been]" (v. 27; emphasis added). In other words, the actions of the children will reverse this downward spiral of life spans so dramatically that human ages will once again, as in the days before Abraham, approach the length of a thousand years.[63] During this time, God's covenant promises will be fulfilled and His chosen people will live in peace and joy as the Lord shows them mercy (vv. 28–31). In the greater context of the original prophecy, then, the "thousand years" of Jubilees 23:27 must be literal, because the overall picture is that of human life spans being restored to those of Abraham's forefathers. The "thousand years" of Jubilees 23:27 is just as literal as the "thousand years" of Jubilees 23:15, and the amillennial view of the "thousand years" in Revelation 20 gains no support from this appeal.

Fourth, when the apostle John intends to express an indefinite quantity in Revelation 20, he does so not by naming a specific number like a "thousand years," but rather by using indefinite expressions like "for a short time" (μικρὸν χρόνον) (v. 3) or "the number of them is like the sand of the seashore" (v. 8).[64] Because John uses indefinite terms to express indefinite amounts in the same immediate context, his six-fold use of the specific number "one thousand" (χίλια) in Revelation 20 stands out in contrast and therefore should be understood as a literal reference to a specific amount of time.[65]

---

[63] James C. VanderKam, *The Book of Jubilees* (Sheffield: Sheffield Academic Press, 2001), 133–34.
[64] This use of indefinite expressions of time is found elsewhere in Revelation as well: "for a little while longer" (ἔτι χρόνον μικρόν) (6:11), "a short time" (ὀλίγον καιρὸν) (12:12), and "a little while" (ὀλίγον) (17:10).
[65] Hoehner, "Evidence from Revelation 20," 249; Thomas, *Revelation 8–22*, 408; Townsend, "Is the Present Age the Millennium?," 214; Sullivan, "Premillennialism," 40. As Feinberg observes, the Greek language knows well how to express "after a long time" (μετά ... πολὺν χρόνον) (Matt 25:19) (*Millennialism*, 333).

A Closer Look at the Symbolic View

To support the non-literal view of the thousand years in Revelation 20, amillennialists point to the symbolic nature of the book of Revelation as a whole. But as George Eldon Ladd notes, "The recognition of the symbolic language of the Apocalypse does not carry with it the corollary that every phrase must involve a symbol."[66] Instead, the interpreter must look for clues in the biblical text which indicate whether a given term—in this case, the "thousand years"—is used literally or figuratively.[67]

According to premillennialists, the only conceivable approach to understanding literature of any kind, the book of Revelation included, is to assume the literal sense unless the nature of the language forces the reader to consider a symbolic interpretation.[68] In other words, even though much of Revelation is indeed symbolic, "as a rule, it is best to begin with the assumption that the language of the [prophet] is to be understood naturally."[69] Not only is this the only conceivable approach, but it also reflects the fact that symbolic language is a departure from the literal, and not vice versa:

> Whenever we read a book, an essay, or a poem we presume the literal sense in the document until the nature of the literature may force us to another level.... The non-literal is always a secondary meaning which presumes an already existing literal understanding of literature. This previous stratum of language is the *necessary* point of departure for the interpretation of all literature.[70]

This includes the use of numbers. As John Davis writes, "Numbers should always be taken at face value and understood as conveying a

---

66 George Eldon Ladd, *Crucial Questions About the Kingdom of God* (Grand Rapids: Eerdmans Publishing, 1952), 148. In the words of Jack Deere, one cannot "secure a symbolic sense for τὰ χίλια ἔτη merely by repeating the shibboleth that Revelation is a symbolic book, for not everything is symbolic in the book, and one must give reasons why a certain passage is symbolic" ("Premillennialism in Revelation 20:4-6," 70).
67 Townsend, "Is the Present Age the Millennium?," 213.
68 Bernard Ramm, *Protestant Biblical Interpretation: A Textbook of Hermeneutics*, 3rd ed. (Grand Rapids: Baker Books, 1970), 123.
69 Walter C. Kaiser, Jr., *Back Toward the Future: Hints for Interpreting Biblical Prophecy* (Eugene, OR: Wipf & Stock Publishers, 1989), 43.
70 Ramm, *Protestant Biblical Interpretation*, 123; emphasis original.

mathematical quantity unless there is either textual or contextual evidence to the contrary."[71]

In contrast, amillennialists take the opposite approach.[72] According to Beale, the reader of Revelation should "expect a predominance of symbolic over literal language, including references to numbers,"[73] and therefore he should approach the Apocalypse with "a nonliteral interpretative method."[74] Even though some parts of Revelation are literal, says Beale, "the essence of the book is figurative," and for this reason, "where there is lack of clarity about whether something is symbolic, the scales of judgment should be tilted in the direction of a nonliteral analysis."[75]

The primary difference between the two approaches, then, can be summarized in terms of their starting points. The premillennialist begins with the assumption that the language is literal unless clear indications compel him to interpret it symbolically, whereas the amillennialist assumes that the language is symbolic unless there is compelling reason to understand it literally. Both approaches recognize the existence of literal and symbolic language in the book of Revelation, but they place the burden of proof at opposite ends of the spectrum.

Despite the difference between the two approaches, however, both of them recognize the need to identify specific criteria by which one can determine whether or not the language in question is symbolic in nature. For example, Beale identifies six "telltale signs" that a biblical author is using figurative language:

> (1) formal linking of two words of totally different meanings so that one is compared to the other (1:20: "the seven lampstands are the seven churches"), (2) use of a key descriptive term to alert the reader to the presence of a comparative relationship (1:20: "The *mystery* of the seven stars"; see also on 11:8: "the great city, which *spiritually* is called Sodom and Egypt"), (3) the impossibility of any intelligible literal interpretation (10:10: "I ate

---

[71] Davis, *Biblical Numerology*, 155.
[72] Beale, *The Book of Revelation*, 52, where he calls for turning the literal approach on its head.
[73] Ibid., 1017.
[74] Ibid., 52. According to Beale, this approach is required by John's use of σημαίνω ("signify") in Rev 1:1, which is said to mean: "to communicate by symbols" (50–52, 1017).
[75] Ibid., 52.

the book"), (4) a statement that would be outrageously false or contradictory if taken literally (11:34: "my two witnesses ... are the two olive trees and the two lampstands"), (5) context that renders a literal interpretation improbable, and (6) clear and repeated figurative use of the same word elsewhere in the Apocalypse.[76]

Ironically, however, even though Beale interprets the "thousand years" in Revelation 20 symbolically, this numerical designation does not appear to meet any of the six criteria he proposes. At the very least, it falls manifestly short of meeting five of the six telltale signs suggested by Beale: (1) the thousand years are not formally linked to another noun as a formal metaphor; (2) there is no descriptive term which alerts the reader to the presence of a comparative relationship; (3) the literal interpretation of the thousand years in Revelation 20 is not impossibly unintelligible; (4) the statement of a thousand-year reign of Christ is not outrageously false or contradictory; and (6) there is no clear and repeated figurative use of "a thousand years" in Revelation outside the immediate context. The only possibility is (5): "context that renders a literal interpretation improbable."

Regarding this fifth criterion, amillennialists typically point to the use of other symbols in Revelation 20—e.g., the key, chain, serpent, bottomless pit, etc.—as evidence that the immediate context renders a literal interpretation of the thousand years improbable.[77] As Samuel Waldron asks, "If the *prison itself and everything associated with it is symbolic*, by what rationale can the prison sentence (the 1000 years) be dogmatically asserted to be literal? The presumption at least must be that it is figurative."[78]

But the weakness of this argument is that it clearly overstates the amount of symbolism in Revelation 20. In addition to "the abyss"—which

---

[76] Ibid., 57; emphasis original. According to Beale, at least three forms of figurative comparison occur in Revelation: formal metaphor, simile, and hypocatastasis. For a similar list of tests by which the intention of the biblical author may be determined, see G. B. Caird, *The Language and Imagery of the Bible* (Philadelphia: The Westminster Press, 1980), 186–97.

[77] Grenz, *The Millennial Maze*, 167; Riddlebarger, *A Case for Amillennialism*, 237; Beale, *The Book of Revelation*, 995; Menn, *Biblical Eschatology*, 356–57; Waldron, *The End Times Made Simple*, 96.

[78] Waldron, *The End Times Made Simple*, 96; emphasis original.

is a technical term referring to a literal spirit prison (see chapter 11)—there are several features in Revelation 20:1–3 alone which should be taken literally: "an angel" (v. 1), "heaven" (v. 1), "the devil" (v. 2), "Satan" (v. 2), the deception (v. 3), "the nations" (v. 3), and "a short time" (v. 3). If the presence of symbolism in Revelation 20 creates a "context that renders a literal interpretation improbable," on what basis does the amillennialist interpret these elements literally? And if the context alone is not sufficient to require a symbolic interpretation of these elements, why is it sufficient as the only indicator of the symbolic nature of the "thousand years"?

Furthermore, it is hermeneutically invalid to assume that if one or more elements in a given prophecy are symbolic, then everything else in that passage must also be symbolic. For example, even though the sword coming from the mouth of Christ in Revelation 19:15 is symbolic, this does not mean that the "nations" later in the same verse should be considered a symbol of something other than actual nations.[79] In the same way, the fact that the chain in Revelation 20:1–3 is not a physical chain does not mean that the thousand years must be figurative.

Rather than taking an all-or-nothing approach to symbolism, one must consider each element of a given passage and determine whether it was intended literally or figuratively. To identify symbolic language in the biblical text, it is helpful to ask three questions. First, *does it possess a degree of absurdity when taken literally?*[80] With symbolic language, there is something inherent in the language itself which compels the exegete to look beyond the literal meaning. This something is a degree of absurdity which causes the interpreter to scratch his head and say, "But how can this be?" As Robertson McQuilkin writes, "If the statement would obviously be irrational, unreasonable, or absurd if taken literally, the presumption is that it is a figure of speech."[81]

---

79 Roy B. Zuck, *Basic Bible Interpretation* (Colorado Springs: David C Cook, 1991), 186–87.
80 This first question aligns with the third and fourth criteria proposed by Beale: "the impossibility of any intelligible literal interpretation" and "a statement that would be outrageously false or contradictory if taken literally" (*The Book of Revelation*, 57). Caird, *The Language and Imagery of the Bible*, 188, refers to this as "impossible literality."
81 Robertson McQuilkin, *Understanding and Applying the Bible*, rev. ed. (Chicago: Moody Press, 1992), 170–71. As McQuilkin writes, "'I am the door,' and 'you are the salt' are obviously irrational if taken literally" (171).

Second, *does it possess a degree of clarity when taken symbolically?* Symbolic language is essentially clear and understandable, vividly portraying what it symbolizes. For this reason, a symbolic interpretation of figurative language naturally brings clarity to the meaning of a statement which initially appeared absurd when taken literally. Even when the initial interpretation of a given symbol proves to be difficult, clarity often arrives when the true significance of the language is eventually identified.[82]

Third, *does it fall into an established category of symbolic language?* Because figures of speech are legitimate departures from the normal use of language, they are limited in number and can be defined and classified in accordance with known examples.[83] For this reason, the interpreter must determine whether the language in question falls into an established category of figurative language, such as simile, metaphor, hypocatastasis, hyperbole, personification, or anthropomorphism.

To illustrate the application of these questions, when Isaiah 55:12 refers to the trees of the field clapping their hands, the language of the verse meets all three criteria for symbolic language—it possesses a degree of absurdity when taken literally (trees don't have hands); it possesses a degree of clarity when taken symbolically (it clearly communicates a time of such joy that even the trees will be clapping); and it falls into an established category of symbolic language (personification in which a human action is attributed to an inanimate object).

In contrast, the "thousand years" of Revelation 20 meets none of the proposed criteria. First, there is nothing absurd or unintelligible about the literal interpretation of the thousand years that compels the interpreter to seek something other than the literal meaning. In fact, if God had wanted to communicate that the imprisonment of Satan and reign of Christ would last for a literal thousand years, how else could He have done it? What else could He have said? Using the number one thousand was the only option available.

Second, there is absolutely no degree of clarity when the thousand years is taken symbolically. Amillennialists typically trace the symbolic

---

[82] For example, the "great chain" in Rev 20:1–3 possesses both a degree of absurdity when taken literally (How can a physical chain bind a spiritual being?) and a degree of clarity when taken symbolically (i.e., it clearly communicates the immobilization of Satan).

[83] Walter C. Kaiser, Jr., *Toward an Exegetical Theology: Biblical Exegesis for Preaching and Teaching* (Grand Rapids: Baker Books, 1981), 122.

significance of the number one thousand back to the number ten,[84] which is said to speak of "highest completeness" when raised to the third degree.[85] As amillennialist Anthony Hoekema explains, "Since the number ten signifies completeness, and since a thousand is ten to the third power, we may think of the expression 'a thousand years' as standing for a complete period, a very long period of indeterminate length."[86] But why exactly would ten to the third power signify highest completeness—why not ten to the fourth or fifth degree, or even ten to the tenth degree?[87] In addition, "One might question why, in attempting to discern the meaning of the number ten, we should investigate the meaning of seven and three instead of, say, six and four."[88] Or one might ask why the number one thousand would drive someone to discern the meaning of the number ten in the first place. What exactly would lead the interpreter to see these kinds of math equations behind John's use of "thousand years"?

Further ambiguity arises when one considers the amillennial view that the thousand years represents "completeness" or "a complete period of time." Put simply, what exactly does this mean? What is completeness (or a complete period of time) and how does it differ from incompleteness (or an incomplete period of time)? To borrow the words of Cornelis Venema, what is exactly "a period of fullness, completion and perfection so far as God's redemptive plan is concerned"?[89] In the simplest of terms, what exactly is being communicated by the six-fold use of "a thousand years" in Revelation 20? Most of the symbolic explanations of the thousand years introduce more confusion than clarity.

---

[84] E.g., Hoekema, *The Bible and the Future*, 227; Riddlebarger, *A Case for Amillennialism*, 237; Beale, *The Book of Revelation*, 995; Morris, *Revelation*, 229.

[85] Richard C. H. Lenski, *The Interpretation of St. John's Revelation* (Minneapolis: Augsburg Fortress Publishers, 2008), 577.

[86] Hoekema, *The Bible and the Future*, 227.

[87] Deere, "Premillennialism in Revelation 20:4–6," 70.

[88] Millard J. Erickson, *A Basic Guide to Eschatology: Making Sense of the Millennium* (Grand Rapids: Baker Books, 1998), 84.

[89] Venema, *The Promise of the Future*, 326. According to Venema, "Just as God's faithfulness is perfect and never failing (unto one thousand generations), so the times within his redemptive purposes are perfect and never failing." But what does it mean that this time period is "perfect" and "never failing"? Conversely, what would it mean for a period of time to be "imperfect" or "failing"? Another amillennialist refers to the "thousand years" as "the complete time that God has determined" (Morris, *Revelation*, 229), but what meaning does this actually communicate? What contribution does it make to John's description of his vision? How could the "thousand years" be anything *but* the amount of time that God has determined?

Third, the symbolic use of the thousand years does not fall into any clear category of symbolic language. Because amillennialists see the thousand years as symbolizing a lengthy period of time, the most likely candidate would seem to be the figure of speech known as *hyperbole*, an obvious exaggeration to communicate a very high number.[90] But John's use of "thousand years" cannot be understood as hyperbole if it refers to a period of time that is already nearly *two* thousand years in length. The number one thousand is not an exaggeration of the number two thousand and therefore cannot be considered hyperbole in Revelation 20.

In the absence of any compelling reason to interpret the thousand years symbolically, the designation should be taken at face value. Therefore, because the duration of the millennial reign of Christ in Revelation 20 is a literal thousand years, the millennium cannot refer to the present age, which is already nearly two thousand years in length. The millennial kingdom of Revelation 20 must take place between the Second Coming (Rev 19) and the eternal state (Rev 21–22), just as premillennialism teaches.

---

90 Although he does not use the word "hyperbole," this appears to be the view of postmillennialist David Chilton, who likens the symbolic interpretation of the "thousand years" to the hyperbolic statement, "I've told you a million times!" (David Chilton, *The Days of Vengeance: An Exposition of the Book of Revelation* [Fort Worth, TX: Dominion Press, 1987], 507). Unlike the "thousand years" in Revelation 20, however, the use of "a million times" in Chilton's example clearly possesses all three of the proposed criteria for symbolic language: (1) it possesses a degree of absurdity when taken literally, for no one has ever said *anything* a million times; (2) it possesses a degree of clarity when taken symbolically, for it effectively communicates that the speaker believes that he has told his hearer this information many, many times; and (3) it falls into an established category of symbolic language, the figure of speech known as *hyperbole*.

Chapter 14

The Chronology of John's Visions

Introduction

The crux of the debate over the timing of the millennium is ultimately found in the chronological relationship between Revelation 19 and 20. The key question is whether (a) the millennium of Revelation 20 follows the Second Coming in Revelation 19:11–21 (the sequential view) or (b) Revelation 20:1–6 goes back in time as a recapitulation of the period between the first and second comings of Christ (the recapitulation view).[1] Premillennialists take the sequential view and insist that the millennium of Revelation 20 will occur after the Second Coming of Revelation 19; whereas amillennialists take the recapitulation view and insist that Revelation 20:1 returns to the beginning of the present age, so that the millennium is taking place here and now.

The significance of this question is acknowledged on both sides of the debate. As amillennialist Anthony Hoekema observes, "If ... one thinks of Revelation 20 as setting forth what follows chronologically after what has been described in chapter 19, one would indeed conclude that the millennium of Revelation 20:1–6 will follow the return of Christ."[2] In other words, if the events of Revelation 19–20 will unfold

---

1 The sequential view is also known as postconsummationism (because the events of Rev 20:1–6 take place *after* the Second Coming), and the recapitulation view is also known as preconsummationism (because the events of Rev 20:1–6 take place *before* the Second Coming).
2 Anthony Hoekema, *The Bible and the Future* (Grand Rapids: Eerdmans Publishing, 1979), 226. Elsewhere Hoekema states that if the sequential view is correct, "We are then virtually

chronologically, the millennial kingdom will occur after the Second Coming and this passage teaches premillennialism. Only by denying the sequential relationship of the events in Revelation 19–20, then, is the amillennialist able to reject the existence of a millennial kingdom between the Second Coming and the eternal state.

The purpose of this chapter is to examine whether clear and compelling evidence exists for a chronological break in Revelation 20:1 so that the millennial kingdom of verses 1–6 coincides with the present age. This examination will demonstrate not only that there is clear contextual evidence for the sequential interpretation of Revelation 19–20, but also that the amillennial arguments for recapitulation provide no convincing reason to depart from the straightforward, chronological reading of these chapters.

The Sequential View of Premillennialism

According to premillennialism, nothing in Revelation 20:1 indicates a chronological break in the events that John describes. Therefore, the most natural way to read Revelation 19–20 is to see a sequential relationship in which the events described in chapter 20 follow those of chapter 19. As Grant Osborne explains:

> There is a distinct progression throughout chapters 19–22, from the return of Christ to the millennium to the final judgment and finally to the descent of the new heavens and new earth. The recapitulation theory does not do justice to this progression and to the difference of details at each level.[3]

In addition to the absence of any clear indication that Revelation 20:1 takes the reader back to start of the present age, the sequential view of Revelation 19 and 20 is supported by a number of key features in the immediate context.

---

compelled to believe that the thousand-year reign depicted in 20:4 must come after the return of Christ described in 19:11" (Anthony A. Hoekema, "Amillennialism," in *The Meaning of the Millennium: Four Views*, ed. Robert G. Clouse [Downers Grove, IL: InterVarsity Press, 1977], 156).

3 Grant R. Osborne, *Revelation*, ECNT (Grand Rapids: Baker Academic, 2002), 715.

The Introductory Καὶ Εἶδον

One of the most common premillennial arguments for the sequential view of Revelation 19 and 20 is John's introductory formula καὶ εἶδον ("and I saw") at the beginning of 20:1.[4] This formula is used 32 times in Revelation—seven of those occurring in chapters 19–21 (19:11, 17, 19; 20:1, 4, 11; 21:1)—usually to introduce the next vision being described by the apostle. According to Harold Hoehner, "Though these words are not as forceful a chronological marker as 'after these things I saw' (*meta tauta eidon*; 4:1; 7:9; 15:5; 18:1), or 'after these things I heard' (*meta tauta ēkousa*; 19:1), they do show chronological progression."[5] In other words, when John uses καὶ εἶδον ("and I saw") to introduce his vision of the thousand years in Revelation 20:1, this establishes a sequential relationship between the events described in chapters 19 and 20.[6]

In response, amillennialists argue that the introductory καὶ εἶδον ("and I saw") certainly indicates the sequence in which John *received* his visions, but not necessarily the historical sequence of the events described in those visions.[7] For this reason, amillennialists insist that the presence of καὶ εἶδον is not relevant to the question of historical progress between Revelation 19:11–21 and 20:1–3, for the only critical issue is the content of the visions themselves.[8]

---

4   John F. Walvoord, *Revelation*, rev. and ed. Philip E. Rawley and Mark Hitchcock (Chicago: Moody Publishers, 2011), 300, 303; Harold W. Hoehner, "Evidence from Revelation 20," in *A Case for Premillennialism: A New Consensus*, eds. Donald K. Campbell and Jeffrey L. Townsend (Chicago: Moody Press, 1992), 247–48; Steve Sullivan, "Premillennialism and an Exegesis of Revelation 20," 4–9, accessed on July 20, 2014, http://www.pre-trib.org/data/pdf/Sullivan-PremillennialismAndA.pdf.

5   Hoehner, "Evidence from Revelation 20," 247–48.

6   Other premillennialists are less dogmatic in making this argument from καὶ εἶδον, but they believe it does place the burden of proof on those who advocate recapitulation (Robert H. Mounce, *The Book of Revelation*, NICNT [Grand Rapids: Eerdmans Publishing, 1977], 361; Craig A. Blaising, "Premillennialism," in *Three Views on the Millennium and Beyond*, ed. Darrell L. Bock [Grand Rapids: Zondervan Publishing], 215; David J. MacLeod, "The Third 'Last Thing': The Binding of Satan (Rev. 20:1–3)," *BSac* 156, no. 624 [Oct 1999]: 472–73; Jeffrey L. Townsend, "Is the Present Age the Millennium?," *BSac* 140, no. 559 [July 1983]: 213).

7   R. Fowler White, "Reexamining the Evidence for Recapitulation in Rev 20:1–10," *WTJ* 51, no. 2 (Fall 1989): 324; Sam Storms, *Kingdom Come: The Amillennial Alternative* (Rossshire, Scotland: Mentor, 2013), 430.

8   White, "Evidence for Recapitulation," 324; White, "Making Sense of Rev 20:1–10?: Harold Hoehner Versus Recapitulation," *JETS* 37, no. 3 (Dec 1994): 540; Storms, *Kingdom Come*, 430–31.

Amillennialists have a point, for it does appear that the chronological sequence of the events in John's visions cannot be proven on the basis of καὶ εἶδον alone.[9] This can be seen in Revelation 20 itself, for even though the vision in verses 4–6 is introduced with the formula καὶ εἶδον, it describes the same thousand-year period of time portrayed earlier in verses 1–3, albeit from a different perspective. For this reason, it cannot be said that John's introductory formula alone proves a chronological progression of events.

At the same time, because καὶ εἶδον almost always indicates historical progression in Revelation—and because recapitulation is clearly the exception and not the rule—the burden of proof falls on those who insist on a chronological break at a given point. In the case of recapitulation in Revelation 20:4–6, for example, the repetition of the "thousand years" makes it clear that the second vision portrays the same time period as 20:1–3. But in the absence of this kind of explicit indication of recapitulation in Revelation 20:1, historical progress should be assumed unless the content of the visions demands a return to the beginning of the present age.[10]

The Content of the Visions

As even some amillennialists recognize, the chronological relationship between the visions in Revelation must ultimately be demonstrated from the *content* of those visions.[11] For this reason, the strongest argument for the sequential view (and against the recapitulation view) is found in the content of the two visions in Revelation 20:1–6. According to amillennialists, the thousand years in this passage coincides with the present age and therefore does not represent an intermediate kingdom between the Second Coming (Rev 19:11–21) and the eternal state (Rev 21–22). But the content of the visions themselves precludes the possibility that this

---

9 Osborne, *Revelation*, 699.
10 As Craig Blaising writes: "The visions of 19:11–21:8 are structured in a unified sequence. *There is no structural indication of a major break within this sequence recapitulating pre-Parousia conditions.* The series is tied together by the frequent use of *kai eidon* ('and I saw'), a recognized structural marker. This phrase, although not determinative in itself of a chronological sequence, nevertheless can be used for such. The content of the visions helps to determine the chronology. The key point, however, is that *kai eidon* does *not* signify a major structural break at one point (such as 20:1), which would be contrary to its use throughout the entire group of visions" ("Premillennialism," 215; emphasis original).
11 White, "Evidence for Recapitulation," 324.

time period represents the present age, and therefore Revelation 20 must not recapitulate the previous chapter.

In the first vision, an angel binds Satan and seals him in the abyss for a thousand years (Rev 20:1–3). Because it is impossible to reconcile the present-day activities of the devil with his incarceration in the abyss, the binding of Satan cannot be a present reality and therefore must be yet future. In the second vision, the saints experience a physical resurrection and live to reign with Christ for the thousand years (Rev 20:4–6), after which unbelievers are resurrected unto the final judgment (Rev 20:11–15). Because Revelation 20 depicts two physical resurrections separated by the thousand years, this time period cannot be the present age and must represent an intermediate kingdom between the Second Coming and the eternal state.

For this reason, all of the previous arguments that the binding of Satan is future (not present) and that the first resurrection is physical (not spiritual) simultaneously function as compelling arguments in favor of the sequential view of Revelation 19–20. The content of Revelation 20:1–6 is simply incompatible with the amillennial view that this passage is a description of the current age, and therefore the events of chapter 20 must follow those of chapter 19.

The Judgment of the "Unholy Trinity"

The third argument for the premillennial view is that the overall flow of thought in Revelation 12–20—specifically concerning the judgment of the "unholy trinity"—points to a sequential relationship between Revelation 19 and 20.[12] In Revelation 12:9, Satan is cast down to the earth where he begins his work of deceiving the whole world. To carry out this deception, Satan enlists the beast of the sea (13:1–10) and the beast of the earth (13:11–18), who is later identified as "the false prophet" (16:13; 19:20; 20:10). The three members of this "unholy trinity"—Satan, the beast, and

---

12 George Eldon Ladd, "An Historic Premillennial Reponse," in *The Meaning of the Millennium: Four Views*, ed. Robert G. Clouse (Downers Grove, IL: InterVarsity Press, 1979), 190; Hoehner, "Evidence from Revelation 20," 247–48; Blaising, "Premillennialism," 219; Craig Blomberg, "Eschatology and the Church: Some New Testament Perspectives," *Them* 23, no. 3 (June 1998): 14–15; John F. Walvoord, "The Theological Significance of Revelation 20:1–6," in *Essays in Honor of J. Dwight Pentecost*, eds. Stanley D. Toussaint and Charles H. Dyer (Chicago: Moody Press, 1986), 229.

the false prophet—are successful in their attempts to deceive, but they are eventually defeated by Christ, who returns to earth, conquers them, and casts them into the lake of fire in Revelation 19:11–20:10.[13]

At the conclusion of Revelation 19, however, only two-thirds of the "unholy trinity"—the beast and the false prophet—has been defeated and cast into the lake of fire. So what about the fate of Satan? This question is answered starting in the first verse of Revelation 20[14]—Satan is imprisoned in the abyss while Jesus reigns on the earth (vv. 1–6); he is released for a short time to resume his work of deception (vv. 7–8); and he is defeated (v. 9) and thrown into the lake of fire, where the entire unholy trinity is tormented for eternity (v. 10). In this way, Christ's victory over the beast, the false prophet, and Satan himself is complete.

The relevant point here is that the fate of Satan—the remaining one-third of the "unholy trinity"—is exactly what the reader would be expecting (and therefore waiting for) at the beginning of Revelation 20.[15] As Harold Hoehner explains:

> Revelation 20:1–10 serves as the final piece of the puzzle in the defeat and ultimate punishment of the utmost enemy of Christ and His saints. Therefore, in order to make sense of the culminating victory of Christ and conclusive defeat of Satan, Revelation 20:1–10 is a logical and chronological necessity to chapters 12–19.[16]

In this way, the judgment of the "unholy trinity" in Revelation 12–20 supports the sequential view of the chronology of John's visions.

William Webb, who sees this as one of the strongest arguments for the sequential view, summarizes it well:

> Throughout the book of Revelation, the beast, the false prophet, and the Dragon/Satan are portrayed as an evil trilogy, a devilish

---

13 This designation "unholy trinity" is used by Blomberg, "Eschatology and the Church," 15, who also refers to them as a "demonic trio." See Rev 16:13–14 where all three are named in succession and are said to deceive the kings of the world and gather them for battle.
14 Blomberg, "Eschatology and the Church," 15.
15 Blaising, "Premillennialism," 219; Walvoord, "Theological Significance," 229. Craig L. Blomberg, "The Posttribulationism of the New Testament," in *A Case for Historic Premillennialism: An Alternative to "Left Behind" Eschatology*, eds. Craig L. Blomberg and Sung Wook Chung (Grand Rapids: Baker Books, 2009), 68.
16 Hoehner, "Evidence from Revelation 20," 247.

troika, seeking to destroy the people of God. As the story-line unfolds, the rider on the white horse and his armies have attacked the rebellious armies led by the evil trilogy. By the end of chapter 19 the armies of the kings of the earth have been destroyed and two of the key leaders (the beast and false prophet) have been captured. Now the anticipated question which the narrative raises is, what will happen to Satan, the "leading figure" of the triad? Will he too be captured? Sure enough, Revelation 20:1–3 depicts just that, the capture of Satan. There is no need to stop the narrative flow at the end of chapter 19 and retrack.[17]

Therefore, as Craig Blomberg argues, "No matter how many flashbacks or disruptions of chronological sequence one might want to argue for elsewhere in Revelation, it makes absolutely no sense to put one in between Revelation 19 and 20 as [amillennalists] must do."[18]

The Use of "Any Longer" (Rev 20:3)

When the apostle John writes that Satan will be sealed in the abyss "so that he would not deceive the nations *any longer* [ἔτι]" (Rev 20:3), his use of ἔτι with the negative particle μὴ indicates the interruption of something already taking place.[19] Because the deception from which Satan is prevented in Revelation 20:1–3 was already taking place prior to his incarceration in the abyss, John's use of ἔτι ("any longer") in Revelation 20:3 points backward in time and connects this vision to the previous context in such a way that indicates a sequential relationship.[20]

---

17 William J. Webb, "Revelation 20: Exegetical Considerations," *The Baptist Review of Theology* 4, no. 2 (Fall 1994): 15. According to Webb, the continuity of this story line is further confirmed through certain word-links which draw together chapters 19 and 20: "For example, the beast and false prophet were 'captured' (ἐπιάσθη) and 'thrown' (ἐβλήθησαν) into the fiery lake. This is followed by Satan being 'seized' (ἐκράτησεν—a very similar semantic field to ἐπιάσθη) and 'thrown' (ἔβαλεν) into the abyss.... So each member of the triad is 'captured/seized' and 'thrown' into a place of confinement, while the plot for the ringleader comes with a little prolonged intrigue. The repeated motif of the 'capture' and 'throwing' of prisoners into confinement strongly suggests that the fate of Satan in Revelation 20:1–3 is a continuation of the battle context of chapter 19" (16).
18 Blomberg, "The Posttribulationism of the New Testament," 67.
19 Richard A. Ostella, "The Significance of Deception in Revelation 20:3," *WTJ* 37, no. 2 (Winter 1975): 237–38; also see *BDAG*, 400.
20 Blaising, "Premillennialism," 219–20.

More specifically, Revelation 20:3 indicates the termination of deceptive activity described throughout Revelation 12-19.[21] In Revelation 12:7-12, Satan—who is described as the one "who deceives the whole world" (v. 9)—is cast out of heaven and thrown down to earth, and he begins working in conjunction with the beast and the false prophet to carry out his deception of the nations. This ongoing work of deception is emphasized throughout Revelation 12-19 (12:9; 13:14; 16:13-16; 18:23; 19:19-20), being highlighted by the repetition of the verb "to deceive" (πλανάω).[22] But this deception of the world comes to a stop when Jesus returns to earth (19:11-19), the beast and the false prophet are thrown into the lake of fire (19:20), and Satan himself is locked in the abyss "so that he would not deceive the nations any longer" (20:3).

Because Revelation 12-19 repeatedly highlights the satanic deception of the nations that will take place throughout the second half of the Tribulation, John's reference to Satan no longer deceiving the nations while in the abyss points to a chronological reading of Revelation 19 and 20.[23] This would be similar to a narrative which contained several chapters describing how a dog barked at a cat, followed by a chapter which then described how a man locked the dog in the garage "so that it would not bark at the cat *any longer*." The most natural way to read such a narrative would be to see this latest chapter as describing an event that took place subsequent to the events described in the previous chapters. In the same way, the most natural way to read the visionary narrative in Revelation is to see chapter 20 as taking place subsequent to the events described in chapters 12-19.

The Description of the Lake of Fire

A fourth argument for the premillennial view is that the description of the lake of fire in Revelation 20:10 points to a sequential relationship between chapters 19 and 20.[24] At the time of the Second Coming, prior to the thousand years, the beast and the false prophet will be "thrown alive into the

---

21 Ibid., 220.
22 Rev 12:9; 13:14; 18:23; and 19:20.
23 Webb, "Revelation 20," 17.
24 Robert L. Thomas, "A Classical Dispensationalist View of Revelation," in *Four Views on the Book of Revelation*, 205-6.

lake of fire which burns with brimstone" (Rev 19:20). Then, at the conclusion of the thousand years, Satan will be "thrown into the lake of fire and brimstone, *where the beast and the false prophet are also*" (Rev 20:10; emphasis added). In light of the progression of these descriptions, the most natural way to read Revelation 19–20 is to see a chronological sequence in which (a) the beast and false prophet are cast into the lake of fire (Rev 19:20); (b) Satan is bound and sealed in the abyss for a thousand years (Rev 20:1–6); (c) Satan is released after the thousand years and defeated by fire from heaven (Rev 20:7–9); and then (d) Satan is thrown into the lake of fire where the beast and false prophet already are (Rev 20:10).

In his response this argument, amillennialist Sam Storms insists that even if Revelation 20:10 indicates that the beast and the false prophet were already in the lake of fire when Satan was consigned to it, "this need only imply that after the war the beast and false prophet were first judged and cast into the lake of fire, a judgment and fate then *immediately* applied to Satan."[25] In other words, isn't it possible that the beast and the false prophet were cast into the lake of fire first and that Satan was consigned there immediately afterward, so that all three were thrown into the lake of fire within moments of each other? Premillennialist William Webb acknowledges that the time lapse between the two consignments to the lake of fire is not specified in verse 10, so it may have been moments or it may have been a lengthy interval. But as Webb argues:

> If Rev 20:7–10 is the same battle as the parousia battle of chapter 19 and all three players in the triad get captured in the same battle (as amillennialists suggest), one might ask why John does not simply have all three players thrown into the lake of fire at the same time.... From a (straight) recapitulation perspective one would expect in Rev 20:10 to read something like, "After the battle of Gog and Magog, Satan was thrown into the lake of fire *along with* the beast and false prophet."[26]

Instead, the consignment of the beast and the false prophet to the lake of fire is separated from the consignment of Satan to the lake of fire in two

---

25 Storms, *Kingdom Come*, 436–37; emphasis added.
26 Webb, "Revelation 20," 15–16.

significant ways: (1) in Revelation 19:20 only the beast and the false prophet are consigned to the lake of fire, and (2) in Rev 20:10 only Satan is consigned to the lake of fire, which is then described as the place where the beast and false prophet had previously been consigned. The recapitulation view has a difficult time explaining the separation of these two consignments, whereas it fits very naturally with the sequential view in which the beast and false prophet are consigned at the time of the Second Coming (Rev 19:20) and Satan is consigned after the thousand years (20:10).[27]

The Future Tense of Βασιλεύσουσιν *in Verse 6*

As a final argument for the sequential view, some premillennialists observe that in describing the reign of the saints with Christ in Revelation 20, the apostle John switches from the aorist-tense verb ἐβασίλυεσαν ("they reigned") in verse 4 to the future-tense verb βασιλεύσουσιν, ("they will reign") in verse 6.[28] Because the beatitude in verse 6 appears

---

27 The primary response of Sam Storms is that this argument for the sequential view is based on a mistranslation of the relative clause ὅπου καὶ τὸ θηρίον καὶ ὁ ψευδοπροφήτης in Rev 20:10. Because this clause contains no verb, most translations supply the verb "are" (NASB; HCSB; NET; ASV; KJV; NKJV) or "were" (ESV; RSV), resulting something like, "where the beast and the false prophet are/were also." According to Storms, however, instead of supplying the copula—as almost all translations do—the verb to be supplied is probably "were cast" (ἐβλήθησαν) from Rev 19:20 (*Kingdom Come*, 436). But unless one presupposes the view that Storms is trying to prove—that Rev 19:20 and 20:10 describe the same event—there is no reason to think that a verb from 12 verses earlier should be supplied in this clause. More feasible—although definitely not certain—is the suggestion of Beale, who sees the elided verb as either "are cast" or "were cast," from the verb ἐβλήθη ("was cast") in regard to Satan earlier in Rev 20:10 (G. K. Beale, *The Book of Revelation*, NIGTC [Grand Rapids: Eerdmans Publishing, 1999], 1030).

Even though Storms and Beale argue from different antecedents, they agree that the verb to be supplied in Rev 20:10 is a plural passive form of βάλλω (either "are cast" or "were cast") and that it indicates that Satan, the beast, and the false prophet are all thrown into the lake of fire at the same time (Beale, *The Book of Revelation*, 1030; Storms, *Kingdom Come*, 436–37). Only one major translation supports the view of Storms and Beale—the NIV, which reads, "where the beast and the false prophet had been thrown"—but it is indeed possible. But even if Rev 19:20 should read "where the beast and the false prophet *were also thrown*," this does nothing to lessen the force of the premillennial argument, for the most natural way to read Revelation 19–20 would still be to see a chronological sequence: (a) the beast and false prophet are cast into the lake of fire (Rev 19:20); (b) Satan is bound and sealed in the abyss for a thousand years (Rev 20:1–6); (c) Satan is released after the thousand years and defeated by fire from heaven (Rev 20:7–9); and then (d) Satan is cast into the lake of fire where the beast and false prophet were previously cast a thousand years earlier (Rev 20:10).

28 Jack S. Deere, "Premillennialism in Revelation 20:4–6," *BSac* 135, no. 537 (Jan 1978): 73; Sullivan, "Premillennialism," 7–8, 40–41.

to be an interpretation of the vision described in verses 4–5, the future tense of βασιλεύσουσιν supports the view that the reign of the saints for a thousand years must be future (cf. Rev 5:10), and therefore that the events of chapter 20 must follow those of chapter 19.[29] Although this argument is not conclusive,[30] the recapitulation view does have difficulty explaining the change from the aorist to the future tense of βασιλεύω in Revelation 20:4–6.

The Recapitulation View of Amillennialism

Amillennialists argue that "the order of the visions in Revelation need not reflect the historical relationship of the events in those visions; it need only reflect the sequence in which John has presented the visions he received."[31] They further argue that the visions in the book Revelation are arranged topically rather than chronologically,[32] and that each of these visions functions like a different camera angle depicting the present age from a unique perspective.[33] This literary technique is known as *recapitulation*.

For many amillennialists, recognizing the use of recapitulation in Revelation is part of a larger interpretive approach called *progressive parallelism*. This approach was popularized by William Hendriksen[34] and subsequently adopted to varying degrees by other leading amillennialists.[35] According to this view, "the book of Revelation consists of seven

---

29 Deere, "Premillennialism in Revelation 20:4–6," 73; Sullivan, "Premillennialism," 7–8, 40–41.
30 Contra Deere, "Premillennialism in Revelation 20:4–6," 73, who sees this as one of the strongest arguments for viewing Revelation 20:4–6 as future.
31 White, "Evidence for Recapitulation," 324; also see Storms, *Kingdom Come*, 404; Kim Riddlebarger, *A Case for Amillennialism: Understanding the End Times*, expanded ed. (Grand Rapids: Baker Books, 2013), 228; Venema, *The Promise of the Future*, 307. As White further explains, "Any historical relationship among the visions must be *demonstrated* from the *content* of the visions, not simply *presumed* from the *order* in which John presents them" ("Evidence for Recapitulation," 324; emphasis original).
32 Riddlebarger, *A Case for Amillennialism*, 228; Venema, *The Promise of the Future*, 305.
33 Riddlebarger, *A Case for Amillennialism*, 228; Venema, *The Promise of the Future*, 305.
34 William Hendriksen, *More Than Conquerors: An Interpretation of the Book of Revelation* (Grand Rapids: Baker Books, 1967), 34–36.
35 E.g., Hoekema, *The Bible and the Future*, 223–26; Venema, *The Promise of the Future*, 306–7; Vern S. Poythress, *The Returning King: A Guide to the Book of Revelation* (Phillipsburg, NJ: Presbyterian and Reformed Publishing, 2000), 179; Riddlebarger, *A Case for Amillennialism*, 228; Storms, *Kingdom Come*, 406.

sections which run parallel to each other, each of which depicts ... the time of Christ's first coming to the time of his second coming."[36] These seven sections—chapters 1-3, 4-7, 8-11, 12-14, 15-16, 17-19, and 20-22—are parallel to each other, but they also reveal a certain amount of eschatological progress, with the final section advancing further into the future than the others.[37]

With this approach, because Revelation 20-22 comprises the last of the seven sections, Revelation 20:1 does not follow the return of Christ in Revelation 19, but rather takes the reader back to the beginning of the present age.[38] In this way, the visions of Revelation 20:1-10 are said to set forth yet another complimentary portrayal of the events between the first and second comings of Christ. For this reason, the visions recorded in Revelation 19:11-21 and 20:1-10 "should be read as parallel descriptions of the same time period."[39] The millennial kingdom of Revelation 20, in other words, is a present reality.

The Case for Recapitulation in Revelation 20:1-10

To make their case for recapitulation, amillennialists appeal to several related arguments: (a) the discrepancy between Revelation 19:11-21 and 20:1-3; (b) the casting down of Satan in Revelation 12:7-11 and 20:1-6; (c) the final battle in Revelation 16:12-16, 19:11-21, and 20:7-10; (d) the theme of angelic ascent/descent in Revelation; and (e) the chiastic structure of Revelation 17-22.

The Discrepancy Between Revelation 19:11-21 and 20:1-3

The initial argument for recapitulation points to the apparent discrepancy between Revelation 19:11-21 and 20:1-3 if those visions are read

---

36 Hoekema, *The Bible and the Future*, 223.
37 Ibid., 226; Hendriksen, *More Than Conquerors*, 36.
38 Hoekema, *The Bible and the Future*, 227. According to Cornelis Venema: "Whether Hendriksen's analysis of the structure of the book of Revelation is entirely correct in all of its particulars is not so important at this juncture. What is important is that it illustrates a commonly acknowledged feature of the book: that it should not be read as a linear description of end-time events. The simple fact that one vision follows another vision in the book does not mean that it does so chronologically. As is often true throughout the book, the events depicted may well parallel and recapitulate events represented in a preceding vision" (*The Promise of the Future*, 307).
39 Venema, *The Promise of the Future*, 305.

in historical sequence.⁴⁰ According to amillennialist R. Fowler White, "It makes no sense to speak of protecting the nations from deception by Satan in 20:1-3 after they have just been both deceived by Satan (16:13-16, cf. 19:19-20) and destroyed by Christ at his return in 19:11-21 (cf. 16:15a, 19)."⁴¹ If all of Christ's enemies are destroyed in Revelation 19:11-21—and if Revelation 20:1-6 describes events *subsequent* to that destruction—there will be no one left for Satan to deceive in Revelation 20:3.⁴²

Moreover, if Revelation 19 and 20 sets forth a sequence of events—and if all the nations are destroyed at the end of chapter 19—where do all the unbelievers come from in Revelation 20:8 when Satan deceives the nations after his release? According to Riddlebarger, the revolt of Revelation 20:7-10 is especially problematic for premillennialism:

> Who are these people who revolt against Christ? Who are these who are consumed by fire? Are these people in unresurrected bodies? If so, where did they come from? How do they pass through the judgment at the beginning of the millennial age? Are these people the redeemed? Such is unthinkable. The presence of evil in the millennial age is a problem from which all forms of premillennialism cannot escape.⁴³

According to amillennialists, this discrepancy introduced by the chronological reading of Revelation 19 and 20 supports the likelihood of recapitulation in Revelation 20:1.⁴⁴

Premillennialists generally respond to this objection in one of two ways. First, some premillennialists claim that not all unbelievers will be destroyed at the Second Coming, and therefore the nations will consist of

---

40 White, "Evidence for Recapitulation," 321. According to White, "Reading the events of 19:11-21 and 20:1-3 in historical sequence does not yield a logically coherent picture."
41 White, "Evidence for Recapitulation," 321. Venema makes the same point: "What sense does it make to speak of nations being protected from Satanic deception, when those nations which were formerly deceived by Satan have now been completely vanquished?" (*The Promise of the Future*, 309).
42 Poythress, *The Returning King*, 179.
43 Riddlebarger, *A Case for Amillennialism*, 249.
44 White, "Evidence for Recapitulation," 321; Riddlebarger, *A Case for Amillennialism*, 230-31; Venema, *The Promise of the Future*, 309; Beale, *The Book of Revelation*, 980-81; Storms, *Kingdom Come*, 431. According to Riddlebarger, "In light of the broader eschatology of the New Testament, the most plausible explanation is that Revelation 19:11-21 depicts the same event as Revelation 20:7-10" (*A Case for Amillennialism*, 231).

(or arise from) unbelieving, non-glorified survivors of the battle in Revelation 19:17–19.[45] But this view appears difficult to sustain, because even though there is clear contextual evidence that not all unbelievers will be killed in the battle of Revelation 19:17–19,[46] Matthew 25:31–46 confirms that any surviving unbelievers will not inherit the millennial kingdom. As Paul Feinberg observes:

> The *complete elimination* of the wicked from entrance into the kingdom rests *not just* on the destruction of the wicked at the descent of Christ at the Second Advent, *but also* on the separation of the sheep from the goats in the judgment that follows (Matt. 25:31–46). While many unbelievers will be slain at Christ's return, two judgments follow to root out all who remain.[47]

---

[45] Mounce, *The Book of Revelation*, 363; Alan Johnson, "Revelation," in *EBC*, ed. Frank E. Gaebelein (Grand Rapids: Zondervan Publishing, 1981), 12:587; Osborne, *Revelation*, 702; Robert H. Gundry, *The Church and the Tribulation: A Biblical Examination of Posttribulationism* (Grand Rapids: Zondervan Publishing, 1973), 166–67; George Eldon Ladd, *A Commentary on the Revelation of John* (Grand Rapids: Eerdmans Publishing, 1972), 257, 262–63. Osborne refers to these survivors as "earth-dwellers who supported but were not part of the army" (*Revelation*, 702) and who therefore were not destroyed in the battle; and Ladd sees them as "nations outside of the scope of this struggle" (*A Commentary on the Revelation of John*, 263). Amillennialist R. Fowler White erroneously claims that this is the *only* premillennial attempt to solve the problem of the alleged discrepancy between Rev 19:11–21 and 20:1–3 ("Evidence for Recapitulation," 323).

[46] The immediate context indicates that the gathering of the nations for this battle "is not a gathering of all their inhabitants but of their armies" (Blaising, "Premillennialism," 220). According to Blaising, this is made explicit in Rev 19:19, which refers to "the beast and the kings of the earth and their armies," but not to the general population of the nations. In addition, Blaising points out that Rev 19:21 "refers to the destruction of these *armies, not all the inhabitants* or even all the wicked inhabitants of the nations" (emphasis original). Even the reference to "all flesh" in verse 18 is most naturally understood as the totality of the armies gathered in opposition to Christ. As Blaising explains: "After 'kings,' 'captains,' 'mighty men,' cavalry ('horses and their riders'), the final reference to 'flesh of all men, both free and slave, both small and great' concludes a reference to the totality of the opposition force. This interpretation is confirmed by the repeat listing in 19:19: 'the beast,' 'the kings of the earth,' and 'their armies.' To read into this global judgment of all unbelievers everywhere on the planet beyond the gathering of these armies is without support in this text" (Craig A. Blaising, "The Kingdom that Comes with Jesus: Premillennialism and the Harmony of Scripture," in *The Return of Christ: A Premillennial Perspective*, ed. David L. Allen and Steve W. Lemke [Nashville: Broadman & Holman, 2011], 152).

[47] Paul D. Feinberg, "The Case for the Pretribulation Rapture Position," in *Three Views on the Rapture: Pre-, Mid-, or Post-Tribulation?* (Grand Rapids: Zondervan Publishing, 1996), 74; emphasis original.

For this reason, it appears difficult to defend the view that some unbelievers will survive the battle of Revelation 19:17–19 and enter the millennial kingdom.

The more likely explanation comes from those premillennialists who see the nations arising from the "the descendants of the tribulation saints who survive the tribulation and enter the millennium in their natural bodies."[48] According to this view, the battle of Revelation 19:19–21 and the subsequent judgment of the nations will indeed result in the death of all unbelievers. But some believers who are converted during the Tribulation will survive the persecution and enter the millennial kingdom in non-glorified bodies. During the millennium, these individuals will produce offspring who will continue in unbelief and eventually give rise to the nations that rebel against Christ after the thousand years.[49]

In the millennial kingdom, the rate of population growth "will be far higher than ever before because physical death will be the exception rather

---

[48] Walvoord, *Revelation*, 314. This is the view of Robert L. Thomas, "The Kingdom of Christ in the Apocalypse," *MSJ* 3, no. 2 (Fall 1992): 133–34; Robert L. Thomas, *Revelation 8–22: An Exegetical Commentary* (Chicago: Moody Press, 1995), 405, 410–11; MacLeod, "The Third 'Last Thing,'" 483; Hoehner, "Evidence from Revelation 20," 252; Sullivan, "Premillennialism," 22–23; Charles E. Powell, "Progression Versus Recapitulation in Revelation 20:1–6," *BSac* 163, no. 649 (Jan 2006): 105. As Sullivan explains: "Christ at his second advent will destroy all those who follow the beast (Revelation 13:7–8, 15–17; 16:13–14; 19:17–21) but the saints will not take the mark of the beast and thus many will be martyred (Revelation 7:9, 13–17; 14:12–13). Some of the saints will survive the Tribulation and will enter the millennium while others will be resurrected to enter the millennium (Matthew 24:38–44; 25:31–46; Luke 17:22–37; Revelation 20:4)" ("Premillennialism," 23). This view is compatible with the pre-tribulation, mid-tribulation, pre-wrath views of the rapture's timing, but not with the post-tribulation view. The first three views allow time for people to be saved after the rapture and therefore enter the millennial kingdom in non-glorified bodies. But according to the post-tribulational view, all the saints will be glorified when they are raptured at the Second Coming (1 Thess 4:13–18; 1 Cor 15:51–52), leaving no non-glorified believers to enter the Millennial Kingdom.

[49] According to amillennialist Floyd Hamilton, Luke 20:34–36 precludes the possibility of believers having offspring during the thousand-year kingdom of premillennialism (Floyd E. Hamilton, *The Basis of Millennial Faith* [Grand Rapids: Eerdmans Publishing, 1942], 137), but this passage refers only to those who have been resurrected and glorified. As stated above, the nations in the millennium will emerge from non-glorified believers who enter the millennial kingdom. Some amillennialists object to the co-existence of glorified and non-glorified people in the messianic kingdom of premillennialism, but the risen and glorified Christ ate and interacted with the non-glorified disciples during the forty days between His resurrection and ascension (e.g., Luke 24:43; Acts 1:3), thus no compelling objection can be sustained.

than the rule throughout this ideal period (cf. Isa. 65:20)."⁵⁰ Therefore, a new set of nations will come to exist on earth in a relatively short period of time.⁵¹ In this way, even though the nations are destroyed in Revelation 19:21, they will be reconstituted later under the messianic King (Isa 2:4; 11:10–16; Zech 14:16–21), consisting of surviving believers and their descendants at the end of the millennium.⁵² The unbelievers among the nations will remain undeceived from external sources until the thousand years are completed (Rev 20:3),⁵³ at which time Satan will be released to deceive them and gather them for the final battle (Rev 20:7–9).⁵⁴

The Casting Down of Satan in Revelation 12:7–11 and 20:1–6

A second argument for recapitulation is found in Revelation 12:7–11, which describes the casting down of Satan in terms very similar to those of Revelation 20:1–6.⁵⁵ Although the details between the two passages are not identical at every point, the parallels are said to "suggest that they depict the same events and mutually interpret one another."⁵⁶ The following seven parallels have been highlighted by amillennialists:

---

50 Thomas, *Revelation 8–22*, 411.
51 Ibid. As premillennialist Charles Powell notes, "It is preferable to see the nations as entities as a whole and not as unbelievers only" ("Progression Versus Recapitulation," 105).
52 Powell, "Progression Versus Recapitulation," 105.
53 Thomas, *Revelation 8–22*, 411.
54 Amillennialist Arthur H. Lewis objects to this view because it is inferential (Arthur H. Lewis, *The Dark Side of the Millennium: The Problem of Evil in Revelation 20:1–10* [Grand Rapids: Baker Books, 1993], 22), but when certain questions are not explicitly answered in Scripture, the interpreter is left to make good and necessary inferences from what is stated clearly. In light of the destruction of all unbelievers in Rev 19:19–21 and the presence of sin and unbelief in Rev 20:7–9, premillennialist Robert Thomas is correct to describe this scenario as "the only viable alternative" (*Revelation 8–22*, 411).
55 Riddlebarger, *A Case for Amillennialism*, 229–30; Beale, *The Book of Revelation*, 992–93; William E. Cox, *Amillennialism Today* (Phillipsburg, NJ: Presbyterian and Reformed Publishing Co., 1966), 61; Samuel E. Waldron, *The End Times Made Simple: How Could Everyone Be So Wrong About Biblical Prophecy?* (Amityville, NY: Calvary Press, 2003), 95; Venema, *The Promise of the Future*, 320–21; Hendriksen, *More Than Conquerors*, 188; Poythress, *The Returning King*, 181; Donald Garlington, "Reigning with Christ: Revelation 20:1–6 and the Question of the Millennium," *R&R* 6, no. 2 (Spring 1997): 72; Jonathan Menn, *Biblical Eschatology* (Eugene, OR: Resource Publications, 2013), 289–90; Dennis E. Johnson, *Triumph of the Lamb: A Commentary on Revelation* (Phillipsburg, NJ: Presbyterian and Reformed Publishing, 2001), 286.
56 Beale, *The Book of Revelation*, 992; also see Riddlebarger, *A Case for Amillennialism*, 229.

Revelation 12:7–11	Revelation 20:1–6
1. heavenly scene (v. 7)	1. heavenly scene (v. 1)
2. angelic battle against Satan and his host (vv. 7–8)	2. presupposed angelic battle with Satan (v. 2)
3. Satan cast to earth (v. 9)	3. Satan cast into the abyss (v. 3)
4. the angels' evil opponent called "the great dragon, … that ancient serpent called the devil or Satan, who leads the whole world astray" (v. 9)	4. the angels' evil opponent called "the dragon, that ancient serpent, who is the devil, or Satan," restrained from "deceiving the nations anymore" (vv. 2–3), to be released later "to deceive the nations in the four corners of the earth" (vv. 3, 7–8)
5. Satan "is filled with fury, because he knows that his time is short" (v. 12)	5. Satan to be "set free for a short time" after his imprisonment (v. 3)
6. Satan's fall, resulting in the kingdom of Christ and his saints (v. 10)	6. Satan's fall, resulting in the kingdom of Christ and his saints (v. 4)
7. the saints' kingship, based not only on the fall of Satan and Christ's victory but also on the saints' faithfulness even to death in holding to "the word of their testimony" (v. 11)	7. the saints' kingship, based not only on the fall of Satan but also on their faithfulness even to death because of their "testimony for Jesus and because of the word of God" (v. 4)

Figure 1. Riddlebarger, *A Case for Amillennialism*, 229.[57]

According to amillennialists, the obvious parallelism between Revelation 12 and 20—and especially the verbal connection in the fourfold identification of the dragon in 12:9 and 20:2–3—indicates that both passages are describing the present age.[58] For this reason, the casting down of Satan in Revelation 12:7–11 is seen as evidence for the present-day fulfillment of Revelation 20:1–3.[59]

---

57 Riddlebarger's chart is adapted from Beale, *The Book of Revelation*, 992.
58 Riddlebarger, *A Case for Amillennialism*, 229; Johnson, *Triumph of the Lamb*, 286; Beale, *The Book of Revelation*, 993.
59 Amillennialist G. K. Beale also believes that Rev 9:1–10 and 20:1–3 are synchronous and portray the same restriction upon Satan, albeit from different perspectives (*The Book of*

The problem with this argument is that it focuses on superficial points of similarity between Revelation 12:7–11 and 20:1–6 while ignoring differences between the two passages which make it impossible for them to be describing the same events or time period. Suppose a news magazine were to publish two separate articles about the president of the United States. The first article described how the president flew on Air Force One from Washington D.C. to London where he spent the day giving a number of public speeches. A subsequent article described how he flew on Air Force One from London to Hawaii where he spent two weeks vacationing with his family out of the public eye. The discerning reader would not assume that the two articles were describing the same flight simply because they both referred to how (a) the president of the United States (b) flew across the ocean (c) on Air Force One. After all, the point of departure is different, the destination is different, and the substance of the trip is different. The two accounts could not possibly be describing the same flight across the ocean.

So it is with the parallels between Revelation 12 and Revelation 20—even though both passages refer to a casting down of Satan, three critical differences preclude the possibility that they refer to the same casting down.[60] First, the origin and the destination of the casting down of Satan are completely different.[61] In Revelation 12 Satan is cast down from heaven to *earth*, but in Revelation 20 he is cast down from earth into the *abyss*. In Revelation 12, Satan no longer has access to heaven because he is confined to earth, but in Revelation 20 he no longer has access to earth because he is confined in the abyss. Unless one is prepared to equate the abyss and the earth, this cannot be the same casting down of Satan. He is on earth in Revelation 12 and in the abyss in Revelation 20, but, as discussed in chapter 11, he cannot be in both places at the same time.

Revelation, 986). But these two visions cannot be synchronous "because Satan cannot be using the key to open the abyss to release demonic forces and at the same time be cast into the abyss and locked in it" (Powell, "Progression Versus Recapitulation," 103). As Powell explains, "While there may be some flexibility in apocalyptic imagery, two visions cannot contradict each other."

60 Powell, "Progression Versus Recapitulation," 103–5; James M. Hamilton, Jr., *Revelation: The Spirit Speaks to the Churches* (Wheaton, IL: Crossway, 2012), 251–52; Webb, "Revelation 20," 24.

61 Powell, "Progression Versus Recapitulation," 103–4; Webb, "Revelation 20," 24.

A second major difference is that the expulsion of Satan from heaven in Revelation 12 has the opposite effect as the casting of Satan into the abyss in Revelation 20.[62] When Satan is cast down to earth in chapter 12, it results in increased deception of the nations (Rev 12:9; cf. 13:14; 16:14; 18:23; 19:20), but when Satan is cast into the abyss in Revelation 20, it prevents him from deceiving the nations any longer (Rev 20:3). How can Satan be described as the one "who deceives the whole world" (Rev 12:9) while simultaneously being sealed in the abyss "so that he would not deceive the nations any longer" (Rev 20:3)? Satan cannot deceive the whole world (Rev 12:9) and yet be unable to deceive the nations of the world (Rev 20:3) at the same time, and therefore the two descriptions are incompatible.

A final difference involves the short amount of time given to Satan in both passages. At the end of Revelation 12:12, John describes Satan being cast down to the earth, "having great wrath, knowing that he has only a short time." In Revelation 20:3, John writes that after Satan is locked in the abyss for a thousand years, "he must be released for a short time." As seen in #5 in the chart above, this parallel—"a short time" (ὀλίγον καιρὸν) in 12:12 and "a short time" (μικρὸν χρόνον) in 20:3—is cited by those who argue for the amillennial view.

The problem is that these two brief periods of time do not line up chronologically. In Revelation 12, Satan is cast down to earth for "a short time," but in Revelation 20 he is cast into the abyss for a *long* time (the thousand years), and then afterward he is released for "a short time." If the amillennial view is correct, the short time in Revelation 12 coincides with the long time in Revelation 20 (the thousand years), which is then *followed* by a short time.[63] The supposed parallel between the

---

62 Johnson, "Revelation," 581; Powell, "Progression Versus Recapitulation," 104; Webb, "Revelation 20," 24.
63 More specifically, the "short time" in Rev 12:12 consists of the three and a half years in the second half of the Tribulation (Rev 11:2–3; 12:6, 14) (Powell, "Progression Versus Recapitulation," 104). Beale denies that the "short time" of Rev 12:12 and the "short time" of Rev 20:3 are identical or synchronous, arguing instead for a temporal overlap in which the "short time" of 20:3 is the final stage of the "short time" in 12:12 (*The Book of Revelation*, 993). The problem is that this makes the "short time" of three and a half years (12:12) much longer than the "long era" of a thousand years (Rev 20:1–6) (Powell, "Progression Versus Recapitulation," 104). As Powell notes, "This overly symbolic approach strips the designations of time of all temporal significance.... Whatever the merits are of literal versus symbolic interpretation of numbers and periods of time, the designation for a brief period of time (three and a half years) should certainly not exceed the designation for a long period of time (one thousand years)" (104–5).

"short time" in Revelation 12 and the "short time" in Revelation 20 offers no support for the amillennial view and actually presents a significant difficulty for it.

Therefore, even though Satan is indeed cast down in both visions, the *destination* of Satan, the *result* of him being cast down, and the *duration* of his restriction (either on earth or in the abyss) are utterly incompatible. For this reason, Revelation 12:7–11 and 20:1–6 must not portray the same events or time period, and a comparison between the two passages provides no evidence for the recapitulation view of amillennialism.[64]

The Final Battle in 16:12–16, 19:11–21, and 20:7–10

A third argument for recapitulation in Revelation 20 involves the decisive war at the end of the present age. Amillennialists believe that three passages in Revelation describe the Battle of Armageddon—Revelation 16:12–16, 19:11–21, and 20:7–10—when Jesus returns to earth with the armies of heaven to destroy His enemies.[65] These passages have different points of emphasis, but all of them are viewed as "complementary portrayals of the second coming of Christ."[66] According to amillennialists, the apostle John is providing, "by means of literary recapitulation, differing perspectives on the same events."[67]

This argument for recapitulation focuses primarily on similarities between the battles described in Revelation 19:11–21 and Revelation

---

64 An additional problem with the amillennial argument is that the scene in Revelation 12 takes place during the tribulation period rather than the present age. But since amillennialists reject this broader reading of the book of Revelation, it is easier to simply demonstrate that Rev 12:7–11 does not describe the same event or time period as Rev 20:1–3.

65 Storms, *Kingdom Come*, 431; also see Poythress, *The Returning King*, 179.

66 Storms, *Kingdom Come*, 431. According to Storms, these passages "differ primarily because chapter 19 is concerned with the war as it relates to the participation and fate of the beast, his followers, and the false prophet, whereas chapter 20 is concerned primarily with the role of Satan. Also, it stands to reason that having given a detailed and vivid description of the war in chapters 16 and 19, John would find it unnecessary to repeat such detail in chapter 20" (*Kingdom Come*, 431–32).

67 Storms, *Kingdom Come*, 434. According to Strimple, "At the heart of the amillennialists' exegetical concern are the many clear evidences that 16:14–16; 19:19–21; and 20:7–10 are not describing three different battles that will take place at three different times, but rather are all descriptions of one and the same battle, with new information about that battle revealed each time" (Robert B. Strimple, "An Amillennial Response to Craig A. Blaising," in *Three Views on the Millennium and Beyond*, ed. Darrell L. Bock [Grand Rapids: Zondervan Publishing, 1999], 273).

20:7–10, which are seen as "one and the same event, each depicted from a different redemptive-historical angle."[68] According to Riddlebarger:

> The battle of Revelation 20:7–10 is a recapitulation of the battle recorded in Revelation 19:11–21, not a different battle that occurs one thousand years later. These are two pictures of the same conflict. If this case can be made with any degree of probability, it goes a long way toward establishing amillennialism as the biblical understanding of the millennial age.[69]

There are three primary reasons that amillennialists believe the battles described in Revelation 16:12–16, 19:11–21, and 20:7–10 are one and the same event: (1) similarities between descriptions of the battle; (2) the use of Ezekiel 38–39 in Revelation 19–20; and (3) the completion of divine wrath in Revelation 15:1.

Similarities Between Descriptions of the Battle

The first reason involves the various similarities in the way that the battles are described.[70] Amillennialists highlight four similarities in particular as evidence that Revelation 16:14–16, 19:19–21, and 20:7–10 "are not describing three different battles that will take place at three different times, but rather are all descriptions of one and the same battle."[71] The first similarity concerns *the identity of the enemies in the battle*. In Revelation 16 they are "the kings of the whole world" (16:14); in Revelation 19 they are "kings" and "commanders" and "mighty men," as well as "all

---

68 Riddlebarger, *A Case for Amillennialism*, 230. According to Riddlebarger, "One reason for the similarity no doubt has to do with the fact that in both texts John drew heavily on the imagery of the prophecy of Ezekiel 38 and 39, which describes the eschatological defeat of the mysterious Gog and Magog" (232). The significance of John's use of Ezekiel 38–39 in Revelation will be considered below.
69 Riddlebarger, *A Case for Amillennialism*, 230; also see Venema, *The Promise of the Future*, 311.
70 Riddlebarger, *A Case for Amillennialism*, 230. According to Storms, because of the similarities between Rev 19:17–21 and 20:7–10, "It seems that John is providing us with parallel accounts of the same conflict (Armageddon) rather than presenting two entirely different battles separated by 1,000 years of human history (as the premillennialist contends)" (Storms, *Kingdom Come*, 431). Venema concurs: "The visions of Revelation 19 and 20 show a similar parallelism in their description of the battle that will terminate the period of history portrayed in them" (*The Promise of the Future*, 311).
71 Strimple, "An Amillennial Response," 273.

men, both free and slave, both small and great" (19:18); and in Revelation 20 they are "the nations that are at the four corners of the earth" (20:8).[72] The similar identity of the enemies in all three battles is viewed as evidence that these battles are one and the same.

In response to this first point of similarity, the identity of God's enemies in these passages is perfectly consistent with the premillennial view. According to premillennialism, Revelation 16:12–16 and 19:11–21 do not describe two different battles.[73] Instead, Revelation 16:12–16 refers to the *preparations* for battle, and Revelation 19:11–21 refers to *the battle itself*, but both passages refer to the same battle.[74] For this reason, when Revelation 16:14 describes the "the kings of the whole world" being assembled in *preparation* for battle, and Revelation 19:19 describes "the kings of the earth and their armies" being *defeated* in battle, this fits perfectly with the premillennial interpretation of these two passages.[75]

In addition, because premillennialists see Revelation 20:7–10 as a separate battle at the end of a millennial kingdom in which Jesus and God's people have reigned on the earth for a thousand years, it makes perfect sense that the enemies gathered for battle are neither kings nor their armies—which will not exist in the millennium (Rev 2:26–27; 3:21; 5:10; 20:4–6)—but simply the nations of the world (Rev 20:8). Therefore, not only is the identity of God's enemies in these three passages perfectly consistent with the premillennial view, but premillennialism has the

---

72 Storms, *Kingdom Come*, 432.
73 When amillennialists argue against the view that these three passages describe "three different battles that will take place at three different times" (e.g., Strimple, "An Amillennial Response," 273), they seem to imply that this is the position of premillennialism, but it is not. Premillennialists see Rev 16:12–16 and 19:11–21 as a single battle which occurs at the Second Coming and Rev 20:7–10 as a second battle taking place after the millennial kingdom.
74 Osborne, *Revelation*, 592, 688; Blaising, "Premillennialism," 219; Thomas, *Revelation 8–22*, 265–66, 396; Johnson, "Revelation," 550–51; Ladd, *A Commentary on the Revelation of John*, 212. As Alan Johnson explains, the sixth bowl in Rev 16:12–16 "is specifically aimed at drying up the Euphrates River and so will allow the demonically inspired kings from the East to gather at Armageddon where God himself will enter into battle with them" ("Revelation," 550).
75 In addition to "kings," Rev 19:18 also refers to "commanders," "mighty men," and "horses ... and those who sit on them," all of which refer to those who comprise the armies of the kings. Even the reference to "all flesh" in verse 18 is most naturally understood as the totality of the armies gathered in opposition to Christ (Blaising, "The Kingdom that Comes with Jesus," 152).

added advantage of being able to explain why Revelation 16:12–16 and 19:11–21 focus on the kings of the earth, whereas Revelation 20:7–10 refers only to the nations of the world.

The second similarity involves *the gathering of God's enemies* to fight in the battle described in the three passages. Not only is virtually identical language used for the gathering of forces in all three descriptions—"to gather them together for the war" (συναγαγεῖν αὐτοὺς εἰς τὸν πόλεμον) in Revelation 16:14 and 20:8 and "assembled to make war" (συνηγμένα ποιῆσαι τὸν πόλεμον) in Revelation 19:19[76]—but also "the gathered forces have been *deceived* into participating" in the battle in all three passages.[77] As Beale writes, "This enforces the impression that Satan's *deception* of the nations in 20:8 'to gather them together for war' is the same event as the *deception* of the nations in 16:12–16 and 19:19."[78]

Because premillennialism sees the gathering described in Revelation 19:19 as a reiteration of what takes place in Revelation 16:14, the similarity between these two passages is to be expected. But as premillennialist Grant Osborne concedes, the language in Revelation 20:8 is indeed "problematic for the premillennial position," especially because the wording is identical to what is found in Revelation 16:14 (συναγαγεῖν αὐτοὺς εἰς τὸν πόλεμον). At the same time, because the binding of Satan in Revelation 20:1–3 prevents a deception that was already taking place, it makes sense that history repeats itself when Satan is released and he returns to deceiving the nations to gather them for battle. Furthermore, in light of all the differences between the battle in Revelation 20:7–9 and the battle of Armageddon in Revelation 16/19, the identical terminology falls short of proving the recapitulation view. As Osborne explains:

> The battle of 16:14–16 and 19:17–21 was led by the beast, this one [in 20:7–9] by Satan. The army of the first [in 16:14–16 and 19:17–21] was destroyed by the sword from the mouth of the Lord, this army [in 20:7–9] by fire coming down from heaven.

---

76 Beale, *The Book of Revelation*, 976, 980; Storms, *Kingdom Come*, 434; Venema, *The Promise of the Future*, 311; White, "Evidence for Recapitulation," 329–30.
77 Beale, *The Book of Revelation*, 980; emphasis original.
78 Ibid.; emphasis original. In addition, Beale observes that "just as the war of Armageddon in ch. 16 is followed by a description of the destruction of the cosmos (16:17–21), so likewise a vision of the dissolution of the world follows the final battle in 20:7–10, which suggests further the synchronous parallelism of the two segments."

At the end of that battle [in 16:14–16 and 19:17–21], the beast and false prophet are cast into the lake of fire; after this one [in 20:7–9], Satan himself is cast into the lake of fire. In other words, the details are sufficiently different to warrant the view of a second battle rather than a recapitulation of the first.[79]

Therefore, even though the identical wording in Revelation 16:14 and 20:8 is the most persuasive argument for the recapitulation view thus far, it fails to overturn the other contextual evidence which argues against it.

The third similarity is *the use of the article* to describe the battle as "the war" (τὸν πόλεμον) in each of the three passages (Rev 16:14; 19:19; 20:8).[80] As amillennialist Robert Strimple explains, "In 16:14 kings are called forth to *the battle*. In 19:19 the beast and the kings of the earth come forth to *the battle*. In 20:8 Satan leads his hosts up to *the battle*. It seems clear that these three texts describe not three battles but one."[81] According to Sam Storms, this use of the article not only "confirms yet again that John had one and the same 'war' in view,"[82] but it also "points to a well-known war, the eschatological war often prophesied in the Old Testament between God and his enemies (cf. Joel 2:11; Zeph. 1:14; Zech. 14:2–14)."[83] Cornelis Venema concurs, stating that the use of the article suggests "that this battle represents a final and conclusive defeat of Christ's enemies."[84] In this way, John's designation "the war" is seen as evidence of recapitulation in Revelation 20.

In response to this argument, it does make good sense to interpret (a) the article in Revelation 16:14 as a reference to a battle which is *well known* because it was prophesied in the Old Testament[85] and (b) the arti-

---

79 Osborne, *Revelation*, 713.
80 Storms, *Kingdom Come*, 432, 434; Venema, *The Promise of the Future*, 311; White, "Evidence for Recapitulation," 328–29.
81 Strimple, "Amillennialism," 125; emphasis original.
82 Storms, *Kingdom Come*, 434. According to Storms, "This point is confirmed when one observes the absence of the definite article in Rev. 9:7, 9; 11:7; 12:7; and 13:7" (432).
83 Storms, *Kingdom Come*, 432.
84 Venema, *The Promise of the Future*, 311.
85 This is what Daniel Wallace refers to as the "well-known," "celebrity," or "familiar" use of the Greek article (Daniel B. Wallace, *Greek Grammar Beyond the Basics: An Exegetical Syntax of the New Testament* [Grand Rapids: Zondervan Publishing, 1996], 225). According to Grant Osborne, "The articular τὸν πόλεμον concretizes this to mean "*the* war," namely

cle in Revelation 19:19 as an anaphoric reference to the same battle. For this reason, the amillennial argument that the article in Revelation 20:8 is also anaphoric—and therefore connects the three wars as one and the same—is formidable and should not be taken lightly.

At the same time, however, "The battle of 20:8 should not be identified with the battle of 19:19 on the basis of the Greek article to the exclusion of the literary context as a whole."[86] Even amillennialist R. Fowler White concedes that this argument from the three uses of τὸν πόλεμον ultimately depends on the larger context and whether the "wording and plot in 16:14; 19:19; 20:8 point most naturally in the direction of identical settings."[87] Because the wording and plot in these passages do *not* most naturally point in the direction of identical settings, the three articular uses of πόλεμος fail to prove the recapitulation view.[88] Even more significantly, if the case for recapitulation fails in Revelation 20:1–6—which it clearly does—then 20:7–10 cannot recapitulate 19:11–21.[89]

Regarding the significance of the Greek article, it is possible, as Harold Hoehner argues, that "the war" (τὸν πόλεμον) does not appear as a single event in Revelation but rather refers to "various facets of the great conflict between Christ with His saints and Satan and his hosts."[90] As Hoehner explains:

> Armageddon (16:16). This end-of-the-world battle was predicted in the OT (Ezek. 38–39; Zech. 12–14; Joel 2:11; 3:2), early Jewish literature (1 Enoch 56.7–8; 90.15–19; 94.9–11; T. Dan 5.10–11; 2 Esdr. [4 Ezra] 13:33–39), and the NT (2 Thess. 2:8), so in a sense the use of the definite article points back to the final battle predicted by the prophets" (*Revelation*, 592).

86 Craig A. Blaising, "A Premillennial Response to Robert B. Strimple," in *Three Views on the Millennium and Beyond*, ed. Darrell L. Bock (Grand Rapids: Zondervan Publishing, 1999), 152.

87 White, "Making Sense of Rev 20:1–10," 547. Stated more fully, White's argument is "that the parallels in wording and plot in 16:14; 19:19; 20:8 point most naturally in the direction of identical settings and hence to an anaphoric usage of the article with *polemos* in 20:8."

88 As Blaising explains, the rebellion in Rev 20:7–10 is described in terms that carefully distinguish it from the state of affairs that existed at the Second Coming: "The latter rebellion occurs on Satan's release from prison, whereas the earlier had occurred after his being cast down from the earth. The latter rebellion surrounds the saints and the beloved city (on earth), while the earlier rebellion gathered to resist the descent of Christ and the saints to the earth. The suppression of the earlier rebellion gave the bodies of the rebels to the carrion birds; the suppression of the latter consumes them by fire" ("Premillennialism," 220).

89 Powell, "Progression Versus Recapitulation," 97.

90 Hoehner, "Evidence from Revelation 20," 259. According to Hoehner, "When we examine Revelation 12–18 as well as Ezekiel 38–39, it seems that it is a prolonged war or a series of battles that last for more than three years." According to Robert Thomas, πόλεμον in

> In Revelation 19–20 this great conflict between Christ and Satan is manifested at the end of the Tribulation and at the end of the Millennium. We should not think that the articular noun always means the same thing in different settings. In 19:17–21 it refers to "the war" between Christ and the beast and the false prophet just before the 1,000 years and in 20:7–10 refers to "the war" between Christ and Satan just after the 1,000 years. The settings of each passage make it clear that they are different times. Though there are parallels, they are not one and the same battle.[91]

In connection with other compelling arguments, the three uses of τὸν πόλεμον would provide additional support for the recapitulation view. But in the absence of such arguments—and in light of the strength and comprehensiveness of the argument *against* the recapitulation view—the three-fold use of "the war" in Revelation 16:14, 19:19, and 20:8 fails to prove the amillennial interpretation.

A fourth similarity involves *God's means of victory over His enemies*. According to Riddlebarger, in both Revelation 19:20 and Revelation 20:9–10, "the fire of God's judgment consumes his enemies."[92] The first vision depicts judgment on the nations, the beast, and the false prophet, and the second vision describes judgment on the nations and on Satan; but both groups of God's enemies "are said to experience the final and eternal wrath of God through the means of burning sulfur."[93] This parallel between the two passages is seen as evidence for recapitulation in Revelation 20.

Rev 16:14 could be translated either "battle" or "war" and could either consist of "a series of conflicts or one major confrontation," depending on how one views subsequent events in Revelation (*Revelation 8–22*, 266). White says that the contexts of Rev 16:14 and 19:19 falsify Hoehner's claim that "the war" refers not to one event but to various facets of the great conflict, because the articular πόλεμος in 19:19 has the same referent as the articular πόλεμος in 16:14 ("Making Sense," 546). But Hoehner agrees that Rev 16:14 and 19:19 refer to the same battle and therefore sees Rev 16:14/19:19 as one facet of the great conflict and Rev 20:8 as another. So it is not clear how White believes Hoehner's view has been falsified by the similarities between Revelation 16 and 19.

91 Hoehner, "Evidence from Revelation 20," 259–60. It is also possible that the article in 16:14 is *well known*, the article in 19:19 is *anaphoric*, and the article in 20:8 is *the article of simple identification* (see Wallace, *Greek Grammar*, 216–20, 225).
92 Riddlebarger, *A Case for Amillennialism*, 233.
93 Ibid.

The initial problem with this argument is that the fire of Revelation 20:9 is the fire of *temporal* judgment, whereas the fire of Revelation 19:20 and 20:10 is the fire of *eternal* judgment. The former is the fire which comes down from heaven and devours Satan and the revolting nations when they attack Jesus and the saints during the "short time" after the millennium (Rev 20:9), whereas the latter is the fire which torments the beast, the false prophet, and Satan for all eternity as an act of everlasting judgment (Rev 19:20; 20:10). Because the fire of Revelation 20:9 does not portray the same act of divine judgment as the fire of Revelation 19:20 and 20:10, Revelation 20:9 has no relevance to Riddlebarger's argument.

This leaves the fire in Revelation 19:20 and 20:10—the fire of everlasting judgment which torments the beast, the false prophet, and Satan forever—as the only possible connection between the two battles.[94] But as discussed above, John's description of Satan's consignment to the lake of fire—the place "where the beast and the false prophet are also" (Rev 20:10)—most naturally leads to the following sequence of events in Revelation: (a) the beast and false prophet are cast into the lake of fire (19:20); (b) Satan is bound and sealed in the abyss for a thousand years (20:1-6); (c) Satan is released after the thousand years and defeated by fire from heaven (20:7-9); and then (d) Satan is thrown into the lake of fire where the beast and false prophet already are (20:10). For this reason, even though the fire of everlasting torment in Revelation 19:20 and 20:10 is indeed the same fire, the context makes it clear that the beast and the false prophet are consigned to this fire *before* the thousand years whereas Satan is not consigned to it until *after* the thousand years (Rev 20:10). The fire in these two passages provides no evidence that the two battles are one and the same.

The Use of Ezekiel 38–39 in Revelation 19–20

The second reason Revelation 20:7-10 is seen as a description of the same battle as Revelation 19:11-21 is because both passages use language

---

94 Riddlebarger does not cite Rev 20:11-15 in this context, but he does refer to the nations as experiencing "the final and eternal wrath of God through the means of burning sulfur" (*A Case for Amillennialism*, 233). But because this judgment of fire is described in Revelation 20 rather than Revelation 19, it fails to provide support that the two battles are the same.

very similar to that in Ezekiel 38–39.[95] In fact, a comparison between the three passages is said to show "that the Apostle John, in his respective descriptions of the rebellion and defeat of the nations in Revelation 19 and 20, is drawing upon identical language and imagery from Ezekiel's prophecy."[96]

This use of Ezekiel 38–39 is presented as evidence of recapitulation in Revelation 20.[97] As White explains, "If John expected us to interpret the revolts in Revelation 19 and 20 as *different episodes* in history, we could hardly expect him to describe them in language and imagery derived from the *same episode* in Ezekiel's prophecy."[98] According to Venema, "A much more plausible reading would conclude that these visions describe the same event and are to be read as parallel descriptions of the same historical period."[99]

Amillennialists believe that the similarities between the visions of John and Ezekiel are unmistakably obvious. For example, in Ezekiel 39:17–20, "the prophet Ezekiel foretold of a gruesome scene in which wild animals and birds are summoned to feast on the remains of God's defeated enemy, Gog."[100] In a similar way, the birds and animals in Revelation 19 are summoned to feast on God's enemies who were crushed by the divine warrior (vv. 17–18, 21).[101] As Riddlebarger writes, "There can be little doubt that the prophecy of Ezekiel 38–39 is fulfilled by the events of Revelation 19:11–21 at the time of our Lord's second advent."[102] The connection of Ezekiel's prophecies to Revelation 20:7–10 is said to be equally strong, for the nations which rebel against Christ at the end of the thousand years

---

95 Poythress, *The Returning King*, 179; Meredith G. Kline, "Har Magedon: The End of the Millennium," *JETS* 39, no. 2 (June 1996): 207, 213–20.
96 Venema, *The Promise of the Future*, 310.
97 White, "Evidence for Recapitulation," 326–28; Riddlebarger, *A Case for Amillennialism*, 232–33; Venema, *The Promise of the Future*, 310; Beale, *The Book of Revelation*, 976, 979.
98 White, "Evidence for Recapitulation," 327. As Venema writes, "It seems hard to believe, accordingly, that the episodes described in these visions are different episodes in history, separated by a period of one thousand years duration" (*The Promise of the Future*, 310).
99 Venema, *The Promise of the Future*, 310.
100 Riddlebarger, *A Case for Amillennialism*, 232.
101 Ibid.; Venema, *The Promise of the Future*, 310; White, "Evidence for Recapitulation," 326; Storms, *Kingdom Come*, 433.
102 Riddlebarger, *A Case for Amillennialism*, 232; also see Venema, *The Promise of the Future*, 310; White, "Evidence for Recapitulation," 326; Storms, *Kingdom Come*, 433.

are referred to as "Gog and Magog" (Rev 20:8), the very titles given to the enemies of God in the prophecies of Ezekiel (38:2; 39:1, 6).[103]

According to amillennialists, this leads to the conclusion that the visions in Revelation 19:11–21 and Revelation 20:7–10 provide two different camera angles of the same battle at the end of the present age.[104] As White summarizes:

> John's recapitulated use of Ezekiel 38–39 in both 19:17–21 and 20:7–10 establishes a *prima facie* case for us to understand 20:7–10 as a recapitulation of 19:17–21. If 20:7–10 is indeed a recapitulation of 19:17–21, then 20:7–10 narrates the demise of the dragon (Satan) at the second coming, while 19:17–21 narrates the demise of the beast and the false prophet at the second coming. Any other interpretation of how to relate these two judgment scenes, both of which are modeled on Ezekiel 38–39, will have to bear the burden of proof.[105]

In response to this argument, there is good reason to deny that Ezekiel's prophecy is fulfilled in the battle of Revelation 20:7–10.[106] The primary indication that Revelation 20:7–10 is not a direct fulfillment of Ezekiel 38–39 is found in the way John alludes to Ezekiel's prophecy. Most interpreters agree that the only explicit connection between the two passages is the reference to "Gog and Magog,"[107] and yet the apostle employs

---

103 White, "Evidence for Recapitulation," 326; Riddlebarger, *A Case for Amillennialism*, 232–33; Storms, *Kingdom Come*, 433; Beale, *The Book of Revelation*, 976, 979. White also discusses the use of Ezek 38:18–22 in Rev 16:17–21 to complete the connection between all three passages in the Apocalypse (Rev 16:17–21; Rev 19:11–21; and Rev 20:7–10) ("Evidence for Recapitulation," 327).
104 Riddlebarger, *A Case for Amillennialism*, 233.
105 White, "Evidence for Recapitulation," 327.
106 Although many premillennialists affirm that Ezekiel 38–39 describes the same battle as Rev 19:11–21, they generally reject the idea that Ezekiel's prophecy is fulfilled in Rev 20:7–10. According to MacLeod, there are at least six different premillennial views on the timing of the invasion of Ezekiel 38–39: (1) The invasion will take place before the Tribulation. (2) The invasion will take place in the middle of the Tribulation. (3) The events will take place at the end of the Tribulation. (4) The events of Ezekiel 38–39 will spread over a period of time, with chapter 38 being fulfilled in the middle of the Tribulation and chapter 39 being fulfilled at its end. (5) The invasion will take place at the end of the millennium. (6) Ezekiel's prophecy will be fulfilled in two events, one recorded in Rev 19:17–21 and one in Rev 20:7–10 (David J. MacLeod, "The Fifth 'Last Thing': The Release of Satan and Man's Final Rebellion (Rev. 20:7–10)," *BSac* 157, no. 626 [April 2000]: 208).
107 Ralph H. Alexander, "A Fresh Look at Ezekiel 38 and 39," *JETS* 17, no. 3 (Summer 1974): 166. Kline points to various similarities between the battles in Ezekiel 38–39 and Rev

this terminology quite differently than the Old Testament prophet. In Ezekiel 38–39, Gog is the prince of Rosh, Meschech, and Tubal (38:2–3), a local power which attacks Israel from the north,[108] and Magog is the land where he is from (38:2; 39:6).[109] But in Revelation 20, "Gog and Magog" are the nations of the world which gather from the four corners of the earth to surround and attack the saints in Jerusalem (vv. 8–9).[110] This distinction alone—Gog as a single ruler and Magog as his homeland vs. Gog and Magog as the nations attacking from the four corners of the earth—is sufficient to indicate that John's allusion should not be understood as a direct fulfillment of the events predicted by Ezekiel.[111]

20:7–10 (Kline, "Har Magedon," 219), but they are much too general to prove that the battles are one and the same.

[108] Several suggestions have been offered for the identity of Gog, including: (1) Gugu or Gyges, a ruthless ruler of Lydia who reigned a century before Ezekiel; (2) Gaga, a mountainous land north of Melitene; (3) Gagu, a ruler of the land of Sakhi, an area north of Assyria; (4) an unidentified ruler whose name is from a Sumerian loan word *gug*, which means "darkness"; (5) an official title for a ruler like a pharaoh or king; and (6) a general term for any enemy of God's people (Alexander, "A Fresh Look," 161; Lamar Eugene Cooper, Sr., *Ezekiel*, NAC vol. 17 [Nashville: Broadman Press, 1994], 331). As Ralph Alexander concludes, the most that can be said with certainty "is that Gog is probably a personage, whether described by a title or by name" ("A Fresh Look," 161).

[109] According to Daniel Block, the land of Gog most likely refers to the territory of Lydia in western Anatolia, but this is less than certain (Daniel I. Block, *The Book of Ezekiel: Chapters 25–48*, NICOT [Grand Rapids: Eerdmans Publishing, 1998], 434).

[110] The expression τὸν Γὼγ καὶ Μαγώγ ("Gog and Magog") is an accusative of simple apposition which refers to τὰ ἔθνη ("the nations") earlier in the verse, contra Alexander ("A Fresh Look," 166–67), who sees τὸν Γὼγ καὶ Μαγώγ in appositional relationship to the entirety of the preceding sentence.

[111] The significance of this distinction has been denied in two ways. First, it is noted that Ezekiel's prophecy identifies nations from the four corners of the earth as members of Gog's entourage taking part in the attack (Ezek 38:5, 6, 13; 39:6) (Alexander, "A Fresh Look," 167; Kline, "Har Magedon," 219). But in doing so, Ezekiel continues to maintain a clear distinction between "Gog and Magog" and the other nations who ally with them (38:2–7, 15, 22; 39:4), and therefore the primary discrepancy between the two passages remains: "Gog" is a single ruler and "Magog" is his homeland in Ezekiel 38–39, but "Gog and Magog" are the nations of the world in Revelation 20. Beale claims that John "universalizes" Gog and Magog without changing Ezekiel's "original contextual intention" (*The Book of Revelation*, 977), but such a modification clearly demonstrates that Rev 20:7–10 is not a direct fulfillment of Ezekiel's prophecy. Second, according to White, because many premillennialists agree that the events of Ezekiel 38–39 are fulfilled in Rev 19:11–21—and because Gog and Magog are identified as the nations of the earth in Rev 19:15—there can be no premillennial objection to Gog and Magog being identified as the nations of the world in Rev 20:7–10 (White, "Making Sense of Rev 20:1–10," 542). But the problem with this argument is that even if Ezekiel 38–39 is fulfilled in Rev 19:11–21—as many premillennialists affirm—this does not mean that Rev 19:15 equates Gog and Magog with the nations of the world. Rev 19:15 portrays the nations of the world taking part in the battle—as does Ezekiel 38–39—but it does not identify the nations as "Gog and Magog" like Rev 20:7–10 does.

But if Revelation 20:7–10 is not the fulfillment of the prophecy in Ezekiel 38–39, what is the significance of the reference to Gog and Magog? The answer begins with the recognition that "John does not always cite the OT with a strictly literal interpretation of proper names and events."[112] For example, when he refers to Sodom (11:8), Egypt (11:8), and Babylon (14:8; 16:19; 17:1, 5; 18:1, 2, 9, 10, 21) elsewhere in Revelation, John does not intend these references to be taken literally—instead he is seeking to convey the classic connotations associated with each of these well-known enemies of God. Therefore, the symbolic significance of these proper names can be traced to the characteristics and/or function of ancient Sodom (moral degradation), ancient Egypt (oppression and slavery), and ancient Babylon (the great enemy of God's people) in biblical history, leading interpreters to identify the intended referents in each case.[113] This is similar to how the prophets Isaiah and Ezekiel apply the name "Sodom" to Judah to highlight the wickedness of the Southern Kingdom (Isa 11:9–17; Ezek 16:46).[114]

In the same way, when John refers to the nations as "Gog and Magog" in Revelation 20:7–9, he is not signaling the fulfillment of the events prophesied in Ezekiel 38–39. Instead, his paradigmatic use of "Gog and Magog" is designed to identify the satanically deceived nations of the world in a way that vividly highlights their role as the enemy of God and His people after the millennium.[115] As Alan Johnson notes, the application of this designation to the enemies of God "has occurred historically through the frequent use in rabbinic circles of the expression 'Gog and Magog' to symbolically refer to the nations spoken of in Psalm 2 who are

---

112 Thomas, *Revelation 8–22*, 424. As William Webb explains, "John uses Old Testament traditions more to paint and color his visions, than to provide a precise 'this is that' kind fulfillment" ("Revelation 20," 11). According to Webb, the differences between Ezekiel 38–39 and Rev 20:7–10 suggest "a broad infusion of imagery" rather than "some kind of specific, detailed fulfillment."
113 Webb, "Revelation 20," 11–12. According to Webb, these are paradigmatic ways to refer to the "classic" enemies of God throughout salvation history without any tight fulfillment formulas. He likens it to the way one might use the terms "Waterloo" and "Alamo" to color descriptions of present-day conflicts. Despite the variety of different referents suggested for Sodom, Egypt, and Babylon in these passages, this general approach to the proper names is taken by interpreters on all sides of the millennial debate.
114 Thomas, *Revelation 8–22*, 93.
115 In this way, John's vision in Rev 20:7–10 "interprets Gog and Magog as symbols of all the nations gathered together in opposition to Christ and his followers" (Osborne, *Revelation*, 712).

in rebellion against God and his Messiah."[116] For this reason, "The most that one can discern from these names is that they are emblems for the enemies of Messiah during the end times,"[117] not that Revelation 20:7–10 fulfills the prophecy of Ezekiel 38–39 and therefore recapitulates the battle of Revelation 19:11–21.[118]

The Completion of Divine Wrath in Revelation 15:1

The third reason that Revelation 19:11–21 and 20:7–10 are viewed as the same battle comes from Revelation 15:1, where John writes: "Then I saw another sign in heaven, great and marvelous, seven angels who had seven plagues, which are the last, because in them the wrath of God is finished." According to amillennialists, John's declaration that "the wrath of God is finished" indicates "that the dispensing of the seven bowls of wrath by the seven angels will bring to a close the outpouring of God's wrath upon the wicked in the course of history."[119] Because amillennialists believe the last of these bowls are also described in both Revelation 16:17–21 and 19:19–21,[120] the vision of Revelation 19 is said to represent "the completion of the course of history and the finishing of God's wrath upon the nations."[121] For this reason, amillennialists claim that the sequential reading of Revelation 19–20 introduces a discrepancy between the *completion*

---

116 Johnson, "Revelation," 587.
117 Thomas, *Revelation 8–22*, 423. According to Webb, "With the Gog-and-Magog imagery (and names) John may be saying (and *only* saying) that these are the enemies of God's people. To argue that John utilizes these traditions beyond a paradigmatic meaning is much more difficult to prove" ("Revelation 20," 12). Beale rejects this view because Gog and Magog—unlike Sodom, Egypt, and Babylon—are part of a specific prophecy about the latter days which has remained unfulfilled (*The Book of Revelation*, 976), but it is not clear how this distinction undermines the argument for the paradigmatic use of "Gog and Magog" in Revelation 20. John does not present Rev 20:7–10 as the fulfillment of Ezekiel 38–39—he simply refers to the nations of the world as "Gog and Magog."
118 According to David MacLeod, during the millennium the defeat of Gog "will become a legend among the nations, something like Napoleon's defeat at Waterloo. Then at the end of the millennial kingdom the Gog and Magog 'legend' is applied to a new historical situation (20:8), with Satan leading the new 'Gog and Magog.' Satan will meet his 'Waterloo'—his 'Gog and Magog'" ("The Fifth 'Last Thing,'" 208). This could be likened to referring to the terrorist attack of September 11, 2001, as the "Pearl Harbor" of today's generation.
119 Venema, *The Promise of the Future*, 312; also see White, "Evidence for Recapitulation," 330.
120 Venema, *The Promise of the Future*, 312; White, "Evidence for Recapitulation," 331; Riddlebarger, *A Case for Amillennialism*, 233; Beale, *The Book of Revelation*, 982.
121 Venema, *The Promise of the Future*, 312.

of God's wrath in 15:1/16:17–21/19:19–21 and the *subsequent outpouring of God's wrath* in 20:7–10.[122] Put simply, if Revelation 15:1 indicates that the outpouring of divine wrath against the enemies of God will be completed in Revelation 19:19–21, how can the divine wrath be poured out once again in Revelation 20:7–10?[123] The amillennial view of recapitulation—in which God's final victory is portrayed in Revelation 16:17–21, 19:11–21, and 20:7–10—claims to avoid this discrepancy because it fits perfectly with the declaration of Revelation 15:1 that "the wrath of God is finished" at the Second Coming.

In reality, however, Revelation 15:1 presents no more of a problem for premillennialism than it does for amillennialism. If Revelation 15:1 is taken to mean that God's wrath will be completed at the Second Coming—never to be expressed again—then the amillennialist has difficulty explaining how the wrath of God can be poured out on unbelievers for all eternity (Rev 20:11–15). This is why amillennialists qualify their interpretation by insisting that Revelation 15:1 refers to the completion of God's "temporal"[124] wrath which is expressed "in the course of history."[125] In doing so, amillennialists can affirm an expression of God's wrath which takes place after the Second Coming (Rev 20:11–15). But by qualifying Revelation 15:1 in this way, amillennialists undermine their own argument against premillennialism. Put simply, if Revelation 15:1 allows for the expression of divine wrath after the Second Coming—as amillennialists concede it does—what objection can be sustained against the

---

122 Ibid.; Riddlebarger, *A Case for Amillennialism*, 233.
123 Venema, *The Promise of the Future*, 312–13; Riddlebarger, *A Case for Amillennialism*, 233. Beale's interpretation of Rev 15:1 is less than clear. In the context of arguing for the recapitulation view, Beale claims that Rev 15:1 means no divine wrath can be directed against the nations after the seventh plague, and therefore Rev 20:8–9 cannot occur after an intermediate kingdom between the present age and the eternal state (*The Book of Revelation*, 982). But elsewhere, when simply commenting on Rev 15:1 itself, Beale says that this verse does not mean God's wrath has ended or reached its completion. Instead, it is a metaphorical way to express that the seven bowls "portray the full-orbed wrath of God in a more intense manner than any of the previous woe visions" (788). According to Beale, Rev 15:1 refers to the seven plagues as "the last" (τὰς ἐσχάτας) to indicate "the order in which John saw the visions and not necessarily the chronological order of their occurrence in history.... Therefore, the bowls do not have to be understood as occurring as the last events of history" (786).
124 White, "Making Sense of Rev 20:1–10," 547.
125 Venema, *The Promise of the Future*, 312. As White explains, "God's wrath, of course, continues interminably in eternity. John's statement applies to divine retribution in history" ("Evidence for Recapitulation," 330).

premillennial view that God will express His wrath against Satan and the unbelieving rebels a thousand years after the return of Christ? If Revelation 15:1 allows for a subsequent expression of God's wrath in Revelation 20:11–15 (according to the recapitulation view), it also allows for a subsequent expression of God's wrath in Revelation 20:7–10 (according to the sequential view).[126]

Revelation 15:1 obviously cannot mean that these plagues exhaust the totality of divine wrath—for the beast, the false prophet, the devil, and unbelievers have not yet been cast into the lake of fire in the final manifestation of God's wrath against sin (Rev 19:20; 20:10, 11–15).[127] Instead, these words must be interpreted in the eschatological context of the outpouring of God's wrath in the time of the great tribulation.[128] According to Revelation 15:1, the seven plagues are the last of God's judgments against the unbelieving nations during the great tribulation—which culminates in the return of Christ—and when these plagues are over, the wrath of God will have been completed (or reached its ultimate goal). But this no more discounts the possibility of divine wrath a thousand years later in Revelation 20:7–10 than it does in the eternal state in Revelation 20:11–15, so this argument from the recapitulation view is not compelling.

The Theme of Angelic Ascent/Descent in Revelation

A fourth argument for the recapitulation view involves the motif of angelic ascent and descent in the book of Revelation.[129] According to this argument, where an angel's ascent or descent begins a new vision sequence elsewhere in Revelation, that vision portrays a course of events from the present time to the return of Christ at the end of the age.[130] In Revelation 7:2, 10:1, and 18:1, for example, "the angelic ascent/descent initiates a vision that temporarily suspends whatever historical or chronological process had heretofore obtained, and introduces an interlude that is

---

126 White argues that God's wrath is not completed within the time frame of the seven last plagues according to the premillennial view of Rev 20:7–10 ("Making Sense of Rev 20:1–10," 547–48), but neither is it completed within that time frame according to the amillennial view of Rev 20:11–15.
127 Ladd, *A Commentary on the Revelation of John*, 204.
128 Ibid.
129 White, "Evidence for Recapitulation," 336–43; Venema, *The Promise of the Future*, 308; Storms, *Kingdom Come*, 437.
130 Venema, *The Promise of the Future*, 308; White, "Evidence for Recapitulation," 336–43.

recapitulatory in nature."[131] Because the vision of Revelation 20 begins with the descent of an angel from heaven, it would fit with this established pattern of recapitulation if this chapter took the reader back to the beginning of the New Testament era.[132] For this reason, the motif of angelical ascent/descent in Revelation is seen as support for the recapitulation view.

The most significant weakness of this argument is the subtlety of the structural pattern supposedly indicated by this angelic motif. In light of the complexity of this argument—and the difficulty of recognizing this pattern even when it is highlighted by the amillennialist—one has to question how likely it is that John intended to signal a recapitulatory interlude with the descent of the angel in Revelation 20:1. Isn't it more likely that the apostle was simply describing the movement of the angel who was sent by God from heaven to lay hold of Satan on earth? And isn't it possible for him to have done so without signaling a chronological break between chapters 19 and 20, especially in light of the previously highlighted progression of these visions?

At issue here is the perspicuity of the book of Revelation (Rev 1:3). Is the claim that these other two angelic descents signal an interlude sufficient to communicate recapitulation in Revelation 20:1?[133] Does the amillennialist believe that the apostle expected his readers to discover this pattern and decipher its intended implications? As Craig Blaising observes, this argument appears to be an artificially constructed typology imposed on the book of Revelation, and one that ignores several textual details in the process.[134]

---

131 Storms, *Kingdom Come*, 437 (emphasis original). According to Venema, "In these instances, the angel's ascent or descent occurs at a time clearly prior to the return of Christ and marks the beginning of a vision whose sequence of events concludes with the coming of Christ in final victory over his enemies" (*The Promise of the Future*, 308).
132 Venema, *The Promise of the Future*, 308.
133 In fairness, it should be noted that amillennialists do not believe that this pattern actually *proves* recapitulation in Revelation 20, but rather that it provides additional support for this view when taken in conjunction with other factors (White, "Evidence for Recapitulation," 336; Storms, *Kingdom Come*, 437).
134 Blaising, "Premillennialism," 217. According to Blaising, this argument fails on literary-structural grounds in several ways. First, in each of the three examples (Rev 7:1; 10:1; 18:1), the angelic ascent/descent is distinct from the indicator used in the larger series, but this is not the case in Rev 20:1. As a result, the angel's coming down in Rev 20:1 is a series item just as much as the opening of heaven in 19:11, as the angel standing in the sun in 19:16, as the assembling of the beast and the kings of the earth in 19:19, etc. Second, each

The Chiastic Structure of Revelation 17–22

A fifth and final argument for recapitulation in chapter 20 involves the broader context of Revelation 17–22. According to G. K. Beale, these chapters form a chiastic structure with sections exhibiting synchronous parallelism:

> A   judgment of the harlot (17:1—19:6)
>   B   the divine Judge (19:11–16)
>   C   judgment of the beast and the false prophet (19:17–21)
>   D   Satan imprisoned for 1,000 years (20:1–3)
>   D' the saints reign/judge for 1,000 years (20:4–6)
>   C' the judgment of Gog and Magog (20:7–10)
>   B' the divine Judge (20:11–15)
> A' vindication of the bride (21:1—22:5; cf. 19:7–9)[135]

According to Beale, this chiastic structure suggests that Revelation 20:1ff does not follow chronologically after Revelation 19:11–21.[136]

The obvious weakness of this argument is that the parallelism is not synchronous in two of the four pairs of the chiasm (A/A' and B/B'), even if one assumes the recapitulatory structure advocated by amillennialists. According to the chiasm, the judgment of the harlot in 17:1–19:6 is synchronously parallel to the vindication of the bride in 21:1–22:5 (A/A'), but the former takes place in the present age while the latter takes place in the eternal state. Furthermore, the divine judgment in 19:11–16 is said to be synchronously parallel to the divine judgment in 20:11–15 (B/B')—but the former is the temporal judgment of the last generation of the wicked

---

of the examples involves a message from the angel explicitly referring to the larger series (7:3; 10:7; 18:2), but no such message appears in Rev 20:1–10. Third, since the angel in Rev 7:2 *ascends* instead of descends, this passage is disqualified from consideration in a *descending* angel typology. Fourth, because this argument ignores the structural significance of Rev 10:11 for the two witnesses' vision in 11:3–13, it fails to see its structural connection to the visions of Rev 12–14. Fifth, this argument's attempt to locate Revelation 18 prior to the bowls judgment in Revelation 16 runs counter to its own typology, because Revelation 18 is not an interlude in the bowls series. Sixth, for all of its focus on the descending angel in Rev 20:1, this argument makes no appeal to Rev 9:1–6—"the only passage that truly offers a parallel description to that of 20:1–3"—which "is *not a recapitulating vision* but rather part of a visionary sequence, just as is the angel of 20:1" ("Premillennialism," 216–17; emphasis original).

135 Beale, *The Book of Revelation*, 983.
136 Ibid.

that takes place when Jesus returns, whereas the latter is the eternal judgment of all the wicked that takes place after the resurrection. Because of the lack of synchronous parallelism in two of the four pairs in the supposed chiasm, this argument provides no support for the recapitulation view of amillennialism.

Conclusion

No other section of Scripture sets forth the eschatological events of human history with the kind of chronological clarity found in Revelation 19–22. At the end of present age, Jesus will return in glory (Rev 19:11–16), bringing judgment to the false prophet, the beast, and the unbelieving armies of the earth (Rev 19:17–21). Satan will be imprisoned in the abyss for a thousand years (Rev 20:1–3), and Jesus will establish His kingdom on earth where He will reign with the saints in perfect righteousness (Rev 20:4–6). At the end of the thousand years, Satan will be released and defeated once and for all (Rev 20:7–10); the wicked will be resurrected, judged, and thrown into the lake of fire (Rev 20:11–15); and the eternal state of the new heaven and earth will begin (Rev 21–22).

In Revelation 20:1–6, then, the apostle John describes the thousand-year reign of Christ as following the Second Coming of Revelation 19 and yet preceding the new heavens and new earth of Revelation 21–22. The inability of amillennialists to demonstrate that the thousand years of Revelation 20 is a present reality leads to the conclusion that this passage affirms an intermediate kingdom between the present age and the eternal state and thereby presents an insurmountable problem for the two-age model of amillennialism.

Chapter 15

Conclusion

To formulate a thoroughly biblical eschatology, one must allow every passage of Scripture to make its own contribution to the doctrine of last things, including the millennium. This means starting in the Old Testament and tracing the prophecies of the coming kingdom from Genesis to Revelation, letting each new biblical passage build upon what was previously revealed. To honor the unity of Scripture, one must recognize that later revelation often supplements and clarifies earlier revelation by providing broader context or additional detail, but it never reinterprets or changes the meaning of those previous passages in the process. In the end, the biblical theologian must harmonize his exegesis of all the relevant passages, being careful not to allow any one of them to silence or distort the contribution of another. This is the only way to construct an eschatology that synthesizes the entirety of Scripture's teaching on the age to come.

In contrast to this approach, the primary argument for amillennialism exalts a handful of New Testament passages to the position of interpretive grid and insists on reading the remainder of Scripture through the hermeneutical lens of the two-age model. This interpretive grid does not allow the amillennialist to see descriptions of an intermediate kingdom in the Old Testament, but the more significant problem concerns Revelation 20. With the two-age model in hand, the amillennialist comes to the last book of the Bible with the assumption that Revelation 20 cannot be allowed to teach a millennial reign of Christ between the Second Coming (Rev 19) and the eternal state (Rev 21). As a result, he is forced to explain away a very straightforward sequence of events described in the final chapters of the Apocalypse.[1]

In one sense, the entire debate can be reduced to a single question: Which is more exegetically feasible—the amillennial interpretation of Revelation 20 or the premillennial insistence on a gap of time between key eschatological events described in the New Testament? This critique has argued that the former consists of a fundamental departure from the meaning of Revelation 20, whereas the latter simply allows subsequent revelation to clarify the existence of a temporal gap between various events prophesied in earlier revelation. The former distorts the meaning of the most significant passage in the millennial debate, while the latter harmonizes the totality of biblical revelation by appealing to a well-attested dynamic known as *prophetic telescoping*.

Amillennialists typically acknowledge the existence of telescoping when moving from the Old Testament to the New, but they are unwilling to let Revelation 20 play a clarifying role within the New Testament itself. As Darrell Bock observes, it is ironic that those who emphasize the prominence of later revelation as definitive in so many other areas would argue for a more limited role of this final New Testament book in the millennial debate.[2] In response, amillennialists usually charge premillennialism with giving too much weight to Revelation 20 by letting this "one obscure passage govern the entire Bible."[3] Sam Storms accuses the premillennialist of allowing the apocalyptic tail to wag the epistolary dog, describing the premillennial approach as making the rest of the Bible "bend to the standard of one text" and "dance to the tune of Revelation 20."[4] Robert Strimple likewise describes it as setting aside the entire New Testament because of this single passage in the highly symbolic book of Revelation.[5]

But the premillennial approach does not use this passage to change

---

[1] Wayne Grudem, *Systematic Theology: An Introduction to Biblical Doctrine* (Grand Rapids: Zondervan Publishing, 1994), 1121.
[2] Darrell L. Bock, "Summary Essay," in *Three Views on the Millennium and Beyond*, ed. Darrell L. Bock (Grand Rapids: Zondervan Publishing, 1999), 298.
[3] William E. Cox, *Amillennialism Today* (Phillipsburg, NJ: Presbyterian and Reformed Publishing, 1966), 65.
[4] Sam Storms, *Kingdom Come: The Amillennial Alternative* (Ross-shire, Scotland: Mentor, 2013), 143.
[5] Robert B. Strimple, "Amillennialism," in *Three Views on the Millennium and Beyond*, ed. Darrell L. Bock (Grand Rapids: Zondervan Publishing, 1999), 120.

or dismiss the meaning of the remainder of Scripture, as amillennialists often claim. Instead, it simply recognizes that Revelation 19–21 contains the fullest and most comprehensive presentation of the eschatological events surrounding the Second Coming. As a result, it allows this section of Scripture to bring greater clarity to the sequence of events that will transpire in the age to come. As George Eldon Ladd notes, "The fact that the relationship of these events ... is made explicit for the first time only in the last verses of the last book of the Bible should pose no acute problem to those who believe in progressive revelation."[6] The only alternative is to silence the unmistakably clear contribution of Revelation 20, which Kim Riddlebarger calls "the most important biblical passage dealing with the subject of the millennium."[7]

If Revelation 20 does indeed teach a millennial reign of Christ between the present age and the eternal state, the biblical theologian must find a way to harmonize this intermediate kingdom with his understanding of the two ages, regardless of what his interpretive grid will or will not allow. Because the Old Testament prophets anticipated a phase of the coming kingdom that corresponds to the millennial reign in John's vision—and because nothing in the remainder of Scripture conclusively excludes the possibility of such a kingdom—there is no reason to reject the plain reading of Revelation 19–21.

The two-age argument for amillennialism will likely continue to be used as a polemic against premillennialism. But as this critique has demonstrated, even though the two ages provide a helpful framework for understanding biblical eschatology, they do not preclude the existence of an intermediate kingdom. The present age will continue until the Second Coming of Christ, which will usher in the age to come. In the initial phase of this coming age, the Lord Jesus will reign on the earth until He has put all His enemies under His feet. And then, after the final enemy is abolished by Christ, He will hand the kingdom over to the Father and the eternal state will begin so that God may be all in all (1 Cor 15:23–28).

---

6 George Eldon Ladd, *Crucial Questions About the Kingdom of God* (Grand Rapids: Eerdmans Publishing, 1952), 182.
7 Kim Riddlebarger, *A Case for Amillennialism: Understanding the End Times*, expanded ed. (Grand Rapids: Baker Books, 2013), 223.

Appendix

The Intermediate Kingdom in Intertestamental Judaism

The difficulty in constructing an accurate picture of intertestamental Jewish eschatology stems from the variety of different viewpoints represented during this time.[1] Moreover, because the ancient sources do not offer systematic descriptions of their views, the eschatological chronology is frequently ambiguous in a given writing, making it difficult to discern a clear sequence of events within a single source, much less among Judaism as a whole.[2] In spite of the ambiguity, however, it is possible to identify a common set of core beliefs, particularly because eschatological thought appears to assume more structure and agreement as it moves toward the end of the intertestamental period.[3]

One such widely embraced belief—solidified later in the era—was the view that there are two distinct ages within the period of redemption, designated "the first age" and "the age that follows" in 2 Esdras 6:6–7.[4] According to this paradigm, redemptive history will unfold in a two-age framework—"this age" inaugurated by creation, and "the age

---

1 J. Julius Scott, Jr., *Jewish Backgrounds of the New Testament* (Grand Rapids: Baker Books, 1995), 284; D. S. Russell, *The Method and Message of Jewish Apocalyptic: 200 BC – AD 100* (Philadephia: The Westminster Press, 1964), 286.
2 Scott, *Jewish Backgrounds of the New Testament*, 284.
3 Ibid., 285. At the same time, Scott continues by issuing the caution that this "must not be allowed to obscure the variety within the intertestamental views of the final age."
4 Ibid., 271–72. According to Scott, these two ages are also attested to in the Dead Sea Scrolls: 2 Esdras 7:3–44, 113; 8:1; 1 Enoch 16:1; 71:15; 2 Bar 14:13–19; 15:7; and Mishnah Aboth 4:1; 6:4, 7 (226, 271).

to come" inaugurated by the Day of the Lord (1 Enoch 71:15; cf. 48:7).[5] Although the attestation of this terminology is limited prior to AD 70, some scholars trace the doctrine of the two ages—as well as the origin of the terminology "this age" and "the age to come"—to the apocalyptic writings of the first century BC.[6] According to Larry Helyer, however, modern scholarship generally "pushes the origins of this concept back into the second century BC, if not earlier."[7]

This distinction between the two ages was fundamental to the intertestamental worldview.[8] The former age was expected to come to an end through direct divine intervention, either the entrance of God Himself into human history or the appearance of God's agent—one or more messianic figures—through whom He would accomplish His will.[9] The latter age was seen as the final culmination of God's victory over hostile forces when He would defeat Satan and the powers of evil and reassert His right to rule over the universe.[10] This concept of the two ages was well established by the time of the New Testament and therefore is simply assumed by Jesus and the biblical writers, as evidenced by the abundance of references to "this age" and/or "the age to come" (e.g., Matt 12:32; Mark 10:30; Luke 18:30; 20:34–35; Eph 1:21).[11]

---

5 Larry R. Helyer, "The Necessity, Problems, and Promise of Second Temple Judaism for Discussions of New Testament Eschatology," *JETS* 47, no. 4 (Dec 2004), 597.
6 Hermann Sasse, "αἰών," in *TDNT*, ed. Gerhard Kittel [Grand Rapids: Eerdmans Publishing, 1964], 1:206–7; Haïm Z'ew Hirschberg, "Eschatology," in *Encyclopaedia Judaica* (New York: The MacMillan Company, 1971), 6:874.
7 Helyer, "Second Temple Judaism and New Testament Eschatology," 598.
8 J. W. Bailey, "The Temporary Messianic Reign in the Literature of Early Judaism," *JBL* 53, no. 1 (1934): 170.
9 Scott, *Jewish Backgrounds of the New Testament*, 272.
10 Ibid. According to Scott, "Intertestamental writers use a number of terms to refer to the whole or a part of that age which was expected to follow God's breaking into human history" (287). Some of the more common ones are "the day," "the day of the Lord," "in that (those) day(s)," "the last days," "the final age," "the messianic age," "the days of Messiah," "the kingdom (of God)," "the coming age," "the world to come," "the hour," and "the time."
11 Helyer, "Second Temple Judaism and New Testament Eschatology," 598; Scott, *Jewish Backgrounds of the New Testament*, 271, 286; W. D. Davies, *The Setting of the Sermon on the Mount* (London: Cambridge University Press, 1963), 182–83; Geerhardus Vos, *The Pauline Eschatology* (1930; repr., Phillipsburg, NJ: Presbyterian and Reformed Publishing, 1994), 14, 16, 28. Sometimes the New Testament refers only to this age (Matt 13:39, 40, 49; 24:3; 28:20; Rom 12:2; 1 Cor 1:20; 1 Cor 2:6, 8; 3:18; 2 Cor 4:4; Gal 1:4; Eph 2:2; 1 Tim 6:17–19; Titus 2:12); other times it refers only to the age to come (Heb 6:5); and still other times it refers to both this age *and* the age to come (Matt 12:32; Mark 10:30; Luke 18:30; 20:34–35; Eph 1:21). As Kaiser writes, "Just as intertestamental Judaism expressed a divine

The fundamental feature common to most intertestamental expectations for the final age was the renewal of the Davidic kingdom in which the Messiah would fulfill the promises of eternal kingship and the nation of Israel would be restored to its previous political, geographical, and spiritual grandeur.[12] As J. Julius Scott explains:

> It was looked to as a time of unparalleled joy and gladness. There would be peace among individuals and nations; the wild beasts would lose their ferocity. The life span of human beings would increase, sickness and pain (including that of childbearing) would be eliminated. Labor and work would lose their tiresome characteristics…. Above all, the messianic age would be a time when the earth shall be cleansed from all defilement and from sin…. All nations will flock to the Jerusalem temple to worship. The rule of the Messiah will be universal and characterized by righteousness, for the dominating mark of the messianic age will be universal obedience to the law.[13]

---

division in time between 'this age' and the 'age to come,' so the New Testament follows suit and uses the same terms and similar concepts" (Walter C. Kaiser, Jr., *Preaching and Teaching the Last Things: Old Testament Eschatology for the Life of the Church* [Grand Rapids: Baker Academic, 2011], xv). Kaiser refers to this as the New Testament writers using "the traditional Jewish concept of the 'two ages'" (ibid.).

12 Scott, *Jewish Backgrounds of the New Testament*, 288–89. According to Scott, "The final resurrection, last judgment, and renovation of nature and the social order were also important components of the final age" (288).

13 Ibid., 289–90; also see Hélène Dallaire, "Judaism and the World to Come," in *A Case for Historic Premillennialism: An Alternative to "Left Behind" Eschatology*, eds. Craig L. Blomberg and Sung Wook Chung (Grand Rapids: Baker Academic, 2009), 39–40. As Scott points out, 2 Baruch 73 summarizes the final age like this: "And it will happen that after he has brought down everything which is in the world, and has sat down in eternal peace on the throne of the kingdom, then joy will be revealed and rest will appear. And then health will descend in dew, and illness will vanish, and fear and tribulation and lamentation will pass away from among men, and joy will encompass the earth. And nobody will again die untimely, nor will any adversity take place suddenly. Judgment, condemnations, contentions, revenges, blood, passions, zeal, hate, and all such things will go into condemnation since they will be uprooted. For these are the things that have filled this earth with evils, and because of them life of men came in yet greater confusion. And the wild beasts will come from the wood and serve men, and the asps and dragons will come out of their holes to subject themselves to a child. And women will no longer have pain when they bear, nor will they be tormented when they yield the fruit of their womb" (*Jewish Backgrounds of the New Testament*, 289–90).

In spite of this consensus on the two-age view of history in general and the primary features of the kingdom in particular, the intertestamental understanding of the age to come also included a great deal of diversity.[14] One of the most significant developments in this era concerned the notion of an intermediate reign of Messiah prior to the eternal state. Although this would be widely affirmed later in the period,[15] the prevailing idea in the earlier stages of intertestamental literature was that the messianic kingdom would come as the final act in redemptive history, the climax which ushered in the eternal enjoyment of God's blessings to His people.[16] As Scott explains, "Those who anticipated the inauguration of the final age and the consummation to occur simultaneously expected the new world to appear immediately."[17] According to this view, when divine intervention brings the present age to a close, the eternal state of the coming age will begin.

This view persisted in the intertestamental period until about 100 BC, when the belief emerged that the blessings of a timeless eternity in heaven would be preceded by a temporary kingdom on earth.[18] Here, for the first time in the literature, a clear distinction was made between the messianic kingdom and the final state of eternity. In the former—eventually

---

14 Russell, *The Method and Message of Jewish Apocalyptic*, 286; Scott, *Jewish Backgrounds of the New Testament*, 290–94.
15 Russell, *The Method and Message of Jewish Apocalyptic*, 286.
16 Ibid. These intertestamental writers affirmed "that with the divine intervention into history the final age (whether it was viewed as the messianic age or the kingdom of God) would begin immediately and be eternal" (Scott, *Jewish Backgrounds of the New Testament*, 292). According to Charles, "Before the year 100 B.C. it was generally believed in Judaism that the Messianic Kingdom would last *forever* on the present earth" (R. H. Charles, *A Critical and Exegetical Commentary on the Revelation of St. John*, vol. 2, ICC [Edinburgh: T. & T. Clark, 1970], 142) (emphasis original).
17 Scott, *Jewish Backgrounds of the New Testament*, 293. According to Russell, "At this stage of writing men were not concerned to look at anything which might lie beyond the kingdom itself. It was an end in itself. This was the climax of history in which the blessings of God, both material and spiritual, would be their portion. It was the religious and political fulfilment of their national history" (*The Method and Message of Jewish Apocalyptic*, 286).
18 R. H. Charles, *Eschatology, the Doctrine of a Future Life in Israel, Judaism, and Christianity: A Critical History* (New York, Schocken Books, 1963), 179–80; Charles, *The Revelation of St. John*, 142; Russell, *The Method and Message of Jewish Apocalyptic*, 291; Scott, *Jewish Backgrounds of the New Testament*, 292. According to Schaff, "It was developed shortly before and after Christ in the apocalyptic literature, as the Book of Enoch, the Apocalypse of Baruch, 4th Esdras, the Testaments of the Twelve Patriarchs, and the Sibylline Books" (Philip Schaff, *History of the Christian Church*, 3rd ed. [Peabody, MA: Hendrickson Publishers, 2006], 2:614).

designated "the days of Messiah" by the rabbis[19]—a temporary intermediate kingdom would be established on earth at the coming of the Messiah. This resulted in a three-fold division of redemptive history: this world (the present age), the times of Messiah (an intermediate kingdom), and the world to come (the eternal state).[20]

As Hélène Dallaire observes, "The notion that the Messiah will rule and reign on earth for a specific amount of time went through major developments in the Jewish literature of the intertestamental and rabbinic periods."[21] The earliest extant reference to a temporary messianic kingdom prior to the eternal state is found in 1 Enoch 91–103 (ca. 168 BC).[22] In 1 Enoch 91:12–17 and 93:1–10, the history of the world is divided into ten periods of time called "weeks," ultimately yielding a chronology of the present age, followed by the messianic kingdom, followed by the eternal state.[23] This view of an intermediate kingdom is also found

---

19 A. Cohen, *Everyman's Talmud* (New York: E. P. Dutton and Co., 1949), 356. Scott, *Jewish Backgrounds of the New Testament*, 292; George Eldon Ladd, *The Presence of the Future: The Eschatology of Biblical Realism* (Grand Rapids: Eerdmans Publishing, 1974), 92.
20 George Foot Moore, *Judaism in the First Centuries of the Christian Era: The Age of Tannaim*, vols. 2 and 3 (Peabody, MA: Hendrickson Publishers, 1960), 2:378.
21 Dallaire, "Judaism and the World to Come," 39.
22 Charles, *Eschatology*, 188; Helyer, "Second Temple Judaism and New Testament Eschatology," 602; Bailey, "The Temporary Messianic Reign," 172; Russell, *The Method and Message of Jewish Apocalyptic*, 291–92; Abba Hillel Silver, *A History of Messianic Speculation in Israel: From the First Through the Seventeenth Centuries* (Boston: Beacon Press, 1959), 5. This conclusion is disputed by some (e.g., Larry Kreitzer, *Jesus and God in Paul's Eschatology* [Sheffield: JSOT, 1987], 32–37), but Helyer ably defends this view ("Second Temple Judaism and New Testament Eschatology," 604–5), and it appears to be the general consensus among scholars.
23 Bailey, "The Temporary Messianic Reign," 172; Charles, *Eschatology*, 188–89; Helyer, "Second Temple Judaism and New Testament Eschatology," 602–4; George W. E. Nickelsburg and James C. VanderKam, *1 Enoch: The Hermeneia Translation* (Minneapolis: Fortress Press, 2012), 10; Russell, *The Method and Message of Jewish Apocalyptic*, 291. In these passages in 1 Enoch—known as "the Apocalypse of Weeks"—the present age starts at biblical creation and runs throughout the first seven weeks; the messianic kingdom is established in the eighth week; the final judgment of the wicked occurs in the ninth week; and the eternal state arrives in the tenth week, ushering in "many weeks without number forever" (Bailey, "The Temporary Messianic Reign," 172–73; Nickelsburg and VanderKam, *1 Enoch*, 10; Russell, *The Method and Message of Jewish Apocalyptic*, 291–92). In this presentation of redemptive history, the Messianic era extends through the eighth and ninth weeks and through the first seven parts of the tenth week, when the new heavens and new earth are created (Bailey, "The Temporary Messianic Reign," 172). Although 1 Enoch 10 and 11 appear to be less definitive than 1 Enoch 91–103, they also reflect the same general conception of a temporary Messianic period followed by a day of general judgment, followed by a period of eternal duration (ibid., 173).

in the Qumran Commentary on Habakkuk (1QpHab 2:3b),[24]—which dates from the second half of the first century BC[25]—and in the Psalms of Solomon (70–40 BC),[26] also composed in the first century BC.[27] In addition, it is possibly found in Jubilees 23:26–31 (153–105 BC), which "mentions, but in a rather ambiguous context, a period of one thousand years."[28] According to D. S. Russell, "In the majority of the later apocalyptic writings especially, the sequence is 'this age' followed by 'the messianic kingdom' followed by 'the age to come.'"[29]

The idea of a temporary messianic kingdom prior to the final state not only continued into the first century AD, but it was also "conceived in more definite and precise terms."[30] Around AD 50, 2 Enoch 25–33 sets forth an intermediate period of one thousand years between the "end of

---

24 Scott, *Jewish Backgrounds of the New Testament*, 293.
25 According to Knibb, "The manuscript dates from the second half of the first century BC, but the work was probably composed before this" (Michael A. Knibb, *The Qumran Community* [London: The Cambridge University Press, 1987], 221).
26 Charles, *Eschatology*, 267–72; Joseph Bonsirven, *Palestinian Judaism in the Time of Jesus*, trans. William Wolf (New York: Holt, Rinehart, and Winston, 1964), 175; Silver, *A History of Messianic Speculation*, 5.
27 Michael Lattke, "Psalms of Solomon," in *Dictionary of New Testament Background*, eds. Craig A. Evans and Stanley E. Porter (Downers Grove, IL: InterVarsity Press, 2000), 853; Charles, *Eschatology*, 267.
28 Scott, *Jewish Backgrounds of the New Testament*, 293; also see Charles, *Eschatology*, 235–40; Bonsirven, *Palestinian Judaism in the Time of Jesus*, 211. According to Bailey, this interpretation of Jubilees 23:26–31 "is apparently correct but cannot be affirmed with absolute certainty" ("The Temporary Messianic Reign," 175); according to Helyer, "While it is possible that the author of *Jubilees* believed in a temporary, messianic kingdom, the evidence is even less certain than in *1 Enoch*" ("Second Temple Judaism and New Testament Eschatology," 605); according to Russell, "We may detect the idea of a temporary kingdom" in the Book of Jubilees and yet the evidence for this kingdom is "much less clear" than in 1 Enoch 91–104 (*The Method and Message of Jewish Apocalyptic*, 292); and according to Charles the messianic kingdom in these psalms is "apparently of temporary duration" (*Eschatology*, 270).
29 Russell, *The Method and Message of Jewish Apocalyptic*, 291. Despite the widespread consensus on the larger issue of an intermediate kingdom, disagreement continued on whether there would be a single final judgment or a series of judgments: "Some seem to have expected the final judgment to precede the arrival of the messianic kingdom and the righteous to be raised to share in it forever. In other writings, such as 1 Enoch 91–104, the judgment comes at the close of the kingdom; but the righteous are not raised to share it, but later enjoy a blessed immortality. Second Baruch 50:4 also seems to allude to a judgment after the conclusion of the kingdom, and 2 Esdras speaks of it in even more detail. The righteous will be accepted into paradise to occupy the high places and to behold the majesty of God. The wicked will be cast into Gehenna, which is characterized by fire and intense suffering" (Scott, *Jewish Backgrounds of the New Testament*, 293–94).
30 Bailey, "The Temporary Messianic Reign," 180.

creation" and the eternal age.³¹ Later in the first century, 2 Esdras (4 Ezra) 7:26–44 indicates that "when the Messiah is revealed, he reigns on earth with the righteous for a period of four hundred years."³² This extended period of peace will be followed by seven days of silence, after which a resurrection of the dead will occur, followed by a day of reckoning known as "the final judgment," which ushers in the eternal state.³³ Also, late in the first century, 2 Baruch teaches that the kingdom of the Messiah is temporary and will endure until the world of corruption comes to an end (24:1–4; 30:1–5; 39:3–8; 40:1–4; 72–74; 44:14).³⁴

According to Helyer, although the evidence just considered appears to indicate that a belief in a temporary, messianic kingdom was confined to sectarian, apocalyptic circles, other texts suggest that the notion was more widespread.³⁵ For example, the Samaritans held a very old tradition

---

31 Ibid., 180–81; Charles, *Eschatology*, 299, 315–20. According to Bailey ("The Temporary Messianic Reign," 181) and Charles (*Eschatology*, 315), this is the oldest passage in Jewish literature which explicitly reflects an intermediate kingdom of one thousand years. Helyer is less dogmatic, referring to 2 Enoch as a "possible candidate" in providing support for the belief in an interim, messianic kingdom ("Second Temple Judaism and New Testament Eschatology," 605). According to Helyer, "There is no explicit mention of a messiah and so we cannot, without qualification, say a temporary, *messianic* kingdom" (606).

32 Helyer, "Second Temple Judaism and New Testament Eschatology," 606; also see Bailey, "The Temporary Messianic Reign," 183–84; Charles, *Eschatology*, 299, 341–42; Dallaire, "Judaism and the World to Come," 41–42; Bonsirven, *Palestinian Judaism in the Time of Jesus*, 211; Scott, *Jewish Backgrounds of the New Testament*, 292–93; Moore, *Judaism*, 2:338–39.

33 Dallaire, "Judaism and the World to Come," 41; Bailey, "The Temporary Messianic Reign," 183–84; Bonsirven, *Palestinian Judaism in the Time of Jesus*, 175, 211; Sasse, "αἰών, αἰώνιος," 206. According to Russell, even though there is some inconsistency in 2 Esdras, the picture presented there is clearly that of an intermediate kingdom on earth lasting 400 years, followed by the eternal state in heaven (*The Method and Message of Jewish Apocalyptic*, 295–96). As Russell writes, "The temporary earthly kingdom passes and the eternal heavenly kingdom is ushered in. The 'days of the Messiah' give place to 'the age to come'" (*The Method and Message of Jewish Apocalyptic*, 296–97). Bailey refers to this as "one of the most significant writings of the entire period" ("The Temporary Messianic Reign," 183).

34 Bailey, "The Temporary Messianic Reign," 182; Charles, *Eschatology*, 322–30; Helyer, "Second Temple Judaism and New Testament Eschatology," 607–8; Russell, *The Method and Message of Jewish Apocalyptic*, 293–95; Scott, *Jewish Backgrounds of the New Testament*, 292; Moore, *Judaism*, 2:339; Bonsirven, *Palestinian Judaism in the Time of Jesus*, 175. At the same time, according to Russell, although 2 Baruch envisions "a temporary kingdom on this earth to be followed by an eternity in heaven," there is some "lack of consistency in its teaching in this regard" (*The Method and Message of Jewish Apocalyptic*, 293). Similarly, Helyer writes, "This composition gives the most detailed description of a temporary, messianic kingdom, though it must be confessed that there are a number of inconsistencies in this regard" ("Second Temple Judaism and New Testament Eschatology," 607).

35 Helyer, "Second Temple Judaism and New Testament Eschatology," 608.

of a temporary, messianic kingdom lasting one thousand years,[36] and the Talmud and Midrash indicate that it had been widely incorporated into rabbinic Judaism.[37] In fact, this belief became so pervasive by the early rabbinical period that the primary debate among the first- and early second-century rabbis concerned not the existence of a temporary earthly kingdom but rather its duration.[38]

The time frames attributed to the messianic age by the rabbis varied between 40 and 7,000 years, depending on their interpretation of canonical and non-canonical texts.[39] Despite the lack of consensus on the length of the messianic era, however, it was agreed that its duration is finite and that it forms an intermediate period between the present age and the

---

36 Ibid., who points to Bailey ("The Temporary Messianic Reign," 179) for references to scholarly studies of this issue.

37 Helyer, "Second Temple Judaism and New Testament Eschatology," 608. At the same time, the earlier Mishnah "is very reticent with regard to eschatological matters and does not mention it at all" (ibid.). Helyer concludes that a temporary, messianic kingdom was also affirmed by the Pharisees of Jesus' day, since the rabbinic sources attribute this teaching to sages descended from the Pharisees (614).

38 Moore, *Judaism*, 2:375-76; Bailey, "The Temporary Messianic Reign," 185; Dallaire, "Judaism and the World to Come," 39-41. There was also significant disagreement regarding the nature of this intermediate kingdom (Silver, *A History of Messianic Speculation*, 14-15). For example, "According to some Jewish authors, during the messianic age, everyone will worship one God and will live in a perfect, harmonious, and peaceful society. According to others, the era between this worldly existence and eternal bliss for the righteous in the world to come will find the earth desolate with God highly exalted over his creation. Both of these views, along with numerous others, appear in rabbinic literature" (Dallaire, "Judaism and the World to Come," 39-40).

39 Dallaire, "Judaism and the World to Come," 40. The estimates of the various rabbis are listed by Bailey, "The Temporary Messianic Reign," 184-87; Helyer, "Second Temple Judaism and New Testament Eschatology," 609; Dallaire, "Judaism and the World to Come," 39-41; Cohen, *Everyman's Talmud*, 356; Jacob Neusner and William Scott Green, eds., *The Dictionary of Judaism in the Biblical Period: 450 B.C.E. to 600 C.E.* (New York: Simon & Schuster Macmillan, 1996), 1:203; Moore, *Judaism in the First Centuries*, 2:375-76; Bonsirven, *Palestinian Judaism in the Time of Jesus*, 212-13; Silver, *A History of Messianic Speculation*, 13-15; Scott, *Jewish Backgrounds of the New Testament*, 292-93; and G. K. Beale, *The Book of Revelation*, NIGTC (Grand Rapids: Eerdmans Publishing, 1999), 1018-19. According to these sources, the rabbis suggested the following durations for the temporary messianic kingdom: Eliezer ben Hyrcanus (ca. AD 90): 40, 100, 400, or 1,000 years; Joshua (ca. AD 90): 2,000 years; Eleazar ben Azariah (ca. AD 100): 70 years; Joseph ben Galilee (ca. AD 110): 60 years; Akiba (ca. AD 135): 40 years; Jose the Galilean (ca. AD 120): 1,000 years; Eliezer ben Joseph of Galilee (ca. AD 150): 400 years; Dosa (AD 180): 400 or 600 years; Judah ha-Nasi (late 2nd century AD): 365 years; Kattina: 1,000 years; Abaye: 2,000 years; and Abimi ben Abbahu: 7,000 years. At the same time, some rabbis—such as Hillel in *Sanhedrin* 99a—denied the possibility of a future messianic age.

eternal state.[40] In addition, in the latter part of the first century "there was also a very definite proposal on the part of certain teachers to place the limit at 1,000 years."[41] Despite the diversity of opinion, all were in agreement that "the Days of the Messiah are of limited duration."[42]

Between 100 BC and AD 100, then, a clear consensus of Jewish thought embraced the concept of a temporary messianic kingdom prior to the eternal state.[43] Despite this widespread agreement, some degree of confusion existed during this time regarding the precise relationship between this temporary kingdom and the terminology "the age/world to come." Sometimes the intermediate kingdom and the "age to come" are clearly distinguished—with the former being portrayed as a transitional stage between this world and the world to come—and other times the two cannot be separated, being either confused or referred to interchangeably.[44]

---

40 Moore, *Judaism*, 2:376; Bailey, "The Temporary Messianic Reign," 185.
41 Bailey, "The Temporary Messianic Reign," 187. For example, the apocalyptic 2 Enoch—usually dated in the late first century AD—indicates a belief that the history of the world will last for 6,000 years and then be followed by 1,000 years of "rest" when God will establish His kingdom (Russell, *The Method and Message of Jewish Apocalyptic*, 293). Russell refers to this as "the beginnings of a belief in a millennium, in the literal sense of a kingdom which is to last 1,000 years." The earliest rabbi to calculate the Days of Messiah to be 1,000 years in length was Rabbi Eliezer ben Hyrcanus (ca. AD 90), "though he probably learned the thousand-year reign from earlier rabbinic tradition" (Beale, *The Book of Revelation*, 1019).
42 Moore, *Judaism*, 2:376.
43 Bailey, "The Temporary Messianic Reign," 187; Charles, *Eschatology*, 167–361; Russell, *The Method and Message of Jewish Apocalyptic*, 297. According to Charles, in the first century AD "in all cases only a transitory Messianic kingdom is expected" (*Eschatology*, 360). Although consulting rabbinic Judaism to identify Jewish thought at the time of the New Testament often leads to reading later ideas back into the first century, the strength of the argument here is found in the consistency among the Jewish writers from the mid-apocalyptic era to the early rabbinic era (100 BC to AD 100) on the existence of an intermediate messianic kingdom.
44 Scott, *Jewish Backgrounds of the New Testament*, 292–93. Also see Russell, *The Method and Message of Jewish Apocalyptic*, 296–97; Neusner and Green, *The Dictionary of Judaism*, 1:203; Joseph Klausner, *The Messianic Idea in Israel from Its Beginning to the Completion of the Mishnah*, trans. W. F. Stinespring (London: George Allen and Unwin Ltd, 1956), 408–19; W. D. Davies, *Paul and Rabbinic Judaism: Some Rabbinic Elements in Pauline Theology* (Mifflintown, PA: Sigler Press, 1998), 316; Cohen, *Everyman's Talmud*, 356; Bonsirven, *Palestinian Judaism in the Time of Jesus*, 205–6; Davies, *The Setting of the Sermon on the Mount*, 182; Ladd, *The Presence of the Future*, 92; Robert H. Gundry, *The Church and the Tribulation: A Biblical Examination of Posttribulationism* (Grand Rapids: Eerdmans Publishing, 1999), 142. This ambiguity does not appear to be reflected in the argument of some who identify the age to come exclusively with the intermediate kingdom (e.g.,

Because of this ambiguity, it is difficult to identify with certainty the precise referent of "the age to come" in Jewish thought at the time of the New Testament. But regardless of whether (a) the age to come = the intermediate kingdom, (b) the age to come = the eternal state (with the intermediate kingdom viewed as a transitional phase between the present age and the eternal state), or (c) the age to come = the intermediate kingdom *and* the eternal state, one thing is clear: The two-age model of first-century Judaism was considered to be perfectly compatible with a temporary kingdom of Messiah between the present age and the eternal state. For this reason, when Jesus and the New Testament writers referred to "this age" and/or "the age to come," this terminology was understood by their original audience as consistent with the belief in an intermediate kingdom of Messiah that would precede the final state of perfection.[45]

Thomas Ice, "Ages of Time," in *The Popular Encyclopedia of Bible Prophecy*, eds. Tim LaHaye and Ed Hindson [Eugene, OR: Harvest House Publishers, 2004], 15; George N. H. Peters, *The Theocratic Kingdom*, vol. 2 [1884; repr., Grand Rapids, Kregel Publications, 1972], 404–5).

[45] When Riddlebarger introduces his two-age model as an interpretive grid which precludes the existence of an intermediate kingdom, he acknowledges that the *age to come* is "a technical term in Jewish eschatology, designating the final state after the messianic reign" (Kim Riddlebarger, *A Case for Amillennialism: Understanding the End Times*, expanded ed. [Grand Rapids: Baker Books, 2013], 298). But he relegates this observation to an endnote, and he fails to comment further on the Jewish background of the two-age terminology or to discuss the implications it may have on the significance of these designations in the New Testament.

Scripture Index

Genesis
1:26	11
1:28	51, 53
3:14	141, 145
3:14–19	143
3:17–19	141, 145
3:22	11
5	33
6:2	188
6:3	33–34
9:1	51, 53
11:7	11
17:6	51, 53
20:16	251

Exodus
1:7	51, 53
12:13	56
20:5–6	245, 254
20:12	51–52
23:16	63
34:22	63

Leviticus
23:33–43	56, 63
23:33–44	55
26:4	56
26:9	51, 53
26:19–20	56

Deuteronomy
1:11	245
4:4	51
5:33	51–52
6:2	51–52
7:9	245, 254
7:14	51, 53
11:8–9	51–52
16:13–17	55–56, 63
25:5	103
28:12	56
28:24	56

Joshua
23:10	245

Judges
15:15–16	251

1 Kings
17:1	56

2 Kings
22:19	71

1 Chronicles
16:15	245
29:21	251

2 Chronicles
15:3	71

Ezra
1:8	252
1:9	251–52
1:10	251–52

Job
1:6	71
1:7	206
9:3	245

Psalms
2	57, 293
2:9	144
8:6	156
28:1	71
30:3	71
33:6	71

40:2	71
45:6–7	11
50:10	245, 254
50:10–11	245, 254
66:3	57
72	21–22
72:1–20	10, 15, 20–22, 83, 92, 105
72:2	82
72:2–4	82
72:4	82
72:7	82
72:7–8	82
72:9	82
72:11	82
72:12	82
72:12–13	82
72:13	82
72:14	82
72:16–17	82
72:19	82
77:16	183
78:15	183
84:10	245, 254
88:4	71
90	253
90:4	245–46, 252–54
90:10	34
105:8	245
106:9	183
110:1	11, 156
142:8	71
143:7	71

Proverbs

1:12	71
3:2	51

Ecclesiastes

5:18–20	252
6:1–2	252
6:1–6	252
6:3	253
6:3–5	252
6:6	246, 252–53
7:28	245

Song of Solomon

4:4	245

Isaiah

2:1–3	10, 15, 20, 23, 25, 83, 92, 105
2:2–4	22–27
2:3	56
2:4	56, 78, 82
6:8	11
9:6–7	13, 112, 214
11	28–30
11:1–9	10, 15, 20, 28–30, 83, 92, 105
11:3–5	82
11:4	57, 82
11:6–8	42, 144
11:6–9	82
11:9	82
11:9–17	293
11:10–16	278
13–23	70
13:6	133
13:9	133
13:13	137
14:12	202
14:12–15	203
14:15	71
24	132
24–25	132
24–27	70, 75, 79
24:1–20	70, 73, 75
24:1–22	132
24:17–20	75, 80
24:20–23	183
24:21	132
24:21–22	132
24:21–23	14, 20, 69–83, 92, 105, 123, 127, 206
24:22	123, 127, 132
25	75, 145
25–27	78
25:6	77
25:6–8	69, 72, 132
25:7	77
25:7–8	39
25:7–9	163
25:8	33–34, 36, 38, 41, 44, 61, 163, 166–67, 169
25:9	70, 76
25:10	77
26:1	70, 76
27:1	70, 76

27:2	70, 76	31:33	26
27:12	70, 76	35:7	71
27:12–13	77		
27:13	70, 76, 168	**Ezekiel**	
29:18	144	16:46	293
30:23–25	144	26:20	71
32:13–15	144	28:11–19	203
33:24	144	31:14	71
34:4	137	31:16	71
35:1	143	34:16	144
35:1–2	144	34:25–29	145
35:1–7	145	34:26–29	145
35:5–6	144	36–39	47
35:7	144	36:6–9	145
38:18	71	36:27	26
40:1–5	13, 214	36:29–30	145
40:26	71	36:35	145
41:18	144	38	283
42:7	71	38–39	59, 283, 287, 289–94
45:12	71	39	283
48:16	11	40–48	64
51:6	137	44:25	144
55:10	183	44:27	144
55:12	260		
60:22	245	**Daniel**	
61:1	11	2:44	137
61:1–2	13–14, 29, 126, 214	4:32	71
63:10	11	6:17	177, 189
65	145	7:1–28	59
65:17	139	7:14	137
65:17–25	10, 15, 20, 31–45, 92, 105, 137–39	7:18	137
		8:10	71
65:18–25	139	9:26–27	59
65:20	51, 61–62, 72, 82–83, 143–44, 170, 278	10:13	71
		11:36–12:17	59
65:22	82, 144	12:2	7, 15, 87, 107–8, 110, 112, 212–14
65:25	144		
65–66	37	**Hosea**	
66:1	240	1:2	11
66:15–16	136	1:7	11
66:22	36, 136	3:4–5	71
66:22–24	35, 137	13:14	166–67, 169
66:24	66		
		Joel	
Jeremiah		1:15	133
29:10–14	13, 214	2:1	133, 168
30–33	47	2:11	133, 286–287
31:12	145	2:21–27	145
31:31–34	63		

2:28–32	13, 214	12–14	287
2:30–31	136	12:1–7	59
2:31	133	12:4	61–62
3	132	14:1–21	48, 67
3:1–17	59, 132	14:2–14	286
3:2	287	14:4	82
3:14	133	14:7	82
3:16	137	14:8–11	54
3:18–21	132	14:9	57, 82
		14:11	143

Amos

		14:12–15	54, 68
4:7–8	56	14:15	61
7:4	183	14:16	82
9:13–14	145	14:16–19	10, 15, 20, 48, 50, 54–68, 83, 92, 105, 144
9:13–15	145	14:16–21	57–58, 62–64, 278
		14:17	68

Obadiah

1–14	133	14:17–19	82, 143–44, 170
15–21	133	14:20–21	62

Micah

Malachi

3:12	23	3:1–2	11
4:1–3	22–27	3:1–3	136
4:2	56	4:1	136
4:2–4	10, 15, 20, 23, 83, 92, 105		
4:3	82		
4:11–5:1	59		

Matthew

		4:1–11	179, 198
		5:17	62

Zephaniah

		12	198, 200
1:4	286	12:25–28	199
1:7	133	12:28	200, 203
1:14	133	12:29	196–201, 203
1:16	168	12:32	3, 6, 87–90, 93, 95, 98, 100, 306
		12:39–42	108

Haggai

		12:43	66
1:11	56	13:19	178, 191
2:6–7	137	13:30	65
		13:39	2–3, 99–100, 107, 306

Zechariah

		13:39–40	115
8:1–3	48, 51–52	13:40	2–3, 99–100, 306
8:1–8	48	13:49	2–3, 99–100, 306
8:3	52	13:49–50	115
8:4	82	21:19	92
8:4–5	15, 20, 48–54, 82–83, 92	22:32	235, 238
8:6–8	51–52	24:1–41	121
8:11–12	145	24:3	2–3, 97, 99–100, 306
9:9–10	13, 214	24:9–13	119
9:10	112	24:14	119
9:14	168	24:31	117

24:38–44	277	8:32	184–85
24:42–51	138	8:33	184–85
24:43	137	8:35	92
25:31–46	7, 15, 55, 87, 107, 114–24, 126, 276–77	8:51	92
		8:52	92
25:46	101	9:56	229, 239
27–28	198	10	202
27:66	177, 189	10:17–18	196–97, 201–3
28:1	60	10:17–20	201
28:18–20	119	10:28	92
28:20	2–3, 97, 99–100, 306	11:17–23	202
		11:26	92

Mark

		11:29–32	108
3:4	229, 239	12:34	92
3:29	89, 92	12:39	137
4:15	178	13:8	92
4:17	150–51	14:14	114
4:28	151	14:16	92
6:44	252	15:32	209
7:5	151	16:7	151
8:25	151–52	16:19–31	73, 122–23, 126
10:22	101	16:24	66
10:28	101	17:22–37	277
10:29–30	89, 101	18:23	101
10:30	3, 7, 87, 93, 97–98, 100–2, 306	18:28	101
		18:29–30	101
11:14	92	18:30	3, 7, 87, 93, 97–98, 100–2, 306
12:26–27	227		
13:32–37	138	20:27–28	103
16:1	60	20:28–33	104
		20:29–30	104

Luke

		20:33	104
1:32–33	137	20:34	97
1:33	91	20:34–35	3, 93, 100, 306
1:55	92	20:34–36	7, 50, 53, 87, 102–5
2:34	210, 219	20:35	113–14
4:1–13	179, 198, 202	20:35–36	98
4:13	199	20:37–38	104
4:16	29	20:38	235, 238
4:16–21	13–14, 214	21:25–36	138
4:18–19	29	22	63
6:9	229, 239	22:31	178
6:51	92	24:43	277
6:58	92		

John

8:12	150–52, 178		
8:26–30	184	3:36	101
8:27	185	4:14	92
8:28	184–85	4:21	111, 214
8:29	185	4:23	111, 214
8:31	78, 81, 178, 184–86, 188	4:38	65

5	236	6:4	224
5:24–30	121	6:4–6	227
5:25	111, 214	6:11	224
5:25–27	228–29	8	141–45, 170
5:25–29	227–28	8:10–11	227
5:28–29	7, 15, 87, 107–12, 212–14, 228–29	8:16–23	129
		8:17	170
5:29	110, 213, 219	8:17–23	7, 15, 87, 142, 170
7:37	66	8:18	170
8:44	178	8:18–23	7, 15, 87, 107, 139–45
11:7	151	8:19	170
11:25	211, 227, 238	8:21	170
12:31	178	8:23	170
12:31–32	196–97, 203–5	9:5	91
12:40	191	10:4	62
13:5	151–52	10:7	184
14:30	178	11:36	91
15:8	51–53	12:2	2–3, 97, 99–100, 306
16:2	111, 214	13:1	229, 239
16:11	178	14:9	209, 238
17:3	101	16:27	91
19:27	151–52		
20:27	150–52	**1 Corinthians**	
		1:20	2–3, 97, 99–100, 306
Acts		2:6	2–3, 99–100, 306
1:3	211, 238, 277	2:6–8	97
2:36	156–57	2:8	99–100, 306
2:41	229, 239	3:18	2–3, 99–100, 306
2:43	229, 239	4:8	156
3:23	229, 239	5:7	63
4:2	113	6:1–3	156
5:3	178	6:9–10	98
7:14	229, 239	7:5	178
9:41	211, 238	8	2–3
15:26	229, 239	8:13	92
17:31	113	10:4	66
17:32	113	12:28	151
23:6	113	15	147, 218–20, 222–23
24:15	7, 15, 87, 107–8, 110, 112, 159, 212–14	15:5	151
		15:5–7	150–51
24:21	113	15:6	151
26:18	178	15:7	151
27:37	229, 239	15:12	113
		15:13	113
Romans		15:18	160
1:4	113	15:20–28	7, 15, 87, 107, 147–61
1:25	91	15:21	113
2:7	101	15:22	217
2:9	229, 239	15:23	162, 167

15:23–26	168
15:23–28	137, 167, 303
15:24	165, 167
15:24–25	164, 167
15:24–26	162, 167
15:24–28	123
15:25	143, 165
15:25–26	132
15:26	167
15:27–28	167
15:42–49	217
15:45	229, 239
15:46	151
15:47	224
15:50	98
15:50–57	7, 15, 87, 107, 147, 161–70
15:51–52	277
15:54–55	148

2 Corinthians

2:11	178
4:3–4	191
4:4	2–3, 97, 99–100, 178, 191–92, 195, 306
9:9	92
11:3	178
11:13–15	178
11:31	91
12:7	178

Galatians

1:4	2–3, 97, 99–100, 306
1:5	91
1:18	151
1:21	151
2:1	151
4:26	24
5:21	98
5:22	51
5:22–23	52–53

Ephesians

1:20–23	156–57
1:21	3, 6, 87–88, 90, 93, 95, 100, 306
2:1	211
2:1–7	227
2:2	2–3, 97, 99–100, 178, 306
2:4–7	211
2:5	224, 227

2:7	3, 91–92
4:27	178
5:5	98
6:11–17	178

Philippians

2:9–11	156
3:11	113–14
3:21	218
4:20	91

Colossians

1:13	66
2:12–13	227
2:15	78, 81, 191, 196–97, 203–5
3:1	224, 227

1 Thessalonians

1:10	138
2:18	178
3:5	178
4:13–18	170, 277
4:17	150–51
5:2	133, 137
5:4	137

2 Thessalonians

1:6–10	7, 15, 87, 107, 114, 124–27
1:7–8	137
2:2	133
2:8	29, 287

1 Timothy

1:17	91
1:20	178
2:13	151
3:10	151
4:1–2	178, 191
6:17	3, 97
6:17–19	2, 89, 99–100, 306
6:19	98

2 Timothy

1:10	169
2:12	156
2:26	178, 191
4:8	138
4:18	91

Titus

2:12	3, 99–100, 306
2:12–13	97
2:13	138

Hebrews

1–2	156
1:3	156–57
1:8	92
1:13	156–57
1:13–14	157
2:1–4	157
2:5	157–58
2:5–8	157
2:7–8	157
2:8	156–57
2:14–15	191, 196–97, 203–5
5:6	92
6:2	113
6:5	3, 100, 306
6:20	92
7:2	151
7:17	92
7:21	92
7:24	92
7:27	151
7:28	92
8–10	218–20, 222–24
8:6–10:9	217
8:13	62–63, 218, 223
10:12–13	156, 158
10:13	157
11:19	113
11:26	66
11:35	114
12:9	150
12:18–24	23, 25
12:22	24
13:4	25
13:21	91

James

3:17	151
4:14	151

1 Peter

1:3	113
1:8	51, 53
1:10–11	126
1:25	92
3:18–20	78, 81
3:20	229, 239
3:21–22	156
3:22	157
4:6	235, 238
4:11	91
5:8	178, 190, 206
5:11	91

2 Peter

2:4	78, 81, 188
3	134–36, 253
3:1–18	136
3:3–4	134–35
3:3–7	253
3:3–13	135, 137
3:4	135
3:5–7	134
3:8	134, 245–46, 252–54
3:9	134–35
3:10–13	7, 15, 87, 107, 129–39
3:11–14	135, 138
3:12–14	138
3:13	35–36
3:14	136

1 John

2:11	191
2:17	92
2:18	111, 214
3:8	191, 197, 203–5
3:8–10	178
3:14	227
4:4	178
5:11–13	101, 227
5:19	178, 191

2 John

2	92

Jude

6	188
7	122
13	92

Revelation

1–3	274

1:1	257	9:1	184
1:3	297	9:1–2	184
1:5	220	9:1–6	186
1:6	92	9:1–10	279
1:10	250	9:2	184
1:13	250	9:3–13	178
1:18	92, 220, 234, 238	9:5	250
1:20	257	9:6	250
2:8	234, 238	9:7	286
2:10	178, 240, 247, 250	9:9	286
2:10–11	235, 240	9:10	250
2:13	234	9:11	184
2:26–27	284	9:13	188
3:1	234	9:15	250
3:10	187	10:1	296–97
3:21	156, 284	10:6	92
4–7	274	10:7	250
4:1	265	10:10	257
4:4	250	10:11	298
4:8	250	11:2	250
4:9	92	11:2–3	281
4:10	92	11:3	250
5:5	250	11:3–13	298
5:10	156, 239, 249, 273, 284	11:6	250
5:13	92	11:7	184, 187, 286
6–19	70, 73	11:8	257, 293
6–22	73	11:9	250
6:9	240–41	11:10	187
6:9–11	235, 240–42	11:11	250
6:10	187, 241	11:15	92, 249
6:10–11	241	11:34	258
6:11	241–42, 255	12	203, 279–82
6:17	250	12–14	274, 298
7	250	12–19	268, 270
7:1	297	12–20	267–68
7:2	296, 298	12:1	66
7:3	237, 250	12:6	250, 281
7:4–8	250	12:7	279, 286
7:9	265, 277	12:7–8	279
7:12	92	12:7–11	197, 205, 278–80, 282
7:13–17	277	12:7–12	197, 270
7:15	250	12:9	192, 267, 270, 279, 281
7:17	234	12:10	250, 279
8–11	274	12:11	229, 233, 279
8:1	250	12:12	255, 279, 281
8:9	229	12:12–13	187
8:12	250	12:14	281
8:13	187	13:1–10	267
9	187	13:2	195, 234

13:4	195	18:23	192, 270, 281
13:5	250	18:24	241
13:7	195, 286	19	15, 73, 83, 262–65, 267–71, 273–75, 282–83, 285, 288, 297, 299, 301
13:7–8	277		
13:8	187, 195	19:1	265
13:11–18	267	19:3	92
13:14	187, 192, 195, 234, 238, 240, 270, 281	19:5	144
		19:7–9	298
13:15	241	19:11	264–65, 297
13:15–17	277	19:11–16	298–99
14:8	293	19:11–18	73
14:10	122	19:11–19	270
14:11	92, 250	19:11–20:10	268
14:12–13	277	19:11–21	120, 125–26, 215, 241, 263, 265–66, 274–76, 282–96, 298
14:13	235, 240		
14:14–16	65	19:11–21:8	266
15–16	274	19:14	210
15:1	283, 294–96	19:15	29, 259
15:5	265	19:16	297
15:7	92	19:17	265
15:18	237	19:17–19	170, 276–77
16	282–83, 285, 288, 298	19:17–21	277, 298–99
16–18	133	19:18	276
16:3	229, 234, 267	19:19	73, 81, 265, 276, 297
16:8–9	137	19:19–20	270, 275
16:10	234	19:19–21	73, 117, 277–78
16:12–16	274, 282–96	19:20	66, 73, 123, 192, 234, 267, 270–72, 281
16:13–14	268, 277		
16:13–16	270, 275	19:21	73, 276, 278
16:14	250, 281	19–20	117, 120, 127, 220, 263–64, 267, 271–72, 283, 288–94
16:15	137, 275		
16:17–21	294	19–21	8, 75, 105, 127, 265, 303
16:19	275	19–22	264, 299
17–19	274	20	1, 4–16, 20, 34, 50, 73, 76–77, 83, 91–93, 95–96, 102, 110, 112, 114, 117, 121, 124, 132–34, 139, 141–43, 148–49, 154, 158, 162–63, 166, 170–71, 175–76, 178–81, 183–85, 187–89, 191–92, 197–207, 210–11, 213, 215–16, 219–23, 226–30, 232, 236, 239, 242–48, 251–52, 254–56, 258, 260–70, 272–75, 279–83, 286, 297, 299, 301–3
17–22	274, 298		
17:1	293		
17:1–19:6	298		
17:2	187		
17:5	293		
17:8	184, 187		
17:10	255		
18	298		
18:1	265, 293, 296–97		
18:2	293	20:1	259, 263–66, 274–75, 279, 297–98
18:8	250	20:1–3	73, 77, 175–206, 259–60, 265–67, 269, 274–76, 279, 282, 285, 298–99
18:9	293		
18:10	293	20:1–6	6–7, 15, 27, 72–73, 83, 127, 175, 215, 263–64, 266–68, 271–72, 274–75, 278–82, 287, 289, 299
18:13	229		
18:21	293		

20:1–10	117, 120, 122, 125, 148–49, 268, 274, 298	20:11–15	74, 76, 115–18, 120–126, 209, 220, 242, 267, 295–96, 298–99
20:1–15	214	20:12–13	118
20–22	274	20:12–15	117
20:2	230, 243, 251, 259, 279	20:13	159–60, 212
20:2–3	279	20:14	66, 79, 122, 148, 166
20:3	237, 243, 251, 255, 259, 269–70, 275, 278–79, 281	20:14–15	216
		20:15	117–18, 120, 122, 220
20:4	156, 227, 243, 251, 264–65, 272, 277, 279	21	15, 50, 121, 218–20, 222, 301
		21–22	20, 74, 77, 83, 91, 93, 96, 262, 266, 299
20:4–5	112–13, 156, 251, 273	21:1	35–36, 117–18, 137–39, 217, 222, 265
20:4–6	77, 159, 170, 207–42, 249, 266–67, 273, 284, 298–99	21:1–4	38, 42, 122, 139, 144–45, 162–63
20:5	117, 159–60, 227, 243, 251	21:1–22:5	298
20:5–6	110–11	21:3	234
20:6	73, 240, 243, 251, 272	21:4	34, 36, 148, 163, 166, 218
20:7	73, 178, 182, 184, 187–89, 205, 243, 251	21:5	234
20:7–8	193, 195, 237, 268, 279	21:6	66
20:7–9	27, 138, 271–72, 278	21:8	218
20:7–10	73–74, 144, 170, 195, 203, 271, 274–75, 282–96, 298–99	21:23	77
		21:24	57
20:7–11	274	21:25	250
20:7–15	73, 298	22	50, 66
20:7–21:1	133	22:1	156, 234
20:8	188, 195, 255, 275	22:1–5	145
20:9	239, 268	22:2	57, 250
20:10	66, 92, 122–23, 202, 216, 250, 267–68, 270–72, 296	22:3	34, 234
		22:5	92, 156
20:11	117–18, 137, 265	22:15	66, 249
20:11–13	220	22:17	6